THE CONSTRUCTION OF REALITY IN THE CHILD

The Language and Thought of the Child (1926)
Judgment and Reasoning in the Child (1928)
The Child's Conception of the World (1929)
The Child's Conception of Physical Causality (1930)
The Moral Judgment of the Child (1932)
The Psychology of Intelligence (1950)
Play, Dreams and Imitation in Childhood (1951)
The Child's Conception of Number (1952)
The Origins of Intelligence in Children (1952)
Logic and Psychology (1953)
The Construction of Reality in the Child (1954)

*Dates given in parentheses are
the first publication dates of the
English translations.*

BASIC BOOKS, INC.
publishers, NEW YORK

JEAN PIAGET

The Construction of Reality in the Child

Translated by Margaret Cook

Contents

INTRODUCTION   xi

CHAPTER I

THE DEVELOPMENT OF OBJECT CONCEPT   3

1. *The first two stages:* no special behavior related to vanished objects 4

2. *The third stage:* beginning of permanence extending the movements of accommodation 13

3. *The fourth stage:* active search for the vanished object but without taking account of the sequence of visible displacements 44

4. *The fifth stage:* the child takes account of the sequential displacements of the object 66

5. *The sixth stage:* the representation of invisible displacements 79

6. The constitutive processes of object concept 86

CHAPTER 2

THE SPATIAL FIELD AND THE ELABORATION
OF GROUPS OF DISPLACEMENTS   97

1. *The first two stages:* practical and heterogeneous groups 101

2. *The third stage:* the coordination of practical groups and the formation of subjective groups 113

3. *The fourth stage:* the transition from subjective to objective groups and the discovery of reversible operations 152

4. *The fifth stage:* "objective" groups 183

5. *The sixth stage:* "representative" groups 203

6. The main processes of the construction of space 209

CHAPTER 3

THE DEVELOPMENT OF CAUSALITY 219

1. *The first two stages:* making contact between internal activity and the external environment, and the causality peculiar to the primary schemata 221

2. *The third stage:* magico-phenomenalistic causality 229

3. *The fourth stage:* the elementary externalization and objectification of causality 256

4. *The fifth stage:* the real objectification and spatialization of causality 271

5. *The sixth stage:* representative causality and the residues of the causality of preceding types 293

6. The origins of causality 308

CHAPTER 4

THE TEMPORAL FIELD 320

1. *The first two stages:* time itself and the practical series 322

2. *The third stage:* the subjective series 327

3. *The fourth stage:* the beginnings of the objectification of time 335

4. *The fifth stage:* the objective series 341

5. *The sixth stage:* the representative series 345

CONCLUSION

THE ELABORATION OF THE UNIVERSE 350

1. Assimilation and accommodation 350

2. The transition from sensorimotor intelligence to conceptual thought 357

3. From sensorimotor universe to representation of the child's world   364

   I. Space and object   364

4. From sensorimotor universe to representation of the child's world   376

   II. Causality and time   376

5. Conclusion   380

Introduction

The study of sensorimotor or practical intelligence in the first two years of development[1] has taught us how the child, at first directly assimilating the external environment to his own activity, later, in order to extend this assimilation, forms an increasing number of schemata which are both more mobile and better able to intercoordinate.

Side by side with this progressive involvement of the assimilatory schemata runs the continuous elaboration of the external universe, in other words, the convergent development of the explicatory function. The more numerous the links that are established among the schemata of assimilation, the less it remains centered on the subjectivity of the assimilating subject, in order to become actual comprehension and deduction. Thus, at the beginnings of assimilatory activity, any object whatever presented by the external environment to the subject's activity is simply something to suck, to look at, or to grasp: such assimilation is at this stage centered solely on the assimilating subject. Later, however, the same object is transformed into something to displace, to set in motion, and to utilize for increasingly complex ends. The essential thus becomes the totality of the relationships elaborated through personal activity between this object and other objects; to assimilate means, thereafter, to understand or deduce, and assimilation is intermingled thereby with the formation of relationships. By virtue of the fact that the assimilating subject enters into reciprocity with the things assimilated, the hand that grasps, the mouth that sucks, or the eyes that look are no longer limited to an activity unaware of itself even though self-centered: they are conceived by the sub-

[1] J. Piaget, *The Origins of Intelligence in Children* (New York: International Universities Press, 1952).

ject as things among things and as sustaining relations of interdependence with the universe.

It is therefore apparent that a development of explicatory accommodation corresponds to the progress of implicatory assimilation. The increasing coherence of the schemata thus parallels
the formation of a world of objects and spatial relationships, in
short, the elaboration of a solid and permanent universe.

We must now study the second aspect of the evolution of sensorimotor intelligence. This new phase of mental development is
of course inseparable from the first; object and causality are nothing other than accommodation to the reality of the schematism
of assimilation. But it is justifiable to study them separately, for
the description of behavior no longer suffices to account
for these new products of intellectual activity; it is the subject's
own interpretation of things which we must now try to analyze.

But, if the study of object concept and the spatial field and of
causality and the temporal field requires that one take the point
of view of awareness and no longer only that of observer, the description we shall give of the child's image of the world characteristic of his preverbal stage will be less venturesome than one
might fear; in order to reconstruct the subject's point of view
it is enough to reverse in some way the picture obtained by observation of his behavior. Through an apparently paradoxical
mechanism whose parallel we have described apropos of the egocentrism of thought of the older child, it is precisely when the
subject is most self-centered that he knows himself the least,
and it is to the extent that he discovers himself that he places
himself in the universe and constructs it by virtue of that fact.
In other words, egocentrism signifies the absence of both self-
perception and objectivity, whereas acquiring possession of the
object as such is on a par with the acquisition of self-perception.

The symmetry between the representation of things and the
functional development of intelligence enables us from now on
to glimpse the directional line of the evolution of the concepts
of object, space, causality, and time. In general it may be said
that during the first months of life, as long as assimilation remains centered on the organic activity of the subject, the universe presents neither permanent objects, nor objective space,
nor time interconnecting events as such, nor causality external to

the personal actions. If the child really knew himself, we should have to maintain that solipsism exists. At the very least we may designate as radical egocentrism this phenomenalism without self-perception, for the moving pictures perceived by the subject are known to him only in relation to his elementary activity. At the other extreme, at the moment when sensorimotor intelligence has sufficiently elaborated understanding to make language and reflective thought possible, the universe is, on the contrary, formed into a structure at once substantial and spatial, causal and temporal. This organization of reality occurs, as we shall see, to the extent that the self is freed from itself by finding itself and so assigns itself a place as a thing among things, an event among events. The transition from chaos to cosmos, which we shall study in the perception and representation of the world in the first two years of life, is brought about through an elimination of egocentrism comparable to that which we have described on the plane of the child's reflective thought and logic. But it is in its elementary and primordial form that we shall now try to grasp this component process of understanding; we shall thus comprehend how it depends on the mechanism of intellectual assimilation.

THE CONSTRUCTION OF REALITY IN THE CHILD

CHAPTER I

The Development of Object Concept

To understand how the budding intelligence constructs the external world, we must first ask whether the child, in its first months of life, conceives and perceives things as we do, as objects that have substance, that are permanent and of constant dimensions. If this is not the case, it is then necessary to explain how the idea of an object (object concept) is built up. The problem is closely connected with that of space. A world without objects would not present the character of spatial homogeneity and of coherence in displacements that marks our universe. Inversely the absence of "groups" in the changes of position would be equivalent to endless transformations, that is, continuous changes of states in the absence of any permanent object. In this first chapter, then, substance and space should be considered simultaneously, and it is only through abstraction that we shall limit ourselves to object concept.

A question of this sort conditions all other questions. A world composed of permanent objects constitutes not only a spatial universe but also a world obeying the principle of causality in the form of relationships between things, and regulated in time, without continuous annihilations or resurrections. Hence it is a universe both stable and external, relatively distinct from the internal world and one in which the subject places himself as one particular term among all the other terms. A universe without objects, on the other hand, is a world in which space does not constitute a solid environment but is limited to structuring the subject's very acts; it is a world of pictures each one of which can be known and analyzed but which disappear and reappear capriciously. From the point of view of causality it is a world in which the connections between things are masked by the relations between the action and its desired results; hence the subject's activity is conceived as being the primary and almost the sole motive power. As far as the boundaries between the self and the external world are concerned, a universe without objects is such that the self, lacking knowledge of itself, is absorbed in external pictures for want of knowing itself; moreover, these pictures center upon the self by failing to include it as a thing among other things, and thus fail to sustain interrelationships independent of the self.

Observation and experimentation combined seem to show that object concept, far from being innate or given ready-made in experience, is constructed little by little. Six stages can be discerned, corresponding to those of intellectual development in general. During the first two stages (those of reflexes and the earliest habits), the infantile universe is formed of pictures that can be recognized but that have no substantial permanence or spatial organization. During the third stage (secondary circular reactions), a beginning of permanence is conferred on things by prolongation of the movements of accommodation (grasping, etc.) but no systematic search for absent objects is yet observable. During the fourth stage ("application of known means to new situations") there is searching for objects that have disappeared but no regard for their displacements. During a fifth stage (about 12 to 18 months old) the object is constituted to the extent that it is permanent individual substance and inserted in the groups of displacements, but the child still cannot take account of changes of position brought about outside the field of direct perception. In a sixth stage (beginning at the age of 16 to 18 months) there is an image of absent objects and their displacements.

§ 1. THE FIRST TWO STAGES: NO SPECIAL BEHAVIOR RELATED TO VANISHED OBJECTS

Among all the impressions which assail his consciousness, the child distinguishes and quickly recognizes certain stable groups which we shall call pictures. That is why we have stated $(O.I.)$[1] that every schema of reproduction assimilation is extended sooner or later in generalizing assimilation and recognitory assimilation combined, recognition being derived from assimilation.

The most elementary example of this process is incontestably that of sucking. The nursling, from the second week of life, is capable of finding the nipple and differentiating it from the surrounding teguments; therein is proof that the schema of sucking in order to nurse begins to be dissociated from the schemata of empty sucking or of sucking at random, and thus results in recognition through acts. So also, after the fifth to the sixth week of life, the child's smile reveals that he recognizes familiar voices or faces whereas strange sounds or images astonish him. In a general way, every functional use (hence all primary circular reaction) of sucking, of sight, of hearing, of touch, etc., gives rise to recognitions.

But none of that proves or even suggests that in the first weeks of life the universe is really cut up into objects, that is, into things conceived as permanent, substantial, external to the self, and firm in existence even though they do not directly affect perception. In itself, recognition is not at all a recognition of objects and it can be affirmed that none of the characteristics mentioned here defines recognition in its beginnings, for they are the product of an extremely complex intellectual elaboration and not of an elementary act of simple sensorimotor assimilation. True, in the associational theory of recognition it could be asserted that recognition merely confers upon the recognized qualities the constitution of the object itself: if, in order to recognize a thing, it is really necessary to have retained the image of that thing (an image capable of being evoked, and not simply the motor schema readapting at each new contact), and if recognition results from an association between this image and actual sensations, then naturally the conserved image will be able to act in the mind when the object itself is absent and thus suggest the idea of its conservation. Recognition will thenceforth be extended into belief in the permanence of the object itself.

[1] J. Piaget, *The Origins of Intelligence in Children* (New York: International Universities Press, 1952); hereafter referred to as *O.I.*

But in the elementary examples now under consideration, recognition does not necessitate any evocation of a mental image. For recognition to begin, it is enough that the attitude previously adopted with regard to the thing be again set in motion and that nothing in the new perception thwart that process. The impression of satisfaction and familiarity peculiar to recognition could thus stem only from this essential fact of the continuity of a schema; the subject recognizes his own reaction before he recognizes the object as such. If the object is new and impedes action, there is no recognition; if the object is too well known or constantly present, the automatism of habit suppresses any opportunity for conscious recognition; but if the object resists the activity of the sensorimotor schema sufficiently to create a momentary maladjustment while giving rise soon after to a successful readjustment, then assimilation is accompanied by recognition. The latter is only the realization of mutual conformity between a given object and a schema all ready to assimilate it. Recognition accordingly begins by being subjective before it becomes object recognition, which of course does not prevent the subject from projecting recognized perception into the undifferentiated universe of his adualistic consciousness (since in the beginning nothing is experienced as subjective). In other words, recognition is at first only a particular instance of assimilation: the thing recognized stimulates and feeds the sensorimotor schema which was previously constructed for its use, and without any necessity for evocation. If this is true, it is self-evident that recognition does not, by itself and without further complication, to lead object concept. In order that the recognized picture may become an object it must be dissociated from the action itself and put in a context of spatial and causal relations independent of the immediate activity. The criterion of this objectification, hence of this rupture in continuity between things perceived and the elementary sensorimotor schemata, is the advent of the behavior patterns related to absent pictures: search for the vanished object, belief in its permanence, evocation, etc. But primary assimilation only implies total continuity between action and environment and does not lead to any reaction beyond the immediate and actual excitation.

Furthermore, independently of recognition, there is no

proof that direct perception is at first a perception of objects. When we perceive a motionless thing we place it in a space in which we are ourselves and thus conceive it according to the laws of perspective; the particular point of view from which we see it does not at all prevent us from imagining its depth, its reverse side, its possible displacements, in short, everything that makes it an object characterized by its form and constant dimensions. When we perceive it in motion or simply removed from its initial location we distinguish between these changes of position and changes of state and thus contrast at every moment the thing as it is with the thing as it appears to our sight; again, this dual distinction leads to the permanence characteristic of object concept. But does the child do the same from the very beginnings of his activity? It is permissible, not to say necessary, to doubt it. Regarding the motionless object, only little by little will a suitable spatial structure make it possible to attribute to it the relief, the form, and the depth characteristic of its objective identity. With regard to the thing in motion, the child has not been given the power from the outset to differentiate between changes of position and changes of state and thus to endow flowing perceptions with the quality of geometric "groups," consequently of objects. On the contrary, failing to locate himself at the outset in space, and to conceive an absolute relativity between the movements of the external world and his own, the child at first does not know how to construct either groups or objects and may well consider the changes in his image of the world as being simultaneously real and constantly created by his own actions.

True, from the earliest stages, certain operations herald the formation of the object: they are, on the one hand, the intercoordinations between heterogeneous schemata which precede the coordination of prehension and of sight (coordination of which creates a special problem) and, on the other hand, the sensorimotor accommodations. These two types of behavior lead the child to transcend the absolutely immediate, and assure a beginning of continuity of pictures perceived.

With regard to the intercoordination of schemata, that of sight and hearing may be mentioned. From the second month of life and the beginning of the third, the child tries to look at the objects he hears (*O.I.*, obs. 44-49), thus revealing the relationship he is establishing between certain sounds and certain visual pictures. It is clear that such coordination endows sensory pictures with a greater degree of solidity than when they are perceived through a single kind of schemata: the fact of expecting to see something instills in the subject who listens to a sound a tendency to consider the visual image as existing before the perception. So also every intersensory coordination (between sucking and prehension, prehension and sight, etc.) contributes to arousing the anticipations which are assurances of the solidity and coherence of the external world.

But that is very far from object concept. The intercoordination of heterogeneous schemata is explained, as we have seen (*O.I.*, Chap. II, §3-4), by a reciprocal assimilation of the presenting schemata. In the case of sight and hearing, therefore, there exists at the outset no objective identity of the visual image with the auditory image (which can also be a tactile or gustatory picture, etc.), but simply a sort of subjective identity; the child tries to see what he hears because each schema of assimilation seeks to encompass the whole universe. Thereafter a coordination of this kind does not yet imply any permanence conceived as independent of present action and perception; discovery of the visual picture announced by the sound is only the extension of the act of trying to see. However, if the act of searching with the glance is, in us adults, accompanied by a belief in the firm existence of the object looked at, we are not justified in assuming that this relation has been obvious from the outset. Just as lip movement or any other functional exercise creates by itself its own object or its own result, so also the nursling may consider the picture which he contemplates as the extension, if not the product, of his effort to see. Perhaps one can reply that the localization of the sound in space, combined with the localization of the visual picture, confer an objectivity on the thing which is simultaneously heard and seen. But as we shall see, the space involved here is still only a space dependent on the immediate action and not precisely an objective space in which things and actions are placed in relation to each other in groups which are independent of the body itself. In short, intersensory coordinations contribute to solidifying the universe by organizing actions but they do not at all suffice to render that universe external to those actions.

Sensorimotor accommodations of every kind often lead not only to anticipations concerning perception (such as the above-mentioned coordinations), but also to extensions of the action related to the image perceived, even after the image has disappeared. Here again it may seem at first that object concept has already been acquired, but a more stringent examination dispels this illusion.

The clearest example is that of visual accommodations; when the child knows how to follow with his eyes an image which is being displaced, and above all when he has learned how to extend that movement of the eyes by an appropriate shift of head and torso, he very quickly reveals behavior patterns comparable to a search for the thing seen which then vanished. This phenomenon, particularly distinct in the case of sight, is also found in connection with sucking, prehension, etc.

OBS. 1. Laurent, as early as the second day, seems to seek with his lips the breast which has escaped him (*O.I.*, obs. 2). From the third day he gropes more systematically to find it (*O.I.*, obs. 4-5, 8, and 10). From 0;1 (2) and 0;1 (3) he searches in the same way for his thumb, which brushed his mouth or came out of it (*O.I.*, obs. 17, 18, etc.). Thus it seems that contact of the lips with the nipple and the thumb gives rise to a pursuit of those objects, once they have disappeared, a pursuit connected with reflex activity in the first case and with a nascent or acquired habit in the second case.

OBS. 2. In the realm of sight, Jacqueline, as early as 0;2 (27) follows her mother with her eyes, and when her mother leaves the visual field, continues to look in the same direction until the picture reappears.

Same observation with Laurent at 0;2 (1). I look at him through the hood of his bassinet and from time to time I appear at a more or less constant point; Laurent then watches that point when I am out of his sight and obviously expects to see me reappear.

Noteworthy too are visual explorations (*O.I.*, obs. 33), alternate glances (*O.I.*, obs. 35) and reversed glances (*ibid.*, obs. 36) which attest to a sort of expectation of some familiar picture.

OBS. 3. Analagous behavior is observable with respect to hearing from the time coordination exists between this function and that of sight, that is to say from the time movements of eyes and head objectively bear witness to some searching. Thus at 0;2 (6) Laurent finds with his glance an electric kettle whose lid I shake (see *O.I.*, obs. 49). When I interrupt the noise, Laurent looks at me a moment, then again looks at the kettle even though it is now silent; hence we may assume that he expects new sounds to come from it, in other words, he behaves with regard to the interrupted sound as he does with regard to the visual pictures which have just disappeared.

OBS. 4. Prehension gives rise to behavior patterns of the same kind. Just as the child seems to expect to see again that which he has just seen and to hear again the sound which has just ceased, so also, when he begins to grasp, he seems to be convinced of the possibility that his hand will rediscover the object it has just relinquished. Thus during the behavior patterns described in *O.I.*, obs. 52-54, Laurent, considerably before knowing how to grasp what he sees, constantly lets go and recaptures the objects he is handling. At 0;2 (7) in particular, Laurent holds a sheet in his hand for a moment, then lets it go and grasps it again soon afterward. Or he holds his hands together, separates them, holds them together again, etc. Finally it may be recalled that as soon as coordination between prehension and sight has been established, the child brings before his eyes everything he grasps outside the visual field, thus revealing expectation comparable to that which we have noted in connection with hearing and sight (See *O.I.*, obs. 85, 89, and 92).

OBS. 5. A reaction slightly more complex than these is that of the child who stops looking at a certain picture and directs his glance elsewhere and who then returns to the first picture; that is the equivalent, in the realm of primary circular reactions, of the deferred reactions which we shall analyze in connection with the second stage.

Thus Lucienne, at 0;3 (9) sees me at the extreme left of her visual field and smiles vaguely. She then looks in different directions, in front of her and to the right, but constantly returns to the place in which she sees me and dwells on it every time for a moment.

At 0;4 (26) she takes the breast but turns when I call her and smiles at me. Then she resumes nursing, but several times in succession, despite my silence, she turns directly to the position from which she can see me. She does it again after a pause of a few minutes. Then I withdraw; when she turns without finding me her expression is one of mingled disappointment and expectation.

At 0;4 (29) same reaction; she is on my lap but with her back to me, and sees my face by turning very much to the right. She then constantly returns to that position.

At first these facts and analogous ones which it would be easy to accumulate seem to indicate a universe similar to ours. The gustatory, visual, auditory, or tactile images that the child ceases to suck, see, hear or grasp seem to exist for him in the capacity of permanent objects which are independent of the action and which the action simply finds again. But in comparing these same behavior patterns with those we describe in connection with subsequent stages, it is apparent how superficial this interpretation would be and how phenomenalistic this primitive universe remains, far from constituting from the outset a world of substances. An essential difference contrasts these early behavior patterns with the true search for objects. True search is active and causes the intervention of movements which do not solely extend the interrupted action, whereas in the present behavior patterns either there is simple expectation, or else the search only continues the earlier act of accommodation. In these latter two cases the expected object is still related to the action itself.

True, in several of our examples there is simply expectation, that is to say passivity and not activity. In the case of the disappearing visual image the child limits himself to looking at the place where the object vanished (obs. 2): thus he merely preserves the attitude of the earlier perception and if nothing reappears, he soon gives up. If he had object concept, on the contrary, he would actively search to find out where the thing could have been put; he would remove obstacles, change the position of the presenting objects at hand, and so on. Lacking prehension, the child could search with his eyes, change his perspective, etc. But that is precisely what he does not know how to do, for the vanished object is not yet for him a permanent object which has been moved; it is a mere image which reenters the void as soon as it vanishes, and emerges from it for no objective reason.

When, on the contrary, there is a search (obs. 1, 3, 4, and 5) it is noteworthy that the search merely reproduces the earlier act of accommodation. In the case of sucking, it is a reflex mechanism which allows the child to grope until he encounters the objective. With regard to observations 3, 4, and 5, the child is content with repeating the act of accommodation just performed. In none of these acts is it possible to speak of the object as existing independently of the activity. The objective is in the direct extension of the act. It is as though the child did not dissociate one from the other and considered the goal to be attained as depending on the action alone and, more precisely, on only one type of action. In the event of failure the child promptly gives up instead of attempting, as he will later do, special steps to complete the initial act. True, during these first stages, the child does not know how to grasp and consequently his potentialities for active searching amount to very little. But if the motor unskillfulness of these initial stages sufficed to explain the child's passivity, in other words, if the child, while not knowing how to search for the absent object, nevertheless believes in its permanence, we should state that search for the vanished object begins as soon as the habits of prehension have been acquired. But we shall now see that this is not the case.

In short, the first two stages are characterized by the absence of any special behavior related to vanished objects. Either the image which disappears immediately sinks into oblivion, that is to say, into the affective void, or else it is regretted, desired, and again expected, and the only behavior pattern utilized to rediscover it is the mere repetition of earlier accommodations.

The latter case applies chiefly to persons, when they have paid too much attention to the nursling and he can no longer bear solitude; he stamps and cries at the disappearance of every image, thus revealing his keen desire to see it reappear. But does this mean that the baby conceives of the vanished image as an object existing in space, remaining identical to itself and escaping sight, touch and hearing because it has been displaced and is masked by various solid substances? In such an hypothesis it would be necessary to attribute to the nursling a most improbable power of spatial representation and intellectual construction, and it would no longer be possible to understand the difficulty he will have, until about 9 or 10 months of age, in searching actively for objects when they are covered by a cloth or a screen of some kind right before his eyes (see the third and fourth stages). But the hypothesis is neither necessary nor does it conform to observations. It is not necessary because it suffices, for the child to hope for the return of the interesting image (of his mother, etc.), that he attribute to it a sort of affective or subjective permanence without localization or substantiation; the vanished image remains, so to speak, "at disposal" without being found anywhere from a spatial point of view. It remains what an occult spirit is to the magician; ready to return if one catches it successfully but obeying no objective law. How does the child go about bringing to himself the image of his desires? Merely by crying at random or by looking at the place where it disappeared or where it was last seen (obs. 2 and 5). It is here that the hypothesis of an object situated in space is contrary to the findings of observation. The child's initial search is not at all an effort to understand the displacements of the vanished image; it is only an extension or repetition of the most recent acts of accommodation.

§ 2. THE THIRD STAGE: BEGINNING OF PERMANENCE EXTENDING THE MOVEMENTS OF ACCOMMODATION

The behavior patterns of the third stage are those which are observable between the beginnings of prehension of things seen and the beginnings of active search for vanished objects. Hence they still are earlier than object concept but mark progress in the solidification of the universe depending on action.

Between three and six months of age, as we have seen elsewhere (*O.I.*, Chap. II, §4), the child begins to grasp what he sees, to bring before his eyes the objects he touches, in short to coordinate his visual universe with the tactile universe. But not until the age of 9 or 10 months does active search for vanished objects occur in the form of the use of grasping to remove solid objects that may mask or cover the desired object. This intermediate period constitutes our third stage.

But, if this long lapse of time is necessary for transition from prehension of an object at hand to true search for a missing object, it is because the interim is filled with the acquisition of a series of intermediate behavior patterns all of which are necessary to proceed from the mere perceived image to the concept of permanent object. In this connection we can distinguish these five types of behavior: 1) "visual accommodation to rapid movements"; 2) "interrupted prehension"; 3) "deferred circular reaction"; 4) the "reconstruction of an invisible whole from a visible fraction," and 5) the "removal of obstacles preventing perception." The first of these behavior patterns merely extends those of the second stage, and the fifth fulfills those of the fourth stage.

Visual accommodation to rapid movements makes possible the anticipation of future positions of the object and consequently endows it with a certain permanence. This permanence of course remains related to the act of accommodation itself, and thus the behavior patterns merely extend those of the second stage; but there is progress in the sense that the anticipated position of the object is a new position and not one observed a moment earlier to which the eyes merely return. Two particular instances are of special importance: reaction to the movement of bodies which disappear from the visual field after having induced a lateral turn of the head, and reaction to falling movements. Both these behavior patterns seem to have developed under the influence of prehension.

OBS. 6. Laurent's reaction to falling objects still seems to be non-existent at 0;5 (24): he does not follow with his eyes any of the objects which I drop in front of him.

At 0;5 (26), on the other hand, Laurent searches in front of him for a paper ball which I drop above his coverlet. He immediately looks at the coverlet after the third attempt but only in front of him, that is, where he has just grasped the ball. When I drop the object outside the bassinet Laurent does not look for it (except around my empty hand while it remains up in the air).

At 0;5 (30) no reaction to the fall of a box of matches. The same is true at 0;6 (0), but then when he drops the box himself he searches for it next to him with his eyes (he is lying down).

At 0;6 (3) Laurent, lying down, holds in his hand a box five centimeters in diameter. When it escapes him he looks for it in the right direction (beside him). I then grasp the box and drop it myself, vertically and too fast for him to be able to follow the trajectory. His eyes search for it at once on the sofa on which he is lying. I manage to eliminate any sound or shock and I perform the experiment at his right and at his left; the result is always positive.

At 0;6 (7) he holds an empty match box in his hand. When it falls his eyes search for it even if they have not followed the beginning of the fall; he turns his head in order to see it on the sheet. Same reaction at 0;6 (9) with a rattle, but this time he has watched the initial movement of the object. The same is true at 0;6 (16) when his eyes have followed the beginning of the fall, at 0;6 (20) etc., etc.

At 0;7 (29) he searches on the floor for everything I drop above him, if he has in the least perceived the beginning of the movement of falling. At 0;8 (1) he searches on the floor for a toy which I held in my hand and which I have just let drop without his knowledge. Not finding it, his eyes return to my hand which he examines at length, and then he again searches on the floor.

OBS. 7. At 0;7 (30) Lucienne grasps a small doll which I present to her for the first time. She examines it with great interest, then lets it go (not intentionally); she immediately looks for it in front of her but does not see it right away.

When she has found it, I take it from her and place a coverlet over it, before her eyes (Lucienne is seated); no reaction.

At 0;8 (5) Lucienne searches systematically on the floor for everything that she happens to drop. When an object is released in front of her, sometimes she searches for it also with her eyes, but less often (an average of one out of four times). The need to grasp what was in her hand therefore plays a role in this reaction to movements of falling; the permanence belonging to the beginnings of the concept of tactile object (of which we shall again speak in connection with interrupted prehension) thus interferes with the permanence arising from visual accommodation.

At 0;8 (12) I again observe that Lucienne tries harder to find fallen objects with her eyes when she has previously touched the objects.

At 0;9 (25) she looks at my hand which I at first hold motionless and then suddenly lower; Lucienne searches for it on the floor for a long time.

OBS. 8. Jacqueline's search for the fallen object took place later. At 0;8 (20) for example, when she tries to reach a cigarette case hanging above her and it drops, she does not search in front of her at all but continues to look up in the air.

At 0;9 (8), same negative reaction with her parrot, which is bulky; it falls on her quilt while she is trying to reach it above her; she does not lower her eyes and continues to search in the air. However the parrot contains a rattle and makes a noise in falling.

At 0;9 (9) on the other hand, Jacqueline makes the same parrot fall by chance on the left of the bassinet and this time, because of the noise, she looks around for it. As the parrot has entered between the quilt and the wicker, Jacqueline perceives only its tail; however she recognizes the object (an instance of "reconstitution of invisible totalities" of which we shall subsequently speak) and tries to grasp it. But by trying to grasp it she wedges it down until she can see it no longer. However, still hearing the rattle inside the parrot, she taps the quilt which covers it and the sound ensues (this is a mere utilization of circular reaction related to this toy). But it does not occur to her to search under the quilt.

OBS. 9. The same day, at 0;9 (9), Jacqueline is seated in her bassinet and looks at my watch which I hold 20-30 centimeters away from her eyes and which I let drop by its chain.

At the first attempt, Jacqueline follows the trajectory, but with a certain tardiness, and finds the watch on the quilt covering her lap. The noise of the fall doubtless helps her and above all the fact that I lower the watch without yet letting it go.

Second attempt; she does not follow the movement, looks at my empty hand with surprise and seems to look around it (this time I have merely let the object go).

Third attempt: she again searches around my hand, then looks on my lap and takes possession of the object.

In order to eliminate the role of sound, I continue with the chain alone; in eight new sequential attempts Jacqueline only once searched on the floor. The other times she was content to examine my hand.

Then I lower the chain slowly, but quickly enough to precede the child's glance; Jacqueline searches on the floor. Then I recommence, merely letting the chain go; six negative attempts. The next two times Jacqueline searches on her lap but with her hand only, while looking in front of her. Finally, during the last attempts, she gives up this tactile search and only examines her hands.

OBS. 10. At 0;9 (10) a new experiment with Jacqueline, but using a little notebook of 8x5 centimeters which I let fall from high up (above her eye level) on to a cushion placed on her lap. This time Jacqueline immediately searches on the floor, although she has not had time to follow the trajectory; she sees only the point of departure and my empty hands.

At 0;9 (11) same experiment with her parrot: she again looks immediately at the floor. With the watch chain, on the other hand, the reaction is completely negative, evidently because the object is less bulky; Jacqueline examines my empty fingers in astonishment. Hence object concept does not yet exist: in the case of the parrot or the notebook it is simply the movement of accommodation which continues, and when the object is too small for the eyes to follow at its point of departure nothing happens.

At 0;9 (16) Jacqueline, seated on my arm, plays with her celluloid duck and lets it fall behind my shoulder. Then she immediately tries to find it again but, and this is very interesting, she does not try to look around my back; she pursues her investigations in front. We shall understand the reason for this error by proving, later on, how difficult it is for the child to take account of screens and to conceive that an object can be "behind" another object.

From 0;9 (18) reaction to falling movements seems to be acquired; falling objects, even when the child has not held them just beforehand, immediately cause the child to look at the ground.

OBS. 11. At 0;9 (6) Jacqueline looks at her duck which I hold level with her eyes and which I move horizontally to the back of her head. She follows it for a moment with her eyes, then loses sight of it. Nevertheless, she continues this movement of accommodation until she finds the duck again. She has searched assiduously for quite a while.

Then I replace the duck before her and repeat the experiment, but in the other direction. Same reaction at first, but then during the search she forgets what she wants and takes possession of another object.

OBS. 11a. In this connection we may mention Lucienne's progress since obs. 5 in remembering positions. It involves a behavior pattern bringing us back to the behavior patterns of the second stage but more complex than they and contemporaneous with those of the third. At 0;8 (12) Lucienne is seated next to me; I am at her right. She sees me, then plays with her mother. Then she looks at me while her mother slowly goes away, on the left, to the door of the room and disappears. Lucienne follows her with her eyes until she ceases to be visible, then, all at once, she turns her head in my direction. She looks at my face at once; she knew that I was there even though she had not looked at me for a few minutes.

OBS. 12. So also Laurent, at 0;6 (0), looks at a rattle which I move horizontally from left to right, at the level of his face. He manages to follow the beginning of the trajectory, then loses sight of the moving object; then he abruptly turns his head and turns it back again 50 centimeters farther. Then I make the object describe the reverse trajectory and he searches for it a moment without recovering it, then gives up.

In the following days the reaction becomes more definite and Laurent rediscovers the object in any direction whatever. Same observation at 0;6 (30), at 0;7 (15), at 0;7 (29), etc.

This capacity for rediscovering the object by following its trajectory develops in Laurent as did the memory of positions in Lucienne (obs. 11a). Thus at 0;7 (11) I am playing with Laurent when his mother appears above him. After she disappears, he throws his head back in order to find her again. He catches sight of her just as she is leaving the room (before he hears the sound of the door). Then he returns to me but always turns around again to see if his mother is still there.

However commonplace these facts may be they are important in forming object concept. They show us that the beginnings of permanence attributed to images perceived arise from the child's action in movements of accommodation. In this respect the present behavior patterns merely extend those of the second stage but reveal essential progress: the child no longer seeks the object only where he has recently seen it but hunts for it in a new place. He anticipates the perception of successive positions of the moving object and in a sense makes allowance for its displacements. But precisely because this beginning of permanence is only an extension of the action in progress, it could only be very limited. The child cannot conceive of just any displacements or just any objective permanence. He is limited to pursuing, more or less correctly, with his eyes or with his hand the trajectory delineated by the movements of accommodation peculiar to the immediately preceding perception; and it is only in the measure in which, in the absence of the objects, he continues the process begun in their presence that he is able to endow them with a certain permanence.

Let us look at this more closely. With regard to Laurent (and to Lucienne, although we have not had the opportunity of understanding the origins of her reaction to falling movements), we prove that at first a search for the fallen object takes place more often when it is the child himself who has let it drop; the permanence attributed to the object is consequently greater when the action of the hand interferes with that of the eyes. Jacqueline's apprenticeship is among the most suggestive. At first (obs. 8) there is no reaction to the fall because the child has not observed the initial movement of the falling object. Then Jacqueline observes that initial movement but instead of extending it when the object perceived leaves the visual field, she returns to the point of departure to search for the toy (obs. 9); however, when the movement is slow or a concomitant sound helps the child in her search, she manages to reconstitute the exact trajectory. In the next phase (beginning of obs. 10), the reaction is positive when the object is sufficiently bulky to have been followed with the eyes long enough, but it remains negative with too slender a chain. Finally only the positive reaction becomes generalized.

It therefore seems clear that the displacement attributed to the object depends essentially on the child's action (movements of accommodation which are extended by looking) and that permanence itself remains related to that very action.

As far as the first point is concerned, it would be impossible to give to the child the concept of autonomous displacements. When we are following an object with our eyes and when, after having lost sight of it, we try to find it again, we have the feeling that it is in a space independent of ourselves; consequently we accept as true that the movements of the object occur without relationship to our own, outside our area of perception, and we strive to move ourselves so as to be reunited with it. On the other hand, everything takes place as if the child, when witnessing the falling movement from the start, is not aware that he moves himself about, in order to follow the movement, and consequently is not aware that his body and the moving object are located in the same space; if the object is not found within the exact extension of the movement of accommodation, the child will give up hope of finding it again. Thereafter, in his consciousness, the object's movement is one with the kinesthetic or sensorimotor impressions which accompany his own movements of eyes, head, or torso; when he loses sight of the moving object the only procedures suitable for finding it again therefore consist either in extending movements which have already been delineated or in returning to the point of departure. Nothing forces the child to consider the object as having been displaced in itself and independently of its movement; all that he is given is an immediate connection between his kinesthetic impressions and the reappearance of the object in his visual field, in short a connection between a certain effort and a certain result. There does not yet exist what we shall later call (Chap. II) an objective displacement.

Then regarding the second point, that is to say the permanence attributed to the object as such, it is self-evident that this permanence remains related to the subject's action. In other words, the visual images the child pursues acquire in his eyes a certain solidity to the precise extent that he tries to follow them, but they do not yet constitute substantial objects. The mere fact that the child does not imagine their displacement as being an independent movement and that he often searches for them (that is to say, when he has not been able to look at them long enough) at the very point where they made their departure, reveals that for him, these images still remain at the disposal of the action itself, and in certain absolute situations. True, that is a beginning of permanence, but such permanence remains subjective; it must produce in the child an impression comparable to that which he experienced in discovering that he could suck his thumb when he wished, see things move when he moved his head, hear a sound when he rubbed a toy against his bassinet or pulled the strings attached to the rattle hanging from its hood, etc. The nature of the primitive object conceived as being at disposal is therefore on a par with the whole of the behavior patterns of this stage, that is to say, with the primary and secondary circular reactions during which the universe presents itself to the subject as depending on his activity. There is progress over the first stages during which the object is not distinguished from the results of reflex activity or mere primary circular reaction (that is to say, the actions exerted by the subject on his own organism to produce some interesting result), but it is a progress in degree and not in quality; the object still exists only in connection with the action itself.

As we shall see later, the proof that the object is still nothing more than this is that the child at this age still manifests no particular behavior pattern related to vanished objects. Lucienne's reaction at 0;7 (30) when I cover her doll with a piece of cloth (obs. 7) already makes this apparent.

This dependence of the object on the action is found again in the second group of acts which we can now emphasize: the acts of interrupted prehension. These observations are in the same relation, in comparison to obs. 4 of the first stages, as are the visual accommodations to rapid movements in comparison to obs. 2 and 5. In other words, the permanence peculiar to the beginnings of the tactile object is still only an extension of accommodation movements, but henceforth the child will try to grasp the lost object in new positions and no longer only in the same place. As soon as prehension becomes a systematic operation, interest in which surpasses all else (between the ages of four to six months), the child learns at one stroke to follow with his hand objects which escape him, even when he does not see them. It is this behavior pattern which permits the subject to attribute a beginning of permanence to tactile objects.

OBS. 13. At 0;8 (20) Jacqueline takes possession of my watch which I offer her while holding the chain in my hand. She examines the watch with great interest, feels it, turns it over, says *apff*, etc. I pull the chain; she feels a resistance and holds it back with force, but ends by letting it go. As she is lying down she does not try to look but holds out her arm, catches the watch again and brings it before her eyes.

I recommence the game; she laughs at the resistance of the watch and still searches without looking. If I pull the object progressively (a little farther each time she has caught it) she searches farther and farther, handling and pulling everything that she encounters. If I pull it back abruptly, she is content to explore the place where the watch departed, touching her bib, her sheet, etc.

But this permanence is solely the function of prehension. If, before her eyes, I hide the watch behind my hand, behind the quilt, etc., she does not react and forgets everything immediately; in the absence of tactile factors visual images seem to melt into each other without substance. As soon as I replace the watch in Jacqueline's hands and pull it back she searches for it again, however.

OBS. 14. Here is a counterproof. At 0;9 (21) Jacqueline is seated and I place on her lap a rubber eraser which she has just held in her hand. Just as she is about to grasp it again I put my hand between her eyes and the eraser; she immediately gives up, as though the object no longer existed.

The experiment is repeated ten times. Every time that Jacqueline is touching the object with her finger at the moment when I cut off her view of it she continues her search to the point of complete success (without looking at the eraser and often dropping it by displacing it involuntarily, etc.). On the other hand, if no tactile contact has been established before the child ceases to see the eraser, Jacqueline withdraws her hand.

Same attempts with a marble, a pencil, etc., and same reactions. My hand does not interest her at all; therefore it is not a shift in interest that causes forgetfulness; it is simply because the image of my hand abolishes that of the object beneath it, unless, let us repeat, her fingers have already grazed the object or perhaps also unless her hand is already in action under mine and ready to grasp.

At 0;9 (22) same observations.

OBS. 15. At 0;6 (0) Lucienne is alone in her bassinet and, watching what she is doing, grasps the material covering the sides. She pulls the folds toward herself but lets them go at each attempt. She then brings before her eyes her hand which is tightly closed, and opens it cautiously. She looks attentively at her fingers and recommences. This goes on more than ten times.

It is therefore sufficient for her to have touched an object, believing she grasps it, for her to conceive of it as being in her hand although she no longer feels it. Such a behavior pattern, like the preceding ones, shows the degree of tactile permanence the child attributes to objects he has grasped.

OBS. 16. So also Laurent, at 0;7 (5) loses a cigarette box which he has just grasped and swung to and fro. Unintentionally he drops it outside the visual field. He then immediately brings his hand before his eyes and looks at it for a long time with an expression of surprise, disappointment, something like an impression of its disappearance. But far from considering the loss as irremediable, he begins again to swing his hand, although it is empty; after this he looks at it once more! For anyone who has seen this act and the child's expression it is impossible not to interpret such behavior as an attempt to make the object come back. Such an observation, combined with the preceding one (Lucienne at 0;6) places in full light the true nature of the object peculiar to this stage: a mere extension of the action.

Subsequently Laurent, to whom I have returned the box, again loses it several times; when he has just held it he is satisfied to stretch out his arm in order to find it again, or else he stops searching altogether (see the next observation).

OBS. 17. As early as 0;4 (6) Laurent searches with his hand for a doll he has just let go. He does not look at what he is doing but extends his arm in the direction toward which it was oriented when the object fell.

At 0;4 (21) also, he lowers his forearm in order again to find under the sheet a stick he held in his hand and which he has just let go.

Same reaction at 0;5 (24) with all sorts of objects. I then try to determine how extensive his search is. I touch his hand with a doll which I immediately withdraw; he is satisfied to lower his forearm without really exploring the surrounding area (see Chap. II, obs. 69).

At 0;6 (0), 0;6 (9), 0;6 (10), 0;6 (15), etc., I observe the same facts. Laurent believes the object has disappeared if he does not find it merely by lowering his arm; the object for which he searches is therefore not yet endowed with true mobility but is conceived as merely extending the interrupted act of prehension. On the other hand, if the fallen object touches the child's cheek, his chin, or his hand, he knows very well how to find it again. It is therefore not motor incapacity which explains the lack of true searching but rather the primitive quality attributed to the object.

At 0;6 (15) I again observe that if the object suddenly falls from his hand Laurent does not search for it. On the contrary, when the hand is about to grasp the escaping object or when the hand displaces the object, shakes it, etc., then a search takes place. Only, in order to recover the object Laurent is always satisfied to raise his arm with no trajectory of true exploration.

At 0;7 (5) he grasps and swings the cigarette box of obs. 16; when he loses it right after having taken it he searches on the coverlet with his hand. However, when he drops it under any other circumstance, he does not try to find it again. I then again offer him the same box above his eye level; he makes it fall by touching it but does not search for it!

At 0;7 (12) he lets go, at his right, a rattle which he was holding in his hand; he searches for it for quite a while without hearing or touching it. He gives up and then begins again to search at the same place. Finally he fails. Next he loses it on his left and finds it twice more because the object is in the direct range of his arm movements.

Finally, from o;8 (8) he truly searches for everything that falls from his hands.

We must first emphasize the difference between these reactions and the behavior patterns of the fourth stage, which consist in searching with the hands for the object disappearing from the visual field. In obs. 13-14 as in obs. 6-12 (accommodation to rapid movements) it is still only a question of a permanence merely extending earlier accommodation movements and not of a special search for the vanished object. The child, holding something in his hand, wishes to keep it when it escapes him; he then merely reproduces the gesture of grasping which he made shortly before. Such a reaction certainly presupposes that the subject expects his gesture to lead to the desired result. But this expectation is merely based on the belief that the object is at the disposal of the act. In this regard obs. 15 and 16 have decisive significance. That does not yet at all imply the substantial permanence of the thing independently of the gesture or the existence of objective trajectories.[2] Proof of this is that the least obstacle advening to change the situation as a whole discourages the child. The child is content merely to stretch out his arm; he does not truly search and invents no new procedure for rediscovering the vanished object. This is all the more striking because, as we shall see, it is along the very lines indicated by the present behavior patterns that such procedures will be formed.

Let us examine a third group of behavior patterns also capable of engendering a beginning of object permanence: the deferred circular reactions. As we have seen, the permanence peculiar to objects of this stage is not yet either substantial or truly spatial; it depends on the action itself and the object merely constitutes that which is at the disposal of that action. We have proved, moreover, that such a situation stems from the fact that the activity of the child at this level consists essentially in primary and secondary circular reactions and not yet in tertiary reactions. In other words, the child spends the better part of his time in reproducing all sorts of interesting results evoked by the sights around him and tries only a little to study new things for their own sake, to experiment. Thereafter the universe of that stage is

[2] See Chap. II, obs. 69.

composed of a countless series of potential actions, the object being nothing more than the material at the disposal of those actions. If this is true, it is to be expected that the secondary circular reactions constitute one of the most abundant sources of elementary permanence; that is what the analysis of deferred circular reactions will show.

It must be noted that sooner or later circular reaction brings with it a sort of revival that prolongs its influence over the child's behavior. We do not, of course, speak of the fact that circular reaction reappears every time the child finds himself facing the same objects (shaking himself when he sees the bassinet hood, pulling the chain when he sees the rattle to which it is attached, etc.) for there deferred behavior patterns are not involved, but rather merely habits revived by the presence of a familiar stimulus. We are thinking exclusively of those acts in the course of which circular reaction is interrupted by circumstances and resumes shortly after without any external stimulus. In such cases the fact that the child returns of his own accord to the position and gestures necessary for the resumption of the interrupted act endows the objects thus rediscovered and recognized with a permanence analogous to those of which we have just spoken. The permanence is even more marked because the rediscovered action, being more complex, gives rise to a proportionately greater solidification of the perceived images.

OBS. 18. At 0;8 (30) Lucienne is busy scratching a powder box placed next to her on her left, but abandons that game when she sees me appear at her right. She drops the box and plays with me for a moment, babbles, etc. Then she suddenly stops looking at me and turns at once in the correct position to grasp the box; obviously she does not doubt that this will be at her disposal in the very place where she used it before.

OBS. 19. At 0;9 (3) Jacqueline tries to grasp a coverlet behind her head, in order to swing it.[3] I distract her by offering her a celluloid

---

[3] This behavior of "swinging" already belongs to the fourth stage with respect to the general development of intelligence (see *O.I.*, obs. 139). But, with regard to object concept, the deferred reaction to which it gives rise in this observation does not yet transcend the level of the third stage. It is apparent that, without considerable artifice, it is impossible to synchronize the corresponding steps of the evolutions peculiar to the various categories

duck. She looks at it, then tries to grasp it, but suddenly stops to look behind her for the coverlet which she did not see.

At 0;9 (13) she tries to grasp with her left hand a bottle which I place beside her head. She succeeds only in grazing it by turning her face slightly. She gives up shortly and losing sight of the bottle pulls a coverlet in front of her. But suddenly she turns around to reapply herself to her attempts at prehension. It all happens as if she has retained the memory of the object and returns to it, after a pause, believing in its permanence.

OBS. 20. Laurent has had many such reactions since 0;6. If the child is interrupted as he pulls the string hanging from the hood, scratches the edge of the bassinet, etc., he will immediately turn in the right direction and rediscover these objects. Let us limit ourselves to describing an observation of him at 0;6 (12), which pertains at the same time to deferred circular reaction, accommodation of the eyes to the movement of falling and tactile-manual search for the object. Without being typical from the point of view of interrupted circular reaction, this observation sums up very well what we have hitherto seen regarding the constitution of the object at that stage.

I place a rattle on the edge of the bassinet hood, barely held in place by a string attached behind it. Laurent at once stirs around in order to swing the object as if it were a toy somehow hanging there; but the rattle falls in front of his face and so close that he grasps it immediately. He replaces the rattle up in the air; same reaction, five or six times in succession. It is therefore possible to consider these acts taken together as constituting a new circular schema: stirring about, making the object fall, and grasping it. What will happen when the cycle remains incomplete, that is to say when the object, instead of falling in a visible place, disappears from the visual field? Will the reaction thus interrupted be extended in deferred reaction and how?

1. When the object falls after having been detached by the movement of the child, his eyes search for it in front of him, at the usual place. If he does not see it he again stirs about, but looking in front of him and not up in the air. If he then hears the rattle, he stretches out his hand and grasps whatever may be there, without true exploration (thus he takes possession either of the rattle itself, if it happens to come under his hand, or of the sheet, the coverlet, etc.).

---

of sensorimotor intelligence, and that temporal displacements are produced, the more comprehensible the farther removed they are from the elementary stages.

2. When the rattle, in falling from the hood, makes a noise in falling, Laurent immediately stretches out his hand in its direction (without seeing it). But if in touching it he pushes it back involuntarily, he does not put his hand forward to follow the trajectory of the object; he merely brings back whatever he finds (the sheet, etc.).

3. When the child has not seen the beginning of the fall of the rattle, he does not search for it in front of him; the object no longer exists. In particular, when it is I who make it fall unexpectedly, its disappearance gives rise to no search. It is therefore only as a function of the total cycle that searching is set in motion.

These behavior patterns are important; their accumulation and systematization will gradually bring with them belief in the permanence of the external world. But they are not in themselves alone enough to constitute object concept. They imply simply that the child considers as permanent everything which is useful to his action in a particular situation under consideration. Thus in obs. 19 Jacqueline, whose attention has been distracted from swinging a coverlet located behind her, returns to the original position, convinced that in the moment of turning she will find the desired object. But in this there is only a global and practical permanence, and nothing yet implies that objects once removed from their context will remain for her identical to themselves; we shall see that when the child begins to search actively for objects which have disappeared from his perceptual field (4th stage), he is still capable only of that entirely practical belief in global permanence. These behavior patterns, therefore, do not go much further than the primitive anticipation arising from visual accommodation to rapid movements or from interrupted prehension. It is not the object which constitutes the permanent element (for example the coverlet), but the act itself (swinging the coverlet), hence the whole of the situation; the child merely returns to his action.

Will reconstructions of an invisible whole from a visible fraction mark progress? Theoretically, behavior patterns like these could be observed at any age, hence from the first stages; it would suffice that the child, accustomed to a certain object as a whole, should try to see it as a whole when he catches sight of part of it. But, in fact, we have not definitely observed such reactions until after prehension has been acquired. Doubtless it is solely the habit of grasping and manipulating objects, of thus endowing them with a relatively constant form, and of locating them in a space that has greater or less depth, that permits the child to form an image of their totality. Nevertheless, it seems to us that this still does not prove that the thing seen or grasped is considered by the subject as being a permanent object of constant dimensions, or, above all, that it is situated among objective displacement groups. It suffices simply to make the child consider it as being a whole, even when he limits himself to looking at it without getting hold of it, and to make him try to see the whole of it when he perceives only a part of it.

OBS. 21. At 0;5 (8) Laurent looks at my hand whose movement he imitates. I am hiding behind his bassinet hood. Several times Laurent obviously tries to see me, his gaze leaving my hand and rising along my arm to the point where my arm seems to issue from the hood; he stares at this point and seems to search for me all around it.

At 0;5 (25) Laurent shakes himself when I place a newspaper partly on the edge of his bassinet hood and partly on the string which connects the hood to the handle (see *O.I.*, obs. 110). If he sees a very small portion of the newspaper he will react in the same way. I observe several times in succession that he looks behind him toward the place where the rest of the newspaper is, as though he expected to see all of it appear.

At 0;6 (17) I offer the child a pencil, and at the moment he is getting ready to grasp it I lower it gradually behind a horizontal screen. At the first attempt he withdraws his hand while he still sees one centimeter of the pencil; he looks at this extremity with curiosity, without seeming to understand. When I raise the pencil one to two centimeters he grasps it at once. Second attempt: I lower the pencil so as to let about two centimeters of it show. Laurent again withdraws his outstretched hand. When three to four centimeters of pencil show he grasps it. Same reactions in a series of sequential attempts; it therefore seems that the child acknowledges the entireness—at least virtual—of the pencil when he sees three or more centimeters of it and believes it is impaired when he sees only one to two centimeters of it. When the pencil is entirely hidden, Laurent of course no longer reacts and even stops looking at the screen.

OBS. 22. At 0;8 (15) Lucienne looks at a celluloid stork which I have just taken away from her and which I cover with a cloth. She

does not attempt to raise the cloth to take the toy. (We shall return
to this phase of the experiment; see obs. 30.) But when a part of
the stork appears outside the cloth, Lucienne immediately grasps this
bit as though she recognized the whole animal.

The proof that this involves a reconstruction of the whole is that
not every partial presentation is equally propitious. The head or tail
immediately gives rise to a search; Lucienne removes the cloth[4] in
order to extricate the animal. But sight of the feet alone arouses great
interest although the child does not try to grasp; Lucienne seems not
to recognize the stork, or at least to consider it as being changed.
These facts cannot therefore be interpreted by saying that the child
grasps anything whatever. Moreover, when Lucienne recognizes the
stork just by its head or tail she expects to find a whole; at first she
raises the cloth, knowing in advance that neither head nor tail is
isolated. Hence it is all the more curious that the child remains incapable of raising the screen when the entire animal is hidden; it
is the sign that the act of reconstructing a totality from a visible
fraction of the thing is psychologically simpler than the act of searching for an object that has completely vanished.

obs. 23. At 0;9 (7) Lucienne reveals analogous reactions but in
connection with a toy hitherto unfamiliar to her. I offer her a celluloid goose which she has never seen before; she grasps it at once
and examines it all over.

I place the goose beside her (Lucienne is seated) and cover it
before her eyes, sometimes completely, sometimes revealing the head
(white head, yellow beak).

Two very distinct reactions.

In the first place, when the goose disappears completely, Lucienne
immediately stops searching even when she is on the point of grasping it; she withdraws her hand and looks at me, laughing.

In the second place, when the beak protrudes, not only does she
grasp the visible part and draw the animal to her, but from the very
first attempts she sometimes raises the coverlet beforehand in order
to grasp the whole thing! The goose is therefore conceived as being
at least a virtual totality, even when only the head appears.

Never, even after having raised the coverlet several times on seeing the beak appear, has Lucienne tried to raise it when the goose
was completely hidden! Here again is proof of the fact that recon-

_____
[4] This act of removing the cloth belongs to the fourth stage in so far as the
function of intelligence is concerned, but the object concept remains characteristic of the third stage.

struction of a totality is much easier than search for an invisible object.

Same reactions at 0;9 (8), that is, the following day.

OBS. 24. No object is more interesting to the child at this stage than his bottle (Jacqueline and Laurent were weaned around 0;6 and were almost exclusively bottle-fed until about 1;0). It is therefore permissible to consider the child's reactions toward it as typical and as characterizing the whole of this stage.

Until about 0;9 (4) Laurent, in whose case particularly I analyzed this phenomenon, manifested three distinct reactions, the sum of which clarifies the three preceding observations and permits an inference free of ambiguity.

1. If the bottle disappears from his perceptual field this is enough to make it cease to exist from the child's point of view. At 0;6 (19), for instance, Laurent immediately begins to cry from hunger and impatience on seeing his bottle (he was already whimpering, as he does quite regularly at mealtime). But at the very moment when I make the bottle disappear behind my hand or under the table—he follows me with his eyes—he stops crying. As soon as the object reappears, a new outburst of desire; then flat calm after it disappears. I repeat the experiment four more times; the result is constant until poor Laurent, beginning to think the joke bad, becomes violently angry.

This behavior pattern is conserved with the same definiteness until about 0;9. Hence it seems apparent that to the child the objective existence of the bottle is subordinate to his perception. This does not mean, of course, that the vanished bottle has been fundamentally forgotten; the child's ultimate rage reveals clearly enough that he believes he can count on the object. But this is precisely because he considers it as being at the disposal of his desires, like the objects of which we have been speaking, and not as having substantial existence under my hand or under the table. Otherwise he would behave quite differently at the moment of its disappearance; he would manifest, at that exact moment, a still more intense desire than during normal perception. That is clearly revealed by the following reaction.

2. When I make only part of the bottle disappear and Laurent sees a small fraction of it near my hand, or a cloth, or the table, the manifestations of his desire are more imperious than when he saw the whole bottle. At the very least, they remain identical: Laurent kicks and cries while staring fixedly at the visible portion of the object. Up to 0;7 (1) he has not stretched out his arms, because he

has not been in the habit of holding his bottle, but from that date on he tries to take it. If I offer it to him half-covered by a cloth, he takes possession of what he sees, never doubting for a single second that his bottle is involved. Thus he reacts as did Lucienne with respect to her stork (obs. 22) or her goose (obs. 23), with the difference that he does not know how to raise the cloth and is content to extricate the bottle from it by degrees and quite clumsily. (As we have noted, the action of removing the cloth or any obstacle belongs to the fourth stage with regard to the development of the intelligence in general; and it appears shortly before the discovery of the object characteristic of the same stage, a discovery which it sets in motion sooner or later.)

Finally, let us note in connection with this second reaction that Laurent recognizes his bottle no matter what part of it is visible. If he sees the nipple, his reaction is natural, but even when he sees the wrong end his desire is the same; hence he admits at least the virtual entireness of the bottle in the same sense as at 0;6 (17) he admitted that of the pencil (obs. 21) and Lucienne that of the swan and the goose (obs. 22 and 23). But, as will be revealed by the third reaction which illuminates the meaning of the first two, this wholeness is considered by the child as only virtual. Everything occurs as though the child believed that the object is alternately made and unmade; if, independently of any screen, the bottle is presented to Laurent upside down he will consider it incomplete and lacking a nipple, at the same time expecting the nipple to appear sooner or later in one way or another. When the child sees a part of the object emerge from the screen and he assumes the existence of the totality of that object, he does not yet consider this totality as being formed "behind" the screen; he simply admits that it is in the process of being formed at the moment of leaving the screen.

3. Let us briefly describe this third reaction, to which we will return in detail in connection with the concept of space and of groups obtained by reversals.

From 0;7 (0) until 0;9 (4) Laurent is subjected to a series of tests, either before the meal or at any other time, to see if he can turn the bottle over and find the nipple when he does not see it. The experiment yields absolutely constant results; if Laurent sees the nipple he brings it to his mouth, but if he does not see it he makes no attempt to turn the bottle over. The object, therefore, has no reverse side or, to put it differently, it is not three dimensional. Nevertheless, Laurent expects to see the nipple appear and evidently in this hope he assiduously sucks the wrong end of the bottle (for more information on this behavior see obs. 78, Chap. II). It is in this sense that we speak of virtual totality from the point of view of object concept; to Laurent the bottle is already a whole, but its various elements are still conceived as being at his disposal and not as remaining organized in space.

Such a reaction confirms the meaning of the first two as well as that of the various preceding observations.

OBS. 25. So also Jacqueline, at 0;6 (29), opens her mouth on seeing the bottle approach. When it is near her, within reach, I hide the bottle with my hand. Jacqueline kicks in anger and impatience; it does not occur to her to remove my hand, but she stares at it with an expression of intense expectation and desire. All this occurs as though the bottle seemed to her to emanate from my hand and as though this emanation having just disappeared, she expected it to reappear.

These behavior patterns surely are a sign of a beginning of solidification of the thing perceived and of a certain permanence attributed to visual and tactile images. But they do not yet prove the existence of objects in general. When a part of a toy is visible the child believes in its material existence but when it is completely hidden the subject ceases to acknowledge that it exists substantially and is merely concealed behind the screen. In other words Laurent, in obs. 21, doubtless does not imagine that I am behind the hood but rather that I am something about to arise from the hood. Neither he nor Jacqueline, in obs. 24 and 25, envisages the bottle behind my hand. As for Lucienne, in obs. 22 and 23, she considers the stork and the goose as entities that somehow issue from the coverlet itself. The concepts of "in front of" and "behind," the idea of an object remaining in substantial form under another object which conceals it are, in effect, of great complexity, for they presuppose the elaboration of groups and of laws of perspective; we have just shown that the latter are far from being formed at the outset, as soon as the capacity to grasp visual objects is acquired.

The following behavior patterns seem, nevertheless, to bear witness to the presence of such concepts. At the outset, the observations we shall describe on "removal of obstacles preventing perception" seem more decisive than they really are, but a careful analysis will show us that they are different from the later behavior patterns with which one might be tempted to compare them. From the age of five to seven months the child becomes capable of practicing a sort of game of hide-and-seek which consists in removing from in front of his face the screen obstructing his view.

OBS. 26. At 0;7 (29) Jacqueline is hidden behind her pillow (which she herself has placed over her face). I call her; she immediately gets rid of this obstacle in order to look at me.

At 0;8 (12) a pillow is placed over her face; she immediately removes it amid peals of laughter and tries at once to see who is there.

At 0;8 (13) Jacqueline has a sheet over her face. Hearing my approaching footsteps she immediately uncovers herself.

OBS. 27. At 0;5 (25) Laurent removes clumsily, but as rapidly as possible, a cushion which I place over his face and which prevents him from seeing. When I place something less irksome over his face, such as his light little pillow, he does not remove it at once but gets rid of it as soon as he hears a voice and tries to see who is in front of him.

At 0;7 (15) he is lying down and spontaneously with both hands pulls his shawl over him, up to his nose. He looks under the shawl with curiosity. I call him; he looks above and behind him but it does not immediately occur to him to displace the shawl. After a moment, however, he displaces it and sees me in front of him. Then he resumes his game and again covers himself up. I call him again; this time he immediately lowers the shawl so as to get a better view. But he does not see me because I am a little nearer his feet than before; it does not enter his mind to lower the screen a little more, although I call him continually.

At 0;7 (28) Laurent is seated and I place a large cushion between him and me so as to make a screen. The cushion remains upright, but sometimes I put it at Laurent's side (10 centimeters from his face), sometimes at my side (20-30 centimeters away from him); when the screen is beside him he lowers it at once, but when it is next to me he does not react. However I disappear and reappear slowly as I had just done when he lowered the cushion at his side, and nothing would be easier for him than to repeat the thing in this new position.

Between 0;7 (13) and 0;8 (0) Laurent discovers the behavior patterns of the fourth stage with regard to the mechanism of intelligence: removing obstacles (*O.I.*, obs. 122-123), etc. From the point of view which interests us here, such behavior patterns precede by several weeks the object construction of the fourth stage, but they lead to it little by little. Thus at 0;8 (1) Laurent with one hand lowers a cushion masking the lower half of a box which I offer him and grasps the box with the other. At 0;8 (8) he goes so far as to lean forward in order to see his bear for a longer time, as I make it disappear behind the cushion, etc. But we shall see presently that during this period of transition (until about 0;9), the child always behaves as though the object which has disappeared altogether from his perceptual field no longer exists (see obs. 32 and 33).

Such behavior patterns, like that of the reconstructions of an invisible whole from a visible fraction, at first seem to show that the child possesses the concept of a substantial object hidden behind a screen. But before reaching this conclusion we should ask at what point the child's action no longer merely extends his earlier or habitual accommodations. In the latter case it would not yet be possible to speak of the concept of objects being displaced in space, but only of a beginning of permanence relative to the perception and the action in progress. Emphasis must be placed on the point that, in the examples just described, the child is trying less to free the object masked by a screen than to free his own perception; if that is what he is trying to do he can succeed without having in advance the concepts of "in front of," "behind," or of objects hidden by one another. Doubtless such a behavior pattern will lead to these concepts, but it does not at all involve them at first.

When Jacqueline and Laurent free their faces from the pillow or from various cloths (obs. 26 and 27), they do nothing more than any baby can do from the age of 6 months. In some excellent experiments Mme. Bühler has shown that on an average from the seventh month the child, even when lying on his stomach, is able to get rid of a cloth placed over his face.[5]

When, later (obs. 27), from 0;7 (15) Laurent removes the coverlet which separates him from me, he is only generalizing what he was learning in a practical way when he removed the cloths placed on his face. This does not yet involve the act

[5] C. H. Bühler and H. Hetzer, *Kleinkindertests* (Leipzig: Barth, 1932), pp. 42-43.

by which the child conceives of one object as remaining permanent behind others; it relates, rather, to a practical schema
which endows objects with no permanence other than that
whose nature we have seen in connection with deferred circular reactions and the other behavior patterns of this stage. The
proof is that, if he knows how to remove the screen sufficiently
to look in front of him, he does not yet succeed in displacing
it in relation to the hidden object. Therein is still a permanence
merely extending accommodation movements and not yet an
objective permanence independent of the action.

In short, none of these facts yet attests to the existence of
objects properly so called. Objects remain, in such behavior
patterns, those things at disposal of which we have spoken,
endowed with a global and completely practical permanence,
that is to say, depending on the continuance of actions as such.
This makes us understand the true nature of the "reconstructions
of invisible totalities from a visible fraction"; either the child sees
a fragment of the object and the action of grasping thus set in motion bestows a totality on the thing perceived, or else he no
longer sees anything and no longer attributes any objective existence to the vanished object. It would therefore be impossible to
say that the half-hidden objective is conceived as being masked by
a screen; it is simply perceived as being in the process of disappearing, the action alone bestowing on it a total reality.

However, it is self-evident that these latter two groups of
behavior patterns and particularly the fifth (obs. 26 and 27)
are those which bring us closest to the true taking possession of
the object, that is to say, to the advent of active search for
the vanished object. It seems to us that this search becomes differentiated, only from the time when it no longer merely extends in an immediate way the movements of accommodation,
but when in the course of the action new movements become
necessary to remove the obstacles (like the screens) intervening
between subject and object. This is precisely what does not yet
happen during the present stage. All the behavior patterns enumerated hitherto merely extend the action in progress. Clearly,
in regard to visual accommodations to rapid movements, interrupted prehensions, and deferred circular reactions, the third
consist merely in returning to the momentarily suspended act

and not in complicating the action by removing the obstacles which arise. The reconstruction of invisible totalities and the removal of obstacles preventing perception both seem to involve this differentiation, but this only appears to be true. When the child tries to get a half-hidden object and, to do this, removes the obstacle which covers the hidden portion, he by no means performs an action as complicated as that of removing a screen masking the entire object. In the latter case the child must momentarily give up his attempt at direct prehension of the object in order to raise a screen recognized as such; in the former case, on the contrary, the child sees part of the object which he tries to grasp, he reconstructs the totality only as a function of the immediate action and in removing the obstacle does nothing more than he always does when he extricates some toy from the coverlet or the cloths clumsily grasped along with it. It is therefore impossible yet to speak of a special behavior pattern consisting in removing the screen. Regarding the removal of obstacles preventing perception we have just seen that this is a question of an object in relation to the subject and not in relation to the object; there is, indeed, differentiation of the action but the obstacle-screen and the object as such are not yet related. From this point of view, the object is still only the extension of the action in progress.

What will happen when the child, trying to grasp some object, sees it completely disappear behind a screen? We have hitherto examined what the child knows how to do during this third stage; it is now important to make clear what he does not know how to do. In the situation we have just posed this striking and essential phenomenon is produced: the child either gives up all searching or searches for objects elsewhere than under the screen, for example around the hand which has just placed them there.

OBS. 28. At 0;7 (28) Jacqueline tries to grasp a celluloid duck on top of her quilt. She almost catches it, shakes herself, and the duck slides down beside her. It falls very close to her hand but behind a fold in the sheet. Jacqueline's eyes have followed the movement, she has even followed it with her outstretched hand. But as soon as the duck has disappeared—nothing more! It does not occur to her to search behind the fold of the sheet, which would be very easy to do (she twists it mechanically without searching at all). But, curiously, she again begins to stir about as she did when trying to get the duck and again glances at the top of the quilt.

I then take the duck from its hiding-place and place it near her hand three times. All three times she tries to grasp it, but when she is about to touch it I replace it very obviously under the sheet. Jacqueline immediately withdraws her hand and gives up. The second and third times I make her grasp the duck through the sheet and she shakes it for a brief moment but it does not occur to her to raise the cloth.

Then I recommence the initial experiment. The duck is on the quilt. In trying to get it she again causes it to slide behind the fold in the sheet; after having looked at this fold for a moment (it is near her hand) she turns over and sucks her thumb.

I then offer her her doll which is crying. Jacqueline laughs. I hide it behind the fold in the sheet; she whimpers. I make the doll cry; no search. I offer it to her again and put a handkerchief around it; no reaction. I make the doll cry in the handkerchief; nothing.

OBS. 29. At 0;8 (2) Jacqueline is seated beside a table and looks at a matchbox which I shake above the table, making as much noise as possible. The box passes slowly under the table, continuing to make a noise; Jacqueline then looks at me instead of searching under the table to see where the noise comes from.

Several attempts, all negative.

At 0;8 (16) while she watches I place her little bells under the coverlet, rolling them up into a ball to facilitate her search. I shake the whole thing to make the bells ring. No reaction. As long as she hears the noise she laughs but then her eyes follow my fingers instead of searching under the coverlet.

Then I pull the string attached to the bells, which has remained visible. She imitates the sound and listens to it but still does not look under the coverlet. I then raise it in order to reveal the object; Jacqueline quickly stretches out her hand, but just when she is about to get it I cover it up again and Jacqueline withdraws her hand. I repeat the experiment but this time hide the bells behind a fold in the sheet; same negative reaction, despite the sound. Subsequent attempts yield nothing more.

At 0;9 (8), at the age when she knows how to remove a screen blocking her view (see obs. 26 and 27), Jacqueline plays with a parrot. I take it away from her and place it behind the fold of the sheet, before her eyes. I tap on it and the rattle sounds. Jacqueline does the same but does not search under the sheet. I then let her glimpse a few millimeters of the end of the tail; she looks at it curiously as though without understanding. She tries to grasp it but picks up the sheet along with the parrot; she jumbles them together without being able to differentiate them.

OBS. 30. At 0;8 (12) Lucienne behaves like Jacqueline at the same age; when she is at the point of grasping an object and it is made to disappear under a handkerchief, a coverlet, or the observer's hand, she immediately gives up.

When I hide her rattle under the coverlet and make it sound she looks in the right direction but merely examines the coverlet itself, without trying to raise it.

At 0;8 (15) Lucienne is seated and tries to recapture a celluloid stork (containing a rattle) which she has just held and shaken (see obs. 22). I place the stork beside her right knee, covering it with the edge of the cloth on which the child is seated; nothing would be simpler than to find it again. Moreover Lucienne has watched each of my movements most attentively and they were slow and clearly visible. However, as soon as the stork disappears under the cloth, Lucienne stops looking at it and looks at my hand. She examines it with great interest but pays no more attention to the cloth.

I extricate the stork before Lucienne's eyes. She takes it, and as she does so her interest is aroused. As a precaution I take pains to repeat this maneuver after each subsequent test. Furthermore, uncovering the stork before the child's eyes should help her; her negative reactions are therefore all the more interesting.

Attempts 2-7: still nothing, except that Lucienne looks at my empty hands with stupefaction.

Attempt 8: After hiding the stork while the child watches, I tap on the cloth. Lucienne hears the stork and taps in turn. But as soon as she hears the sound thus produced, she looks at my hand (which is on the edge of the bassinet 30 centimeters away), as though the stork should be there still, or should be there again.

Attempts 9-12: partial presentations, described in obs. 22.

Attempts 13-15: When the stork is again completely hidden Lucienne resumes her negative reactions. She begins again to look at my hand when she hears the stork under the cloth. Twice in succession she even happens to tap on my hand as she has just done with the stork covered by the cloth; new proof that she thinks the stork should emanate from that hand.

At 0;8 (16), the next day, the same experiment yields the same result: Lucienne continues to search in my hands when she has herself tapped on the stork covered by the cloth.

OBS. 31. At 0;9 (7) Lucienne tries to grasp a celluloid goose, which I cover either completely or partially. We have seen, in obs. 23, the beginning of these reactions: Lucienne is able to grasp the goose with precision when she perceives the beak (in this case she extricates it from the coverlet and even raises the latter in advance) but she remains incapable of searching for the object when it is entirely covered up.

At the end of the experiment I facilitate things as follows: the animal is lying under the coverlet and Lucienne has withdrawn her hand; I tap on the goose which then rattles very distinctly. Lucienne imitates me at once, taps harder and harder, and laughs; but it does not occur to her to raise the screen. Then I again let the beak emerge; Lucienne at once raises the coverlet to look for the animal. I cover it up again; she taps, laughs, looks at my hands for a moment, but does not again touch the screen.

OBS. 32. Laurent, as we have seen (obs. 24), ceases to cry at 0;6 (19) and until about 0;9, at the time when he sees the bottle he desired disappear; everything occurs as though the child believed that it ceased to exist in substance. In particular, at 0;7 (3), when Laurent has been on a diet for a week, he cries from hunger after each meal and clings frantically to his bottle; however if I hide it slowly behind my arm or my back this is enough to calm Laurent. He screams on seeing it disappear, but at the precise moment when he can no longer see it at all he ceases to react.

At 0;7 (28) I offer him a little bell behind a cushion (the cushion in obs. 27); so long as he sees the little bell, however small it may be, he tries to grasp it from above the screen which he lowers more or less intentionally. But if the little bell disappears completely he stops all searching.

I then resume the experiment, using my hand as a screen. Laurent's arm is outstretched and about to grasp the little bell at the moment I make it disappear behind my hand (which is open and at a distance of 15 cm. from him); he immediately withdraws his arm, as though the little bell no longer existed. I then shake my hand, always revealing the back of it and gripping the little bell in my palm; Laurent watches attentively, greatly surprised to rediscover the sound of the little bell, but he does not try to grasp it. I turn my hand over and he sees the little bell; he then stretches out his hand toward it. I hide the little bell again by changing the position of my hand;

Laurent withdraws his hand. In short, he does not yet have the concept that the little bell is "behind" my hand for he has no concept of the "reverse side" of it (see obs. 24, reaction 3).

Afterward I put the little bell before him, but at the moment he is about to grasp it with outstretched hand I cover it with a thin cloth; Laurent withdraws his hand. He taps on the little bell with his index finger, through the cloth, and the little bell rings; Laurent watches this phenomenon with great interest, then his eyes follow my hand as I withdraw it open and look at it for a moment (as though the little bell were going to arise from it). But he does not raise the cloth.

obs. 33. From about 0;8, as we have seen (obs. 27), Laurent begins to remove the screen or even to lean forward to look over it. But during this entire phase intermediate between the third and the fourth stage he never once succeeds in raising the screen when the object has entirely disappeared. Thus at 0;8 (8) he is incapable of finding my watch under his little pillow, placed before him. This is all the more curious because he has just searched with his hand (outside the visual field) for the watch which escaped him ("tactile object" and "interrupted prehension": see obs. 17). But when I put the watch under his eyes, and at the moment he is about to grasp it I cover it with his small pillow, he withdraws his hand, whimpering. It would, however, be very easy for him to raise his pillow as he always does in play.

At 0;8 (25) Laurent watches me when I place a cushion against my face. He begins by pushing himself up in order to look at me over the screen, then he pulls the screen away (therefore he knows I am there). But when I lie down before him with the cushion over my head he does not raise it, even if I say "coucou." He simply looks at my shoulder at the place where I disappear under the cushion and no longer reacts. Similarly, the objects he sees me hide under the cushion give rise to no reaction. It is only after 0;9 that he applies himself to searching for the object in such circumstances.

In short, so long as the search for the vanished object merely extends the accommodation movements in progress, the child reacts to the object's disappearance. On the other hand, as soon as it is a question of doing more, that is, of interrupting the movements of prehension, of visual accommodation, etc., in order to raise a screen conceived as such, the child abandons all active search; he is content to look at the examiner's hand as though the object should emanate from it. Even when he hears the object under the cloth which serves as a screen he does not seem to believe in its substantial permanence.

How, then, can the whole of the behavior patterns of this stage be interpreted? They surely mark notable progress over those of the preceding stage. A greater degree of permanence is attributed to vanished images, since the child expects to find them again not only in the very place where they were left but also in places within the extension of their trajectory (reaction to falling, interrupted prehension, etc.). But in comparing this stage to the following ones we prove that this permanence remains exclusively connected with the action in progress and does not yet imply the idea of a substantial permanence independent of the organism's sphere of activity. All that the child assumes is that in continuing to turn his head or to lower it he will see a certain image which has just disappeared, that in lowering his hand he will again find the tactile impression experienced shortly before, etc. Moreover he shows impatience or disappointment in the event of failure. He always knows, in the end, how to search for the image in its absolute position, that is, where he saw it at the beginning of the experiment (in the hands of the experimenter, for instance); but this return to the initial position is still determined by the activity itself, the advantage of this position rising merely from the fact that it characterized the beginning of the action in progress.

Two explanations could account for this apparent limitation of objective permanence. In the first place it could be maintained that the child believes as we do in a universe of substantial objects; but he would pay attention only to the things on which he can act, disregarding the other things and forgetting them at once. According to the second explanation, on the other hand, the images perceived would be endowed with true permanence only to the extent that they would depend on the action itself; the child would thus imagine the existence of these images as resulting in some way from the very effort put forth to utilize and find them again.

If it is impossible to decide between those two hypotheses when only the factors of the present stage are under consideration, examination of the entire evolution of object concept seems to impose the choice of the second, especially with reference to the hidden implications on which each hypothesis in reality rests. If the first were true it would have to be maintained that the child from the outset conceives of the universe as being external to the action itself and thus distinguishes it from the relations existing among things as such. Furthermore and by virtue of that very fact, it would be necessary to maintain that the initial universe is at first spatial not only to the extent that it is perceived, but also to the extent that vanished objects are deemed to occupy a determined position. On the other hand, the second hypothesis attributes to the child a sort of practical solipsism such that external images are not immediately dissociated from the activities which utilize them and such that the self knows nothing of itself as subject, and therefore fuses into objects the impressions of effort, tension, desire, and satisfaction which accompany acts. The primitive universe, therefore, would not be organized spatially except as a function of the action in progress, and the object would exist for the subject only to the extent that it depends on that very action. If the problem is stated in these terms everything seems to favor the second solution. On the one hand, we do not see how the child would dissociate from his activity the universe insofar as it is permanent, precisely since he does not yet try to concern himself with vanished objects and therefore in no way experiences their resistance to himself. On the other hand, we shall see that the most significant behavior patterns stand in the way of attributing to the child belief in a motionless and general space which invisible objects would occupy along with other bodies, and his own, as well as things. In reality the subject does not exist in his own consciousness and still less is he situated in space; from this time, things are arranged spatially only in the immediate action and remain permanent only as a function of that action.

In effect, at this stage the child does not know the mechanism of his own actions, and hence does not dissociate them from the things themselves; he knows only their total and undifferentiated schema (which we have called the schema of assimilation) comprising in a single act the data of external perception as well as the internal impressions that are affective and kinesthetic, etc., in nature. So long as the object is present it is assimilated in that schema and could not therefore be thought of apart from the acts to which it gives rise. When it disappears, either it is forgotten because it is not sufficiently dynamogenic or else it gives way to a feeling of disappointment or expectation and to the desire to continue the action. Then that which is the essential of circular reaction or reproductive assimilation is produced: a conservation effort. This effort radiates as always in movements extending the action in progress, and if the vanished image is rediscovered it appears merely as the completion of that action. None of this implies substantial permanence: the permanence in question is still only that with which circular reaction in general is impregnated, that is to say definitively the assimilatory activity itself. The child's universe is still only a totality of pictures emerging from nothingness at the moment of the action, to return to nothingness at the moment when the action is finished. There is added to it only the circumstance that the images subsist longer than before, because the child tries to make these actions last longer than in the past; in extending them either he rediscovers the vanished images or else he supposes them to be at disposal in the very situation in which the act in progress began.

Proof that this interpretation is the right one, however painful it may be to our realism, is that the child makes no attempt to search for the object when it is neither within an extension of the gesture made, nor in its initial position; here obs. 28-33 are decisive.

But could not the latter facts be accounted for simply by the lack of motor skill or defects of the child's memory? We do not at all see how. On the one hand it is not difficult for a baby of seven to nine months to lift a cloth, a coverlet, etc. (as he does in obs. 26 and 27). On the other hand we shall see in studying the behavior patterns of the fourth stage that the formation of the object is far from finished when the child begins to look under screens; at first he does not take account of the displacements perceived and always searches for the object in its initial position!

But then could it not be said that the object exists in substance from the very beginning, only its localization in space being subject to difficulties? As we shall see later such a distinction is in fact devoid of meaning; to exist as object is to be ordered in space, for the elaboration of space is precisely the objectification of perceived images. A reality which merely remains at disposal of the action without being situated in objective displacement groups is therefore not an object; it is only a potential act.

A final remark: The state of affairs at the end of this third stage is still inconsistent. On the one hand, the child tends to attribute a certain visual permanence to images extending his accommodations of sight. On the other hand, he tends to rediscover what falls from his hands and thus to form a sort of tactile object. But there is not yet a merging of these two cycles; the child still does not try to grasp an object that disappears from his visual field without having been in contact with his hands shortly before. It will be the task of the fourth stage to bring about this coordination.

§ 3. THE FOURTH STAGE: ACTIVE SEARCH FOR THE VANISHED OBJECT BUT WITHOUT TAKING ACCOUNT OF THE SEQUENCE OF VISIBLE DISPLACEMENTS

An essential acquisition marks the beginning of this fourth stage. The child is no longer content to search for the vanished object when it is found in the extension of accommodation movements; henceforth he searches for it even outside the perceptual field, that is, behind screens interposed between the subject and the image perceived. This discovery rises from the fact that the child begins to study displacements of objects (by grasping them, shaking them, swinging them, hiding and finding them, etc.) and thus begins to coordinate visual permanence and tactile permanence, which, as we have just noted, remain unlinked during the preceding stage.

But such discoveries, however it may seem, do not yet mark the definitive advent of object concept. The experiment shows that when the object disappears successively in two or more distinct places, the child still confers on it a sort of absolute position; he does not take note of the sequential displacements, although they are quite visible, and seems to reason as if the place where the object was found the first time remains where he will find it when he wants to do so. In the fourth stage, therefore, the object remains intermediate between the thing at disposal of the preceding stages and the object properly so called of the fifth and sixth stages.

At what age does the child begin to search for the object hidden behind a screen? According to our observations, this occurs between the ages of 8 and 10 months.[6] But it is hard to determine with precision the boundary between the third stage and the fourth and, if one adheres to a precise criterion, that is, the advent of the behavior pattern which consists in raising the screen in order to find the objective, it is only around 0;9 that the present stage begins, that is, with a well marked temporal displacement as compared to the corresponding stage of the development of intelligence (*O.I.*, Chap. IV).

OBS. 34. At 0;8 (29) Laurent plays with a tin box (see *O.I.*, obs. 126). I take it from him and place it under his pillow; whereas four days previously the child did not react in a similar circumstance (see obs. 33), this time he grasps the pillow and perceives the box of which he immediately takes possession. Same reaction at the second test. But is this chance or is the behavior intentional? It is doubtless merely an attempt on Laurent's part and not yet real anticipation. Proof of this is his inertia as soon as I slightly modify the conditions of the experiment. At the third test I place the box 15 centimeters away from him, and as soon as he extends his hand I cover the object with the same pillow as before; he immediately withdraws his hand.

The next days, analogous reactions, difficult to interpret. At 0;9 (17) on the other hand, it suffices that he see a cigar case disappear under a cushion for him to raise the screen and discover the object. At the first attempts the case was completely hidden; nevertheless Laurent found it easily. Then I let a fraction of the object appear; the effort is increased tenfold, Laurent displacing the cushion with one hand and trying to catch the case with the other. In a general

---

[6] See obs. 0;9 cited by Stern, *Psychol. der frühen Kindheit* (4th ed.), p. 97.

In their *Kleinkindertests* Mmes. Bühler and Hetzer consider as characteristic of the 9th and 10th months the behavior pattern which consists in finding a toy under a folded cloth when this toy has been hidden before the child's eyes (see test 7 of Series IX, p. 49). After the 8th month, it is true, the children observed by these writers can find an object half hidden in a pocket (test 8 of series VIII, p. 47, Fig. 15), but as part of the toy remains visible it involves a behavior pattern comparable to our third stage.

way, when the object disappeared completely Laurent showed less animation but the search continued until the end.

At 0;9 (20) in the same way he finds my watch under a quilt, under a cloth, etc. At 0;9 (24) he searches for a little duck under his pillow, under a spread cloth, etc. The behavior pattern has now been acquired and is accompanied by a growing interest.

OBS. 35. As we have seen, up to 0;9 (22) Jacqueline has manifested reactions typical of the third stage (see obs. 8-9, 13-14, 25 and 28-29). Nevertheless, from 0;9 and even from 0;8 (15) some sporadic searching for the hidden object is observable.

The most elementary searches derive merely from the removal of obstacles preventing perception, of which we have spoken in connection with obs. 26 and 27; at a given moment instead of removing a pillow or sheet only when it covers her own face, she manages to remove it when it covers someone else.

For example, at 0;8 (14) Jacqueline is lying on my bed beside me. I cover my head and cry "coucou"; I emerge and do it again. She bursts into peals of laughter, then pulls the covers away to find me again. Attitude of expectation and lively interest.

At 0;8 (16) she faces a coverlet raised between her and me, within reach of her hand but not touching it. I am behind this screen and call her. She responds to each sound but it does not occur to her to lower the coverlet. I rise and reveal myself as briefly as possible, then disappear behind the coverlet. This time she pulls it down with her hand and stretches her head to see me. She laughs at her success. I recommence, lowering myself still further; she again pulls the coverlet down. Jacqueline finally removes it when it completely conceals me.

Obviously these two behavior patterns belong to the fourth stage with regard to the mechanism of intelligence since there is subordination of means to ends with coordination of heterogeneous schemata. On the other hand, with regard to object concept (the elaboration of which naturally lags behind the progress of the intellectual function in general, since it results from this progress instead of engendering it by itself), these behavior patterns remain midway between the third and fourth stage; it is evident that Jacqueline assumes my presence in the sheets or the coverlet, and in this she is already in the fourth stage, but the movements she makes to find me again extend those of obs. 26-27 in such a way that they still belong to the third stage. Let us note, furthermore, that the object searched for in the course of these two behavior patterns is a person, and that persons are obviously the most easily substantiated of all the child's sensorial images; hence it is natural that as early as 0;8 (15) Jacqueline behaves as we have just seen toward her father when she does not find some toy hidden under a screen.

Concerning the search for inanimate objects which disappeared under screens, Jacqueline's first attempts took place at 0;9 (8) and at 0;9 (20). At 0;9 (8), that is, right after the events in obs. 29, Jacqueline is seated on a sofa and tries to get hold of my watch. I place it under the edge of the coverlet on which the child is seated; Jacqueline immediately pulls the edge of the coverlet, spies the watch, and takes possession of it. I again hide the object, she finds it, and so on eight times in succession.

On the days following, she lapses into disinterest in vanished objects. At 0;9 (20), on the other hand, I hide her parrot under her quilt after she has amused herself by raising this spontaneously; she again grasps the quilt, raises it, perceives the parrot, and seizes it. At the second attempt, the same game but with a certain slowness. At the third attempt the search seems no longer to interest her at all.

At 0;9 (21) and at 0;9 (22) Jacqueline lapses into the behavior patterns characteristic of the third stage (see obs. 14), then, at 0;9 (23) makes fresh progress.

OBS. 36. At 0;9 (23), the day after the last observation made on her related to interrupted prehension (obs. 14), Jacqueline reveals a reaction which clearly belongs to those of the fourth stage while extending those of the third.

We recall that, at 0;9 (21) and 0;9 (22) when Jacqueline tries to grasp an object on her lap and I place a screen between her hand and the object, she renounces her attempt unless her fingers have already grazed the object. At 0;9 (23), placed in the same situation, she pursues her search, provided always that the movement of grasping has already been made before the visual disappearance of the object.

Thus I place an eraser on her lap and hide it with my hand at the moment she stretches out her hand. Jacqueline's hand is at least five centimeters from the eraser and has therefore not yet touched it; however she continues to search under my hand until she has been completely successful. It also happens that she has her hand over mine when I hide the eraser; she also searches under this hand. However, if the movement of grasping has not been made before I hide the eraser, it is not set in motion after the event.

OBS. 37. At 0;10 (3) I resume the same experiment. I place a small sponge on her lap and hide it with my hand. Contrary to what took place several days before, Jacqueline immediately grasps my hand and casts it aside, then takes possession of the object. This happens a great many times with any object at all: pliers, pipe, etc. Moreover, even if Jacqueline has made no movement before I hide the object, she searches for it once it is hidden.

A moment later I place her parrot under a coverlet; she immediately raises it and searches for the object.

Same reactions at 0;10 (6) and the days following. At 0;10 (12) she scratches a sheet from the outside and every time she does so I take my index finger out from under the sheet, which makes her laugh. At a given moment she scratches but I do not take out my hand again; then she raises the sheet to look for it. A moment later, new disappointment; she again raises the sheet, but as she still does not see my hand, which I purposely withdraw further, she raises the sheet still higher until she sees my fingers.

It is therefore very clear that she believes in the substantial existence of the vanished object, whatever screen may be placed between it and herself.

OBS. 38. At 0;9 (25) Lucienne, like Jacqueline at the same age, manifests behavior patterns which are intermediate between those of the second and third stages. Moreover Lucienne's intermediate behavior patterns are interesting in that they foretell that which is characteristic of the present stage: the difficulty in conceiving of sequential positions of the vanished object. We shall distinguish between two phases of the experiment, I and II.

1. Lucienne is seated on a cloth. I place under its edge a familiar rubber doll which she likes to suck and nibble. Lucienne watches me (I work slowly and visibly), but she does not react.

Second attempt: This time I let the doll's feet emerge: Lucienne grabs them at once and pulls the doll out from under the blanket.

Third attempt: I again hide the object completely. Lucienne pulls the cloth about and raises it as though she were discovering this new procedure in the very course of her groping, and perceives an extremity of the doll; she leans forward to see better and looks at it, much surprised. She does not grasp it.

Attempts 4 and 5 (the doll is henceforth completely hidden each time): negative reaction.

Sixth attempt: Lucienne again pulls the cloth about and makes half the object appear. This time she again looks at it with great interest and at length, as though she did not recognize it. Then she grasps and sucks it.

Seventh attempt: Lucienne searches at once, grasps the cloth and the doll together and has difficulty in dissociating them.

Eighth attempt: She raises the cloth right away but still leans forward in order to have a close view of the doll before grasping it, as though she were not sure of its identity.

II. *First attempt:* I now place the doll under a coverlet 10 centimeters from the original place. I raise the coverlet, put the doll on the floor, and cover it slowly and visibly. As soon as the doll is hidden Lucienne manifests her anger, although it is just as easy for her to find the doll as it was before. She whimpers for a moment but does not search anywhere.

Second attempt: I again place the doll under the original cloth; Lucienne immediately searches for it and finds it.

Third attempt: I again place the object under the coverlet. A strange thing happens. Lucienne not only makes no attempt to raise the coverlet but again pulls the cloth about and ends by raising it!

Attempts 4-6: same reaction. That evening, same experiment; Lucienne searches only under the cloth and never under the coverlet!

It is evident that obs. 34, 36, and 38 are transitional between the preceding stage and the present one. There is certainly something new in the sense that in each of those observations, in obs. 36 and 38 as well as in obs. 37, the child undertakes an active search for the vanished object; he is not content to extend a movement of accommodation (such as lowering the eyes, turning the head, etc.) but he removes the screen which masks the object or searches under the screen. But in obs. 36, the child undertakes this search only if he has previously made the movement of prehension while the object was still visible. Hence everything occurs as though the child still did not have enough faith in permanency to press a search that was not begun in the presence of the object! So also in obs. 38, the child tries only gradually to search under the screen, and when he has found the thing desired he examines it as though doubtful of its identity. Subsequently, however (obs. 37 and end of obs. 38), the search always takes place, at least within the boundaries we shall now define.

The chief interest of this stage is that the active search for the vanished object is not immediately general, but is governed by a restrictive condition: the child looks for and conceives of the object only in a special position, the first place in which it was hidden and found. It is this peculiarity which enables us to contrast the present stage with the succeeding stages and which should be emphasized now.

The procedure is as follows, at least in the most characteristic period of the stage. Suppose an object is hidden at point A: the child searches for it and finds it. Next the object is placed in B and is covered before the child's eyes; although the child has continued to watch the object and has seen it disappear in B, he nevertheless immediately tries to find it in A! We shall call this the typical reaction of the fourth stage. Toward the end of the stage a reaction appears which we shall consider residual. It is as follows: the child follows with his eyes the object in B, searches for it in this second place, and if he does not find it immediately (because the object is buried too deeply, etc.) he returns to A.

Let us begin by describing the typical reaction. It is noteworthy that this reaction was presaged from the third stage by a series of signs which were doubtless noticed. It has been observed, for example, that in obs. 28-30, showing that the child at the third stage gives up searching for the object hidden behind a screen, the subject does not actually abandon all investigation but searches for the object in the same place where it was found before it was put under the screen. Thus Jacqueline, in obs. 28, searches for the duck on top of her quilt and even resumes wriggling to make it fall, although she saw it slide down under a fold in the sheet. In obs. 30 Lucienne, after having seen me place a stork under a cloth, looks at my hand to see if the stork is still there. Such behavior patterns seem to show us that the object is not yet at this stage a substantial thing remaining in the place to which it was moved but a thing at disposal in the place where the action has made use of it. This is precisely what happens during the whole of the fourth stage: the child learns to search for the object behind a screen—and thereby makes progress over the second stage—but he always returns to the same screen, even if one moves the object from one location to another, because the original screen seems to him to constitute the special place where the action of finding is successful.

OBS. 39. At 0;10 (3) after the events recorded in obs. 37 on that day, Jacqueline looks at the parrot on her lap. I place my hand on the object; she raises it and grasps the parrot. I take it away from her and, before her eyes, I move it away very slowly and put it under a rug, 40 centimeters away. Meanwhile I place my hand on her lap again. As soon as Jacqueline ceases to see the parrot she looks at her lap, lifts my hand and hunts beneath it. The reaction is the same during three sequential attempts.

II. I then simplify the experiment in the following way; instead of hiding the parrot under the rug I place it in plain view on the edge of a table, 50 centimeters away. At the first attempt Jacqueline raises my hand and obviously searches under it, always watching the parrot on the table.

Second attempt: She raises my hand from her lap without looking under it and without taking her eyes from the parrot.

Third attempt: She stops looking at the parrot on the table for a moment and searches carefully under my hand. Then she again looks at the object while removing my hand.

Fourth attempt: She removes my hand without looking at it any more. As this last reaction might be due to automatism I give up the experiment and several days later devise the following:

OBS. 40. At 0;10 (18) Jacqueline is seated on a mattress without anything to disturb or distract her (no coverlets, etc.). I take her parrot from her hands and hide it twice in succession under the mattress, on her left, in A. Both times Jacqueline looks for the object immediately and grabs it. Then I take it from her hands and move it very slowly before her eyes to the corresponding place on her right, under the mattress, in B. Jacqueline watches this movement very attentively, but at the moment when the parrot disappears in B she turns to her left and looks where it was before, in A.

During the next four attempts I hide the parrot in B every time without having first placed it in A. Every time Jacqueline watches me attentively. Nevertheless each time she immediately tries to rediscover the object in A; she turns the mattress over and examines it conscientiously. During the last two attempts, however, the search tapers off.

Sixth attempt: She no longer searches.

From the end of the eleventh month the reactions are no longer as simple and become of the type we call "residual."

OBS. 41. As early as 0;9 (25) Lucienne, as we recall, refused to search for a doll under a coverlet after having previously found it under another cloth. She even searched for the doll under the cloth after having seen it being covered up by the coverlet (*ibid.*, II, third attempt).

I. A few days later, at 0;10 (3), Lucienne is seated with a coverlet over her lap and a cloth spread on the floor, at her left. I hide her rubber doll under the coverlet, in A; without hesitation Lucienne raises the coverlet and searches. She finds the doll and sucks it. I immediately place the doll under the cloth in B, taking care to have Lucienne see me. She looks at me until the doll is entirely covered up again, then without hesitation looks at A again and raises the coverlet. She searches for a while in disappointment.

Same reaction with perfect regularity in four sequential experiments; failure does not seem to discourage her at all.

II. In what follows I modify the experiment so as to simplify it and compare it to obs. 39, series II. Once Lucienne has searched in A for the object hidden in B, I again raise the cloth at B in order to show her that the doll is still there, then I cover it up again; but Lucienne looks at the doll in B and, as though motivated by a new impetus, returns to A to pursue her search!

Following attempts: same preparations and same reactions. Thus it may be seen that the reaction in obs. 39, series II, was not attributable to perseveration alone.

OBS. 42. At 0;10 (9) Lucienne is seated on a sofa and plays with a plush duck. I put it on her lap and place a small red cushion on top of the duck (this is position A); Lucienne immediately raises the cushion and takes hold of the duck. I then place the duck next to her on the sofa in B, and cover it with another cushion, a yellow one. Lucienne has watched all my moves, but as soon as the duck is hidden she returns to the little cushion A on her lap, raises it and searches. An expression of disappointment; she turns it over in every direction and gives up.

Same reaction three times in succession.

At 0;10 (26) Lucienne is seated. I place a pencil between her knees in A, under a coverlet. She raises the cover and takes the pencil. I then place it in B under the same coverlet but on her left; Lucienne watches what I do, looks at B for a while after the object has disappeared, then she looks for it in A. Subsequently the reaction changes slightly and becomes of the residual type (see obs. 49).

OBS. 43. At 0;9 (16) Laurent swings in his hammock. In the cords above him I attach a chain which makes a noise at each swinging. Laurent looks at it constantly, with great interest. I then take the chain and bring it very slowly behind my back. Laurent watches this displacement of the object. As soon as the chain is hidden I shake it and it makes a noise; Laurent then stops looking at me and searches for it in the air for a while, disregarding the direction from which the sound emanates. This first observation, although not related to the manual search for the object, shows how Laurent, at the beginning of this stage, is still unaware of the order of successive displacements of the object when he tries to locate it.

From 0;9 (17), that is, the next day, I find the same behavior in manual searching as revealed by the following observations.

OBS. 44. At 0;9 (17), just after having discovered a box under a cushion (see obs. 34), Laurent is placed on a sofa between a coverlet A on the right and a wool garment B on the left. I place my watch under A; he gently raises the coverlet, perceives part of the object, uncovers it, and grasps it. The same thing happens a second and a third time but with increasing application. I then place the watch under B; Laurent watches this maneuver attentively, but at the moment the watch has disappeared under garment B, he turns back toward coverlet A and searches for the object under that screen. I again place the watch under B; he again searches for it under A. By contrast, when for the third time I again place the watch under garment B, Laurent, whose hand is outstretched, raises the screen at once without turning to A; he finds the watch immediately. I then try a fourth time to put the watch under B, but at the moment when Laurent has both hands in the air; he watches my gesture attentively, then turns and again searches for the watch in A!

We see that with the exception of the attempt at the beginning of which Laurent's hand was already directed toward screen B, the child has regularly searched for the object in A, even when he has just seen it disappear under B.

OBS. 45. A quarter-hour later I resume an analogous experiment with Laurent. He is seated on a sofa between cushion A on his right and cushion B. At first he busies himself with raising B before I hide anything under it. I then place my watch under A; Laurent, who has watched me do this, searches indolently under A without finding it, then grasps cushion B and plays with it. Twice in succession I put the watch back under A; he searches for it and finds it. Afterward I put it under B; he raises B and finds it. I put it back under A; he looks for it there immediately. Finally I place it twice under B but each time he turns back to A.

Does this series of reactions mark progress over the preceding (the number of correct responses is greater than before) or does it simply attest to the absence of systematic reaction, an absence caused both by relative indifference and by the fact that the habit of searching for vanished objects is still too recent? We shall see that this second interpretation is the right one; during the few weeks that follow the harder Laurent tries to rediscover the vanished object the more he searches for it in the original location A.

At 0;9 (20) for example, Laurent is in his bed and watches me when I hide a celluloid duck under his quilt A on his right. Laurent finds it immediately but when I take it from him to hide it on his left under sheet B he watches it and then turns and looks under A. I replace the duck in A; Laurent grasps it there. I again place it in B; Laurent, after having seen cloth B cover up the object, follows my hand with his eyes and searches there for the duck. At the third attempt, the duck being again in B, Laurent looks for it in A.

At 0;9 (21) Laurent is seated between pillow A and napkin B. Three times in succession I hide my watch under A where Laurent finds it. Then I place it alternately under A and under B. Every time the watch is under A, the child finds it there. But the first two times it is under B he looks for it under A. The third time, on the other hand, he raises B, but his hand was already two centimeters from that napkin at the time the watch disappeared under it.

At 0;9 (23) Laurent is seated between bib A and pillow B. I hide my watch chain twice in succession under A, then alternately under B and under A. Every time it is under A Laurent finds it there. By contrast, out of five attempts with the watch chain under B he returns four times to look under A and tries only once to search under B. This last movement is perhaps explainable as before by virtue of the fact that it was begun before the object disappeared entirely from the visual field.

At 0;9 (26) the child is seated between bib A, and cloth B. I hide a penknife under A twice in succession; Laurent finds it there. Afterward I hide it alternately ten times under A and ten times under B. When the penknife is under A, Laurent looks for it there each time without hesitation. On the other hand, out of ten attempts under B, Laurent searches for the object eight times under A (although he has seen it disappear under B every time) and only twice under B.

At 0;9 (28) Laurent is seated between two pillows A and B. I hide my watch alternately at A and at B (beginning once under A, which is on the left); out of five times under B not one attempt is successful as the child returns each time under A!

So also at 0;9 (30) Laurent watches alternately disappear under each pillow sometimes my watch, sometimes the celluloid duck, sometimes the plush cat he has just received. Despite the attraction of these objects he looks for them only under A and not once under B, although he sees them disappear there!

The same applies at 0;10 (4) and until 0;10 (16).

Thus it may be seen that if Laurent's reactions are a little less systematic than those of Jacqueline and Lucienne, they are no less definite. On the whole it may be said that, between 0;9 (17) and 0;10 (16) when the object is moved from an initial position A to a later position B, Laurent searches for it in A much more often than in B. When he searches for it in B it is often because the movement of prehension directed toward B was already made and thus is merely extended. But several instances remain in which the child searches immediately in B without returning to A. Do these instances arise from the fact that Laurent, being on the average more advanced than his sisters, goes through the present stage more rapidly, or to the fact that his interest in searches of this type has been less great, it seems to us, than was the case with his older sisters? It is hard to tell without a comparison with a sufficient number of other cases. The only sure thing is that Laurent within a month searches for the object in A much more often than in B and that his reactions are thus comparable to those of our two other subjects. Unfortunately during the months following we were unable to extend the analysis of his case from the point of view of the object, as we focused all our attention on the problems of space itself.

These typical reactions of the fourth stage, observed in our three children over a period of two to four weeks, could not show more clearly that the object still retains a special position; seemingly the child has not taken note of the displacements he has witnessed, but searches for the object in the original place. Later the child makes progress; he searches for the object in the second position (in B). But in the next few weeks if he does not find the vanished thing immediately or if the problem is complicated by the introduction of a third position (C), it will cause the child to return to position A and search there for the object as though nothing had happened in the meantime! This residual reaction seems to us sufficiently related to the preceding one to be classed in the same stage. Hence we shall state that the fifth stage begins only when the child once for all abandons searching in A for the object which he has seen being displaced into B or C. The boundary line is not easy to draw with certainty, because these residual reactions may appear again quite late and may, through temporal displacement, overlap the later stages.

Here are a few examples.

OBS. 46. At 0;11 (7) Jacqueline is seated between two cushions, A and B. I hide a brush under A. Jacqueline raises the cushion, finds the brush and grasps it. I take it from her and hide it under B, but quite far down. Jacqueline searches for it in B, but indolently, and then returns to A where she pursues her investigations with much more energy.

At 0;11 (15) Jacqueline holds a trumpet which I take from her in order to put it under an eiderdown quilt on her left, in A. She finds it, then I hide it in B, that is to say, on her right under the same quilt. Jacqueline searches for it in B, but does not find it. She then returns to A and searches for a moment. Then she goes back to B and after a few seconds abandons all attempts.

I resume the experiment by hiding the object in A, then, after she has found it again, in B, but less far down; Jacqueline immediately searches for it in B and finds it again.

Third attempt: The trumpet is first put in A; Jacqueline searches for it and takes it. Then I place it in B; Jacqueline begins by searching in A, and only after this tries in B. She finally returns to A and gives up.

OBS. 47. At 0;11 (21) Jacqueline is in an armchair and I hide a celluloid swan on her right, in A; she finds it. I then put it on the left, in B; she finds it there too. Then I take the swan and, before her eyes, let it fall to the floor. She sees it fall, even leans over to watch it (but not far enough); not having caught sight of it, she immediately looks for it in B, under the left-hand cushion.

A moment later I make the swan reappear, bring it before her eyes, then let it fall again. She leans over once more and not seeing it, returns to B to look for it under the cushion.

OBS. 48. At 1;0 (0) Jacqueline swings in a hammock suspended from the ceiling. The same day she has received a doll made of celluloid balls, trimmed with a rattle which sounds at the slightest movement. I place the doll above Jacqueline among the cords that hold up the hammock. Jacqueline swings herself, the doll immediately makes a sound and the child raises her eyes; she recognizes the doll and smiles. Afterward I take the doll and very slowly put it behind my back. I make it sound; Jacqueline smiles, leans over in order to see behind me and, not succeeding in doing so, raises her eyes to look attentively at the place where the doll hung.

Same reaction three times in succession, then a negative reaction.

OBS. 49. I. At 0;10 (26), that is, just after the last reaction in obs. 42, Lucienne searches for a pencil between her knees, in A, where I hid it. After she has found it I place the pencil in B, under the same coverlet, but on her left. This time Lucienne immediately looks in B and finds the object.

After that I place the pencil in succession in A, in B, then in C, that is, under the same coverlet but on her right. Lucienne searches properly and finds the pencil in A, then in B. However, as soon as she sees the pencil disappear in C, she searches for it in A!

II. I now hide my watch chain in A; Lucienne searches for it and finds it. Then I place it in B, but quite far down; Lucienne searches for it, but not finding it at once, she gives up her investigation and resumes searching in A! Same reaction in the remainder.

III. This time I hide my watch in A, then in C, without making any further use of position B. Lucienne finds the watch in A, but never once tries to find it in C despite repeated tests; when she sees the watch disappear in C, she immediately searches for it in A. Hence there is a return to the reaction of obs. 41 and 42, as soon as one more position is added!

OBS. 50. Here are the last residual reactions of the third stage observed with Lucienne in the same situation, which will not prevent these reactions from reappearing in other circumstances, as we shall see (obs. 51). It is worthwhile to describe these last events in order to analyze the manner of extinction of such a systematic behavior pattern.

At 0;10 (27) Lucienne is sitting with her legs apart. I place the watch chain between her knees and cover it with a pillow (A); she searches for it and finds it. I then place it on the left, under a cloth (B); Lucienne looks for it there but barely raises this cloth and immediately resumes looking under the pillow in A. At the second attempt she searches at greater length under the cloth B and finds the object. But when I put it in a third place, C, she searches only under the pillow or the cloth, that is, in A or in B.

At 0;11 (3), same experiment. Lucienne searches and finds it in A. When the object is in B she looks at length at B, then searches indolently in A, and returns to B.

At 0;11 (26) when the object is in B, Lucienne searches in B but does not find it at once; then she again returns to A but without conviction and as though to relieve her conscience. Same reaction three times in succession, but as though she were performing a rite.

The next day, at 0;11 (27), same attitude. I put a ball in A, under a rubber sheet on her left; then after she has found it I bring the ball slowly under the bassinet. Lucienne tries to see by pushing herself up, then immediately returns to A, under the rubber sheet, and moves the sheet. She still seems to be searching, but indolently.

Here is the last reaction of the same type. At 0;11 (30) Lucienne, seated in her bassinet, searches for my watch, which always interests her deeply, under a cloth on her left, in A. Then I make the watch disappear under the bassinet, on the right, in B. Three sequential attempts:

1. She looks in B and searches in the right direction. She leans over to see better. Then an expression of resentment; she even whimpers. Then, as though an idea occurred to her, she searches in A, under the cloth, with some persistence; she gives up.

2. Exactly the same reactions but she only searches very rapidly on the right, as though to relieve her conscience. There is no longer any real searching.

3. Same reactions, but Lucienne is content to grip the cloth in A, without raising it or searching; therefore she no longer believes in what she is doing there!

In the following attempts, Lucienne enters the fifth stage.

Before discussing the totality of these events it is fitting to cite several examples of residual reactions analogous to the preceding ones but reappearing in the course of the subsequent stages because of a temporal displacement which is explained by the difficulty of the problems involved. Examination of these tardy reactions will help us to understand the true nature of the foregoing facts.

OBS. 51. At 1;3 (9) Lucienne is in the garden with her mother. Then I arrive; she sees me come, smiles at me, therefore obviously recognizes me (I am at a distance of about 1 meter 50). Her mother then asks her: "Where is papa?" Curiously enough, Lucienne immediately turns toward the window of my office where she is accustomed to seeing me and points in that direction. A moment later we repeat the experiment; she has just seen me 1 meter away from her, yet, when her mother pronounces my name, Lucienne again turns toward my office.

Here it may be clearly seen that if I do not represent two archetypes to her, at least I give rise to two distinct behavior patterns not synthesized nor exclusive of one another but merely juxtaposed: "papa at his window" and "papa in the garden."

At 1;6 (7) Lucienne is with Jacqueline who has just spent a week in bed in a separate room and has gotten up today. Lucienne speaks to her, plays with her, etc., but this does not prevent her, a moment later, from climbing the stairs which lead to Jacqueline's empty bed and laughing before entering the room as she does every day; therefore she certainly expects to find Jacqueline in bed and looks surprised at her own mistake.

At 2;4 (3) Lucienne, hearing a noise in my office, says to me (we are together in the garden): "That is papa up there."

Finally, at 3;5 (0) after seeing her godfather off in an automobile, Lucienne comes back into the house and goes straight to the room in which he slept, saying, "I want to see if godfather has left." She enters alone and says to herself, "Yes, he has gone."

We know the little game which consists in saying to children: "Go look in my room and see if I am there," and we know how often the child yields to the suggestion. Jacqueline and Lucienne have never been taught the custom by us, but Lucienne has let herself be taken in by it after the foregoing observation. It seems probable that there is here some residual reaction analogous to the preceding.

OBS. 52. Let us cite an observation made not on our children but on an older cousin who suggested to us all the foregoing studies. Gérard, at 13 months, knows how to walk, and is playing ball in a large room. He throws the ball, or rather lets it drop in front of him and, either on his feet or on all fours, hurries to pick it up. At a given moment the ball rolls under an armchair. Gérard sees it and, not without some difficulty, takes it out in order to resume the game. Then the ball rolls under a sofa at the other end of the room. Gérard has seen it pass under the fringe of the sofa; he bends down to recover it. But as the sofa is deeper than the armchair and the fringe does prevent a clear view, Gérard gives up after a moment; he gets up, crosses the room, goes right under the armchair and carefully explores the place where the ball was before.

The general fact common to all these observations is that the child, after seeing an object disappear under a screen B, goes to look for it under screen A under which he searched for it and found it a moment before. In obs. 39 to 45, characterizing what we have called the typical reaction of this fourth stage, the child searches for the object in A as soon as he has seen it disappear in B and without first trying to find it in B. In obs. 46 to 50 characterizing the residual reactions, the child searches first in B and, if he fails, returns to A. Or again, accustomed to searching indiscriminately in A or in B, he does not search in C if the object has been put in this third place, but returns to A or to B (obs. 49 and 50). Finally, in obs. 51 and 52 the child, even after having transcended this fourth stage (this is certain with respect to Lucienne and very probable with respect to Gérard) relapses, in certain circumstances, into residual reaction.

How are these facts to be interpreted? Three interpretations seem possible to us according to whether one attributes these strange behavior patterns to difficulties of memory or of spatial localization, or to the incomplete formation of object concept.

The first explanation seems to be the simplest from the point of view of adult psychology. Everyone, in a moment of absentmindedness, has behaved somewhat like our children. For example I take my clothesbrush out of the small bag in which it is usually kept and place it on a table; afterward when I want to use it I look for it in its bag and cannot understand its disappearance. Or else I go to look for a necktie in my closet, place it before me, and when ready to put it on, return to my tie rack; I see my pipe on my desk, put it in my pocket, then hunt for it on the desk, etc. This is not, fortunately, either confusion related to the constitution of objects as permanent substances or confusion related to spatial localization; I have merely forgotten the sequential displacements of the object, and left without it, I search for it in the place where my attempts are ordinarily crowned with success or else in the place where I noted its presence on the last occasion. So also it could be stated that Gérard (obs. 52), having known perfectly well at first that the ball had left the armchair and was to be found under the sofa, little by little lost all memory of the events; no longer knowing very well what he was doing under the sofa, he remembered having found the ball under the armchair and immediately followed his impulse. In the example in obs. 51, there is no doubt that the habit of seeing her father at the office window, of seeing Jacqueline in bed or of seeing her godfather in the guest room is important in Lucienne's reactions; it could therefore be affirmed that she forgets what she has just seen and reverts to her habitual schema. In residual reactions in general it is permissible to think that the child, after having failed to find the object in B, no longer remembers the order of events very well and tries at all events to seek the object in A. In typical reactions one could go so far as to believe that, faced with the disappearance of the object, the child immediately ceases to reflect; in other words, he does not try to remember the sequence of positions and thus merely returns to the place where he was successful in finding the object the first time.

The second explanation pertains to the constitution of space. It can be asserted that between the ages of 9 and 12 months the child still has too much difficulty in elaborating objective displacement groups for him to take note of the localization of invisible objects. Surely, if he saw the object uninterruptedly, nothing would be easier for him than to form the two following groups (we shall designate by M the position of the object when it is at rest in the child's hand and by A and B the other positions of the same object):

(1) $M \to A$; $A \to B$; $B \to M$, or
(2) $M \to A$; $A \to M$; $M \to B$; $B \to M$.

But precisely because in normal times he sees the object uninterruptedly, the child does not need to be aware of such groups; he puts them into action without thinking about them. In other words, the child grasps the object where he sees it or else where he has just seen it without needing to retrace his itinerary mentally. If such were the case, that is, if the "group" remained chiefly practical without being a concept to him, it could very well be that the localization of objects in space would remain a matter of mere sensorimotor schemata, hence of immediate and not considered actions. There would, consequently, be no image of localizations but merely an empirical use of localization. The hierarchy of behavior patterns would therefore be the following: the object would first be sought where it is seen, then where it was seen and finally where it was found behind a screen for the first time. But when the object disappears behind a second screen the child would use up the series of these behavior patterns in the first place before searching for it behind this new obstacle; no longer seeing it, but having already seen and found it in a first position, the child would therefore return to A merely through failure to vary his action of searching and to vary it in relation to the sequential positions. This is seen, for example, when the subject manages to search in B but refuses to search in C (obs. 49 and 50): the search in A and in B having been successful, it is useless to try in C ! In other words, there would be no localization from the point of view of object but solely from the point of view of action. The object would have a special position merely because the group remains practical or subjective and is not yet entirely objective or representative.

With this hypothesis it would be easy to explain the chronological order of the behavior patterns observed. The child would begin with the typical reaction for the reasons just demonstrated: having previously found the object in A and not trying to imagine its localization in B, he would return to A as soon as the object disappears in B. In the second place the child, discovering gradually and empirically the failure of his procedure, would begin to search for the object also in B; but unaware as he still is of objective localization, if he did not succeed at once he would return to his search in A. Residual reaction would therefore indicate the persistence of practical or subjective localization or its primacy in relation to objective localization. Finally, in obs. 51, the belated resurrection of this behavior pattern would stem from the fact that, as the object has a very unyielding practical or subjective localization (for reasons of habit), the objective and representative localizations would momentarily pass over to the second plane.

But still a third explanation is possible with regard to the constitution of object concept. It is possible that during this third stage the object is still not the same to the child as it is to us: a substantial body, individualized and displaced in space without depending on the action context in which it is inserted. Thus the object is, perhaps, to the child, only a particularly striking aspect of the total picture in which it is contained; at least it would not manifest so many "moments of freedom" as do our images. Hence there would not be one chain, one doll, one watch, one ball, etc., individualized, permanent, and independent of the child's activity, that is, of the special positions in which that activity takes place or has taken place, but there would still exist only images such as "ball-under-the-arm-chair," "doll-attached-to-the-hammock," "watch-under-a-cushion," "papa-at-his-window," etc. Certainly the same object reappearing in different practical positions or contexts is recognized, identified, and endowed with permanence as such. In this sense it is relatively independent. But, without being truly conceived as having several copies, the object may manifest itself to the child as assuming a limited number of distinct forms of a nature intermediate between unity and plurality, and in this sense it remains a part of its context. Obs. 51 permits us to understand this hypothesis: when Lucienne looks for me at the window when she knows that I am beside her two behavior patterns are obviously involved, "papa-at-his-window" and "papa-in-front-of-oneself"; and, if Lucienne does not hesitate to consider the two papas as being one and the same person, she nevertheless does not succeed in abstracting this person from the total pictures with which he is connected sufficiently to refrain from looking for him in two places simultaneously. *A fortiori*, in obs. 52, the child who does not find the "ball-under-the-sofa" does not hesitate to look for the "ball-under-the-armchair" since here there are two distinct totalities. Whereas we think of the ball as able to occupy an infinitude of different positions, which enables us to abstract it from all of them at once, the child endows it with only a few special positions without being able, consequently, to consider it as entirely independent of them. In a general way, in all the observations in which the child searches in A for what he has seen disappear in B, the explanation should be sought in the fact that the object is not yet sufficiently individualized to be dissociated from the global behavior related to position A.

Such then are the three possible explanations for the phenomenon: defect of memory, defect of spatial localization, or defect of objectification. But far from trying to choose among them, we shall on the contrary try to show that these three explanations, seemingly different, in reality constitute only a single explanation, seen from three distinct points of view. It is only if one retained one of the three explanations to the exclusion of the two others that it would be disputable. But if all three are accepted, they are complementary.

First, the defect of memory. The great difference between the behavior of the ten-month-old child and our own seemingly analogous behavior (looking for the brush in its usual place when we have just put it somewhere else) is that we could very well keep the memory of the sequential displacements if we paid attention whereas, by hypothesis, the child cannot. If we change the order of movements of the brush, the necktie or the pipe, it is because we are absentminded; but being otherwise quite capable of remembering the sequential displacements of the things which surround us, we attribute to them by virtue of this fact an objective structure, and by extension we conceive of the brush, etc., in an identical way even in moments of the worst absentmindedness. On the contrary, in obs. 39 to 52 the child manifests the *maximum* of attention and interest of which he is capable, and if one may refer to absentmindedness in certain events of obs. 51, this could not be involved when the child is trying by every means to find the hidden object he wants. In particular in the instances of typical reaction (obs. 39 to 46), the child is watching the object with the greatest fixity as it disappears in B, yet immediately afterward he turns to A; it would therefore be unrealistic to admit that he forgets the displacements out of mere absentmindedness. Thereafter to the extent that a defect of memory intervenes it would only involve a systematic difficulty in arranging events in time and, consequently, in noting the sequence of displacements. Seeing the object disappear, the child would not try to reconstruct its itinerary; he would, without reflection or memory, go straight to the position where his action had already succeeded in finding it. But then in this hypothesis, the spatial and objective structure of the universe would become, at the same stroke, entirely different from what it is for us. Let us suppose the existence of a mind which retained no memory of the order of displacements: its universe would consist in a series of total pictures whose coherence would pertain to the action itself and not to the relations sustained by the elements of the different pictures with each other. This first interpretation is tantamount to the next two: the construction of objective groups of displacements presupposes time and memory, just as time presupposes a universe spatially and objectively organized.

With regard to the second explanation, it is equally true, provided it includes the first and third. It is perfectly accurate to say that the child searches for the object in A when it has disappeared in B, simply because the practical schema prevails over the objective group of displacements. The child does not take note of those displacements and when (in the residual reactions) he begins to note them, he still subordinates them to the schemata of immediate action. But if that is the case it must be concluded, first, that the memory of the positions does not play a decisive role and, second, that the object remains linked with a global context instead of being individualized and substantiated as an independent and permanent body in motion.

Hence we are brought to the third solution inasmuch as it really involves the first two solutions and vice versa. In a word, during this fourth stage the object remains a practical object rather than a substantial thing. The child's reactions remain inspired in whole or in part by a sort of phenomenalism mixed with dynamism. The object is not a thing which is displaced and is independent of those displacements; it is a reality at disposal in a certain context, itself related to a certain action. In this respect the behavior patterns of the present stage merely extend those of the preceding one. They are phenomenalistic since the object remains dependent on its context and not isolated in the capacity of a moving body endowed with permanence. They are dynamic, moreover, since the object remains in the extension of the effort and of the feeling of efficacy linked with the action by which the subject finds the object again. From this dual point of view the progress made by the child in learning to search for the object behind a screen has not yet sufficed to cause him to attribute an objective structure to the things which surround him. In order that these things really become objects the awareness of relations of position and displacement must be acquired. The child will have to understand the "how" of the appearance and disappearance of these objects and thus will have to abandon belief in the possibility of their mysterious reappearance at the place they have left and where action itself has discovered them. In short, a truly geometric rationalism will have to supersede the phenomenalism of immediate perception and the dynamism of practical efficacy.

§ 4. THE FIFTH STAGE: THE CHILD TAKES ACCOUNT OF THE SEQUENTIAL DISPLACEMENTS OF THE OBJECT

From the end of the first year of life until toward the middle of the second there extends a stage characterized by the progressive acquisition of spatial relations whose absence during the stage just passed prevents the definitive formation of object concept. In other words, the child learns to take account of the sequential displacements perceived in the visual field; he no longer searches for the object in a special position but only in the position resulting from the last visible displacement. This discovery we consider the beginning of the fifth stage.

Thus characterized, the behavior patterns of the present stage are of great interest in connection with the questions raised with respect to the fourth stage. To the extent that these behavior patterns bear upon visible displacements they reveal a nascent geometric rationalism; this constitutes the new element peculiar to them. True, to the extent that they remain incapable of making allowance for invisible displacements (those which the child does not see) they conserve an element of mixed phenomenalism and dynamism. But such a complication does not alter in any way the regularity of the development. Far from disappearing entirely the practical and egocentric object defends foot by foot the terrain which the geometric relationships will conquer. In a general way, it may be said that every complication in the problems encountered and particularly the complication resulting from invisible displacements causes the habits of the preceding stages to reappear through temporal displacement. This circumstance does not make it easier to describe the behavior patterns of the present stage; but if we follow the chronological order of their manifestations, the mechanism of the patterns will be intelligible.

The first acquisition of the fifth stage (which marks its advent) is signified by the success of the tests whose initial failure is described in obs. 39 to 52: when the object is hidden under a first screen under which the child finds it, and then under a second screen, the subject no longer searches for the object under the first screen, but only under the second one.

OBS. 53. At 1;0 (20) Jacqueline watches me hide my watch under cushion A on her left, then under cushion B on her right; in the latter case she immediately searches in the right place. If I bury the object deep she searches for a long time, then gives up, but does not return to A.

At 1;0 (26), same experiment. At the first attempt Jacqueline searches and finds in A where I first put the watch. When I hide it in B Jacqueline does not succeed in finding it there, being unable to raise the cushion altogether. Then she turns around, unnerved, and touches different things including cushion A, but she does not try to turn it over; she *knows* that the watch is no longer under it.

Subsequent attempts: Jacqueline never succeeds in finding the watch in B because I hide it too deep, but neither does she ever try to return to A to see if it is still there; she searches assiduously in B, then gives up.

At 1;1 (22) new experiments with different objects. The result is always the same.

OBS. 54. Laurent, at 0;11 (22) is seated between two cushions A and B. I hide the watch alternately under each; Laurent constantly searches for the object where it has just disappeared, that is, sometimes in A, sometimes in B, without remaining attached to a privileged position as during the preceding stage.

It is noteworthy that the same day Laurent reveals a very systematic mind in searching for the vanished object. I hide a little box in my hand. He then tries to raise my fingers to reach the object. But, instead of letting him do this and without showing the box, I pass to him with two fingers of the same hand a shoe, a toy, and finally a ribbon; Laurent is not fooled and always returns to the proper hand despite its displacements, and at last opens it and takes the box. When I take it from him to put it in the other hand, he searches for it there immediately.

At 1;0 (20) likewise, he searches sequentially in both my hands for a button I am hiding. Afterward he tries to see behind me when I make the button roll on the floor (on which I am seated) even though, to fool him, I hold out my two closed hands.

At 1;1 (8) etc., likewise, he takes note of all the visible displacements of the object.

OBS. 54a. Lucienne also, at 1;0 (5), no longer looks for the object only in B and does not return to the initial place, even in the event of continuous failure.

Same observations at 1;0 (11) etc.

On this point phenomenalism has certainly yielded to awareness of relation; the child takes account of all the visible displacements he has observed and dissociates the object from its practical context.

But if we interpose the simplest possible of invisible displacements the phenomena of the preceding stage immediately reappear. In this connection we have tried the following experiment: hiding an object not directly under the screen, but in a box without a lid; box and object are made to disappear under a screen and the box brought out empty. The child does not succeed in understanding, except by luck, that the object can have been left behind under the screen.

OBS. 55. At 1;6 (8) Jacqueline is sitting on a green rug and playing with a potato which interests her very much (it is a new object for her). She says "po-terre" and amuses herself by putting it into an empty box and taking it out again. For several days she has been enthusiastic about this game.

I. I then take the potato and put it in the box while Jacqueline watches. Then I place the box under the rug and turn it upside down thus leaving the object hidden by the rug without letting the child see my maneuver, and I bring out the empty box. I say to Jacqueline, who has not stopped looking at the rug and who has realized that I was doing something under it: "Give papa the potato." She searches for the object in the box, looks at me, again looks at the box minutely, looks at the rug, etc., but it does not occur to her to raise the rug in order to find the potato underneath.

During the five subsequent attempts the reaction is uniformly negative. I begin again, however, each time putting the object in the box as the child watches, putting the box under the rug, and bringing it out empty. Each time Jacqueline looks in the box, then looks at everything around her including the rug, but does not search under it.

II. At the seventh attempt, I change the technique. I place the object in the box and the box under the rug but leave the object in the box. As soon as I remove my empty hand Jacqueline looks under the rug, finds and grasps the box, opens it and takes the potato out of it. Same reaction a second time.

III. Then I resume the first technique: emptying the box under the rug and bringing it forth empty. At first Jacqueline looks for the object in the box, and not finding it there, searches for it under the rug. Hence the attempt has been successful. This occurs a second time but from the third attempt on, the result becomes negative again, as in I. Is this due to fatigue?

OBS. 56. The next day, at 1;6 (9), I resume the experiment but with a celluloid fish containing a rattle. I put the fish in the box and the box under the rug. There I shake it and Jacqueline hears the fish in the box. I turn the box upside down and bring it out empty. Jacqueline immediately takes possession of the box, searches for the fish, turns the box over in all directions, looks around her, in particular looks at the rug but does not raise it.

The next attempts yield nothing further. I do not use technique II of the preceding observation.

That evening I repeat the experiment with a little lamb. Jacqueline herself puts the lamb in the box and when the whole thing is under the coverlet she says with me, "Coucou, lamb." When I take out the empty box she says, "Lamb, lamb," but does not look under the coverlet.

Whenever I leave the whole thing under the coverlet she immediately searches for the box and brings out the lamb. But when I start again, using the first technique, she no longer looks under the coverlet!

OBS. 57. At 1;0 (16) Lucienne looks at my watch chain which I place in my own hand; she opens my hand and takes the chain. I recommence, but after having closed my hand I place it on the floor next to the child (Lucienne is seated), and cover my fist with a coverlet. I take out my fist and extend it to Lucienne, who has watched the whole thing most attentively; Lucienne opens my hand, finds nothing, looks all around her but does not raise the coverlet.

Attempts 2-4: Same reaction.

Fifth attempt: Lucienne raises the coverlet mechanically or by chance, and perceives the chain. This must not have been intentional since it did not affect the rest of the behavior.

Attempts 6-10: Return to the initial reaction. Lucienne searches attentively around my hand, looks at the coverlet but does not raise it.

This reaction could not, however, be attributed to boredom; Lucienne seems to be very much interested.

These first failures are significant. For example, Jacqueline knows very well how to search for an object hidden behind a screen, as we have established to be the case for more than six months. But she succeeds in keeping track of only the visible displacements of the object and locates it only where she has actually seen it. In the experiment now under discussion an invisible displacement is involved (the object leaves the box or the hand when both are under the rug) and the object occupies a space where it has not been directly perceived (under the rug); these are two new conditions of the experiment. In effect, so long as the child sees the box or the hand disappear under the rug he knows that the object is in the box and the box under the rug; but from this he does not succeed in concluding that, when the box comes out empty, the object has been left under the rug. Hence the search for the object as yet makes allowance only for observed displacements and positions in which the object has actually been seen.

It is true that series II and III of obs. 55 end in the child's success. But precisely by virtue of the fact that in series II I have left the box under the rug, Jacqueline has acquired the movement of searching for the object under this screen; afterward she will therefore look there for the same object when she does not find it elsewhere. But as we have seen, this discovery is not generalized, and on the next day (obs. 56), the attempts are all negative. Hence this was only a practical schema and not yet an awareness of relations or an image of what I was doing under the screen: removing the object from the box. Yet, as we have seen, such a movement is familiar to the child.

Nevertheless, after a few days the child succeeds in solving the problem. But this new acquisition is immediately accompanied by a reappearance, on the new plane thus discovered, of the earlier phenomena of reversal of the order of displacements. Here are made most clearly manifest the temporal displacements mentioned at the beginning of this section.

Let us first analyze how the child discovers the result of the invisible displacement. Does it occur through awareness of relations, in which case there would really be a utilization of the unseen displacements, or merely through empirical or practical apprenticeship, in which case there would not be a true image of invisible displacements. The second solution seems to us the right one, precisely since the discovery is immediately accompanied by the resurrection of earlier behavior patterns, displaced chronologically by one or several steps.

obs. 58. At 1;6 (16) Jacqueline looks at a ring which I place in my left hand. She opens my hand by raising my fingers and finds the object, all with great pleasure and even a certain agitation.

I. *First attempt:* I ostensibly place the ring in my left hand, then press the left hand against the right and extend both hands closed, the ring having passed into the right hand. Jacqueline searches in the left and, astonished, says, "Ring, ring, where it is?" but it does not occur to her to look in the right hand.

Second attempt: She searches directly for the ring in the right hand, finds it and laughs. Is this luck, or does the gesture of pressing one hand against the other suggest to her to begin with the right one?

Third attempt: This time I place the ring in the right hand and then pass it into the left one. Jacqueline looks in the right hand, astonished at not finding anything, then grasps the left one and laughs at her success.

Attempts 4 and 5: Same reaction (changing hands each time).

II. I now place the ring in my hand, then put my hand in a beret placed between Jacqueline's knees. After having left the ring in the beret I withdraw my hand and extend it closed.

1. By a lucky chance, Jacqueline had not paid sufficient attention to my closed hand and immediately turns to the beret, as when I merely hid an object under a screen. Of course she finds the ring and laughs. But this chance occurrence, which might have falsified the result of the experiment, on the contrary serves to emphasize the interest of the following reactions: despite this first success Jacqueline did not, in fact, succeed immediately in understanding the ring's itinerary.

2. Jacqueline's first movement is again to turn toward the beret. But seeing my fist come out of it, she grasps it and opens it. Much surprised to find nothing, she repeats over and over, "Where it is, where it is?" but it does not occur to her to look in the beret.

3 and 4. Same reactions.

5. Still not finding the ring in my hand, Jacqueline looks all

around her, sees the beret but without any idea of looking inside it. On the other hand, it does occur to her to look inside my other hand, even though she does not see it (I am leaning on it). I hold my other hand out to her, she opens it, then gives up all search.

6. She gives up right away.

III. Three hours later I resume these two experiments. That of series I yields no more than immediately positive results: Jacqueline now understands that I can pass the ring from one hand to the other. With regard to the experiment in series II, here are the results (five attempts):

1. Negative reaction: Jacqueline opens my hand, searches all over, but does not think of the beret into which she has, however, seen me slip my hand.

2. Same beginning, then she looks at the beret. She perceives it at the very moment in which she is examining my hand all over. She grasps the beret, looks inside it and finds the ring. Laughs.

3. Opens my hand, searches for a moment, then without hesitation searches in the beret.

4 and 5: Same reaction.

OBS. 59. Lucienne at 1;1 (4) finds a watch chain in my fist. I then replace the chain in my hand and slip this hand under a pillow. I leave the chain under the pillow and bring my hand out closed.

1. *First attempt:* Lucienne looks in my hand, then finding nothing, looks at me, laughing. She resumes searching, then gives up.

Attempts 2-5: Same reactions. I use the watch instead of the chain to increase her interest; same difficulty.

Sixth attempt: This time, sudden success. Lucienne opens my hand as soon as I take it out from under the pillow. After having examined it a moment she stops, looks around her, then suddenly looks under the pillow and finds the watch.

Subsequent attempts: Same reaction.

II. Then I resume the experiment with a quilt which is on the child's right. Lucienne begins by looking in my hand which I have removed closed from under the quilt. After having opened and explored it for a moment Lucienne searches under the quilt without hesitation.

Subsequent attempts: Same success.

But I did not yet try that day to pass rapidly from the quilt to the pillow or vice versa in order to see if there were memory of the localizations. This experiment will be found later.

It may be seen that this discovery of the result of invisible displacements appears to be the effect of practical learning rather than a representation of the relations themselves. Thus, in obs. 58, series I, if Jacqueline looks in the second hand for the ring which is gone from the first one, it is doubtless merely because seeing the other hand incites her to repeat with it the behavior applied to the first hand. Proof of this is that subsequently (series II, attempt 5) she happens to search for the object in my other hand, which played no role in the experiment with the beret. It therefore seems that Jacqueline is guided by the memory of the movements which succeeded rather than by awareness of the actual relationships. In the experiment with the beret (series II), the good luck of the first attempt is far from having been utilized from the outset in the following attempts; it is necessary to resume the experiment three hours later to succeed in the goal. It therefore seems that all of this is the work of practical learning and not a deduction of the relations themselves. With regard to Lucienne (obs. 59), her discovery seems, on the contrary, to result from invention through a mental combination of the relations involved. But we shall see that neither she nor Jacqueline escapes the reappearance by temporal displacement of the phenomena of reversal of the order of displacements, proof that the representation of the object's itinerary is not yet dependable.

In effect, as soon as the behavior pattern consisting in making allowance for the invisible displacement was acquired, we tried the following experiment: combining this new schema of the transfer of objects outside the visual field with the schema of the order of sequential positions. In other words, we have tried to correlate the experiments made in connection with the third stage (to cause searching for the object in two sequential positions) with those of which we have just spoken. For example, let the child be seated between cushion A and cushion B. I put the object in one hand and the hand under A. I bring my hand out closed; thereafter the child knows he must look in A as soon as he has ascertained that my hand is empty. But when I repeat these same procedures in B, will the child immediately search in B, or, through a resurrection of the behavior patterns of the third stage, will he return to A? The experiment has shown that over a longer or shorter period, it is the latter behavior pattern which presents itself first.

OBS. 60. Jacqueline, at 1;6 (16), that is, after the experiments of obs. 58, undergoes three new series of tests.

I. In order to check on the firmness of the recent acquisitions I take a key in my fist, place my fist in a beret, leave the key in the beret and finally throw it on the floor at the end of the room. Jacqueline runs toward the beret but as I say, "Key, key, look for the key," she turns around, looks at me laughingly, looks at my hands which are open and, resuming her idea, goes toward the beret. She picks it up and without hesitation puts in her hand and removes the key.

II. I seat Jacqueline on a bed between a pillow A, 50 centimeters away from her on her left, and a quilt B, 50 centimeters on her right.

1. I put the key in my right hand, put my hand under the pillow and withdraw it, empty and closed; Jacqueline opens the hand and searches. Then she takes my left hand (cf. obs. 58, series I and II, attempt 5). When she ascertains that my left hand also is empty, she says: "Where it is, where it is?" I put my hands behind my back. She looks at the bed, and seeing the pillow rushes forward and finds the key underneath.

2. I repeat the whole process with the quilt. Jacqueline looks first in my right hand at quite some length, then in my left hand (which has not come into the experiment). Afterward she looks at the quilt and searches under it.

3. Same reactions with the pillow.

Thus it seems that Jacqueline's behavior is entirely correct with respect to screens A and B and that there is no reappearance of the difficulties of the third stage. But might this not be due to the lengthy preliminary procedures, that is, to the fact that she searched in my left hand after having found nothing in my right? Thus she might have forgotten the sequential positions of the object under the screens and gone directly to the correct place, not through reflection but, on the contrary, through automatism. This seems indicated by what follows: as soon as Jacqueline gives up searching both my hands in sequence she reverses the positions in relation to A and B.

III. Two hours later I put Jacqueline back on her bed between pillow A and quilt B. She holds a flower in her hands, freshly picked and highly valued by her. I take it from her, put it in my right hand, put my hand under pillow A and bring it out empty and closed. Jacqueline says spontaneously, "Search, search," and opens my hand.

Then, instead of looking under the pillow in A, she turns to the other side and plunges under quilt B!

The next day, at 1;6 (17) I resume the experiment with a tape measure rolled up; I place it in my hand, put my hand under pillow A and bring it out closed. Jacqueline opens my hand, says: "Where it is, look," and goes straight under quilt B. Same reaction with a button.

OBS. 61. I. Fearing that the last reaction might have resulted from chance or from automatism, I interrupt the experiment for three days and resume it on 1;6 (20). I abandon the quilt for the same reason and put Jacqueline between garment A and cushion B.

1. I place the object in my hand, put my hand under A and bring it out closed. Jacqueline searches in my hand, looks at it all over, then looks at me with astonishment, examines the floor, and as though enlightened by her thought, turns over garment A. She takes the object and laughs.

2. I repeat the same gestures in B. Jacqueline opens my hand, again hesitates for a moment, then returns to A without hesitation! The reaction is very definite, with an attitude of sustained attention.

II. At 1;7. (1) Jacqueline, who has not been tested since series I, is seated on a bed between pillow A and quilt B.

1. I place the object in my hand, the hand under pillow A and bring it forth closed. Jacqueline looks in my hand, then under A and finds the object.

2. I repeat the experiment in B. Jacqueline watches me, opens my hand and searches. Afterward she pauses, seems to reflect for an instant, then goes straight to pillow A. She raises it, examines the under part of it attentively and, only then and after a pause, searches under quilt B where she finds it.

3-5. Experiment in B. Always the same reaction; she begins by searching in A and only then goes to B.

OBS. 62. Finally, here are three new behavior patterns observed with Jacqueline in slightly different circumstances; the mechanism of these patterns is analogous to that of the preceding ones.

1. At 1;7 (7) Jacqueline finds an adult's slipper and puts it on her foot. I take it from her, put my watch inside it and shake it. Jacqueline hears the noise, searches, and finds the watch. Then I place the watch in the slipper, the slipper under my leg and empty the slipper of its contents. The watch falls to the floor under my leg, making a very distinct noise. I withdraw the slipper and say to Jacqueline, "Search." Jacqueline has followed each of my movements very at-

tentively. First she explores the inside of the slipper. But finding nothing she stretches out her hand immediately, not under my outstretched leg, but into my vest pocket from which I took the watch at the beginning of the game! She therefore has no concern for the object's itinerary, which was, however, very easy to reconstruct.

II. At 1;7 (9) Jacqueline is sitting on me and I am lying on a sofa. She has in her hand a piece of yellow paper which she holds in high regard. I hide it in my hand, while she watches, of course, put my hand under a coverlet behind her (she turns around and is watching my movements). I withdraw my hand closed and hold it out to her. She opens it, feels it, then turns around, looks under the coverlet and finds the paper.

After which I put the paper back into my hand, put my hand under my vest, in front of her, and hold my hand out to her, closed; Jacqueline opens it, feels it, turns around and extends her hand halfway toward the quilt. Then, a sudden turnabout, and her hand searches under the vest.

Hence this time there is complete success but with a residue of preceding behavior patterns. The same applies to the following series:

III. At 1;7 (11) Jacqueline is seated on a bed.

1. I place a pebble in my hand, put my hand under quilt A and withdraw it closed. Jacqueline opens my hand, then searches under A and finds the pebble.

2. Same experiment under my vest B. Jacqueline opens my hand and goes under vest B at the first try. Consequently success ensues.

3. I place the pebble in my hand and press this hand against the other one in C, leaving the pebble there. Jacqueline searches in my first hand, then under vest B, then finally under the quilt A. She takes no account of position C, although she has watched each of my movements.

4. I repeat the same experiment (3). This time Jacqueline looks in my first hand, then under quilt A, then at last under vest B, but still takes no account of my other hand.

The complication of the problem has therefore caused merely empirical reactions to reappear at once.

OBS. 63. At 1;1 (18) Lucienne is seated on a bed, between shawl A and cloth B. I hide a safety pin in my hand and my hand under the shawl. I remove my hand closed and empty. Jacqueline opens it at once and looks for the pin. Not finding it, she searches under the shawl and finds it.

After which I place the pin in my hand and my hand under cloth B. Lucienne looks at my hand but does not open it, guessing right away that it is empty, and after this quick look immediately searches under shawl A!

At 1;1 (24) Lucienne watches me put a ring in my hand and my hand under A, then, after she has found the ring, under B; the experiment is successful.

But, with a beret, things become complicated. I put my watch in the beret and the beret under pillow A (on the right); Lucienne lifts the pillow, takes the beret, and removes the watch from it. Then I place the beret, again containing the watch, under cushion B on the left; Lucienne looks for it in B but, as it is hidden too far down for her to find it at once, she returns to A.

Then, twice, I raise cushion B so that Lucienne sees the beret obviously containing the object; both times she resumes looking in B but, not finding the watch right away, returns to A! She searches even longer in A than in B after having seen the object in B!

These results seem to us to have a certain interest from two points of view. In the first place, they furnish us with a good example of the law of temporal displacements; when an operation passes over from one plane of consciousness or of action to another, it has to be relearned on this new plane. In particular, the group of displacements of the object which, at the beginning of this fifth stage, had been constituted on the plane of direct perception of relationships of position, must be formed anew as soon as it has been transferred to the plane of representation of these relationships. In effect, when an invisible displacement of the object intervenes, the child relapses into the same difficulties which he has already overcome when visible displacements were involved. The unobserved displacement must be imagined, since it is not directly perceived.

In the second place, such results are interesting from the point of view of object concept. They show us that the object, although already constituted as permanent substance when visible displacements are involved, still remains dependent on its context as a phenomenalistic whole and on the practical and dynamic schema which it extends when it is subjected to invisible displacements.

It is true that in a particular case, memory may play a much greater role than in the experiments described in connection with the third stage: it is more difficult to remember four or five sequential displacements than only two, especially if some of them have not been perceived but inferred. But here, as before, it does not seem to us that the child's memory can be called upon independently of the spatial elaborations whose orderly arrangement in time is only one of the elements inseparable from the others; memory is only a construction of temporal relationships, and if it fails to bring order to these relationships in the course of experiments which hold the child's interest it is apparent that the failure pertains to the actual content of these relationships, that is, to the nature of the events and not only to their sequence.

In other words, if the child does not remember the order of displacements, it is because in such cases he does not construct a coherent spatial group. But then it is apparent that for the child the object is not yet entirely what it is for us. From the moment when the child takes account of the visible displacements (obs. 53-54a), the object is certainly dissociated from its phenomenalistic and practical context and consequently endowed with substantial and geometric permanence. But from the moment that the displacements are too complicated to be arranged in groups accessible to representation (and to memory), the object again becomes dependent on the context of the whole and on the practical schema leading to its possession. There is nothing contradictory in this dual nature of the object during the fifth stage since two different planes are involved. The child who speaks, or even the adult, may alike bestow the quality of object on the things which surround them and yet find themselves incapable of so doing with regard to the stars or other distant bodies; the discovery of the singleness of the sun or the oneness of the moon during its different phases is a good example of this, as many children of four to six years of age are far from having made the discovery. There is therefore nothing surprising in the fact that the child of 12 to 16 months of age considers as objects only those images that are near and remains doubtful with regard to bodies subjected to invisible displacements.

§ 5. THE SIXTH STAGE: THE REPRESENTATION OF INVISIBLE
   DISPLACEMENTS

After the sixth stage the child becomes capable of constructing
objects when the displacements are not all visible. That of course
does not signify that this discovery is immediately generalized
to include the whole universe, since we have just seen that during
the years following this is still not the case. It merely means that
the child succeeds in resolving the problems raised in the course
of the preceding experiments and has resolved them by means of
a new method: that of representation. This success became systematic in Jacqueline's case at 1;7 (20) and in Lucienne's at 1;3
(14).

OBS. 64. I. At 1;7 (20) Jacqueline watches me when I put a coin
in my hand, then put my hand under a coverlet. I withdraw my
hand closed; Jacqueline opens it, then searches under the coverlet
until she finds the object. I take back the coin at once, put it in my
hand and then slip my closed hand under a cushion situated at
the other side (on her left and no longer on her right); Jacqueline
immediately searches for the object under the cushion. I repeat
the experiment by hiding the coin under a jacket; Jacqueline finds it
without hesitation.

II. I complicate the test as follows: I place the coin in my hand,
then my hand under the cushion. I bring it forth closed and immediately hide it under the coverlet. Finally I withdraw it and hold it
out, closed, to Jacqueline. Jacqueline then pushes my hand aside
without opening it (she guesses that there is nothing in it, which is
new), she looks under the cushion, then directly under the coverlet
where she finds the object.

During a second series (cushion and jacket) she behaves in the
same way.

I then try a series of three displacements: I put the coin in my
hand and move my closed hand sequentially from A to B and from
B to C; Jacqueline sets my hand aside, then searches in A, in B and
finally in C.

Lucienne is successful in the same tests at 1;3 (14).

OBS. 65. At 1;7 (23) Jacqueline is seated opposite three object-
screens, A, B, and C (a beret, a handkerchief, and her jacket)
aligned equidistant from each other. I hide a small pencil in my

hand, saying, "Coucou, the pencil." I hold out my closed hand to her, put it under A, then under B, then under C (leaving the pencil under C); at each step I again extend my closed hand, repeating, "Coucou, the pencil." Jacqueline then searches for the pencil directly in C, finds it and laughs.

I repeat the experiment nine times in succession, always taking the following precautions: 1) I show the child my closed hand every time I withdraw it from under one of the three object-screens, and especially after having brought it out of the third one. 2) I vary the order in each experiment, taking care to begin by putting my hand under the object-screen under which the child found the pencil during the preceding test. For example, the first attempt having been made in the order A, B, C, the second test will follow the order C, A, B (the pencil being in B), the third, B, C, A, etc. 3) Each time I move the object-screens; sometimes the beret is on the left, sometimes in the middle, sometimes on the right, etc. 4) Each time the pencil is left under the last screen under which I passed my hand.

During the first eight experiments Jacqueline constantly searches for and finds the pencil under the last object-screen under which I put my hand. At the ninth attempt she searches for it under the next to the last one and at the tenth she recommences without hesitation to investigate under the last one. Moreover she makes one characteristic hesitation at the sixth attempt; she first touches the handkerchief (under which the pencil was hidden the time before) but without turning it over, then passes spontaneously to the beret (correct), as though mentally correcting her mistake. Attention and interest are very lively throughout, except during attempts 8 and 9 (fatigue). Effort revives in attempt 10.

At 1;7 (24), the next day, I repeat the experiment under the same conditions. Jacqueline continues to turn over the last screen only. However, sometimes she hesitates and touches sequentially the next to last screen (without turning it over), then the last one (finally turning it over), as though with reflection and mental association. During test 7, Jacqueline even touches the three screens in succession, following the order in which I myself had slid in and withdrawn my closed hand, but she again turned over only the last screen.

Clearly, there is definitely a system here. These facts cannot be explained by chance alone, given the modifications I introduce each time in the order followed. Moreover, it is impossible to state that the child remembers the third position only; the hesitations he often reveals show, on the contrary, that he mentally retraces the order followed. Finally, the longer the experiment lasts the harder it is to remember the last position because of the increasing interference of memories.

OBS. 66. At 1;7 (23) Jacqueline reveals herself to be equally capable of conceiving of the object present under a series of superimposed or encasing screens.

1. Before her eyes I put a pencil in a strainer (which I turn over on the floor). I place a beret on the strainer and a coverlet on the beret; Jacqueline raises the coverlet at once, then the beret, then the strainer, and takes possession of the pencil.

Then I put the pencil in a closed matchbox which I cover with the beret and the coverlet. Jacqueline raises both screens, then opens the box.

I put the pencil back in the box, put a piece of paper around it, wrap this in a handkerchief, then cover the whole thing with the beret and the coverlet. Jacqueline removes these last two screens, then unfolds the handkerchief. She does not find the box right away but continues looking for it, evidently convinced of its presence; she then perceives the paper, recognizes it immediately, unfolds it, opens the box and grasps the pencil.

II. I now complicate the test by juxtaposing two screens on the same plane, for example, the pencil in the paper (Jacqueline watches me attentively), and put the box beside the paper. I wrap both objects in a handkerchief which I place beside a beret and cover handkerchief and beret with my coat. Jacqueline removes the coat and immediately goes to the handkerchief, which she unfolds without hesitation. The box appears first; Jacqueline opens it, looks inside it at length, turns it all over, then returns to the handkerchief. Then she perceives the paper, grasps it hastily, unfolds it, and finds the pencil. It is therefore proven that Jacqueline has forgotten the exact location of the pencil. Nevertheless she does not question its substantial permanence or its presence within the object-screens; not finding it in the box she looks for it again in the handkerchief, and the sight of the paper at once reinforces her conviction.

I resume the experiment a moment later, somewhat modifying the conditions. I put the pencil back in the paper and the paper next to the box, but I put them both under Jacqueline's jacket and not under the handkerchief. The handkerchief is placed beside the jacket, and the whole thing is covered by my coat. Jacqueline, who has observed all these maneuvers attentively, at first lifts my coat, then takes up the handkerchief, apparently through perseveration, given the conditions of the preceding experiment. After having explored the handkerchief at length she goes to the jacket and takes the box and the paper out of it simultaneously. She grasps the box and throws it back without opening it (and without shaking it to hear the sound, as she has happened to do lately when she knew the box contained some object), then unfolds the paper until she finds the pencil.

Here again is proof that Jacqueline remembers only a part of the incasements observed. But whatever may be the basis of her memories, she assumes the presence of the hidden object despite all complications, and directs all her search as a function of this image. She knows, moreover, how to choose an object by its contents (cf. the paper and the box in the second attempt, etc.).

It may be seen how such behavior patterns differ from those of the preceding stage. In general terms it can be said that the child has become capable of directing his search by means of representation. Sometimes he takes note of the invisible displacements of the object and shows himself able to deduce them as well as to perceive them, sometimes, through thought, he masters a series of incasements too complex not to give rise to a true awareness of relationships.

The simplest case is that of obs. 64: looking for the object under a screen under which the child saw my closed hand disappear, but without having directly perceived the displacements of the object. It has been proven previously (obs. 55-57) that the child at the fifth stage shows himself to be at first incapable of succeeding in such an experiment; he clearly sees that the object is placed in receptacle R (hand, box, etc.), that R is put under screen E (coverlet, etc.), and that R is removed empty; but he does not search for the object under E. True, a little later the child becomes able to look under screen E for the vanished object (see obs. 58-59); but, as we have observed, this ability seems the result, first of all, of practical learning and empirical groping rather than of an actual image of the itinerary followed by the object (hence of invisible displacements). It has sufficed to hide the object under two different screens E^1 and E^2 for behavior patterns analogous to those of the fourth stage to reappear (obs. 60-63). From the point of view of representation such a result entails an obvious conclusion: the child still knows how to arrange only the series of directly perceived displacements and if the intervention of invisible displacements can give rise to a practical adaptation it is still not occasion for true representation. Now, obs. 64, which marks the beginning of the present stage, reveals a very different method of search; the child henceforth imagines the whole of the object's itinerary, including the series of invisible displacements. Thus it can be said that the object is definitively constituted; its permanence no longer depends at all on the action itself but obeys a totality of spatial and kinematic laws which are independent of the self.

Obs. 65 is a valuable indication of this. It bears witness to an obvious capacity for representation. By searching for the object only under the last screen under which I slid my closed hand, Jacqueline follows a system and follows it consciously; given the growing interference of memories (the test is repeated ten times) she finds herself obliged each time to retrace the order I followed in order to recall under which screen I passed my hand last. Such a system, although remaining the simplest possible, presupposes the representation of invisible displacements of the object. With regard to the object itself, it is clear that such behavior patterns imply the postulate of its permanence, since the law of its displacements is entirely dissociated from the action itself.

Obs. 66 gives rise to analogous remarks. True, in such a case the child has directly perceived all the elements of the problem; the object is not extracted from a bottle or from a fist outside the perceptual field as before (obs. 64 and 65) but is placed in a receptacle in which it remains, and this receptacle is itself placed, before the child's eyes, under a series of superposed screens. Moreover the child does not need to recall the procedures in detail, since, in case of initial failure, he can grope until success has been attained. Nevertheless we believe such a behavior pattern entails representation and deduction, given the necessity, in order to reach the object, of putting into relationship with each other all the "direct connections" at work in the experiment. When the child sees some object disappear into a receptacle or under a screen it can be said that the act of searching for it presupposes nothing more than a direct connection, since the act of turning over the screen or opening the receptacle is already coordinated in itself and the desire of attaining the object merely sets that act in motion. But when the receptacle or the screen is itself hidden in other receptacles or under other screens and thus becomes an object for search while remaining receptacle or screen as it was at first, the child is forced to take note of their dual natures simultaneously. Such a relation is therefore complex or indirect and transcends the level of simple direct connections which have just been discussed; it is analogous to that of P. Janet's "basket of apples" which is simultaneously a thing to grasp, like any object, and a receptacle in relation to the apples. Confronted by a series of incasements such as those of obs. 66, to direct his search the child must necessarily subordinate the whole of his procedures to the representation of the hidden object; even if it is not accompanied by a precise memory of the positions, such a behavior pattern thus involves a sort of "multiplication of relations" or of sensorimotor deduction comparable to those we have analyzed in connection with the sixth stage of the development of intelligence (*O.I.*, Chap. VI).

From the point of view of object formation each of our observations thus leads to the same conclusion: the object is no longer, as it was during the first four stages, merely the extension of various accommodations, nor is it, as in the fifth stage, merely a permanent body in motion whose movements have become independent of the self but solely to the extent to which they have been perceived; instead, the object is now definitely freed from perception and action alike and obeys entirely autonomous laws of displacement. In effect, by virtue of the very fact that it enters the system of abstract or indirect images and relations, the object acquires in the subject's consciousness, a new and final degree of liberty. It is conceived as remaining identical to itself whatever may be its invisible displacements or the complexity of the screens which mask it. Doubtless this representation of the object which we call the characteristic of the sixth stage is already budding in the preceding stages. As soon as the child at the fourth stage begins to search actively for the vanished object it can be claimed that there exists a sort of evolution of the absent object. But never until the present stage has this behavior led to real evocation, because it has merely utilized a system of signs linked with the action; searching for an object under a screen when the subject has seen it disappear there (stages IV and V) does not necessarily presuppose that the subject "imagines" the object under the screen but simply that he has understood the relation of the two objects at the moment he perceived it (at the moment when the object was covered) and that he therefore interprets the screen as a sign of the actual presence of the object. It is one thing to assume the permanence of an object when one has just seen it and when some other object now in sight recalls its presence, and it is quite another thing to imagine the first object when there is nothing in sight to attest its hidden existence. True representation therefore begins only when no perceived sign commands belief in permanency, that is to say, from the moment when the vanished object is displaced according to an itinerary which the subject may deduce but not perceive. That is why up to the fifth stage inclusively as soon as the displacements are not all visible the child searches for objects in the place where they were found the first time, as though they were always at the subject's disposal, whereas from this sixth stage he takes account of all possible displacements, even if they are invisible.

Can it be said that this difference between the behavior patterns of the sixth stage and those of the fifth concern only the construction of space and not the permanence of the object as such? In this hypothesis an object whose displacements it is impossible to reconstruct would nevertheless be conceived as being as invariant and as identical to itself as if all its movements were known. For example, even though I cannot imagine or deduce the course of a small stone which I toss down the irregular slope of a mountain, I know that it remains somewhere as an object and that its properties (or those of its parts, in the event of fragmentation) have remained identical to what they were at the moment of the fall. But let us beware of too facile comparisons. If the adult can lend the quality of objects to bodies whose trajectory he does not know or to bodies he has seen only for a moment, it is by analogy with others of whose displacements he is already aware, whether these are absolute or related to the movements of the body itself. But, sooner or later, representation and deduction enter into this knowledge. With regard to the baby at the fifth stage, to the extent that he does not know how to imagine or to deduce the invisible displacements of bodies he remains incapable of perceiving these bodies as objects truly independent of the self. A world in which only perceived movements are regulated is neither stable nor dissociated from the self; it is a world of still chaotic potentialities whose organization begins only in the subject's presence. Outside the perceptual field and the beginnings of objectivity which are constituted by the organization of perceived movements, the elements of such a universe are not objects but realities at the disposal of action and consciousness. On the contrary, the representation and deduction characteristic of the sixth stage result in extending the process of solidification to regions of that universe which are dissociated from action and perception; displacements, even invisible ones, are henceforth envisaged as subservient to laws, and objects in motion become real objects independent of the self and persisting in their substantial identity.

A final consequence essential to the development of representation is that henceforth, the child's own body is regarded as an object. Thanks to imitation, for example, and in particular to the behavior patterns of the present stage (these are characterized by the fact that imitation becomes embedded in representation), the child is now able to see his own body as an object by analogy with that of another person. Moreover, nascent spatial, causal, and temporal images permit him to locate himself in a space and time reaching beyond him everywhere, and to consider himself as mere cause and mere effect among the totality of the connections he discovers. Having thus become an object among other objects at the very moment when he learns to conceive of their true permanence even outside all direct perception, the child ends by completely reversing his initial universe, whose moving images were centered on an activity unconscious of itself, and by transforming it into a solid universe of coordinated objects including the body itself in the capacity of an element. Such is the result of object construction on the sensorimotor plane, until reflection and conceptual thought pursue this elaboration on new planes of creative intelligence.

§ 6. THE CONSTITUTIVE PROCESSES OF OBJECT CONCEPT

We have hitherto limited ourselves to describing merely the historical development of object concept. The time has come to attempt an explanation of this development by attaching it to the whole of the intellectual evolution peculiar to the child's first two years of life.

To understand the formation of initial sensorimotor objects it may not be useless to compare the elementary processes of the child's intelligence to those used by scientific thought to establish the objectivity of the beings it elaborates. For if the structures employed by thought vary from one stage to another and, *a fortiori*, from one mental system to another, thought remains constantly identical to itself from the functional point of view. It is therefore not illegitimate to elucidate one of the terms of intellectual evolution by the directly opposite term, that is, the construction of practical objects by that of scientific objects, provided that the first term, when it is sufficiently understood, elucidate the second in return.

Now three criteria seem to us to contribute to the definition of the object peculiar to the sciences: in the first place, every objective phenomenon permits anticipation, in contrast to other phenomena whose advent, fortuitous and contrary to all anticipation, permits the hypothesis of a subjective origin. But, as subjective phenomena also can give rise to anticipation (for example, the "illusions of the senses") and moreover as unexpected events are sometimes those which mark the failure of an erroneous interpretation and thus entail progress in objectivity, a second condition must be added to the first: a phenomenon is the more objective the more it lends itself, not only to anticipation, but also to distinct experiments whose results are in accordance with it. But that is still not enough, for certain subjective qualities may be linked with constant physical characteristics, as qualitative colors with luminous waves. In this case, only a deduction of the totality succeeds in dissociating the subjective from the objective: only that phenomenon constitutes a real object which is connected in an intelligible way with the totality of a spatio-temporal and causal system (for example, luminous waves constitute objects because they have a physical explanation, whereas quality is dissociated from the objective system).

These three methods are found to be the very same which the little child uses in his effort to form an objective world. At first the object is only the extension of accommodation movements (anticipation). Then it is the point of intersection, that is, of reciprocal assimilation of multiple schemata which manifest the different modalities of the action (concordance of the experiments). Finally, the object is fully constructed in correlation with causality to the extent that this coordination of schemata results in the formation of an intelligible spatio-temporal world endowed with permanence (comprehension related to a deductive system of the totality).

The first contact between the acting subject and the environment, that is, taking possession of things through reflex assimilation, does not at all imply awareness of the object as such. Even if, as we have asserted, such an activity involves a capacity for repetition, generalization, and recognition, nothing as yet forces the child to dissociate the action itself from its point of application. What he recognizes when he finds the nipple, for example, is a certain relation between the object and himself, that is, a global image in which all the sensations connected with the act in progress intervene. Such recognition has nothing in common with a perception of objects. The same is true of the activity characteristic of the first schemata to be acquired. When the child rediscovers his thumb when he wants to suck it or finds familiar images because he wishes to look at them, etc., nothing as yet leads him to make of these sensorial images substances detached from the activity itself; so long as the action succeeds, as far as the subject is concerned his objective is one and the same thing as his awareness of desire, of effort or of success.

The question of the object's independence and permanence begins to be raised only when the child perceives the disappearance of desired objects and applies himself to searching for them actively. Here the first method of constructing the object makes its entrance: the effort of accommodation and the anticipations which spring from it.

During the first two stages the behavior of the subject shows how much he is already aware of the periodic disappearance of objects. The newborn child who is nursing manifests emotion when the breast is taken from him, and the nursling, as soon as he has learned to smile, knows how to express his disappointment when his mother suddenly leaves his visual field. But the subject's only positive reaction for finding lost objects consists in reproducing the latest accommodation movements he has made; he sucks the air or stares at the place where his mother's image disappeared. The object is still only the extension of the action; the child counts only on the repetition of his accommodation movements to realize his desire and, in case of failure, on the efficacy of his passion and his anger. He is acquainted only with actions which succeed at once and others which fail momentarily, but up to now the failure has not sufficed to permit distinction between permanent objects and an activity being exerted on them. At most, the effort of accommodation arising at the moment of the object's disappearance foretells the advent of the need for conservation which will subsequently constitute the object itself.

This elementary permanence is accentuated when, in the course of the third stage, the child no longer limits himself to searching for the object only where it has just disappeared but extends the accommodation movement in the direction it followed up to then (reaction to the fall, etc.). The act of losing contact with the object momentarily to find it in a new position apparently marks progress in the dissociation of action and object, hence in the autonomy conferred upon the latter. But, as we have emphasized in discussing the nature of these behavior patterns, so long as the search for the object consists merely in extending accommodation movements already made in its presence, the object cannot yet show either an independent trajectory in space or consequently intrinsic permanence. It is therefore not yet an object.

On the other hand, progress is made in the consolidation of objects when the accommodation of a single series of schemata (visual, tactile, etc.) is followed by a search involving the coordination of multiple primary schemata. We may cite as an example of this second process of elaboration of the object the behavior patterns of "deferred circular reaction," of search for the whole when only a part of the object has been seen, and the suppression of obstacles preventing perception (end of the third stage). In those cases the child is no longer limited to following some object in motion with his eyes or hand; he combines visual and tactile searching. This coordination of two or more distinct series of accommodations certainly reinforces the consolidation and externalization of the object (the dissociation between the object and the action). Mr. Szuman has shown this in his interesting studies of object concept.[7] The telereceptive sphere of perception, he says following Sherrington, entails, from the moment the baby knows how to grasp what he sees, a sort of motor restlessness which is appeased only by prehension and the perceptions belonging to the sphere of contact. The polysensory complexes which thus determine the dynamic association among the various sensory impressions and above all between sight and prehension would then themselves form objects whose different characteristics would spring from the multiple and sequential varieties of activities made possible by the initial coordination (sensory or primary characteristics, functional ones and those acquired through imitation).

But however exact Mr. Szuman's analyses may be, we do not believe that the coordination of schemata suffices to explain the permanence belonging to the object. So long as the child does not undertake special searches to find objects which disappear, that is, so long as he does not succeed in deducing their displacements in space when he no longer sees them, one should not yet speak of object conservation. Even when the child succeeds in pursuing interrupted actions (deferred circular reaction) because of progress in coordination between sight and prehension, he merely conceives of the object as being connected with his behavior patterns and with the special positions which characterize them, without attributing to it either an independent existence or an independent trajectory. Hence there exists elaboration of practical objects—which constitute, according to Mr. Szuman's definition, centers of possible experiences or points of crystallization of each characteristic sphere of activities—but not yet permanent substances.

We can say the same of the excellent observations of Mmes. Rubinow and Frankl [8] on the objectification of the bottle. Like Mr. Szuman, these writers characterize the object not by its

[7] S. Szuman, "La Genese de l'objet," *Kwartalnik Psycholog.* (Poznan, 1932), Vol. III, No. 3-4.
[8] Rubinow and Frankl, "Die erste Dingauffassung beim Saugling," *Zeitschrift f. Kinderforschung*, Vol. 133, Chap. 34, p. 1 (with a conclusion by C. Bühler).

substantial permanence but by its practical qualities. Thus if during the fourth month every solid body approaching the nursling's face sets sucking in motion, during the fifth month only pointed bodies produce this effect. A primary characteristic of the object "bottle" would thus be constituted first in connection with the movement (the object must approach for its point to be noticed), then statically (the pointed thing as such setting sucking in motion). But although it is accurate to consider these phenomena as characterizing stages in object construction (since they show us how the objective characteristics gradually become detached from accommodation movements after having been formed through coordination between sight and sensations of contact), it seems to us that the practical object thus elaborated is still far from the true object or permanent substance with a spatially defined trajectory.

Real permanence begins only with a third process in object construction: the search for the vanished object in a comprehensible spatio-temporal universe. We recall that the three steps of this search characterize our last three stages: simple search without taking account of objective displacement groups, then search based upon the group of perceived displacements, and finally search involving representation of displacements not perceived. The problem is, therefore, to understand how the child succeeds in elaborating such relations and thereby even constructing permanent objects under the moving images of immediate perception.

At its point of departure this active search for the vanished object merely extends the behavior patterns of the first three stages. The child begins to pursue invisible objects only after he has made the movement of grasping when they are in sight. But even when this schema becomes generalized and searching takes place independently of this condition, the object is at first sought only in a special place—where it was found the first time. Therefore it still depends on the action and constitutes only a practical object; it is not differentiated from the outset but is part of the whole situation in which it gave rise to a successful search. The only progress consists in pursuing the object behind a screen and no longer only when it is partly visible, as during the third stage.

But this progress, if at first it presupposes no profound transformation of behavior, nevertheless entails two important consequences. The first is that the object gradually becomes detached from the activity: the fact that the child succeeds in conceiving of objects as existing behind screens leads him to dissociate, far more than in the past, subjective action from the reality on which it bears. Henceforth reality resists the subject's effort in a new way; there is no longer only resistance through the opposition of forces as in the contacts between muscular activity and a solid mass,[9] but also resistance through complication of the field of action and intervention of obstacles preventing the subject from perceiving the objective. Hence the second result: the action ceases to be the source of the external world and becomes merely a factor among other factors, one that is central, no doubt, but of the same order as the various elements which make up his total environment. Henceforth the child places his own hand movements among those of external bodies, endowing the latter with an activity complementary to his own. In short, to the extent that objects become detached from the action, the body itself becomes an item among other items and is thus brought into an aggregate system. This step marks the beginnings of true objectification.

Objects are constructed to the extent that this transition operates, from the complete and unconscious egocentrism of the first stages to the localization of the body itself in an external universe. To the extent that things are detached from action and that action is placed among the totality of the series of surrounding events, the subject has power to construct a system of relations to understand these series and to understand himself in relation to them. To organize such series is to form simultaneously a spatio-temporal network and a system consisting of substances and of relations of cause to effect. Hence the construction of the object is inseparable from that of space, of time, and of causality. An object is a system of perceptual images endowed with a constant spatial form throughout its sequential displacements and constituting an item which can be isolated in

[9] Maine de Biran thought he saw in this first type of resistance the constitutive process of objectification. But the subject can very well incorporate the sensation of the obstacle into the schema of his own activity, granted that all bodily action is limited and is accompanied by the more or less clear consciousness of this limitation.

the causal series unfolding in time. Consequently the elaboration of the object is bound up with that of the universe as a whole. To understand this genesis it would thus be necessary to anticipate the next chapters and show how displacement groups as well as temporal and causal structures are formed. But since, inversely, it is only by achieving belief in the object's permanence that the child succeeds in organizing space, time, and causality, we must begin our analysis by trying to explain the behavior patterns which tend to construct the object as such. How then does the child come to search for the object not only in a special place but by taking account of displacements observed sequentially, then even displacements occurring outside the perceptual field?

To understand this process let us first say what it is not: it is neither an *a priori* deduction nor training by purely empirical associations. Next we shall see what it is: an actually constructive deduction.

That it does not consist in a simple deduction emerges clearly from the fact of the gropings necessary to learn the relationships of displacements. The child begins (fourth stage) by searching for the object where he has already found it the first time. Then, when he knows how to find it in the last position in which he saw it (fifth stage) he must still learn the possibility of transfer; the object placed in a box which one empties under a coverlet will be sought in the box, then where it was previously found but not in the place where it disappeared. Once the habit of searching under that coverlet has been acquired it will be necessary to learn again to take into account sequential displacements, etc. Such gropings in fact sufficiently demonstrate the necessity for active experience in order to build up sequential perceptions; that is, for the child to understand that the object constitutes an independent body in motion which is capable of multiple displacements, perception and action must constitute a single whole in the form of sensorimotor schemata, and these schemata must, thanks to the action itself, proceed from the global or dynamic state to the analytic state or the separation of spatio-temporal elements. To explain this evolution of schemata and account for the fact that the individualized and permanent object supersedes the undifferentiated and merely practical object it would therefore be useless to invoke a mechanism of identification envisaged as innate and consubstantial with all thought. What is innate in identification is simply the function of assimilation and not the sequential structures which that function elaborates and among which identification is only one simple example in particular. How are we to account for object construction from the laws of the schemata of assimilation?

Such construction is not the act of an *a priori* deduction, nor is it due to purely empirical gropings. The sequence of the stages which we have distinguished testifies much more strongly to progressive comprehension than to haphazard achievements. If there is experimentation, the experiments are directed: in finding the object the child organizes his motor schemata and elaborates his operative relationships rather than submitting passively to the pressure of events.

The solution to the problem, therefore, seems to us to be the following: the permanence of the object stems from the constructive deduction which from the fourth stage is constituted by reciprocal assimilation of the secondary schemata, that is, the coordination of schemata which have become mobile. Until this level has been reached the object merely extends the activity itself; its permanence is only practical and not substantial, because the universe is not detached from the action nor objectified in a system of relationships. The coordination of the primary schemata, in particular that coordination between sight and prehension which gives rise to the secondary circular reactions, does indeed result in a relative externalization of things; but so long as the secondary schemata remain global or undifferentiated instead of being dissociated the better to unite, this externalization does not go far enough to constitute a substantial permanence. On the contrary, from the fourth stage onward the secondary schemata become mobile through a reciprocal assimilation which permits them to combine among themselves in different ways; it is this process of complementary dissociation and regroupment which, by engendering the first acts of intelligence properly so called, enables the child to build a spatio-temporal world of objects endowed with causality.

As we have seen (*O.I.*, Chap. IV, §3), the mobile schemata resulting from the coordination of secondary reactions constitute not only some kinds of motor concepts that may be arranged in practical judgments and reasonings, but also some systems of relations that permit an increasingly precise elaboration of the objects on which these behavior patterns bear. The reciprocal assimilation of the schemata therefore entails the construction of physical connections and consequently of objects as such. Thus the union of the schemata of prehension with those of striking, which explains the behavior pattern consisting in removing obstacles (*O.I.*, Chap. IV, §1-2), permits the child to construct the relations "above," and "below," "hidden behind," etc., and leads him to base his belief in the permanence of the object on truly spatial relations. But above all, the combinations of the mobile schemata make possible a better accommodation of behavior to the specific characteristics of objects. The fact that the schemata can henceforth adjust themselves to each other leads the child to observe the detail of objects much more closely when his action bears upon them than when the objects are absorbed in the acts as a whole and remain undifferentiated. For this reason the behavior patterns of "exploration of new objects" appear at the fourth stage and, during the fifth, are extended in tertiary circular reactions, that is, in experiments in order to see. It is in this context that, from the fifth stage on, the true object will be elaborated.

It may be recalled that the specific behavior patterns of the fifth stage—"discoveries of new means through active experimentation"—are explainable precisely by this union of the coordination of schemata and of tertiary reactions. The union of this progressive accommodation with the reciprocal assimilation of the schemata constitutes, with respect to the intelligence, a process of learning which should not be considered as either purely experimental or purely deductive, but which partakes simultaneously of experience and mental construction. Sensorimotor intelligence, having arrived at this level, is therefore essentially the construction of relations or constructive deduction.

This process explains, it seems to us, the discovery of the object's real permanence. After having established during the fourth stage that the vanished object remains behind a screen, the child succeeds during the fifth stage in bestowing on that object an autonomous trajectory and consequently a truly spatial permanence. This discovery simultaneously presupposes two things: 1) experience, since only the failure of his initial search teaches the child that the object is no longer where it was found the first time but rather where it was last hidden, and 2) deduction, since without the reciprocal assimilation of schemata the child would not succeed in assuming the existence of objects hidden behind the screen nor in postulating their permanence, once and for all, particularly when he has not found them where he first looked for them. In short, object conservation, which is the first of the forms of conservation, results like all the others in the close union of a rational or deductive element and an empirical element, indicating that deduction is constantly at work in close relation to things or at their suggestion.

We shall see this still better in studying the more truly spatial characteristics of the solid object, such as its form and constant dimensions; the constitution of these characteristics, linked with that of all space, predicates the constant collaboration of experience and the reciprocal assimilation of the schemata.

Finally, during the sixth stage, the coordination of the schemata is internalized in the form of mental combinations, while accommodation becomes representation. Thereafter deduction of the object and of its spatial characteristics is achieved in the construction of a collective universe in which displacements that are merely indicated are inserted among observed movements and complete them in a truly coherent whole.

CHAPTER II

The Spatial Field and the Elaboration of Groups of Displacements

It can be said that the formation of object concept is correlated to the organization of the spatial field. The aggregate of facts established in the preceding chapter will therefore be useful to us from this new point of view.

The conclusion to which the analysis of object concept has led us is that in the course of his first twelve to eighteen months the child proceeds from a sort of initial practical solipsism to the construction of a universe which includes himself as an element. At first the object is nothing more, in effect, than the sensory image at the disposal of acts; it merely extends the activity of the subject and, without being conceived as created by the action itself (since the subject knows nothing of himself at this level of his perception of the world), it is only felt and perceived as linked with the most immediate and subjective data of sensorimotor activity. During the first months the object does not, therefore, exist apart from the action, and the action alone confers upon it the quality of constancy. At the other extreme, on the contrary, the object is envisaged as a permanent substance independent of the activity of the self, which the action rediscovers provided it submits to certain external laws. Furthermore, the subject no longer occupies the center of the world, a center all the more limited because the child is unaware of this perspective; he places himself as an object among other objects and so becomes an integral part of the universe he has constructed by freeing himself of his personal perspective.

The history of the elaboration of spatial relations and of the formation of the principal groups exactly parallels the foregoing. At first there exists only a practical space or, more precisely, as many practical spaces as are predicated by the various activities of the subject, while the subject remains outside of space to the precise extent that he does not know himself; thus space is only a property of action, developed as action becomes coordinated. At the other extreme, space is a property of things, the framework of a universe in which all displacements are located, including those which determine the actions of the subject as such; therefore the subject includes himself in space and puts his own displacements into relation with all the others, counting them as elements among those of the groups which he succeeds in representing to himself.

This transition from a practical and egocentric space to the represented space containing the subject himself is not an accident in the elaboration of displacement groups; it is the *sine qua non* of the representation and even of the direct perception of groups, for we shall see that it is one thing to act in conformity to the principle of groups and another to perceive or conceive of them. Hence it is fitting to focus our attention on this central question with regard to the genetic description of behavior patterns relating to space; it is the understanding of space and not its physiology which we shall try to study here.

But one sees at the same time how much our analysis of the child's space perception is simplified by parallelism between the process just indicated and the processes of formation of object concept. Just as during the first weeks of life the object is confused with the sensory impressions connected with elementary action, so also at birth there is no concept of space except the perception of light and the accommodation inherent in that perception (pupillary reflex to light and palpebral reflex to dazzle). All the rest—perception of shapes, of sizes, distances, positions, etc.—is elaborated little by little at the same time as the objects themselves. Space, therefore, is not at all perceived as a container but rather as that which it contains, that is, objects themselves; and, if space becomes in a sense a container, it is to the extent that the relationships which constitute the objectification of bodies succeed in becoming intercoordinated until they form a coherent whole. The concept of space is understood only as a function of the construction of objects, and it was necessary to start by describing the latter in order to understand the former; only the degree of objectification that the child attributes to things informs us of the degree of externality he accords to space.

We shall place the description of behavior patterns relative to space in the framework prepared by the six stages in the evolution of object concept. This is not arbitrary but imposed by the facts.

In effect, an initial stage during which space consists of heterogeneous and purely practical groups (each perceptual bundle constitutes a space) corresponds to the first stages of object concept (no behavior pattern relative to vanished objects). There are groups in the sense that the child's activity is capable of turning back on itself and thus of constituting closed totalities which mathematically define the group. But the child does not perceive these groups in things and does not become aware of the entirely motor operations by means of which he elaborates them; hence the groups remain entirely practical.

To the third stage of object concept (the beginning of permanence extending accommodation movements) corresponds a space whose groups intercoordinate and become subjective. The groups intercoordinate under the influence of prehension (which connects visual space to tactile and gustatory space) at precisely the time when prehension guarantees the object a beginning of permanence. On the other hand, by manipulating things the child becomes capable of imparting systematic movements to them and thus of perceiving groups in the universe itself. But as objects are not yet endowed with substantial permanence and the subject is ignorant of his own displacements with the exception of those of his hand, these groups, although perceived in the universe, remain dependent upon sensory appearance and related, without the subject's knowledge, to the child's own perspective. We call them subjective to mark their parallelism with the permanence still dependent on the action itself which characterizes the object at this stage; they are, therefore, groups which connect a subject who does not know himself with a semi-permanent object, and not groups uniting objects as such with each other.

To the fourth stage of object concept (active search for the vanished object but in a special position and without taking account of its sequential displacements) there corresponds an essential progress in the group concept: the child becomes capable of hiding and finding, etc. In short, he elaborates the reversible operations which constitute the beginning of the objective group. But, not yet noting the object's sequential displacements, he does not transcend the level of these elementary groups and does not arrive at the objective group in all its generality. It is therefore the stage of the "group of simply reversible operations."

To the fifth stage of object concept (permanence of the object throughout its displacements) there corresponds the advent of the objective group and to the sixth stage (representation of invisible displacements), the elaboration of "representative" groups.

The parallelism we have just outlined is self-evident if one adheres to the concept of group regarding space. There is a mutual dependence between group and object; the permanence of objects presupposes elaboration of the group of their displacements and vice versa. On the other hand, everything justifies us in centering our description of the genesis of space around that of the concept of group. Geometrically, ever since H. Poincaré this concept has appeared as a prime essential to the interpretation of displacements. Psychologically, the group is the expression of the processes of identification and reversibility, which pertain to the fundamental phenomena of intellectual assimilation, particularly to reproductive assimilation or circular reaction.

Therefore we have good reason to emphasize primarily in this chapter the "groups" themselves, appending to our elaboration of them various other aspects of the construction of space, such as the evaluation of depth, the understanding of displacements, the representation of body movements, etc. From the point of view of intelligence, which interests us here, in contrast to that of perception, it is the problem of groups which remains primary. But it is necessary to remember that we shall attribute the widest meaning to this concept for if, as recent works have shown, the logical definition of the group is inexhaustible and involves the most essential processes of thought, it is possible, purely from our psychological point of view, to consider as a group every system of operations capable of permitting a return to the point of departure. Considered thus, it is self-evident that practical groups exist prior to any perception or awareness of any group whatever. They exist from the beginnings of postural space and, one might go so far as to say, even from the most elementary spatial and kinetic organizations of the living being. In this sense it is possible to speak of the *a priori* nature of this concept; it merely attests to the fact that every organization forms a self-enclosed system. Moreover from the time that the circular processes of assimilation are applied to the sensory and kinetic data which constitute the raw material of space, this functioning takes the form of groups. But, and in this a true construction of space must be acknowledged, this *a priori* functioning must be structured to give rise to real organizations, and it is the history of this structuring that we shall now try to give, paralleling what we have noted concerning the object and following the development of the six stages of sensorimotor intelligence.

§ 1. THE FIRST TWO STAGES: PRACTICAL AND HETEROGENEOUS
    GROUPS

Until the age of three to six months, that is, until the prehension of visual objectives, the child's main activities, from the point of view of space, merely lead him to analyze the content of sensory images: analysis of forms as a whole, or of figures, positions, and displacements. Each behavior pattern or each class of behavior patterns thus results in the formation of a particular category of perceptual clusters which are more or less stable but are not yet realized in objects and are of a type corresponding to spaces: the gustatory or "buccal" space of Stern, visual space, auditory space, tactile space and many others (postural and kinesthetic spaces, etc.). These spaces can be more or less interconnected according to the degree of coordination of the sensorimotor schemata which engender them (regarding those coordinations, see *O.I.*), but they remain primarily heterogeneous, that is, they are far from constituting together a single space in which each one would be situated. Consequently they do not yet suffice at all for the evaluation of sizes, of distances, of related positions, or above all for the elaboration of objective displacement groups. By virtue of the very fact that there is no single space there could be no question of the subject locating his own activities in space and thus understanding them as related to the displacements of objects. Quite to the contrary, far from knowing himself to be in space, the subject confers on his perceptions only those spatial qualities whose reality is created, as needed, by the immediate action, and he conceives of displacements of things only as extensions of his activity. If there are groups they are therefore only practical, unaware of themselves, and do not include the subject as such; in short, action creates space but is not yet situated in it.

In his famous analysis of the concept of space[1] intended to show its origins in experience and in the very constitution of the human mind, Henri Poincaré considers as elementary the distinction between changes of position and changes of state. Among the changes presented in the external world some can be corrected by body movements which lead a perception back to its initial state (for example turning the head to find an object which has passed before the eyes), others cannot; therefore the first constitute changes of position, the second changes of state. Thus, from the outset, according to Poincaré, this elementary distinction places the spatial in opposition to the physical and at the same time attests to the primitive nature of the concept of "group."

There is no doubt that changes of position are gradually differentiated from changes of state during the earliest months of life. From the chaos of sensory impressions the child comes sooner or later to find certain stable elements in the changes perceived and thus to dissociate irreversible changes from those which can be compensated by body movements. For example, when

[1] H. Poincaré, *La Valeur de la science* (Paris: Flammarion), Chaps. III and IV.

Jacqueline at 1;7 (sixth stage of the evolution of object concept) finds a hidden object by noting its successive and partly invisible displacements, it is clear that she is distinguishing changes of position from changes of state—that is, she considers the vanished object not as being altered in structure or as having returned to nothingness, but as having been subjected to displacements constituting a coherent "group."

But can one, like Poincaré, consider this distinction as primitive? Can one consider the act of readjustment which makes it possible to find displaced objects as nothing more than an awareness of displacements? And above all, can one infer from the motor adaptation to displacements the sign of an immediate perception of groups? Our analysis of the development of object concept raises doubt as to the simplicity of these various questions. By stating that the distinction between changes of position and changes of state is present at the very first, Poincaré seems to have reconstructed the elementary stages of spatial concepts more logically than psychologically, which is tantamount to saying that he has endowed primitive consciousness with postulates presupposing an already refined mental elaboration. There is nothing to prove that sensorimotor adaptation to displacements immediately brings with it the concept of changes of position and, above all, there is nothing to prove that an activity, even if its constitutive operations proceed by groups from the observer's point of view, leads the subject to perceive displacements as such. Let us emphasize those two points, beginning with the problem of changes of position, and we shall better understand what space must be to the child at this first stage.

In the first place, in order that a change of position may be distinguished from a change of state, the subject must be able to conceive of the external universe as being solid, that is, composed of substantial and permanent objects; otherwise the act of finding a displaced image would be confused, in the subject's consciousness, with the act of recreating it. If there are no objects which are displaced and if sensory images are considered stable only to the extent that they are at the disposal of an action which repeats or follows its course, then of necessity the universe will be perceived as being continuously torn down and built up, and the act of following a moving image will be confused with that of creating it or making it last.

In the second place, and by virtue of that very fact, in order that a change of position may be opposed to changes of state, the external universe must be distinguished from personal activity. If the perceived phenomenon and the acts of accommodation necessary for its perception were not dissociated, there could be no consciousness of the displacement. Poincaré says that we are apprised of changes of position by the muscular sensations which inform us of our movements: in this way it could be asserted that even if the child simply follows spots of light with his eyes, without perceiving them as objects, he would be conscious of their displacements. But, to thought which has not distinguished an external world formed of substantial objects from an internal world attached to the body itself, the impressions of every kind emanating from this body can be attached to perceived movements whatever they may be: therefore the subject will be unable to know when it is things that are displaced and when it is only himself, and will be unable to attribute objective laws for their displacements, that is, to distinguish them from changes of state.

In the third place, as this last remark makes clear, to conceive of a change of position is tantamount to locating oneself in a spatial field conceived as being external to the body and independent of the action. It consists, therefore, in understanding that in finding the displaced object one displaces oneself as the observer localized in space, the displacement of the object and that of the subject being relative to each other. In order that accommodation to displacements may engender an image of these displacements, a radical reversal of direction is imposed; this results in the formation of a space encompassing the subject himself, whereas the initial perception, on the contrary, projected his activity on the moving images which precede any stable framework.

But as we have seen in the analysis of object concept, none of these three conditions is present during the first stages. Far from consisting of objects, the universe depends on personal action; far from being externalized, it is not dissociated from subjective elements; and far from knowing himself and placing himself in relation to things, the subject does not know himself and is absorbed into things.

With regard to the concept of "group" it therefore seems clear that, even if the subject's movements constitute groups from the point of view of the observer, the subject himself is unable to imagine them as such. A group is a closed circle of operations that return to the point of departure through an operation of the group as a whole. In this respect it is certain that from the observer's point of view every coordinated activity of the subject will involve the existence of displacement groups. But this is true only if the observer locates the subject as well as the objects in a single space and describes the movements of object and subject in relation to each other. If from this point of view external to the action one moves to that of the subject himself, things change entirely. In order for the subject to understand the observed displacements correctly and thus to conceive of them as groups, two conditions must be met. In the first place, the objects which are displaced must be considered as moving in relation to each other or in relation to certain landmarks; an aggregate of spatial relations must therefore be established between them. In the second place, the subject must conceive of himself as an object among the other elements involved and must see his own displacements as relative to those of the surrounding things. These two characteristics constitutive of the "group"—relations among things and relativity between one's movements and those of the object—presuppose exactly the three conditions we have just attributed to the distinction between changes of position and changes of state: permanence of objects, differentiation between one's own movements and those of things, and representation of one's own displacements. If these conditions are not met, there can be no question of a perception of groups from the beginning of the construction of space.

Nevertheless, like Poincaré, we shall not hesitate to speak of groups to designate the child's behavior patterns to the extent that they can be reversed or corrected to bring them back to the initial point. The only objection to Poincaré's description is that he considered such groups as capable of being immediately extended in adequate perceptions or images, whereas in fact they remain in the practical state for a long time before giving rise to mental constructions.

This distinction makes it possible at the same time to answer the objection which logicians or mathematicians might raise, whether the qualities just described as conditions for the appearance of groups may, on the contrary, be considered their result. Actually, these qualities are developed in the use of practical groups but are requisite in the elaboration of the conscious groups; the circle of psychological facts is therefore not at all vicious from the logical point of view.

Let us look at this more closely by examining the different groups.

The first of the schemata constitutive of the child's space is that which Stern has called *buccal space*. The displacements of the mouth in relation to objects for sucking or of objects in relation to the mouth accordingly constitute the simplest practical groups it is possible to observe in the child. In this respect we can distinguish three aggregates of events: displacements of the mouth in the search for the nipple, the reciprocal adjustment of thumb and mouth, and the adjustment of objects seized for the purpose of sucking. Let us sum up in a single observation these factors which are very familiar to us through the behavior patterns described in *O.I.*

OBS. 67. I. From 0;0 (2) and 0;0 (3) Laurent searches for the nipple when it escapes his lips. From 0;0 (12) he searches systematically on the side where he felt contact between the breast and his lips (see *O.I.*, obs. 5). At 0;0 (21) he describes with his mouth a curve tangential to the breast, alternately going away from and approaching the nipple which he seeks, grazes, and goes beyond to recommence in the other direction in an accelerated rhythm (*O.I.*, obs. 8). So also, at 0;0 (24) he raises his head when he knocks against the nipple with his upper lip (same obs.).

II. From 0;1 (3) there is coordination between hand and mouth in thumb sucking: the hand goes toward the mouth at the same time as the mouth seeks the hand (*O.I.*, obs. 18). See also obs. 19 and 20, showing how the hand acquires the right position to enter the mouth, how it wanders over the nose, cheeks and eyes when the baby lies on his back, to rediscover its route when the child is raised up. Finally, see in obs. 21 how the mouth has oscillated at 0;1 (21) between the right and left thumbs.

III. From 0;2 (28) Laurent knows how to carry to his mouth an object grasped independently of sight and how to adjust it empirically (O.I., obs. 66 repeated); for example, he puts a rattle between his lips. At 0;3 (5) he puts a clothespin in his mouth, adjusting its position so that he may suck it.

As revealed in their elementary simplicity, such movements are already arranged in groups of displacements if one adheres to the description of the behavior itself, that is, from the observer's point of view. For example, when the child describes a series of movements of approach around the nipple in order to reach it with his lips, he corrects his displacements to the right by displacements to the left and thus arranges the aggregate of his movements into a system which includes the group. Then when he coordinates the movements of his mouth with those of his hand, he describes in space trajectories that depend on one another and are capable of repetition and reversibility. In these trajectories group structure is also found. This is particularly clear from the time when movements of the mouth are related to those of the hand; the mouth can approach the hand as well as the hand can approach the mouth. In a general way, the group is constituted by every coordinated totality of displacements capable of returning to the point of departure and such that the final state does not depend on the route followed; the simple accommodations of the mouth to the nipple and the elementary coordinations of mouth and hands are in this category.

But if the child thus acquires from the very beginning a sense *sui generis* of positions and displacements, of forms and dimensions, it is evident that for him, that is, from the point of view of his perception or his representation, such systems of displacements do not constitute groups, for the reasons indicated above. First of all, as we have seen in connection with the first stage of object concept, the breast or any other objects for which the child searches do not constitute, for him, immobile things around which he turns, nor moving things which he tries to catch; to him they are only more or less stable sensory images which extend his own effort at accommodation. In the second place, and by virtue of that very fact, he does not dissociate his own movements from those of the object or the movements of his mouth from those of his hand, and thus does not establish any relativity between them. Finally and most important, he does not locate either himself or his movements in the same space as that of the objects perceived; his own movements constitute for him an absolute which is foreign to space and not a system of displacements capable of being perceived or represented from without. On the whole, buccal space is a practical space which permits the child to rediscover positions, perform movements, adapt himself to forms and dimensions, but which does not at all allow him to apply such schemata beyond the immediate action.

Just as he does not conceive of things as permanent objects, so also the child at this stage does not conceive of spatial relations as independent of acts. For example, we shall see (obs. 76) that Laurent still, at 0;4 (6), while knowing how to adjust his mouth to an outstretched object, is unable either to return the object or adjust it systematically to his mouth, and is satisfied to displace it by chance; buccal space is therefore for him only a practical schema of mouth or hands and not a property of the things themselves. In short, there are no permanent spatial relations among things any more than there are permanent things in space; the absence of an objective group is the same thing as the absence of objects.

These remarks enable us to understand the real nature of *visual space* and the exaggeration it would be to believe, like Poincaré, that any subject capable of following objects with his eyes inserts them in experimental groups. In reality, accommodation to visually perceived movements presupposes an activity which is arranged in groups, and in this sense it is possible to speak of practical groups, but the child neither perceives nor conceives of the movements of things in the form of objective groups because he does not place himself in space in relation to them.

The main practical groups in which the child unknowingly finds himself inserted by his visual accommodations are those which result from these three operations: following movements of translation, finding the position of objects, and estimating distances in depth.

With regard to the perception of objects in motion we have

noted (*O.I.*, obs. 28-32) how, from the end of the third month, the child learns to watch movements of translation or to fix his glance on a stationary object by correlating the movements of his eyes or his head; therein, as Poincaré has ably demonstrated from the observer's point of view, is a constant elaboration of the group of displacements.

Concerning the localization of vanished objects we have seen (see above, obs. 2 and 5) how the child, after losing sight of an object propelled by too rapid a movement or especially after having stopped looking at an image in order to look elsewhere, knows how to find them again, either by extending the movement of the vanished object or by replacing it in its initial position. The latter behavior pattern presupposes the elaboration of more or less complex groups, so that the child, starting from position P, moves successively to positions Q, R, S, etc., to return at one stroke to position P.

With regard to visual estimation of depth, it presupposes, in addition to the factors of a purely perceptual kind which writers have always emphasized, a relating of the displacements of objects to one another which alone supplies a practical estimate of their respective distances. For example, let us suppose a mountain 3 kilometers away from me, trees 30 meters distant, and my worktable 30 centimeters away. I perceive them one above the other. On the slightest movement of my head to one side, I see the table as most displaced, the trees a little less, and the mountain very little; from this I might conclude that the mountain is the most remote of the three objects and the table the least, even if I had no other experience concerning their relative distances. The group of displacements thus formed makes it possible to evaluate the parallaxes of objects instead of locating them on a plane without depth. To the extent that the child accommodates his vision to objects at different depths and follows them when they are displaced on different planes, it can be said that he utilizes such groups; from the observer's point of view the movements he makes to watch an object in motion in the background (a person in the room) or in the foreground (a watch 30 centimeters away from his eyes) are capable of forming practical or physiological groups.

But do these three kinds of groups exist in the child's consciousness? We may doubt it. When the child watches a movement of translation, even independently of the relative depth of the objects, there is nothing to prove that he has the impression of displacing himself as a function of the object; and when his glance, too slow or too fast, loses sight of the object and then recovers it, there is nothing to indicate that the subject is aware of a relationship between two displacements. He has no image of his own movements as trajectories in space and merely has the feeling of always recovering, through his own effort, a visual image that tends to disappear. Here is proof that, as we established in connection with the first stages of object concept, the vanished image is rediscovered only if it is within the extension of the accommodation movement immediately preceding; if it is in the least removed from its initial trajectory it is neither rediscovered nor even sought. Regarding his own movements of eyes or head how can one expect the child to perceive them or represent them as movements in space, since, as we shall see in connection with imitation,[2] he does not even have any visual knowledge of his own face during these first months of life?

As for the localization of vanished objects, this does not in the least involve perception or representation of a group of displacements, any more than does accommodation to their visible movements. In effect, the only thing of which the child is capable during the second stage—besides the action of rediscovering the object in the extension of the movement of accommodation —is returning to that object in the initial position in which he perceived it (for instance, obs. 5). But if such a return involves the intervention of a group from the observer's point of view, for the subject himself it constitutes only a quite simple operation of reproductive assimilation or of sensorimotor memory; it is not the objects which the subject finds in reality, it is his own initial position. If the subject passes through positions P, Q, R, and S to return to P, he does not have an image of any of them and has practical knowledge only of position P. Therein is neither perception nor representation of groups.

In the third place, if perception of objects being displaced on planes of different depth presupposes the use of groups of dis-

[2] J. Piaget, *Play, Dreams and Imitation in Childhood* (New York: Norton, 1951).

placements, those groups are surely not perceived as such by the child. As we have seen, it is only during the fourth stage of object concept (9 or 10 months of age) that the child searches for things one behind another or behind screens. Furthermore, as we shall see in connection with the third stage, it is the prehension of objects seen which will make it possible to acquire concepts of "in front of" and "behind"; hence it is very probable that during the first two stages the objects perceived are not located behind one another.

At most it is possible to speak of organic accommodations, momentary and isolated in depth, but the absence of any other behavior related to that depth seems to reveal that, even in nearby space, one cannot talk of a conscious coordination of the spatial field regarding distance; the child certainly perceives at various depths, but there is no indication that he is conscious of these depths or that he groups the perceived displacements on different planes in totalities which are consistent in regard to the objects themselves. Moreover, even in simple accommodation to depth, binocular convergence is not at all systematic until about the age of nine months. It appears at the end of the first month as does the accommodation of the crystalline lens to short distances. But it is not regularized until much later.

OBS. 68. At 0;8 (13) Jacqueline still manifests internal strabismus of the left eye when looking at a person who is one meter away from her, even when she has not just previously examined a nearby object. An hour later, internal strabismus of the right eye, in the same circumstances. At 0;8 (14), internal strabismus of both eyes when looking at an object placed at a distance of 30 centimeters. At 0;8 (16), when looking at an object 20 centimeters distant the right eye is accommodated, the left eye divergent; same observations until about 0;9 (15).

In the first months of life, binocular divergence is daily observable in her.

This lack of systematic binocular convergence is therefore frequent, as Preyer had already noted, during the first two stages and often until the end of the third stage (until about 8-9 months). True, there may be, independently of sight, a tactile depth due to movements of the hand in relation to objects grasped or felt. But this, too, remains purely practical and does not yet correspond to any visual perception.

In short, if perception of visual space involves the presence of practical groups, nothing warrants the assertion that the child perceives, or *a fortiori* has an image of, the displacements of objects in the form of groups; objects are not yet perceived either in their interrelations or in relation to the body itself conceived as a mobile in space.

The same is true of *auditory space, tactile space*, etc. If the child quickly learns to localize sounds (*O.I.*, obs. 44-49), to find the relinquished object with his hand (*O.I.*, obs. 52-54 and see above obs. 4) etc., that does not prove in any way that he arranges perceived positions and displacements in groups; he is capable of following a displacement or of finding a position connected with his own attitudes but not of objectifying these factors in groups which are independent of the action. This can be said even more strongly of kinesthetic or postural space, that is to say, of the equilibrium of the body itself.

In conclusion, two main aspects characterize these first two stages from the point of view of knowledge of spatial relations: the purely practical nature of the presenting groups and the relative heterogeneity of the different spaces.

Each kind of space involves the existence of groups. Whether he finds a displaced sensory image by means of mouth, eyes, ear, or hand, the child puts to work movements of his organism which are arranged in groups, since they are capable of constantly returning to the initial situation, speaking absolutely or relatively to the object. But the child is not yet capable either of perceiving things in space in conformity to this group structure or, still less, of having an image of the groups thus formed; he puts the group into practice without having either direct or indirect knowledge of it, just as he acts causally without perceiving or conceiving of causal relations.

Moreover, these practical groups remain heterogeneous among themselves. As yet, no constant relation exists between visual and buccal space or between tactile and visual space. True, auditory and visual space are already coordinated, as are buccal and tactile space, but no total and abstract space encompasses all the others. Hence each activity gives rise to an ordination *sui generis* of reality in space, but perceived spatial relations are not unified, and, above all, there is no specifically geometric and kinematic representation that would make it possible to place them in a common environment.

§ 2. THE THIRD STAGE: THE COORDINATION OF PRACTICAL GROUPS AND THE FORMATION OF SUBJECTIVE GROUPS

Space, in the first two stages, is but the development of sensori-motor schemata envisaged from the point of view of accommodation, and perception of space in no way transcends the perception of sensory images to which the child accommodates pragmatically. Hence the child perceives neither the spatial relations of things to one another nor his own displacements in relation to things. His own movements are known to him only through internal sensations projected in images of the external world; the displacements of things themselves thenceforth appear to him as being the extension of these internal sensations. Consequently it would be impossible to speak either of objective groups connecting the displacements of bodies to each other, or of subjective groups involving perception of active relations which the subject establishes between things and himself.

What will happen in the third stage, which we have described as beginning with the coordination of sight and prehension and ending with the search for hidden objects? The new element in this stage is the coordination of different practical groups among themselves, hence of buccal space with visual space, of visual space with tactile and kinesthetic space, etc. The essential factor in such coordination is the development of prehension; once prehension is coordinated with sight, then tactilo-kinesthetic space, visual and buccal space begin to form an aggregate to which other forms of spatial accommodation will gradually be added. This fact is of considerable importance in the elaboration of groups of displacements. Without as yet detaching these latter from the action itself and placing them among things, prehension nevertheless makes it possible to transcend the level of the simple practical group and to form what we shall call the subjective group.

In effect, two essential acquisitions result from the development of prehension. In the first place the child, learning to use his hands to act upon things, begins to make use of the relationships of things among themselves in contrast to the simple relations of things with the functioning of organs. This acquisition, which defines what we have called (*O.I.*, Chap. III) the secondary circular reaction, is important from the point of view of space since it leads the subject to become interested in the spatial relations which unite perceived objects to each other. In the second place, by virtue of the very fact that through prehension the child intervenes in the detail of displacements and of spatial connections, he begins to watch himself act; he observes his hands, his arms, and the contacts of his hand with the objects grasped. Even without being aware of himself in the totality of his action and even without taking account of his displacements as a whole or those of his glance, the child can henceforth relate certain movements of his own to those of the environment. Whence a new repercussion of prehension on the groups of displacements.

The projection of the practical group into the perceptual field circumscribed by the action itself thereby determines what we shall call the subjective group. But such progress does not yet suffice for the elaboration of objective groups for, beyond the immediate action, the child still does not take into account the spatial interrelations of objects or the displacements of the body itself in its totality. Hence the subjective group constitutes a simple transition from the practical group to the objective group; it involves an incipient objectification but within the limits of the momentary activity.

Let us begin by describing the elementary groups, half-practical, half-subjective, which, during this third stage, merely extend the purely practical groups of the second one. Then we shall describe the subjective groups belonging to the present stage and shall end by showing how they differ from the objective groups.

The simplest groups of the third stage are those which correspond to what we have called "interrupted prehension" with regard to object concept (Chap. I, §2, obs. 13-15): having dropped an object from his hands, the child searches for it in the extension of his earlier movements of prehension. In such cases, groups may be said to be present, since the subject tries to adjust the displacements of his hand to those of the object. But it is apparent that these groups are neither perceived nor conceived as such. The proof is that if the movement of prehension is not sufficiently delineated before the object disappears, the child behaves as though the object has reentered the void. The incipient perception to which these groups give rise therefore does not transcend the level of subjective groups.

OBS. 69. At 0;5 (24) Laurent, having touched with his right hand a doll which I immediately withdraw (all of this outside the visual field) searches for it at once but confines himself to lowering his arm without exploring the surrounding space, as though the doll could have been displaced only in the extension of the movement of prehension. Furthermore, if he extends his arm farther at the moment of search, he actually advances it only 2 or 3 centimeters and consequently does not even endow the vanished object with a rectilinear trajectory.

So also, at 0;6 (0) having relinquished a box which I take away from him without his having seen it, he searches for it but without putting his hand forward and merely scratches where his hand is. Finally he waves his hand in the surrounding space but without systematic exploration.

At 0;6 (9) his right hand touches a rattle placed under his sheet (he does not see it). In trying to grasp it he involuntarily pushes it away. But even so, he does not stretch out his arm to follow the trajectory.

At 0;6 (10) I touch his hand with a matchbox; he immediately extends his hand in a straight line, merely lowering the forearm, but he searches neither left nor right. Same observation at 0;6 (15), etc. (see obs. 17).

OBS. 70. Here are some examples of coordination between the tactile space belonging to these groups and visual space.

At 0;6 (0) when he lets a box escape him, he looks to left and right of his head, while searching for the object with his hand. But as he does not succeed in touching the box he does not coordinate his glance with the movements of his hands.

At 0;6 (9) he directs his eyes toward the object after having touched it. But he cannot see it because of various screens. Same reaction at 0;6 (10), etc.

At 0;6 (30) he lets go of a toy as he raises his right arm (he is lying down). The toy falls to the level of his waist; he searches for it at once with his hand, lowering his forearm without displacing his upper arm (he knocks against the object as it happens to be located in the trajectory of his hand). Throughout the whole search his glance is aimed in the right direction, but he does not succeed in seeing the object. Next, Laurent loses the object on his left at the level of his hair; he searches for it simultaneously with his hand and by looking. But in trying to grasp it he gradually pushes it above his head. Although he is the cause of this movement it does not occur to him that the object has been displaced and he continues to look for it where he saw it just before.

At 0;7 (12), etc., he also coordinates his glance and his tactile search, the latter remaining independent of the former when the child cannot see the object but being oriented by it when the object is visible.

Behavior patterns of this kind form groups that are partly practical and partly subjective. At first, groups exist to the extent that the interconnected movements of object and child form a closed cycle, or at least tend to do so; the child loses an object, finds it, and brings it toward himself. But in order to classify these groups as practical, subjective, or objective it is necessary to find out how the child himself perceives or conceives of them. Does he already have the concept that fallen objects follow a trajectory independent of himself and that his hand meets them merely by following another route? In that case he would perceive or conceive of the group as a closed cycle of displacements of the object, and the group would be classed among objective groups. On the other hand, is the child limited to experiencing vague impressions of relinquishing and recapturing—or of "no longer holding" and of "holding again"—without perceiving in the form of groups either the movements of the object or those of his hand? In that case the group would remain purely practical, that is, only the observer would succeed in discerning a closed cycle in the movements of the child who experiences only a sort of internal impression of return or rhythm (something like alternating disappointment and satisfaction). Or again, does the child conceive of the group in a way intermediate between these two extremes, that is, by objectifying his own action enough to perceive it partially from without, but not objectifying the moving object enough to make a real "object" of it? In that case the object would be considered a sort of extension of the action, and its trajectory would be comparable to that followed by the child's hands; such a group, located halfway between the practical group and the objective one, would be what we call a subjective group.

Once these definitions have been made it seems clear that the groups described in obs. 69 and 70 still belong in part to the practical groups, and in part constitute subjective groups. None of them corresponds to the concept of the objective group. The reason is that in none of the behavior patterns examined does the child behave as though the objects followed an independent trajectory; in order to recover them he confines himself to lowering his forearm but does not try to search either on the left or the right, or even to stretch his arm farther when he does not succeed in touching the object or when he pushes it away while trying to grasp it. The object is, therefore, not yet a real "object"; it is merely a sensory image at the disposal of actions and merely extends the activity (Chap. I, §2). Thereafter the child does not in the least imagine the trajectory of his hands as meeting outside that of the object or constituting a group with it, that is, a totality of movements returning to their point of departure.

With regard to determining whether such groups remain purely practical or reach the level of subjective groups, this is a matter of degree. In the simplest cases the child reclaims the lost object without a detached perception of his own gesture; behavior of this type does not differ at all from that of the first stages. But in other cases, particularly when the subject tries to watch what he is doing (see obs. 70, the examples of coordination between visual and tactile space), he arrives at an elementary perception of the group, that is, he discovers the subjective group.

What does such a discovery mean? So long as the child succeeds in seeing in a continuous way the object which escapes and the hand which overtakes it, the displacements he perceives are arranged in a group; the aggregate of the movements of the object and those of the hand constitutes a coherent self-limited cycle. When, on the other hand, the object leaves the perceptual field, either the child considers it as momentarily annihilated or else he merely compares its trajectory with that of his hands. On the whole, if the object thus begins to be deployed in space, this space remains delimited by the child's zone of action; space, therefore, does not yet consist in a system of relationships between objects but is only an aggregate of relations centered on the subject.

The accommodation of the glance to movements of translation perpendicular to itself furnishes a second example of this situation and thus makes it possible to extend the preceding analysis somewhat.

The only practical progress achieved in this realm, in relation to the behavior patterns of the second stage, consists in the fact that the child henceforth succeeds in finding objects even when they move too rapidly for the eyes to follow them. We have described these observations in connection with object concept (see obs. 6-12). Is the improvement such as to permit the child to elaborate subjective or even objective groups, or do such acts remain on the level of purely practical groups? With regard to accommodation to rapid movements (see the observations cited), it is very doubtful whether the child perceives anything of the presenting groups; if he perceives his own movements during his search for the vanished object it is in the form of kinesthetic and muscular impressions and not yet as displacements in space. On the other hand, by slowing down the speed of the moving object, does one give the child the opportunity to perceive groups, and what is the nature of such groups?

OBS. 71. For instance Laurent, at 0;6 (8) is lying in his bassinet opposite a wide window behind which I appear. I place before him, against the window, a large cushion which can hide me completely. Then I appear at A, on the right of the cushion, at the child's right, and tap on the window pane; Laurent looks at me and smiles. Then I hide and emerge at B, on the left of the cushion. Laurent sees me again and laughs. Finally I move sideways still further to the left, until I disappear from his horizon at C. Then, instead of expecting my return at C or B he turns immediately in direction A and searches for me there.

Two hours later I resume the experiment without the cushion and in the opposite order. I appear at C at the extreme left of his visual field, then go to B, to A and finally disappear at the extreme right, at A; Laurent searches for me immediately at C!

Laurent therefore does not attribute to me any rectilinear trajectory, if my visible displacements end at the left and the right of the window and if I displace myself too slowly for him to pursue his own movement of accommodation; he therefore searches for me only where he saw me at first, the group thus remaining linked with his action alone.

OBS. 72. At 0;7 (13) Laurent is seated in his bassinet opposite my office door. I open the door, appear, make him laugh, then go slowly to the end of the room; Laurent's eyes follow me, but even before he sees me disappear from his visual field he turns toward the door and waits.

At the second and third attempts he watches me until he can see me no longer, then searches for me in the direction of the door (hence the opposite direction).

At the fourth attempt he looks at me until I disappear. Then he waits for a moment and turns again to the door.

It seems, in such examples, that the child consciously begins to arrange the perceived displacements and consequently to become aware of groups. It is certain that the child is not yet aware of either his eyes or his head, and therefore it is not in relation to them that he localizes the movements observed. But through the development of prehension he surely has some spatial concept of the action itself and can appreciate, in relation to it, the changes in position of the object in motion.

What, then, is the nature of the groups thus constructed? The behavior patterns of which we have just given two examples and which are frequently observed spontaneously provide a decisive answer in this respect; they are subjective groups and not yet objective ones. So long as the child directly perceives the moving object and readjusts his movements of eyes and head in such a way as to stare at it, it is impossible to determine accurately whether the group is objective or subjective, since in this case the behavior of the child gives no clue regarding his awareness of the displacements thus arranged. But as soon as the momentary placing of the moving object forces the subject to reveal his concept of the group of displacements, one discovers how far removed this concept still remains from that of truly objective groups.

Concerning the perceived moving object, it is noteworthy that the child does not endow it with an independent trajectory (in the present case, a rectilinear course). It is only when the object moves rapidly and the child loses sight of it momentarily that he searches for it in the extension of the straight line observed; but, as we have noted, this involves only an extension of the act of accommodation itself. When the moving object really disappears the child does not endow it with the power to continue its course and to follow the trajectory delineated; he searches for it immediately at the point of departure of its trajectory. The moving object is therefore not yet an object endowed with autonomous movements; the child still does not perceive and still less does he imagine the movements of objects in relation to each other. Can it be said that perceiving a person in a doorway or next to a cushion, etc., amounts to the same thing as putting one object (the person) into relationship with other objects (the door or the cushion)? We do not believe so, given all that the analysis of object concept has shown us. The door and the cushion do not constitute spatial landmarks in relation to which the moving object is displaced; they are still only qualitative terms in a practical and subjective space, in other words guidemarks of the very act of accommodation by means of which the child's eyes find the object again.

Concerning the subject of the behavior patterns under discussion, to the extent that he is unaware of himself as a body located in space, he distorts the spatial field in which the moving object is displaced and thereby signifies true awareness of the group. If the child considered himself a body in space he would understand that the moving object goes away from him along an independent trajectory, and in order to recover it he would at once try to displace himself or to orient his glance as a function of that trajectory; hence the group thus formed would be objective. But the child at the present stage knows nothing of himself except his own activity experienced from within and certain visible movements from without, such as those of prehension. Therefore the moving object appears to him as the mere extension of that activity and its displacements are conceived only as relative to it; as soon as the moving object leaves the perceptual field the child searches for it where he first perceived it as though the group were self-enclosed in relation to the subject and not in relation to the object.

The nature of the subjective group again becomes clear; it is not a system of relations between objects but an aggregate of relationships centered on the subject. These relationships constitute groups in so far as they induce the subject's activity to revert to the point of departure in order to rediscover the object. These groups, moreover, are no longer purely practical, since the subject is partly conscious of his regulatory activity and is no longer limited to experiencing it at most from within. But such groups do not yet lead to the formation of an objective space, that is, of a field independent of the body itself and in which the body is displaced as an object among other objects.

These conclusions coincide completely with those suggested to us by the acts of interrupted prehension and tactile ordination of space. We shall find them again in various forms in connection with each of the behavior patterns of this stage.

The same applies, at first, to the *positions* of objects which the child rediscovers, after having ceased to look at them, through the mechanism of deferred reaction (see above, obs. 18-19). Therein is manifest undeniable memory of position, which seems at first to attest to the presence of stable objective groups. But in reality, progress beyond the behavior patterns of the second stage is merely quantitative; that which the child rediscovers is still only his own initial position related to the object and not yet that of the objects themselves in relation to each other. The proof is that during the fourth stage the child still does not take into account, in his search for vanished objects, the sequential displacements witnessed by him. Hence the group exists only in the movements of the child, who does not perceive it as characterizing the interrelations of things. In other words, the positions of objects are still conceived only as relative to an action which begins to evoke awareness of space, but not as relative to their actual displacements in a common and objective space.

Here are some examples.

OBS. 73. Let us begin by citing one or two cases of groups of displacements leading to a correct result, that is, permitting the child to find the object where it actually is.

At 0;5 (21) Laurent looks at a new rattle attached to his hood; he busies himself with it for a moment (waves his hands, etc.), then goes on to something else but looks back at it constantly.

At 0;6 (1) during an automobile trip he examines a lemon in a net (above him). He shakes his head while looking at it, etc. Continually distracted by the landscape, noises, and other things, he nevertheless unhesitatingly finds the position of the lemon as soon as he is unoccupied.

At 0;7 (0) he has an object in each hand. By chance he lets go the object in his left hand (his arm is outstretched). With the empty hand he is about to grasp the second object from his right hand when he suddenly turns his head and looks for the first object which has fallen beside him.

These are typical groups. But are they objective, that is, related to displacements of the objects as such, or subjective, that is, depending on the action? The following observations make it possible to answer in support of the second solution.

OBS. 74. At 0;9 (9) Jacqueline is seated on my lap but turns her back to me. I say "coucou" in her left ear and she laughingly turns her head until she sees my face. Then I say "coucou" in her right ear; she laughs again but looks for me on the left, although as a rule she localizes sounds accurately.

Likewise, after a moment, when I begin at the right and proceed to the left she turns to the right to search for me systematically.

All this occurs as though my face had an absolute position in relation to the action of the child and as though she did not take into account the contingent unobserved displacements. This observation, from the point of view of position, coincides with what the preceding observations have taught us in regard to movements of translation.

OBS. 75. At 0;6 (14) Laurent sees me emerge from a large curtain from behind which I have called to him, at the left of his visual field (he is seated on a sofa and can see nearly the whole room). I remain motionless for a moment, then move to the right and finally disappear; Laurent immediately turns to search for me in the curtain. Then he tires of this. I call him from the extreme right of his visual field; he immediately turns again to the left.

Subsequently, however, he searches for me in the direction of the sound.

At 0;7 (2) and at 0;7 (4) Laurent is seated in his bassinet opposite the curtain behind which I hide. I cry "coucou"; he arches
back, waves his arms, etc. I leave; he laughs contentedly (impression
of success). I leave slowly on his left (opposite direction from the
curtain) and cease to be visible; he wriggles again, facing the curtain.

It is useless to comment on these observations; their result is
identical to the preceding ones with the sole difference that here
is involved memory of positions connected with a circular activity of the child (Jacqueline's game of hide-and-seek, procedures such as arching his back, waving his arms, etc., in Laurent's case).

A fourth type of actions will occupy us longer because they
are more complex and more characteristic of this stage; they are
the groups related to buccal space which are formed in coordination with tactile and visual space and which determine the
movements of *rotation*. When objects brought to the mouth
have a side particularly favorable to sucking, the child is able
to turn them around to find the "good part." Such a reversal of
the object implies a group from the mathematical point of view.
But what is the psychological level of this group at the present
stage of mental evolution?

First, here are the facts.

OBS. 76. At 0;4 (6) Laurent tries to suck a paper knife which he
has just grasped and holds against his face. He begins by holding it
simultaneously against his forehead, nose, and chin without being
able to reach his lips; then he moves it at random, finds one end of
it with his mouth, and sucks it at once. Subsequently he tries to put
hand and object together into his mouth. Then he moves the object
away while searching left and right with his mouth. At each new
attempt he finishes by grasping the desired end with his lips (because it is the only end suitable for sucking). But he does not succeed in systematically turning over the object himself; he moves it by
chance, trying to suck it, and retains only those of his gropings
which are successful.

At 0;5 (8) on the other hand, he seems systematically to find the
end of a stick in order to suck it; he grasps the stick with both hands
and, after having tried to suck the middle part, shifts it until he
reaches one of the two ends. For instance he raises his head and
mouth as high as possible while he lowers the stick with his hands.

Or else, on the contrary, he raises the stick and bends his head down to reach the lower end. Or his lips follow the edge of the stick until he grasps one of the ends. But during each of these behavior patterns Laurent gives the impression of being guided exclusively by impressions of mouth and fingers; he does not perceive a rotation of the object as such but merely coordinates his movements of head and hands until he finds the special position he seeks. This coordination gives the illusion of a systematic rotation but it is only empirical.

So also, at 0;5 (25), he turns in every direction a large crumpled piece of paper almost forming a ball until his lips attain an angle suitable for sucking. He succeeds each time, guiding himself by perceptions of mouth and fingers.

Same reaction at 0;6 (0); he turns a notebook over until his lips grasp one of the four corners. The object in question, having a more regular shape than the crumpled paper, gives the impression of being turned for its own sake, like the stick at 0;5 (8). But in reality it is only a question of groping made systematic through coordination of mouth and hands.

OBS. 77. At 0;6 (6) Laurent turns a rattle over and over, without looking at it, until he can suck the handle; this he perceives tactually by passing the rattle from one hand to the other and immediately directs the handle toward his mouth. The next day he grasps the rattle by the base (the knob), he straightens it accidentally and perceives the handle; he then tries at once to put the handle in his mouth in order to suck it (one sees here the role of sight in the "reversing" group). But in trying to steer the handle to his mouth he catches it on his arm (he sees this happen); he pulls harder and harder but does not succeed in correcting the movement by turning the rattle in the other direction. This limitation is important; it shows us at the outset that during this stage the only systematic reversals of which the child is capable are observed half-reversals (bringing to himself a side of the object which has already been perceived), any total reversal (bringing to himself intentionally the reverse side of the object) being as yet impossible.

At 0;6 (10) Laurent manipulates the same rattle; he turns it over by chance, and as soon as he sees the handle he brings it toward his mouth with his left hand.

At 0;6 (16) Laurent explores a new toy (a swan surrounded by a ring and attached to a handle), happens to reverse it in passing it from one hand to the other, and sees the handle; he lowers the toy immediately, turning the whole thing over, and sucks the handle. I give Laurent the same rattle a series of times always in the same way, by the side opposite the handle. Laurent never turns the object over right away but each time when he perceives the handle he turns it over.

Same observations at 0;6 (24) with a doll whose feet he likes to suck, at 0;7 (12), at 0;8 (16), etc.

Such movements of rotation given to objects surely constitute new groups which the child masters on the plane of action; by putting the object back into its initial position the subject coordinates his own movements in self-enclosed entities. But are such movements accompanied by perception or representation of the group, in other words, is the child able to perceive or imagine the rotation of the objects which he knows how to turn over in a practical way? It is clear that in turning the object over the child perceives differences between the sides, whether those differences are gustatory, tactile, or visual. But concerning the mouth, which in this respect is what Stern[3] very accurately calls an "organ of control," it is impossible to speak of rotation; there is simply a special position (contact of lips with the nipple of the bottle or with the handle of the rattle) and the child finds it again, without imagining how he does so, by simple motor accommodation to the object. Buccal space therefore does not by itself give rise to any perception or representation of this new group.

Could it be said, on the other hand, that from the tactile point of view there is perception of rotation? We do not believe this either so long as sight does not direct the movements themselves. It should be noted that when a child of this age holds an object he passes it almost constantly from one hand to the other; in the course of this manipulation he notices whether the side he brings to his mouth is pleasant to suck or not. The hand does not intentionally turn the object over; it adapts it to the mouth, and it is to the observer that this adaptation consists in a rotation. Even in the case when, at 0;5 (8) Laurent skillfully turns a stick over, the coordination of the impressions of his hand and his buccal perceptions suffices to explain his behavior; here he

[3] *Psychol. d. früh. Kindheit* (Leipzig: Quelle & Meyer, 4th ed.; 1927), pp. 90-91.

elaborates a schema analogous, though slightly more complex, to that of thumb-sucking and the primary schemata without perception of the movements of the object. To be sure, such behavior patterns constitute groups, but there is as yet no authority for assuming that the child places them in a space which is such that he perceives simultaneously the movements of the object and those of his hands.

The visual perception of rotation is more complex. When the child looks at the object which he turns over he certainly perceives different sequential aspects of it. In the late stages this interest will even lead him to rotate the object systematically in order to study its outlines and surfaces. From this point on, it is possible to speak of an objectification of this group of displacements, that is, a perception of the group in the object itself. But in the present stage this interpretation is impossible. Either the child searches with eyes or mouth for the special side he has just noticed, and in that case there is no complete reversal or rotation, or else he examines impartially all that the object has to offer but turns it over without purpose or system, by means of mere motor combination. In neither case does the child perceive the displacements in themselves, arranged in groups, even if he executes in a practical way the movements which constitute such groups.

OBS. 78. An excellent example of this is furnished by the child's bottle, for in the rotation of this object various kinds of inter-coordinated space intervene: visual, tactilo-kinesthetic, and buccal. Analysis of the rotation of the bottle makes it possible, therefore, to determine precisely at which point the child perceives the group he is capable of constituting in a practical way. It is therefore expedient to analyze this behavior in some detail, given the importance of the question it raises with regard to the concept of the reverse side of objects, the constancy of their shape, their substantial and spatial permanence, etc.

From 0;7 (0), when Laurent begins to hold his bottle[4] while drinking, I systematically make the following experiment; I hold out the bottle upside down (the nipple being invisible) to see if Laurent will

[4] This bottle is cylindrical, 18 centimeters long, and regular in shape. Therefore if the bottom is shown, the nipple is invisible, but the slightest tilt in relation to the child's eyes makes it appear.

know how to turn it over. Until about 0;9 Laurent has behaved as though once the nipple disappeared it no longer existed, in other words as though the object had no reverse side. Systematic reversal occurs in this period only after the nipple has been wholly or partly perceived.

At 0;7 (4) I present the bottle in a vertical position to Laurent (it is full of milk, just before the meal); he looks at it from bottom to top, sees the nipple and immediately brings it toward his mouth. He sucks. I take it from his hands and present it to him horizontally; Laurent easily turns the bottle in a quarter-circle and puts the nipple into his mouth. At the third attempt I present the bottle in such a way that it must be simultaneously lowered and turned from left to right; Laurent succeeds at once. At the fourth attempt I present the bottle upside down, Laurent seeing only the bottom and no longer perceiving the nipple; he looks at it for one or two seconds and begins to howl without making any attempt at reversal. Fifth attempt (same position); Laurent looks, begins to suck the glass (the bottom), and howls again.

At 0;7 (5), same reactions.

At 0;7 (6), I repeat the experiment after the evening meal when Laurent still demands food (he is never satisfied so long as he sees his bottle), but without nervousness. He begins by turning the bottle over and, no matter what position it is in, adjusting it very accurately as soon as he sees the right end. Particularly when I present him with the bottle almost upside down but letting him see a band of the rubber of the nipple, 2-3 millimeters wide, he succeeds at once in making the nearly complete reversal of the nipple necessary to adjust it; this fact adequately demonstrates that it is not the technical or motor difficulty which stops the child when he no longer sees the right end. Once these preliminary attempts have been made I present the bottle to Laurent upside down; he looks at it, sucks it (hence tries to suck the glass!), rejects it, examines it again, sucks it again, etc., four or five times in succession. Then I remove the bottle and present it to him in a vertical position, 30 centimeters from his eyes; Laurent considers it with great interest and alternately examines the top (the nipple) and the bottom (the wrong end). I turn it over; his glance again oscillates between the top (the wrong end) and the bottom (the nipple). Once he has sufficiently considered the object and thus seems to have understood, I tilt the bottle slowly and present it to him by the wrong end; he looks at it, then tries to suck, looks again, sucks again, and finally becomes discouraged. He has therefore understood nothing, despite his extensive examination of the object when it was completely visible.

At 0;7 (11), he again turns the bottle over very well as soon as he sees the nipple (in any position whatever) but still fails to understand at all when he ceases to see it. Same reactions at 0;7 (17), at 0;7 (21), etc.

At 0;7 (30), Laurent looks at his full bottle before the meal. I show him the whole thing at a distance of 30 centimeters, then bring it closer to him, turning it very slowly; so long as he sees the nipple he holds out his hands, but as soon as it disappears from his visual field he begins to howl and withdraws his hands. He no longer tries to suck the glass as before, but pushes the bottle away, crying. Same reaction three times in succession. Falsification of the object definitely still exists. However, when I move the bottle a little farther away, he looks at both ends very attentively and stops crying; he is certainly interested in the problem intellectually (and no longer merely practically). He extends his hand when I bring the object closer, then withdraws it when he no longer sees the nipple.

Same reaction at 0;8 (2), at 0;8 (15) and up to 0;8 (24). Finally at 0;9 (9), the behavior is modified, and from the particular point of view which concerns us here, Laurent enters the fourth stage.

OBS. 78a. Without, unfortunately, having made similar experiments with Jacqueline, I have, however, observed reactions of the same kind. At 0;8 (8) for example, she still does not seem to recognize her familiar celluloid duck when it is presented to her by the base (white surface). As soon as she perceives the back or the head she grasps it with both hands and looks at it for a moment (as though convincing herself of its identity) before sucking it. But when she sees only the base, she does not react. However it is clear that, left to herself, she turns it over constantly in transferring it from one hand to the other (see the next observation).

OBS. 79. The foregoing observations show the difficulties in intentional rotation even when visual, tactile, and buccal spaces are intercoordinated; everything takes place as though the object had no reverse side. The child well knows how to bring to the front visible parts in the background, but invisible parts do not give rise to search or, consequently, to voluntary rotation.

To corroborate this conclusion we may examine how the child behaves toward objects which he studies as he turns them over, no longer trying to suck the "right" end. Does he turn them over merely for the sake of the movement or to reach their invisible side?

At 0;6 (0) Laurent holds a matchbox which he passes back and forth from one hand to the other. He looks successively at the yellow side and the blue side, but without method of any kind; he obviously is satisfied to turn the box over for the sake of turning it over and to examine the various transformations, but there is not yet any search for the reverse side of the object.

At 0;6 (1) he turns over a box of lozenges at least three times before shaking it or rubbing it against the edge of the bassinet. He also turns over a stick eight times in succession, transferring it from one hand to the other, before sucking one end of it. But in both cases an essentially motor pleasure is involved, accompanied, it is true, by a visual interest in the modifications in the object's appearance, but there is not yet either a search for the "wrong side" or true exploration of shapes or perspectives.

At 0;6 (14) when confronted with a new doll he turns it over only twice before applying to it his habitual secondary schemata (O.I., obs. 110). At 0;6 (18) a pipe holds his attention longer but he turns it over only by chance, in passing it from one hand to the other. Only when he perceives the end does he turn it over intentionally (in order to suck it), but he does not search for it when he no longer sees it. It is noteworthy, moreover, that in transferring the object from one hand to the other, Laurent separates his hands to lengthen the trajectory; such an act is confirmation that reversal of the object remains essentially motor and reveals no exploration of the object as such. Afterward Laurent shakes the pipe, knocks it, rubs it against the edge of the bassinet, etc.

At 0;6 (30), at 0;7 (0), at 0;7 (12), etc., Laurent turns over a toy mushroom, a lamb, etc., while passing them back and forth from one hand to another. But if he begins to look at various sides of them, and especially the reverse side, he does not search systematically and confines himself to considering them when they turn up fortuitously.

Such observations seem to us to admit of two definite conclusions. In the first place, so long as the child perceives visually the parts he wishes to reach with his mouth or to examine more closely, he is capable of giving the object a movement of rotation. The group of displacements he elaborates is, therefore, not only practical but still at least subjective since it is accompanied by a perception of the movements of the object and perhaps also those of the hand which makes the object move. But, in the second place, in this regard it would be impossible to speak of the objective group, for the child remains incapable of conceiving of a complete rotation of the object leading to a search for its reverse side. When the child turns the object completely over, it is always partly by chance; either it takes place without plan, as the object is passed from one hand to the other, or else it occurs when a chance displacement brings into view the part of the object which is sought (for instance, the nipple of the bottle when the child perceives it because of a slight tilt of the bottle). On the other hand, if chance movements are eliminated, the child shows himself incapable of any search for the reverse side of the object. Thus in obs. 78 Laurent intensely desires the nipple of his bottle in order to eat or merely to suck, but he does not succeed in turning it over; as soon as the nipple appears he knows quite well how to turn the bottle over, but when the nipple becomes invisible he does not understand that it is "behind." The group cannot therefore be considered as relative to the object; it remains dependent on a certain perspective, that of the subject.

Let us note, in this respect, the way in which such a behavior pattern concerns object concept. As we tried to establish in Chapter I, the child at the third stage does not yet reveal any special behavior patterns in relation to vanished objects; it all happens as though the objects had been annihilated or changed by being covered with a screen. Observation 78, concerning the bottle, confirms this interpretation most clearly. When the nipple leaves the perceptual field it is not conceived as being on the object's "reverse side" or "behind" the visible part; the child behaves, on the contrary, as though it were reabsorbed in the object and ceased to exist spatially so as to remain simply at the disposal of the appropriate actions. That is why Laurent sucks the wrong end of the bottle, strikes it, etc., as though this would make the nipple appear. The object is therefore not yet endowed with substantial permanence; it has neither constant form nor solidity and is conceived only as being what it appears to be on immediate perception. Having no reverse side it is not yet capable of objective rotation. The subjective quality of the spatial group is thus seen to be equivalent to the absence of true objects.

Finally let us note how much these observations confirm what we have seen in *O.I.* concerning the absence of true "explorations" during the third stage. It is only in the fourth stage that the child begins to explore the object in order to understand its real nature and only during the fifth that he begins to experiment upon it by means of tertiary circular reactions. The rotations we have just described therefore constitute neither tertiary reactions nor even explorations; they are only secondary reactions. Iet us then examine the latter from the point of view of group concept.

If neither accommodation of the glance to rapid movements, nor memory of positions, nor rotations are sufficient to prove the existence of objective groups, could it not be asserted that, in the very center of the visual field perceived by the child at the moment of his action, displacements are arranged in groups? After this, in the *secondary circular reactions*, when the child modifies through prehension the detail of the visually perceived phenomena, does not the group change in structure? Moreover we have defined secondary circular reaction in relation to primary reaction as an activity constructing and utilizing the relationships of things to each other and no longer merely the relationships of things to the functioning of organs; is this not an essential source of objectification of groups?

For example, Laurent pulls on a chain in order to shake the hanging rattles attached to it (*O.I.*, obs. 98); Jacqueline and Lucienne shake their bassinet hood by shaking the hanging dolls (*O.I.*, obs. 100-109), etc. Or witness, above all, reactions consisting in shaking, swinging, rubbing, etc., objects held in the hands (*O.I.*, obs. 102-104). It is apparent that each of these movements can give rise not merely to a practical or motor group but also to a perception of groups.

In such behavior patterns, groups undeniably exist precisely because these reactions are circular, that is, the movements permitting the child to pull, to move, to shake, to swing, etc., are so adjusted that they are always able to return to their point of departure and they act upon objects for the sake of this repetition of the action. So it is that Lucienne, shaking a rattle she has in her hands (*O.I.*, obs. 102), constantly moves her arm forward and pulls it back, correcting one set of movements by means of another. This is a very elementary group but it is nevertheless a group, if one analyzes the particulars of the operations.

OBS. 80. For example, Laurent at 0;5 (24) suddenly perceives in front of him the string which habitually hangs from his bassinet hood; he immediately grasps it to shake the rattles and the whole hood. At a certain moment he relinquishes the string. I take advantage of this by shaking the hood without revealing myself. He watches with astonishment, then his glance goes directly from the hood to the usual location of the string (at the height at which he usually grasps it), while his right hand delineates a movement of prehension. In shaking the hood I have managed to remove the string; Laurent then really looks for the string; it is not the sight of it that distracts him from looking at the hood or that directly attracts his gaze.

Here is the beginning of a group; the action of pulling the string is conceived as being connected with the movements of the hood so that perception of the latter in turn sets in motion search for the string—for the string is not yet a detachable object—or rather, sets in motion the tendency to reproduce the act of pulling the string. The circular quality of this secondary reaction is thus extended into a group one.

Contrary to the case in which the eyes alone, the mouth or hand follow an object without knowing their own spatial displacements, such behavior patterns presuppose a perception of the group as a given phenomenon in the visual field.

For instance, the rattle which Lucienne shakes appears to her as an object endowed with more or less regular forward and backward movements, and the proof that they appear to her thus is that she corrects and directs them. Moreover these interventions seem known to her not only through the muscular sensations, affective states, etc., which accompany her movements, but through the very sight of her hands. The same thing applies to each of the secondary circular reactions just mentioned: in each of these cases the child perceives movements that can be repeated with the manipulated objects and perceives the movements as governed by his action. To be sure, he does not yet understand anything about the "how" of these connections, but this matters little. From the time he becomes interested in the external result of the acts it is enough that he recognize the permanent aspects and kinematic regularities for him to perceive in objects at least a trace of the structure characteristic of groups. The group is therefore in process of being objectified and of being transferred from the action itself to the displacements perceived in objects as such.

But it is not yet possible to conclude from this that objective groups exist. One part of the child does not know how to take account of displacements of the object independent of the action; to the child, if objects leave the perceptual field, they reenter the void, or if their movements deviate from the habitual pattern, they cease to be regulated and understood. On the other hand, if the child has acquired the power to correct the movements of things with his hand and if he thus perceives his own displacements at the same time as those of the object, he is still far from placing these manual movements in relation to those of his head and his glance. Space, therefore, does not yet contain the whole subject and remains dependent on the action in progress. That is why we can still consider as subjective the groups at issue here; they remain intermediate between practical and objective groups (as if the object of this third stage still has permanence only relatively to the action itself, although it has acquired through the act of prehension a solidity superior to that of the primitive object). It is necessary to bear in mind that if the secondary circular reaction leads the child to put things into relationship with one another, these relations are not immediately objective. It is the subject's action which still forms the real link between the various objects intervening in the course of such a behavior pattern. The proof of this is that, in the very absence of any spatial contact, the habitual reactions utilized by the child to obtain a certain result are set in motion by perception of familiar objectives; the secondary circular reaction is thus extended in magico-phenomenalistic procedures stripped of any physical and spatial character (see *O.I.*, Chap. III, obs. 112-118). The groups which define the present level do not yet at all concern the interrelations of objects; they merely connect a subject partly unaware of himself with objects that are semi-permanent and not spatially arranged in relation to each other. Consequently the two conditions constitutive of the "objective" group are lacking.

We shall now try to demonstrate this by analysis of the spatial interrelations of objects. If the groups formed by the development of secondary circular reactions were of the objective type, two results would necessarily follow: 1) objects would be arranged in relation to others in depth and not only in two dimensions; 2) objects would at one stroke acquire constant size and form. To the observer, the groups elaborated by the activity of the child of this stage fulfill these two conditions. Does this also apply to the subject? The absence of any behavior pattern related to objects masked by screens shows immediately that the question arises: everything happens as though the child still did not know that the object's displacements are arranged according to various planes of depth. If from the point of view of practical groups the child who grasps what he sees moves in the third dimension, one may ask whether, in regard to the perception or knowledge of groups and also the understanding of shapes and sizes, he has turned this fundamental experience to account.

It is expedient first to examine accommodation to *depth* and to find out what, in this respect, is introduced in the present stage (defined by the coordination between prehension and sight), as compared to the "groups" of the first stage.

Nothing is more obscure than the question of perception of distances, or the third dimension, so long as no distinction is made between behavior—that is, what the subject knows how to do in relation to a space wholly constituted in the observer's mind—and the subject himself, that is, the way in which he interprets his own behavior in regard to space. From the point of view of behavior, it is relatively easy to determine the extent to which the child accommodates his eyes and hands to depth and how he behaves with respect to objects arranged according to the third dimension. But whatever the complexity of the practical groups thus revealed may be, the whole problem remains to determine whether or not these groups correspond to conscious groups and whether they are objective or merely subjective in nature. It is very possible that to a correct accommodation to depth there corresponds a consciousness incapable of arranging displacements of objects in groups involving depth, just as a correct accommodation of the glance to movements of translation perpendicular to it does not entail the capacity to arrange these movements in independent groups. That is the problem which interests us here. It matters little whether the child perceives distant objects as well as near ones or even whether he gives up trying to grasp them when they are too far away from him, if he does not arrange them in sequential planes and knows nothing about their relative positions. The problem is therefore to discover how, from his actions bearing on distances, he will draw an awareness of the third dimension capable of interconnecting things in a spatially organized universe. As Berkeley said, it is necessary to distinguish vision as a sensory factor from the judgments we bring to bear upon it. That is why we shall carefully distinguish here the point of view of behavior or of practical groups from that of the subject or of subjective groups. Doubtless it is only through study of behavior that we shall manage to determine the latter. But this is no obstacle if one distinguishes the tests in which the subject could not succeed without our spatial representation (tests related to hidden objects, for instance) from the current behavior patterns common to all levels of spatial perception (looking at or grasping objects at different distances, etc.).

Let us begin by describing the facts of behavior involving nothing more than practical groups. In this connection the important innovation of this stage is the coordination of prehension and sight. During the preceding stage the eye already accommodates to distances, with the limitations we have noted. But this accommodation is not yet reflected at all in the child's action, since the movements of the hand remain independent of the visual field (except the inhibiting or accelerating actions of the glance; see *O.I.*, Chap. II, §4). Henceforth, on the contrary, it is possible to find in the behavior of the hands or the entire body the effect of visual perceptions of depth. From this point of view two classes of facts are to be analyzed: accommodations of the hand and total displacements of the child.

OBS. 81. I. Ever since she has begun to grasp perceived objects, Jacqueline has appeared to show discernment between nearby objects and distant ones; a ball, a doll, a rattle, etc., presented in the field of prehension are grasped sooner or later, whereas the same objects presented at the end of the bassinet or at the height of the hood give rise to no movement of prehension properly so called.

II. Moreover the experiment described by Stern[5] and cited by him to substantiate correct perception of distance yields the same re-

Psychol. d. früh. Kindheit (4th Ed.; 1927), p. 95.

sults as those of this writer. Between 0;6 (15) and 0;7, if Jacqueline is lying on her back and is confronted with an object at a distance which is gradually brought closer to her, she really stretches out her hands to grasp only from the moment when the object enters the field of prehension.

III. In the third place, she learns little by little to bring distant objects closer to her. At 0;7 (17) she has stretched her mouth toward the object I hold; this displacement, though related to buccal space, involves an intervention of visual space. At 0;8 (8) the thing is repeated, this time through coordination between prehension and sight. Jacqueline, trying to take possession of a powder box at her left on the edge of the bassinet, sits up straight, leaning at first to the side, without immediately trying to grasp the object; she seems, therefore, to have measured the distance right away. Same observation the same day with a rattle hung above her head; she at once arches back to grasp it.

At 0;8 (9), after having palpated and hit the observer's thumb, and in particular explored the nail with an expression of curiosity, Jacqueline manifests a reaction of disappointment while looking at the other thumb placed on the edge of the bassinet. She does not try to grasp it and immediately starts a series of movements of the whole body intended to bring it closer.

At 0;8 (21) she is lying on her stomach in front of a window and tries to see better; she pushes herself forward with both feet and knees.

OBS. 82. In the preceding observation we have described the main behavior patterns that seem to indicate Jacqueline's correct perception of distances during this stage. Here are facts which indicate the opposite and which are such as to permit us to state precisely that subjective groups of displacements related to depth correspond to the foregoing practical groups.

I. First let us note that if, around 0;6 and 0;7, distant objects do not at first give rise to attempts at prehension, neither are all near objects grasped immediately. For instance, at 0;6 (23), Jacqueline opens her mouth on seeing her bottle at a distance of 10 centimeters but if it is not given she is satisfied to kick with her foot without making the least effort to grasp it herself; since she does not touch it she therefore has no idea it is subject to prehension on her part.

II. As to distant objects, she tries to grasp them in certain circumstances: when a given habit intervenes, when the object's position creates an illusion of accessibility, or when its newness sets in motion a lively interest and suppresses all awareness of possible obstacles. Here are the examples of each of these three categories.

At 0;7 (21) Jacqueline looks at my fingers which I gently move one meter away from her; she immediately tries to grasp as though the resemblance between my hand and hers facilitated the contact (cf. Laurent, *O.I.*, obs. 74, who knew how to grasp my hand before any other object).

At 0;7 (27) she tries to grasp directly a duck placed on top of a quilt outside her field of prehension; here the intermediary of the quilt facilitates things. So also, at 0;8 (8) Jacqueline looks at the duck through the semi-transparent hood of the bassinet; she does not move her arms, but as soon as the duck appears in the free space 50 centimeters distant from her, she holds out her hands to grasp it. At 0;8 (11) she tries in the same way to reach a piece of material located more than 50 centimeters away from her but placed on a support.

Here are examples of objects giving rise to keen desire and thus evoking movements of prehension. At 0;8 (12) Jacqueline wriggles with joy at sight of a person who interests her very much; she holds out her hands as though to grasp, swinging them in the air, whether the person appears next to the bassinet or at the window of the floor above (above the balcony where the bassinet is placed). These do not seem to be mere movements of desire, but also attempts at prehension. At a given moment Jacqueline looks at her own hand, then opens and closes it alternately, meanwhile examining it most attentively. This behavior pattern would be difficult to understand (since she is well acquainted with this spectacle) if at that moment some frustrated desire to grasp were not intervening.

At 0;9 (17) Jacqueline is carried onto the balcony, toward evening. She sees the moon and immediately stretches out her arms. Here again there does not seem to be a mere movement of desire; Jacqueline obviously looks over the whole situation, alternately examines the house and the sky, stops looking at the moon and returns to it with new movements. She seems to have lost all points of reference and appears to try at all costs to grasp the interesting object. Surely, as Stern has noted, this is not pure "reaching for the moon." But it is hard to see what these movements of desire might be without hope of grasping.

III. Regarding near objects, they do not at all immediately give rise to a precise accommodation of movements of prehension considered from the point of view of depth. At 0;7 (11), for instance, Jacqueline does not succeed in grasping a duck several centimeters away from her face because she searches for it farther away; she does not bring her arm close enough to touch the object. In most cases, on the contrary, she reaches between the object and herself, failing to gauge the object at its true depth, and gropes before encountering it.

So also Lucienne, at 0;6 (5), tries to grasp my finger with both hands at once when it is 20 centimeters away from her face. At the first attempt she measures too short a distance and closes her hands between the finger and her face. Second attempt: same mistake. Third and fourth attempts: opposite mistake, her hands join behind mine. Fifth attempt: grazes my finger and immediately adjusts her movements.

iv. Noteworthy, too, are the illusions to which the child is victim when he believes he is able to grasp objects that are too far away, or has the impression that he is coming closer to them.

At 0;8 (10) Jacqueline tries to grasp a finger 60 centimeters from her. She then grabs whatever is within reach, her foot, her bootee, etc. Her expression varies according to the situation. Sometimes everything takes place as though she considered her gesture as accomplished and satisfactory, as though she had really caught what she desired (that is, the finger). At other times she manifests something which resembles surprise or disappointment.

Same reaction with Lucienne at 0;5 (10): she tries to grasp a rattle about one meter away. First she extends both hands parallel (what Stern calls the gesture of desire), then ends by taking one hand in the other.

At 0;8 (12) Jacqueline performs a series of movements designed to bring closer an object placed on the edge of the bassinet 40 centimeters from her. She moves, draws up her torso, etc., and continues to stretch out her arms as if able to grasp it. Actually she remains stationary and does not perceive the inefficacy of her movements; the kinesthetic impression of effort and movement make her believe in an actual displacement.

Same reactions at 0;8 (13); she tries to grasp my thumb by drawing herself up and by holding her hand out toward it; but she raises herself up vertically and not obliquely when the thumb is on her right.

obs. 83. Laurent has occasioned observations exactly parallel to those of Jacqueline. We shall divide them also into two groups, those which favor the hypothesis of a correct evaluation of distances and those which reveal a different meaning. We shall use the same methods for both.

i. Ever since the coordination of prehension and sight, toward the middle of the fourth month, Laurent seems able to distinguish near objects from distant ones; he grasps the former at a distance of 10-15 centimeters from his face and makes no attempt to grasp the second (beyond 15-20 centimeters). But it must immediately be noted that until about 0;6 [6] he remains very reserved and timid in his attempts at prehension, even with regard to near space. Not only does he not try to take everything that is offered but it takes him a while to decide to put his hand on the things he wants. Furthermore a sort of gradation in the time of latency is observable, as a function of the familiarity of the objects; he grasps my hand quite quickly, whereas he hesitates when confronted by a less familiar box and cannot decide about a new rattle until I touch each of his fingers with it.

Finally, let us note that the behavior patterns characteristic of the fourth stage of prehension (grasping the object only when the hand is perceived in the same visual field) have frequently reappeared in the fifth, by a sort of temporal displacement due to the preceding factors; at 0;6 (10) certain new objects have still been grasped only after having been seen at the same time as the hand.

II. Same reaction as Jacqueline, but not until about 0;6, with respect to objects brought close to him; he stretches out his arms only when the objects penetrate his field of prehension (about 10-15 centimeters).

III. Laurent has begun to draw objects to him at 0;5 (25). He tries to grasp a stick hanging in front of him (at a distance of 35 centimeters from his face); he shakes his arms, manifests real anger, then twists himself about, creeping on his back little by little. The effort is certainly due to the desire to grasp, for the child pauses often in order to try again to touch the object. But it seems apparent that he is not conscious of displacing himself; at most he thinks that the object approaches him.

Analogous observations the following weeks, but at 0;6 (27) he is still incapable of stretching out his arms full length when he fails to grasp; he merely directs them toward the object but does nothing to make them reach their maximum length.

On the other hand, from the time he knows how to sit (about 0;7) he rapidly learns to straighten himself up and lean slightly forward toward the object. I note this at 0;7 (2), etc.

IV. In this connection, let me mention a curious observation. At 0;7 (11) and the days following, I note that Laurent sits up straight in order to approach the object each time I present him with the

_____

[6] That is to say, until the time he tries precisely to grasp distant objects.

rubber bear or the rubber lamb with which he learned how to sit up. On the other hand, familiar objects which he has frequently grasped and manipulated but in the presence of which he has not yet sat up, prompt this behavior pattern only very slowly; for example, Laurent sits up only after 100 seconds to grasp a matchbox, a doll, etc. Other objects which he only grasped late, the bottle, for instance, do not induce him to sit up.

The schema of sitting up, like that of prehension, is not immediately generalized; it is only by steps that it is applied to everything, all things being equal, of course, with regard to the distance at which the proffered object is located.

v. Let us mention another observation on Laurent which seems to support the idea of a correct perception of distances. At 0;7 (2) Laurent bursts out laughing when I approach him and press my face against his chest. After two repetitions I resume very slowly; he merely smiles when I am at a distance but bursts out laughing as soon as I come closer than about 30 centimeters. Hence he seems to gauge distance very well. He is lying on his back and I approach him in the direct line of his gaze; these are not changes in perspective but only in size which permit him to predict the moment I will reach his body.

This often repeated experiment always yields the same result.

obs. 84. Here are the unfavorable examples.

i. Laurent has not yet grasped his bottle up to 0;7 (0), even when it was offered him at a distance of 5 centimeters; he cried but did not move his hands!

ii. From 0;5 (25) Laurent has tried to grasp objects located outside the field of prehension. He tries to reach a box, a watch, etc., at a distance of 40 centimeters from his face, without yet knowing how to move closer to it.

At 0;6 (7) and at 0;6 (15) I note that Laurent gives up trying to seize the object as soon as I bring it near the hood of his bassinet; if a box is presented at a distance of 20-30 centimeters from the hood, Laurent ceases to hold out his arms and begins to shake his head, raises himself, waves his hands, or shakes himself, etc. (as though a hanging object were involved; see *O.I.*, obs. 112, 115, 118, etc.). But the same objects, situated at a distance of 30-40 centimeters in free space, give rise to attempts at prehension. When he notes his failure, he begins to draw himself up again.

At 0;7 (4) Laurent is seated and I present him with a rubber monkey at the end of his bassinet. He shakes himself, shakes his arms, his head, etc., as though he were immediately measuring the distance and were abandoning the idea of grasping the object in favor of acting upon it according to magico-phenomenalistic procedures. But, as the monkey no longer moves (since I hold it myself), Laurent then tries to grasp it; he extends his hands (the gesture of desire), then joins them in trying to embrace the object (the typical gesture of prehension).

So also, at 0;7 (30) Laurent attempts to reach directly a little box placed before him at a distance of 40 centimeters. He sits up and leans forward, but there remains a space of at least 20 centimeters between the object and his hands.

As with Jacqueline, after two to three months of coordination between sight and prehension the effort to grasp inaccessible objects is more frequent than at the beginning.

III. Finally I noted that Laurent has the same difficulties as Lucienne in measuring near distances at first glance. At 0;4 (6), for instance, before grasping he looks alternately at his hands and at the object as though to measure the depth, then he joins his hands on this side of the object. It is only through groping related to the third dimension that he touches the object.

Such mistakes remain very common until the time, around 0;7, when he knows how to sit up and stretch his arms full length in the direction of the object (see obs. 83, III). But even then many faults remain. Thus at 0;7 (4), after having tried directly to reach a monkey placed at the end of his bassinet, Laurent looks at it from a distance of 20 centimeters. He even touches it with his left hand; he would reach it if he stretched out his arms a little. Nevertheless he does not try it; he merely directs his two hands toward the object and closes one hand on the other. He repeats this gesture two or three times before leaning forward correctly.

At 0;8 (8) he still pushes a box back while trying to grasp it; he does not have the notion of grasping it from behind, even though it is possible to do so, and he pushes it farther away at each new attempt.

What do these facts prove? On the one hand, it seems that the child distinguishes in general what he can and cannot grasp; in this respect he evidences measurement of depth. Moreover, he learns to approach the distant object (obs. 81, III, and obs. 83, III), which reveals the same thing. But on the other hand, he also behaves as though he did not know how to measure the presenting distances with certainty; sometimes he tries to obtain objects that are out of his reach (obs. 82, II, and 84, II), he commits continued errors with regard to near objects (obs. 82, III, and 84, III), and he often believes he is moving closer when he remains in place (obs. 82, IV).

An easy solution would be to say, as is sometimes done, that the child immediately perceives depth but, without a special apprenticeship, does not succeed in correctly evaluating specific distances. We confess that we cannot well understand such a distinction if it is tantamount to saying that the child, without knowing how to estimate various depths, nevertheless is conscious of depth as such and does not confine himself merely to an accommodation of his visual or tactile organs. What, in effect, is perception of distance if not the orderly arrangement according to the third dimension of perceived objects as being situated at various depths? It is therefore hard to conceive of depth in itself, independent of specific distances; and consciousness of depth could be acquired only as a function of the evaluations of these distances. But does this merely mean that the child, while knowing practically how to accommodate his glance and his prehension to various depths, does not know how to adjust them objectively in relation to each other? If this is the meaning of the first solution then it is reduced to that which we shall now defend.

In order to understand this second interpretation it is necessary to invoke the distinction just established between the points of view of observer and subject, or of behavior and consciousness. From the point of view of behavior, it is apparent that the child accommodates his eyes and hands to distance; even if he makes some errors of judgment his appraisal is on the whole accurate. But in what respect does such behavior prove that from his own point of view the child considers the difference between near objects and distant ones as a difference in depth? We have stated above that the child's own movements remain unknown to him as spatial displacements and that subjective groups or even incoherent perceptions far removed from our objective groups can thus correspond to the apparent movements of objects. May this also apply to depth? Here analysis of the errors in estimation is revealing; it shows us that perceptual knowledge corresponding to practical accommodations to depth must in reality be interpreted as a function of subjective groups peculiar to this stage and in no way as a function of objective depth.

First let us note that the impetus to grasp objects is far from being solely a function of their distance. There are numerous objects which the child does not try to grasp, even when within his reach. There are, for instance, the familiar things which he has always looked at in a practical situation which excluded prehension. Jacqueline's and Laurent's bottles (obs. 82, 1, and 84, 1, respectively) are good examples of this; the child knows his bottle better than any other object, but, not having held it himself, he does not think of grasping it when it is not put between his lips. There are, on the other hand, things that are not very familiar or that are presented in abnormal circumstances (cf. Laurent, obs. 83, 1). Let us accept as true that distant objects, while being recognized by the child, seem to him to be precisely what they are in crude and uncorrected perception—diminished, distorted, and linked to a context in which direct prehension has never intervened. It is very possible that, without awareness of distance as such, the child does not try to grasp them merely because they are different from when he touches or grasps them ordinarily. It is noteworthy that, if the child learns at the beginning of this stage to coordinate prehension with sight, he does not at once generalize the prehension of seen objects with his whole universe. He begins by being circumspect and timid, and lively interest is required for him to grasp the thing offered by the observer. It is only little by little that the behavior pattern will become generalized. Besides, let us note carefully, it is precisely around 0;6-0;7 rather than around 0;3-0;6 that the child begins to wish to grasp distant objects, as though regression had occurred, whereas there is merely generalization of prehension. It is therefore understandable that the distant object does not immediately arouse the action of grasping. On the one hand, it is strange and altered; on the other, it is perceived in a visual context in which prehension has never yet been ventured. This visual context of distant objects, even if not perceived as distant and deep, is in effect easily recognized by the child as being the realm of secondary circular reactions and procedures for making an interesting spectacle last. For this it suffices that the child perceive distant objects in the same totality as the hood or the edges of the bassinet or the room in general instead of perceiving them in the ordinary context of his hands, so that even if he places all his aggregates on planes badly organized in depth, he does not try to grasp things at a distance. This is the case with Laurent (obs. 84, II); he shakes himself when he sees objects at the same time as he sees the bassinet hood, whereas he grasps them when they are before him.

This preliminary remark shows that it is impossible to draw from the difference in reactions toward near and distant objects a decisive argument in favor of the correct knowledge of distances. The facts contained in obs. 82, II, indicate the same; if Jacqueline holds out her hands in the direction of objects 0.50-3 meters from her, or even in the direction of the moon, it is because she is little aware of the obstacles which separate her from them. True, Stern has differentiated movements of desire (merely outstretching the arms) from those of prehension (joining arms and hands), but all the intermediates exist between them. It is impossible to state that the contrast between near space and distant space is immediately apparent to the child as being related to distance or to depth. It is, rather, for him a practical distinction, near space being that of objects of normal size and shape on which prehension has already been brought to bear, and distant space that of diminished or distorted objects, situated in a context in which secondary circular reactions and "procedures for making an interesting spectacle last" have shown themselves to be immediately fruitful.

This does not mean, however, that all externality is absent from space at this stage; on the contrary. But it is constructed gradually through subjective groups which are superimposed on practical groups. To understand this, one may compare the "distant space" of the child at this stage, that is, space beyond the field of prehension, with the celestial space of the uninformed adult or of immediate perception. The sky seems to us a big spherical or elliptical cover on whose surface move images without depth which alternately interpenetrate and detach themselves: sun and moon, clouds, the stars as well as the blue, black, or gray spots which fill the interstices. It is only through patient observations relating the movements of these images and the way they mask each other, that we arrive at the kind of elaborating subjective groups which satisfied mankind until the constitution of objective groups was made possible by the Copernican image of the earth and of the solar system.[7] At first, with regard to immediate perception, there exist neither conscious groups nor permanent solids (the celestial bodies seem to be reabsorbed in each other and not to hide behind one another), nor even depth; there is only accommodation of eyes, head, and body which enables us to follow the movement of some cloud or of the moon, or to perceive a faint star, but the practical groups which we thus utilize are not yet extended into any subjective group.

Let us suppose that during the first two stages, until the prehension of visual objectives, the child's whole space considered from the point of view of distances is analogous to the celestial space of immediate perception which we have just described: a fluid mass without depth (although the eye accommodates to various distances), traversed by images which interpenetrate or become detached without laws and alternately separate and reunite. In this initial state a certain number of practical groups intervene in relation to the movements the child executes in order to follow or rediscover interesting images, but neither objective nor even subjective groups yet exist. With the coordination of prehension and sight (third stage), on the other hand, things change; the movements of the hand give the child the opportunity to make actual experiments with depth and then the subjective groups involving awareness of that depth are superimposed on simple practical groups. Thereafter space, hitherto not externalized, becomes dissociated into two zones, "near space" accessible to the construction of subjective groups related to depth, and "distant space" which inherits all the remnants of the space of the first stages (absence of planes of depth and of subjective groups).

How, then, can we form an image of this space of the third stage? To resume our comparison, distant space remains analogous to the sky in immediate perception, whereas near space is comparable to our perception of the terrestrial environment in which planes of depth are regulated by the action. But here the sky must be envisaged as closely enveloping the subject and re-

[7] See Conclusions, §3.

ceding very gradually. Before the prehension of visual objects the child is in the center of a sort of moving and colored sphere, whose images imprison him without his having any hold on them other than by making them reappear by movements of head and eyes. Then when he begins to grasp what he sees the sphere expands little by little and the objects grasped are regulated in depth in relation to the body itself; distant space merely appears then as a kind of neutral zone in which prehension is not yet ventured, while near space is the realm of objects to be grasped. Doubtless it is only toward the end of this stage—after the establishment of planes of depth makes it possible to adjust objects in near space in relation to prehension—that distant space really appears distant, that is, a background in which relative distances remain undiscernible.

Of this distant space we have nothing to say except that it is identical to space in general in the first two stages before the prehension of visual objects. As to near space, let us see how prehension makes it possible to arrange this in subjective groups in regard to depth. The essential advantage of coordination between sight and prehension is thus constituted by the acquisition of concepts of "in front" and "in back." Take, for example, the child (obs. 82, III, and 84, III) who tries to reach an object several centimeters from his face; he joins his hands either too near or too far and so sees the object pass sometimes behind, sometimes in front of his hands. Surely such groping must be at first purely motor and kinesthetic, but sooner or later it imposes on sight itself the concepts at issue. For instance when at 0;4 (19) Laurent (*O.I.*, obs. 103) makes the hanging rattles swing by striking them, he well knows when his hand pushes or strikes them "from the front" and consequently when they are "in back." The perception of movements of the object combined with perception of the hand which operates thus constitutes a group of displacements involving depth. Moreover repetition of these experiments will gradually give the child the opportunity to estimate the distances of objects in near space. But are the subjective groups thus formed immediately capable of being extended into objective groups? We do not believe so, for the reasons which follow.

In the first place, when the child simultaneously perceives his hand and the object, he still knows nothing of himself but this hand and he is unaware of himself as visual subject. True, he begins to approach objects leaving his field of prehension (obs. 81, III, and 83, III), but he is aware only of the internal and kinesthetic aspect of this displacement of his body; the proof is that he sometimes believes he has achieved his purpose even though he has made the effort without displacing himself (obs. 82, IV).

In the second place, if the movements of the hand around the object occasion a discovery of the elementary concepts of in front and in back, this discovery does not go very far and is not enough to constitute the idea of object-screen completely masking the object. We have seen in connection with the object (Chap. I, §2) to what extent the behavior patterns of this stage related to screens (obs. 26-27) remain rudimentary and incapable of being extended in objective groups. The child does not yet have the concept of objects placed behind others.

Finally and most important, the evaluation of distances does not forthwith produce the concept of the position of objects relative to each other or the arrangement of planes of depth. Let us recall in this connection that at least three conditions are essential to the adult perception of depth: the number of objects interposed between the perceived object and the subject (a mountain seems farther away if there is a series of hills between it and us), the superposition of objects and the different speeds of displacements which we observe by moving the head or the whole body (displacements which enable us to evaluate the parallax of distant objects). None of these conditions is as yet realized; the only thing known by the child at this stage is the distance of objects in near space in relation to his body, and he does not locate himself bodily among the objects and thus estimate the relative distances between them. True, neither do we perceive immediately the distance between objects and ourselves: "The only thing we know directly," says Poincaré, "is the relative position of objects in relation to our body," [8] for "to localize an object merely means to imagine the movements which must be made in order to reach it";[9] as to positions of objects in relation to each other, we infer them from these first data. But we

[8] H. Poincaré, *La Valeur de la science* (Paris: Flammarion), p. 79.
[9] *Ibid.*, p. 80.

infer them from groups of displacements in which we place our own movements; now that is precisely what the child cannot do in the stage we are examining. The child learns how to grasp, hence to localize, objects in relation to himself, but he has no definite concept of the position of objects in relation to one another: in the next stage he will still look for objects in two places at once or will look for them in their old place without taking note of their sequential positions. Such groups are necessary in order that the data of immediate perception may be understood: the number of objects separating the subject from the perceived object, the superposition of these objects, and their relative movements when the subject is displaced. Such data remain bereft of meaning for anyone who does not locate himself among the groups of displacements and who does not correct perceived displacements by displacements accurately imagined.

In conclusion, if, beginning with this stage, perception of distances involves the intervention of subjective groups it does not yet go so far as to constitute objective groups.

This leads us to examine a final question, which we shall not be able to resolve until the next stage, that is, in retrospect: at the third stage, does the child have the concept that perceived objects have *permanent form and dimensions?* The whole elaboration of object concept and that of groups of displacements converge on this point. It is noteworthy that the object's permanence is constituted only through an objective group of displacements; but, inversely, this permanence is necessary for the construction of the groups. Therein is a "genetic circle" as J. M. Baldwin would say, so that all the questions hitherto under discussion are definitively summarized in those we now raise.

But except with regard to the rotation we have already studied (obs. 78 and 79), it is unfortunately extremely difficult to decide the question experimentally during the present stage. What we do know, through H. Frank's excellent studies, is that as early as 0;11, that is, during the next stage, the concept of constant size is acquired. Observation reveals, moreover, that during the fourth stage the child undertakes by himself many experiments on the apparent and constant dimensions of objects. These facts are in full agreement with what we know from experimentation relating to hidden objects. Since it is during the fourth stage that the child begins to search for things behind screens and thus to constitute the simplest groups of objective displacements, it is natural that at this same time he should begin to attribute constant form and dimensions to objects themselves, and that permanence of the size and form of solid bodies should not exist at all throughout the present stage.

On examination of all the "subjective groups" described hitherto, nothing indicates the presence of the concept of the object of constant shape and dimensions, and everything substantiates the contrary hypothesis. We have not yet been able to establish the existence of any objective group during this stage; such an interpretation of the facts, if accurate, entails the conclusion that the child is still ignorant of the permanence of the object's spatial qualities. For instance, when he turns in all directions, or in a special direction, the things he holds in his hands (obs. 76 and 77 and 21-25), the child does not seem to explore their shape for its own sake, as he will do later in the tertiary circular reactions or experiments in order to see. True, when he grasps a part in order to have the whole (see Chap. I, obs. 21-25), he seems to reconstruct the object's total form and thus to consider it as permanent; but it is one thing to try to complete a whole from a directly visible fraction and quite another to attribute constant spatial qualities to that whole. Proof of this is the absence of any search connected with the reverse side of objects (obs. 78 and 79); such a fact in itself reveals how far removed the child is, at this stage, from attributing a constant form to the object. Moreover, all that we have seen concerning perception in depth can be interpreted without belief in the permanence of dimensions and even seems to indicate the absence of that belief. If it is not because of a correct evaluation of distances that the child fails to reach for objects in distant space, but because of alterations of these objects themselves, this is because shapes and dimensions are not considered constant.

But above all, as Stern puts it very well,[10] it is impossible to see by what procedures the child would acquire the concept of the permanence of the object's spatial qualities before knowing how to displace himself and, let us add, before locating himself in objective groups of displacements. Thereafter Stern states that, if

[10] *Psychol. d. früh. Kindheit* (4th ed.; 1927), pp. 96-98.

the permanence of dimensions is acquired with regard to near objects which can be directly grasped, it remains doubtful at that age as soon as distant objects are involved. In this connection Stern cites an important observation made on Günther at 0;7 in the course of which the child, being hungry, cried loudly for a tiny bottle, a toy belonging to his sister, which he took for a bottle of normal dimensions.

In conclusion, all the facts discussed in connection with this stage seem to show that though the child has grown capable of constructing subjective groups he remains unable to perceive or imagine objective groups.

The subjective group is the perception of an aggregate of movements which return to their point of departure, but only in so far as this aggregate remains related to the action and is not located among larger aggregates that would include the subject himself as an element and would coordinate displacements from the point of view of objects. The subjective group is therefore that of apparent movements in which the five- to six-year-old child still believes when he says that the moon is following him, in contradistinction to objective groups in which the subject will locate his own movements in relation to the real movements of the object. During the third stage the subjective group is superimposed on the practical group wherever the child perceives that his action can introduce or rediscover a repetition in the images perceived: turning the object over, subjecting it to circular reactions, rediscovering the object on different planes of depth, etc.

The subjective group thus extends the practical group and remains midway between the latter and the objective group. The practical group being formed by a reversibility in the child's acts, although neither this reversibility nor its results is perceived or imagined, it is apparent that the subjective group extends the practical group in a direct line; the only added element is a perception of the group as such, but the group does not yet concern the interrelations of objects. On the other hand, this perception heralds the objective group but does not join it since it remains related to the activity itself. We have, in effect, considered certain conditions as necessary to the establishment of objective groups: the existence of substantial objects, the differentiation of external displacements and the movements themselves, and the externalization of spatial relations so that the subject is capable of locating himself "in" space. But none of these three conditions is as yet entirely fulfilled. Concerning the third, the child discovers during the present stage the distance of objects and their arrangement in depth in relation to his body. But thus to locate his body in the center of space, is it enough to locate it "in" a motionless space, independent of himself? Obviously not: it is solely his hand that the child localizes in space and not his entire body, to the extent that his hand is capable of displacements and above all to the extent that it imposes a particular perspective on his glance and his vision of things. With regard to the second condition, will the child know how to differentiate his own movements from external movements and apparent movements from real ones? It is likely that such distinctions, easy with respect to the hand, are still impossible for the child with respect to movements of his head and eyes.[11] Furthermore, not yet noting displacements that are not directly perceived and not knowing how to search for vanished objects, the child does not yet know how to construct a system of real movements capable of correcting appearances and of furnishing a criterion of differentiation between his own movements and those of things themselves. Finally, with regard to the permanence of objects, we have seen (Chap. I, §2) how, during the third stage, it remained related solely to action.

In short if, during this third stage, space begins to be objectified to the extent that it is externalized, it is not yet in any way an immobile environment in which the body evolves, an environment presupposed by the objective group of displacements constitutive of geometric space. If the child locates objects in relation to his body and as a function of his acts of prehension, he does not locate them in relation to each other and does not postulate their permanence outside his field of action. He has, therefore, no criterion at his disposal for differentiating the displacements of his own body from those of external bodies. Space at this stage is always imbued with a sort of solipsism or at least egocentrism, but an egocentrism unaware of itself.

[11] See below, obs. 88-91.

§ 3. THE FOURTH STAGE: THE TRANSITION FROM SUBJECTIVE TO
OBJECTIVE GROUPS AND THE DISCOVERY OF REVERSIBLE
OPERATIONS

The kind of behavior pattern whose influence dominates the whole of the preceding stage is the secondary circular reaction. Compared to the primary reactions, this behavior marks essential progress: it involves a beginning of setting things into relation with one another and no longer only a utilization of reality as a function of the activities of the body. It therefore leads the child to perceive certain groups in the midst of external reality and thus to transcend the level of purely practical groups. But the relations he establishes among things remain global and primarily active, so that the groups perceived by the child are regulated from the point of view of the subject and not yet from the point of view of objects. These we have called subjective groups.

In contrast, the type of behavior pattern which is the starting point for the manifestations of the fourth stage is the application of familiar means to new situations. We will recall that this behavior consists not in constructing new isolated schemata or in constructing them otherwise than by primary and secondary circular reaction, but in applying and intercombining them in a new way. Up to now the primary or secondary schemata formed new global totalities each of which was applied as a unit in the presence of suitable objects and was generalized to the extent that new objects could be directly merged with the old ones. From now on, however, the child tries to accommodate certain of these same schemata to situations different from those in which they arose. In other words, confronted by new problems, he tries to utilize the schemata already acquired, either by adjusting them separately to given circumstances or by subordinating them to each other in a complex act. Whence two essential consequences. One is that accommodation to things becomes precise and thus the objective conditions of reality begin to surpass the merely active relations. The other is that the schemata adapt to each other and cease to function separately in the capacity of global units. From the point of view which interests us here, that of the formation of the spatial field, these two consequences both signify that relationships are being woven among the things themselves, whereas hitherto such relations were wrapped up in those of the totality established by the action. Instead of merely reproducing successful gestures without understanding how, the child now begins to busy himself with contacts and to intercombine the resulting displacements of objects. When, for instance, the subject removes the material obstacles interposed between himself and his objective, or when he uses someone else's hand in order to act upon things, he intercoordinates not only the schemata separated up to then but the objects themselves, and thus opens the way to the elaboration of groups much more precise than before. True, these groups remain limited to the case of reversible displacements, but even within these limits they attain objectivity.

Hence it is this beginning of creating relationships among objects as such which explains the main characteristics of space of the fourth stage: the discovery of reversible operations, of the constant size of solids, of the perspective of relations of depth, and, above all, of the permanence of the object masked by a screen.

In regard to objects the major innovation of this stage (see Chap. I, §3) is that the child begins to search for moving objects behind a screen even when they have completely disappeared from the visual field, without extending a single movement of prehension already made. Let us note first that this behavior pattern, some aspects of which we have studied by means of experiments designed to evidence the object's permanence, gives rise to spontaneous manifestations on the child's part. At 10 or 12 months of age, the child spontaneously hides toys to find them again and thus forms some very characteristic groups of displacements.

OBS. 85. At 0;11 (3) Lucienne hides her feet under a coverlet, then raises the coverlet, looks at them, hides them again, etc.

Same observation at 0;11 (15) with a rattle which she slips under a rug to bring it out and put it under again endlessly.

Same observations on Jacqueline between 0;11 and 1;0.

Here is a well-defined group of displacements. After leaving the child's hand the object is placed under a screen and found again, after displacement of the latter, by means of an operation like the first one. Hence there is reversibility of operation, that is, formation of an elementary group. Is such a group objective or still subjective? Considered by itself, it is objective: the subject's hand and the displacements of that hand constitute elements of the group properly placed in relation to the other elements, and the relationship of the object and the object-screen are completely understood. Moreover, when instead of letting the child act one experiments on him, and the object passes successively from the child's hand into that of the observer, from the observer's hand to under the screen, and from there back into the child's hand, one witnesses the elaboration of objective groups psychologically more complex and yet perfectly correct. It can therefore be asserted that the child in this way succeeds for the first time in forming an objective group of displacements. It is interesting to note that this progress is exactly correlative to that observed with regard to the formation of object concept. It is because of the substantial permanence beginning to be conferred on the object that such groups are elaborated, and it is because of their elaboration that this beginning of permanence is constituted.

But if the two symmetrical movements of hiding an object and recovering it form an objective group, it is noteworthy that this group remains elementary;[12] as yet it is only a question of a reversible operation and not of a system of three self-enclosing displacements. But if from the psychological point of view this consciousness of reversibility appears as progress toward the system in question, it does not lead to it directly. If, as we recall (see Chap. I, §3), the object is put in two sequential positions, this is sufficient to make the child's behavior less facile; instead of searching for the object in the second position, that is, where he saw it placed the last time, he searches for it in its first position without taking the last displacements into account. As we have seen in connection with objects, this reaction can be typical (the child immediately returns to position A after having seen the object disappear in B) or residual (the child searches first in B,

[12] Geometrically speaking, that is why it is already a group, although three operations are necessary for the existence of any structure of this kind; it can be said that the product of the two operations of hiding and rediscovering is equal, in this particular case, to the "identical" operation (holding the object in the hands).

then, if he does not find it at once, he returns to A), but it lasts one or two months. Concerning the structure of groups of displacements, what can be concluded from this except that the objective group discovered by the child still retains a subjective quality, or that the group in question, the group of reversible operations, remains midway between the subjective type and the objective type?

If we have recourse to our three habitual criteria this intermediate situation cannot be in doubt. In the first place, the substantial permanence of the object is almost acquired, since the child searches for his toy under a screen even if no movement of prehension or accommodation had been delineated at the moment of its disappearance. But such permanence still remains linked to the action itself, since the object in the second position is still sought where the child found it previously. In the second place, the displacements of the object are henceforth dissociated from those of the subject, since the object exists even when it is not directly perceived. But the law of these displacements still conserves some subjectivity, since the object is sought only where the child has previously succeeded in taking possession of it. Finally, space is externalized (hidden objects being henceforth endowed with substantial existence) to the extent that the action itself must be conceived by the subject as inserting itself into a ready-made world and no longer as continually engendering that world. But nothing proves that the subject already places himself as an object among other objects and thus conceives of his spatial perspective as being relative to his own position and to his displacements as a whole, precisely because he does not yet take account of either the sequence of perceived displacements of objects or *a fortiori* of the displacements not directly visible. For all these reasons it seems clear to us that the typical group of this stage remains midway between the subjective group and the objective group.

To clarify this situation let us first try to describe the other acquisitions of this stage; then we shall see what is lacking in the whole of these behavior patterns for the formation of the geometric space defining groups that are objective and purely representative.

The second acquisition characteristic of this stage seems to be constancy of shapes and dimensions. H. Frank [13] was able to train a child of 0;11 to choose with regularity the larger of two boxes; even when that box seemed the smaller from the point of view of immediate perception, that is, of the retinal image, the child was able to maintain his choice without error. The success of such a test at 0;11 shows what the child must be capable of in his current perceptions. Observation confirms that this is a question of a recent acquisition belonging to this stage.

OBS. 86. Lucienne, at 0;10 (7) and the days following, slowly brings her face close to objects she holds (rattles, dolls, etc.) until her nose is pressed against them. Then she moves away from them, looking at them very attentively, and begins over and over again.

At 0;10 (12) she does the same, bringing close to her and moving slowly away with her hand a chick, a stick, a rattle, etc.

OBS. 87. As early as 0;9 (6) Laurent, during the exploration of new objects, seems to study the object's shape as a function of its position. He slowly displaces in space the toys he is holding, either perpendicularly to his glance or in depth. In the latter case I cannot manage to decide whether the movements imparted to the object by the child are systematic or not. But even though unintentional at first, they seem to give rise to deliberate repetitions.

At 0;10 (2) he slowly displaces a plush cat in front of him or above him. The cat has been familiar to him for several days. Here again I believe I distinguish among his movements several trajectories in depth.

At 0;10 (11) he moves away and brings close to himself a box of matches while looking at it as though it were an entirely new object, whereas he knows it well. This time there is surely involved a systematic study of the apparent shape of the displaced object.

At 0;10 (12) he systematically displaces a notebook and carries it to and from his eyes. Sometimes it is the object itself he moves thus, sometimes his own face.

At 0;11 (0) he does the same with a box, etc.

These behavior patterns which also belong to the group of reversible operations (moving forward and backward) are easy to interpret: the child is studying (by exploration, then by tertiary circular reaction) this fundamental fact, that an object whose tactile dimensions are constant varies in visual shape

[13] H. Frank, *Psychol. Forschung*, VII (1925), 137-145.

and size according to whether it is moved toward or away from his face. True, another interpretation could be proposed: it would not be at all absurd to state that the child, in moving away from and approaching the thing perceived, has the impression of really modifying it by his actions. But this interpretation, which would be very likely if such observations were made during the preceding stage, becomes implausible at the age of about 10 months. On the one hand, the child begins to know himself sufficiently well (he imitates, recently, facial movements) to understand that he is moving his face as he approaches the object and that these are changes of position and not changes of state. Moreover, these movements made by the child to study shapes and sizes as a function of distance constitute only a particular case among other analogous activities. We shall see that at this stage the child studies perspectives in the same way and that it is difficult to interpret his experiments in this respect as other than experiments in solid geometry. It can therefore be said that in contrast to the behavior patterns of the third stage, the child at the present stage acquires the concept of constancy of the size of objects, at least in the realm of near space. That does not, of course, mean that he immediately generalizes this schema to apply to everything; on the contrary, we shall see that through the fifth stage the errors remain frequent with respect to distant space.

It is noteworthy, too, in connection with obs. 86 and 87, that the child seems to equate displacements of his face toward the object with those of the object toward his face. But it would be premature to conclude that the subject knows himself as an object and in general locates his own displacements in a common and motionless space; we shall soon see proof of the opposite. On the other hand, from the existence of such behavior patterns we may conjecture that the child has discovered the possibility of modifying his view of things by giving his head certain reversible movements. This leads us to a third point: the concept of perspective.

The third acquisition of the stage seems to be the discovery of *perspective* or *changes in shape resulting from different positions of the head*. But one must be very prudent in interpreting such behavior patterns and must not attribute either too much or too little to the child. Too much must not be attributed to him because obviously the child at this stage remains incapable of locating himself, as a body considered as a totality, in a motionless space in which he would displace himself. He is therefore unable to conceive of his own perspective as relative to the position he occupies; his discovery consists merely in observing that changes in the shape and position of objects correspond to the displacements of his head (and not of his whole body). But this is already a great deal, and the importance of such an observation should not be underestimated. If one analyzes the attempts related to perspective which belong to this stage they appear to be quite different from analogous attempts observable during the preceding stage. During the third stage the child often shakes his head in order to study the results of the action on the surrounding visual images. But this is a matter of very rapid movements in which the child certainly does not distinguish what comes from himself and what pertains to the displacements of external objects. During the present stage, on the contrary (and doubtless from the end of the preceding one, as it is apparent that the various acquisitions of a stage are not exactly contemporary!), the child systematically and slowly moves his head as if trying to analyze the effect of his own movements in relation to the shape of things. In other words, it is again a question of a formation of the permanent shape of objects.

Let us cite some examples, beginning each time by contrasting the acts of this fourth stage with those of the third (we have not spoken of this question in connection with the earlier stage in order to simplify the account and to condense the whole discussion here).

OBS. 88. From 0;2 (21), that is, the second stage, Laurent begins to look behind him when he is lying down. He takes great pleasure in this behavior (*O.I.*, obs. 36). But it is apparent that at this age he does not distinguish at all, in such an experience, between changes of position and changes of state. In looking upside down he witnesses a transformation of the world which he cannot know is due to his own perspective.

At 0;3 (23), that is, at the beginning of the third stage (he has known how to grasp what he sees since the beginning of the month), Laurent shakes his head sideways in front of a hanging rattle. He shakes it harder and harder, then seizes the string to shake the rattle itself. One may ask whether in shaking his head Laurent was merely trying to transform the image of the rattle or to act upon the rattle itself. The context of this observation seems to indicate that the second solution is the right one; the act of shaking the head is directly extended in the action of pulling the string, as though there were, for Laurent, two equivalent procedures, the first sufficing to shake the rattle but not to make it sound. In other words, it does not seem that Laurent distinguishes the rattle itself from the view he has of it according to his own perspective.

From 0;5 (15) he shakes his head sideways much more often and more systematically and with much greater rapidity and motor skill; he does it while looking at his bassinet hood, etc. At 0;6 (0) he does this in an unfamiliar room while looking at the furniture, etc., at 0;6 (1) in an automobile while watching the roof, the net, etc.

It is only at 0;8 (26) that I observe the reaction of the fourth stage; he is in his bassinet and leans to the side in order to look at the corner of the room. He remains motionless for a few seconds, then straightens up very slowly. At 0;8 (27) he does the same in his hammock, pausing to lean over and from that position to examine the chandelier, a big table, etc.

On the following days the behavior becomes increasingly frequent, but he does not yet seem to vary the perspectives; Laurent merely leans to the right and the left and remains motionless while looking at an object.

At 0;9 (16), on the other hand, it seems to me that Laurent leans alternately to left and right but with a pause between the two positions. This reaction becomes increasingly frequent during the following weeks.

OBS. 89. Similarly between 0;4 and 0;8 Lucienne has made rapid lateral movements of the head when confronted by various objects: hanging rattles, my hand, my face, etc. At 0;7 (30) she still sometimes bursts out laughing when making this gesture, which clearly shows that this is still a secondary "procedure."

From 0;9 (8) on the other hand, she manifests a clearly different reaction; she looks at the objects (hanging rattles, bassinet hood, etc.) bending her head slowly from side to side and studying in detail the effect produced. Same observation at 0;10 (7) and at 0;10 (12) in the presence of a plush duck and other toys.

OBS. 90. Jacqueline has presented during the third stage the same reactions as Lucienne and Laurent. At 0;9 (1), on the other hand, the reaction peculiar to the fourth stage begins. She is seated on my right arm and brings her head close to my shoulder caressingly. She lifts herself up and repeats this a number of times through motor pleasure (conquest of equilibrium). But doing this, she perceives the transformations of the image of the objects; she remains erect but bends her head left and right alternately while staring fixedly at a point in the room (the corner of a piece of furniture?).

A moment later she is seated, leaning against a sofa cushion. Same reaction: she turns her head in one direction and the other, then bends it left and right, very slowly, while looking in front of her.

OBS. 91. At 0;11 (23) Jacqueline is in her baby swing and perceives her foot through one of the two openings for the use of the legs. She looks at it with great interest and visible astonishment, then stops looking to lean over the edge and discover her foot from the outside. Afterward she returns to the opening and looks at the same foot from this perspective. She alternates thus five or six times between the two points of view.

In reading these observations it seems that an essential difference contrasts the reaction of this stage with that of the preceding stages: the presenting groups, from being subjective or even purely practical, tend to become objective. But to understand this transformation two questions must be singled out: first, in shaking his head, does the child have the impression of truly acting upon the objects perceived or merely of seeing them from another angle, and, in the second place, in such a phenomenon does the child distinguish between his own movements and those of the things as such?

Concerning the first question, it seems difficult not to concede that until the reaction of the fourth stage (that is, the slow reaction during which the child studies the result of his gesture) the subject has the impression that by shaking his head he really makes things move. When, at 0;3 (23), Laurent pulls the string of a rattle just after having shaken the image, so to speak, of this same rattle by shaking his head in front of it, it is undeniable that his sole interest is to make the object move. Moreover, the rapid lateral head movement of the three children betwen 0;5 and 0;8 has been employed so often as a procedure to make an interesting spectacle last (cf. *O.I.*, obs. 117 and 118) that one cannot conceive of how it could be devoid of any idea of efficacy in the examples cited in obs. 88-91. For the rest, the fact that this concerns a rapid movement whose rapidity seems to be regulated by the child (as when the child pulls a string harder and harder in order to augment the effect obtained) reveals sufficiently that a causal procedure is involved and not an experiment in simple solid geometry. On the contrary, the slow reaction manifested by Laurent at 0;8 (26), by Lucienne at 0;9 (8), and by Jacqueline at 0;9 (1) gives the impression not of an effort by the subject to act upon things but of an interest related to the properties of the things themselves. In other words, the difference between the rapid reaction of the third stage and the slow reaction of the fourth is the same as that between secondary circular reactions and explorations (not to speak of tertiary circular reactions); the former, while attesting to an interest in things and their relations, tend merely to reproduce the results obtained by means of those things, whereas the second tend to explore things for their own sake and to understand new properties in them. Therefore the first are essentially actions upon the object, whereas the second constitute, rather, research or experiments. So also, the slow reaction of which we now speak comprises an attempt to understand, much more than an effort of production. If such is the case, it is permissible to suppose that when the child moves his head he no longer has the illusion of putting things in motion and that he simply tries to analyze their various aspects. In short, the reaction of the fourth stage compared to that of the third can be defined as an effort to grasp the different shapes of things and no longer as an effort to act upon them. That is most important, since this analysis of the apparent forms of the object results in the construction of its permanent form.

But what conclusion can be reached from this in respect to the second question: does the child distinguish between his own movements and those of the thing itself? Two possibilities are to be observed here: when the child moves his head either he is merely conscious of a muscular effort without understanding that a displacement in space corresponds to that effort, or else he is aware of an actual displacement of his own head. Let us note that to each of these two attitudes concerning the object there is a corresponding attitude concerning the subject. When the sub-

ject has the impression of moving the object by his own movements, either he imagines his movements as real displacements
(as is the case of the child who thinks he pushes forward the
moon or the mountains as he walks), or else he is aware only of
his kinesthetic displacements without realizing that he changes
his position. Moreover, when he has the impression of studying the object's various aspects, either he knows he changes
his position or he knows nothing of it. What do obs. 88-91 say
about this? In the rapid reactions of the third stage nothing
entitles us to believe that the child is conscious of his own displacement since he knows nothing about his own face. By contrast, after the slow reactions of 0;9 to 0;10 it is very likely that
the child discovers his own displacements of the head; when in
obs. 90, for example, Jacqueline notices at 0;9 (1) the changes
in the shape of objects when she leans over and straightens up,
she can notice only these changes in position; *a fortiori*, in obs.
91, when, at 0;11 Jacqueline looks at her foot from two points of
view sequentially, she performs movements sufficiently complex
to cause awareness of them as displacements.

In conclusion, it seems that the slow reactions of the fourth
stage described in obs. 88-91 constitute objective groups of displacements. Moving the head laterally in front of an immobile
object so as to examine its various perspectives, the child is at
once aware of his own displacements and of the immobility of
the object; thereafter the movements he makes in relation to the
object are arranged in a completely objective group. During the
third stage, on the other hand, the same group is accompanied
by a dual illusion, that of the movements and alterations of the
object conceived as real and doubtless that of the subject's relative immobility; also, the group of the third stage remains subjective.

But if the groups of the fourth stage, constituted by the slow
reactions just described, are thus of an objective kind, nevertheless they do not transcend the level of merely reversible operations. The subject passes alternately from G to D and from D
to G by a lateral movement of the head and finds in each position a particular aspect of the object, but he does not yet arrange
three movements among them. It is therefore impossible as yet
to speak of objective groups in the full meaning of the term,

particularly as awareness of lateral movements of the head does not yet involve awareness either of advance and recoil or *a fortiori* that of body movements (if both are to be considered as displacements in space and not only as muscular efforts).

The preceding observations relating to the search for different aspects of the object lead us to the study of groups obtained by *rotations* which are connected with acts of analogous purpose. We recall that during the third stage the child succeeds in turning objects over, but either he does it in order to rediscover a special side which he perceives during the rotation, or else he turns it over in order to turn it over, without awareness of the group thus obtained; the rotation therefore remains relative to the subject and does not yet constitute an "objective" group. During the fourth stage, on the contrary, the child learns to turn things over in themselves and thus acquires the concept of the "reverse" side of the object and consequently of its constant shape.

Here are some examples.

OBS. 92. At 0;8 (6) Laurent still reacts toward his bottle in the manner described in obs. 78. When I present the bottle very obliquely, the wrong end foremost, he does not try to turn the nipple backward (although it is slightly visible). In contrast, when I withdraw the object 30 centimeters, thus permitting him to compare the two ends, and when I slowly replace it in its former position, he tries twice in succession to see the nipple. But this phenomenon is only an episode and is not reproduced at 0;8 (15) or at 0;8 (24).

On the other hand, at 0;9 (9) when I present his bottle to him upside down, he grasps it immediately and it seems to me that he turns it over intentionally. Unfortunately the thing has happened too quickly to permit a positive interpretation; as soon as the bottle is displaced Laurent perceives the nipple and is guided by it in reversing the object, which he already knew how to do during the third stage. But the very rapidity of the reaction attests an intentional rotation.

The next day, at 0;9 (10), no doubt remains. I present to Laurent his full bottle at meal time, but upside down so that he cannot see the "good" end. Laurent no longer tries to suck the wrong end, as before; he does not abandon all attempts, as he sometimes did, while crying or struggling; he immediately displaces the wrong end with a quick stroke of the hand, while *looking beforehand* in the direction of the nipple. He therefore obviously knows that the extremity he seeks is at the reverse end of the object.

At 0;9 (17) same reaction. Laurent holds the empty bottle wrong end foremost: he immediately looks for the nipple while with his other hand he displaces the bottle and thereby brings the right end into his visual field. Then he easily turns the object over.

At 0;9 (21), as soon as I present the bottle to him upside down he leans sideways in order to see the nipple at the other end. He behaves as if confronted by an object masked by a screen, behavior typical of the present stage. Objective rotation has therefore been acquired as well as the concept of the reverse side of the object.

OBS. 93. Here are some more examples of Laurent's behavior which confirm the foregoing interpretation.

At 0;9 (17) Laurent holds in his right hand a box of matches one of whose sides is yellow and the other blue. Instead of turning it over haphazardly, as at 0;6 (0) by transferring it from one hand to the other (see obs. 79), he turns it over five or six times without changing hands and examines it very closely from both sides (by supination and pronation). His attention is continuous until the end; his mouth is open and his lips protrude. It is definitely, therefore, an intentional rotation with exploration of the object and search for the reverse side, and no longer a secondary reaction as at 0;6 (0).

Likewise at 0;9 (26) in exploring a bath thermometer he discovers that the handle is pleasant to suck, and when I present the object to him by the other end he immediately turns it over intentionally to find the handle again. Hence this behavior pattern combines in itself the foregoing one and that of the bottle: exploration has led to intentional rotation and to the concept of the reverse side of the object.

At 0;10 (2) Laurent handles a tobacco tamper; he turns it over continuously in order to touch one of its ends, decorated with a border which amuses him. As soon as he has touched the end with the border he looks at the other end and begins over again.

At 0;10 (3) he turns over a round metal box in the same way in order to rediscover one of the two surfaces, decorated with a design. As soon as he has seen it he looks for the other surface, then returns to the first one.

At 0;10 (11) he alternately examines the green back and yellow belly of a little celluloid frog (with outstretched legs, in other words, of a flat and not a squat shape). He turns it over very systematically.

Subsequently, in the next stages, this behavior pattern develops increasingly. I note at 1;0 (8) that Laurent turns over a pocket mirror very well and finds the correct side of it. But the group becomes complicated when applied to objects with several surfaces and thus ceases to consist in a system of merely reversible operations.

OBS. 93a. Without having systematically studied similar reversals with respect to Lucienne I have observed in her the following spontaneous behavior patterns which are doubtless related to them. From 0;10 (26), as soon as she is in possession of a chain, a string, etc., she winds it around her thumb or hand. She does this with both hands alternately and looks at the result; she holds the string in one hand and winds the other around, making a spool. At 0;11 (30) she rolls my watch chain around her knee.

It is impossible to compare these behavior patterns to the corresponding acts of the third stage without being struck by the progress which marks their evolution. On the one hand, instead of turning objects over only by chance or when the desired part is already visible, the child is thereafter capable of intentionally giving them a complete rotation. From being subjective because related to the subject's perspective, the group therefore becomes objective because related to the moving object itself. On the other hand, and in correlation with this first acquisition, the moving object acquires the character of a permanent three-dimensional object: henceforth it is endowed with an invisible reverse side which completes intellectually the immediate data of perception by placing them in a constant and consequently intelligible "shape." Thus we rediscover Frank's conclusions related to the constancy of shapes and dimensions.

But however positive this progress may be, the "group" thus discovered remains reducible to a mere system of reversible operations. It is only when the child holds the object in his hands that he is capable of reversing it. As we shall see later, the child at this stage does not yet know how to turn objects over in relation to each other.

With regard to perception of *movements of translations* in the plane which we have discussed in connection with the last stages, it is easy, given the various acquisitions just described, to understand how it progresses during the present stage. On the one hand, since the subject is better aware of himself as a body located in space (he is aware of certain movements of his head and trunk and no longer only of those of his hands), and since he attributes more permanence to external objects, he will be better able to distinguish changes of position from changes of state. Thus a movement of translation perpendicular to his glance will appear to him as being the displacement of a body in relation to himself and he will be aware of displacing himself in order to be able to follow it. This does not mean that he yet knows how to localize the object when its sequential displacements need to be arranged in time, but it does mean that the directly perceived displacements are apprehended in the form of simple objective groups and no longer only in the form of subjective groups.

The first statement to be made in this connection is that during this stage the child begins spontaneously to impart to objects movements of translation, horizontal and in depth, in order to study the latter. Just as he hides objects in order to find them again, moves them away from him and toward him in order to examine their apparent transformations, so also does he displace them simply to study their movement.

Let us first cite some examples before indicating how they differ from the corresponding acts of the preceding stage and the following one.

OBS. 94. Until about 0;9 I have not observed in Laurent intentional displacements of objects designed to study their movements. To be sure, throughout the third stage he has sometimes, when examining new or familiar objects, passed and repassed them from one hand to the other, and on this occasion has lengthened their trajectory by separating his hands—see obs. 79, at 0;6 (15), the example of the pipe; but this is simply motor pleasure and not yet exploration of the object as such.

On the other hand, from 0;8 (29), that is, from the beginning of explorations (see *O.I.*, obs. 137), I observe that he displaces a notebook very slowly before his eyes, as though he were studying its movement. At 0;9 (6) no doubt remains: when confronted by a series of new objects (a man doll, animals, a case for a box of matches, etc.) he sometimes, in the course of his explorations, displaces them slowly at eye level with no other concern than to watch them in motion or to follow their trajectory. At 0;9 (30) I find the same reaction toward a new toy.

Between 0;9 (10) and 0;10 (0) I also observe several times that Laurent displaces very familiar objects in the same way (his rattles, etc.), interrupting habitual circular reactions.

Let us recall that from 0;7 (28), in the course of the "application of familiar schemata to new situations" (see *O.I.*, obs. 123), Laurent has known how to displace objects impeding his desires and that from 0;8 (7) he has known how to move another person's hand nearer to the objects on which he wishes it to act (see *O.I.*, obs. 128, and the present volume, obs. 144). Finally, it is noteworthy that the schemata related to the swinging of objects (*O.I.*, obs. 138) began with him at 0;8 (30).

OBS. 95. In correlation with those displacements which the subject spontaneously imparts to objects we should note the new manner in which the child at this stage follows movements of translation independent of himself.

We recall that during the third stage the child is capable of following rapid movements of translation but on condition that they merely extend movements of accommodation; once it has left the trajectory thus fixed in advance, the object is no longer sought or followed by the glance (see obs. 71-72). Whence the difficulty of marking the position of the vanished object (obs. 74-75). Henceforth the child whose eyes follow a rapid movement and who loses sight of the object searches for it whatever its trajectory may be and independently of the direction of the initial movement of accommodation.

This may first be noticed by observing the way in which the child obtains the object being displaced before him. Not only does Laurent react correctly, from about 0;8 (15), to all the tests in obs. 71-75, but from 0;9 his eyes follow the most complex movements. At 0;9 (16), for example, Laurent is on my lap during my lunch and attentively watches the spoon which goes from the soup plate to my mouth (he is seated facing the table and is therefore obliged to execute the most inconvenient movements in order to follow the object). I amuse myself by making the spoon describe the most varied trajectories; he always finds it. At 0;9 (20) and 0;9 (30) I displace before him, by hanging them on a string attached to a stick, various silent toys; he really searches for them and always finds them. The same applies even more strongly to movements of falling.

But the pertinent experiment is one that can be made by displacing objects in a straight line behind the child (cf. obs. 74). For instance,

at 0;9 (12) Laurent is in the garden, seated in a carriage and unable to see behind it because of the half-raised hood; nevertheless when
someone walks quietly from left to right or vice versa behind his
carriage, he follows the movement on his left with his eyes to the
point where he no longer sees anything, then turns abruptly to the
right to rediscover the moving object. At 0;9 (20) he is sitting in
his bed and I pass behind him various objects suspended on a stick;
he turns his head very accurately in order to see them.

I have also noted that from 0;9 (27), when Laurent is taken
from one room to another down a long hall, he looks alternately
before and behind him, as though to study the movement which
animates him.

These observations seem to leave no doubt concerning the
fact that the child henceforth distinguishes changes of position
from changes of state. During the first two stages of the development of space we have, on the contrary, shown that everything occurs as though this distinction had not yet been established by the child's consciousness. Regardless of the opinion of
H. Poincaré, the subject begins by confusing his own movements
with the movements of the object and from then on considers
the vanished or distant object as annihilated or actually altered.
During the third stage the situation remains intermediate between
the initial lack of differentiation and the present state. On the
one hand, the groups of displacements belonging to the third
stage remain subjective and the moving object is hence not conceived as being animated by an independent movement. On the
other hand, the object at this same stage is not yet endowed
with substantial permanence and remains capable of multiple
alterations (see in particular obs. 78 concerning the bottle's rotation). These two correlative reasons surely prevent the child
from clearly distinguishing changes of position from changes of
state. On the contrary, the whole of the behavior patterns of the
fourth stage, and in particular the present observations, attest to
the existence of a dissociation between these two types of
changes. On the one hand, the object of the fourth stage has
become permanent and constant in shape. On the other hand,
the child's searchings with regard to movements of rotation and
translation show that he considers moving objects capable of fol-

lowing autonomous trajectories independently of his own action. The objective group is thus constituted.

But let us remark that this group, like most of the groups of the present stage, remains reducible to simple reversible operations, at least with respect to the movements which the child spontaneously imparts to the object. When the child slowly displaces a moving object before him this is merely a matter of reciprocating motion. It is only during the fifth stage that the child places objects upon each other in a series of sequential displacements (see below, obs. 109 and 110). Furthermore, we recall that if one hides an object under a screen and then displaces it under a second screen, the child at this fourth stage searches for it under the first screen, thus attesting to the paucity of groups he is able to elaborate.

It is now fitting to describe the child's reactions to "interrupted prehension": these reactions are closely related to the preceding ones and lead to the analysis of depth.

We recall that during the third stage the child is able to follow the lost object with his hand, if the trajectory of the object follows the movement of prehension already outlined, or a simple movement of the forearm (see obs. 69 and 70); thus the child, having relinquished the object he was holding, confines himself to lowering his forearm to recover it without searching to the right or left in case of failure. It is as though the object were not conceived as an independent moving body with some sort of trajectory. On the contrary, from the fourth stage the child behaves in the event of interrupted prehension as we have seen him behave in accommodation to movements of translation visually perceived: he really searches with his hand for the vanished object.

OBS. 96. At 0;9 (2) and the following days, I give Laurent the following test. When his right hand is eclipsed from his view by some sort of screen (pillow, etc.), I take from him the object he is holding or I brush his fingers with an object and then make the object describe the most varied movements. But, inversely to what he did between 0;5 and 0;7, Laurent knows perfectly well how to explore the spatial field with his hand on all sides and particularly in depth. Thus he succeeds in finding the object every time.

These last remarks lead us to examine the behavior patterns of the fourth stage related to *depth*. All that we have seen hitherto concerning the groups of the present stage (in particular the examples of perspectives, of rotation, etc.) shows that the child achieves a series of important improvements with respect to arranging the various planes of space, including distant space, according to the third dimension.

We recall that during the third stage space manifests itself to the child as comprising two regions: one beyond the field of prehension and the other defining the field itself. If the near space of the third stage actually implies a certain perception of distances in relation to the body itself (since the child practices grasping visual objectives), this perception does not yet lead to any ordination properly so-called of the planes of depth nor to any determination of the distances separating objects from one another. With regard to the distant space of the third stage, this constitutes a sort of unique plane analogous to celestial space in our immediate perception, without perception of distances or still less any ordination of planes of depth.

The various acquisitions of the fourth stage transform this state of affairs. Concerning near space the progress of prehension (which toward the end of the third stage is generalized in such a way that the child tries to grasp anything whatever, at increasing distances in depth) insures a better evaluation of distances. This conquest of depth is particularly accelerated by the fact that the child begins to displace himself and without knowing how to walk nevertheless learns to approach objects. Moreover, the child searches for objects behind other objects and thus inaugurates an effective ordination of the planes of depth. Things are not only in front or in back, but they are in front of or behind such and such a landmark, and they continue to exist even when actual screens mask them.

Little by little this progress pertaining to near space is extended to distant space, abolishing all structural differences between these two regions of the child's universe.

In the first place, the generalization of attempts at prehension as well as the progress in the child's motility eliminate the barriers between the two spaces. On the one hand, the child succeeds in grasping increasingly distant objects and thus in constructing the concept of greater and greater distances. On the other hand, truly inaccessible objects acquire a character of actual distance; they are no longer, as in the third stage, merely altered or strange objects in the presence of which prehension must give way to procedures connected with the efficacy of the gesture, but are located in a distant space by virtue of the very fact that they acquire permanent dimensions despite their apparent reduction.

In the second place, the ordination in depth of the planes of "near space" and above all the search for objects masked by screens are generalized little by little until they apply, by constant extension, to distant space. In other words, the superposition of objects in the perceptual field begins to acquire for the child the same meaning as for us: that of a sequence of planes according to the third dimension. True, the child, not yet knowing how to walk, is unable to verify experimentally the existence of such planes. But by virtue of the very fact that he has acquired in near space the concept of objects located behind others and the concept of the screen, he knows how to interpret, even in distant space, certain total or partial disappearances as being due to a sequence of planes. Here are some examples.

OBS. 97. As early as 0;8 (1) Jacqueline, in striking the quilt of an adult's bed on which she is seated, perceives by chance a thin ray of light coming from a lamp on the other side of the quilt; she strikes the quilt harder and harder while looking exclusively at the lamp. It is true that in this observation there is nothing to prove that to the child the lamp is indeed "behind" the quilt, but such behavior foretells genuine ordinations. In effect, if this first example constitutes merely a case of transition and consequently a doubtful case, in the following months the same kind of behavior gives rise to distinct generalizations, first in near, then in distant space.

Thus at 0;9 (7) Jacqueline plays with a doll which she passes back and forth before her eyes. By a chance combination she happens to place the doll on her head; looking up in the air she then sees the bottom of its feet. She hastens to make the doll advance, retreat, disappear behind her, in short she studies its transformations.

At 0;9 (20) likewise, Jacqueline is lying down and holds her quilt with both hands. She raises it, brings it before her face, looks under it, then ends by raising and lowering it alternately while looking over the top of it: thus she studies the transformations of the image of the room as a function of the screen formed by the quilt.

At 0;11 (7) Jacqueline is seated on a sofa. I make an object disappear under the sofa; she bends over to see it. This action shows that for her the vanished object is located on a plane deeper than that of the edge of the sofa, the latter plane itself belonging to distant space (inaccessible to prehension).

So also at 1;0 (0) when I make a noisy rattle disappear behind my back (see Chap. I, obs. 48), Jacqueline leans sideways to see behind my back. I am about two meters from her; therefore she is distinctly able at this moment to see three planes of depth properly arranged; the space located in front of me, the space I occupy, and the space behind my back (the latter plane being that on which she first localizes the vanished rattle).

OBS. 98. At 0;9 (7) Lucienne is seated in her bassinet and looks at my hand. I let my arm hang down; she raises herself immediately in order to see my hand again, her eyes following the line of my arm. She therefore thinks of the edge of the bassinet as a screen; she locates the object on a plane which is deeper and partly invisible, and, in order to solve the problem, she displaces herself. This totality of behavior patterns is therefore very characteristic of the fourth stage.

At 0;9 (8) also, she raises herself, then approaches in order to see me better when I squat and appear against the edge of the bassinet. She manages to perform the same behavior patterns when I merely call, in an analogous position, but without revealing myself.

OBS. 99. At 0;7 (29) Laurent looks at a box which I slowly lower behind a cushion. At the moment it disappears he raises his head the better to see and even leans slightly forward. The same experiment, often attempted during the preceding weeks, had not given rise to such a reaction until this day. Doubtless the appearance of this behavior pattern should be correlated with the fact that for the past two or three days Laurent raises himself in bed and looks over the edge.

But it is noteworthy that again at 0;7 (29) Laurent is incapable of raising himself in this way to see over a screen when it is more than 50 centimeters from him. It is as though the ordination of planes of depth begins in near space and only later is extended to distant space.

At 0;8 (7) I note that Laurent, seated in his swing and leaning

far back, straightens up in order to see me over the edge when I
lie on the ground and call him.

At 0;8 (25) he raises himself to look at me over a cushion however far away this may be. At 0;9 (10) he also leans sideways to
see me behind a cushion (or a door).

At 0;9 (30) he leans sideways to see his bottle hidden behind my
raised arm. Moreover we recall that from 0;9 (21), when I present
his bottle to him upside down, he leans sideways in order to see the
nipple.

All these behavior patterns attest to the existence of an ordination
of planes in depth.

Such observations are sufficiently revelatory of the extent to
which the ordination of planes in depth, which begins with near
space as a function of the movements of prehension and the
search for objects masked by screens, ends by concerning distant space. The latter therefore ceases to expand in a single
undifferentiated plane and becomes arranged in regions of different depths.

In the third place, it should be noted how much the behavior
patterns of which we have just spoken, as well as the generalization of prehension (aided by displacements of the child's whole
body), accord with the acts relating to perspective which were
considered a little earlier. We have seen that toward 0;9 the child
begins to displace himself systematically, to lean, for example,
to the right and to the left, in order to study the distortions
of the image of things as a function of these various points of
view. The relationship existing between such behavior patterns and those of obs. 97-99 is immediately apparent: in both
cases the child discovers that a change of form results from his
own changes of position. Now this dual discovery permits the
subject to elaborate a new method of evaluation and orientation
of depth—that which we have treated in connection with the first
two stages (§1 of this chapter) and which consists in determining the parallax of distant objects as a function of their displacements in relation to each other. As we have said, a lateral movement of the head is sufficient to perceive an equal displacement
in the opposite direction of the table 30 centimeters away from
the eyes, a lesser displacement of trees 30 meters away, and a
very slight displacement of the mountain 3 kilometers away:

these are movements which make it possible to arrange the planes when direct perception does not supply other clues. But it is obvious that without any thought of such a phenomenon, a child of 9 to 12 months can profit from it in a practical way, if he combines the discovery of changes of perspective with the knowledge of relations of object-screens to masked objects. This knowledge being acquired at the age of 9 to 10 months, it seems probable that the child is henceforth able to construct groups of displacements related to depth. These objective groups, like the preceding ones, remain limited to merely reversible operations (lateral movements of the head, etc.), but nevertheless they mark considerable progress over those of the preceding stage.

But this series of acquisitions, whose essence derives from the discovery of the reversibility of operations (hiding and searching for an object under a screen, moving the head or object forward or backward to compare the apparent dimensions with the constant dimensions, moving the head from right to left in order to study the perspectives, etc.), does not entail the formation of complex objective groups or, consequently, of a motionless space in which the subject would place himself *in toto*. In effect, if the child conceives of the object's displacements in relation to himself and establishes objective groups from that point of view, he still does not generalize this discovery with respect to the interrelations of objects when these relations transcend simple reversibility. It is this circumstance which explains why, after finding an object under screen A, the child does not search for it under screen B, although he saw the object placed in B: as we have already established, the child at this stage searches for objects in A without noting their sequential displacements. In regard to space such behavior obviously indicates that the subject continues to locate things in relation to himself and not in relation to each other; the object has, in a way, an absolute position, that in which the child attained it the first time. The sequence of displacements does not yet constitute a group. Space is far from forming a homogeneous environment such that bodies may displace themselves in it in relation to each other. It still consists in qualitative aggregates arranged as a function of the action, and as images of the whole objectified as a whole and not

in their elements. In this space the body itself always plays an illegitimate, because privileged, role.

Whence two consequences. The first is that the child is incapable of perceiving his own displacements outside the simple
groups of reversible operations. He knows how to move his
hands or his head, to turn to follow an object in motion behind
him, to advance his whole trunk in order to approach the objects to be grasped, but he does not yet consider himself capable
of performing movements of the whole. Moreover, even in situations in which reversible operations would suffice, he does not
succeed in understanding the relationship between his own
movements and those of objects.

OBS. 100. At 0;10 (8) Lucienne's head is caught between a wall and
a taut vertical string. She tries to extricate herself by pushing the
string but does not succeed. It would be very easy for her to back
out either by withdrawing her head or by straightening her torso
but this does not occur to her.

So also Laurent, between 0;9 and 0;10, does not know how to displace himself properly in order to find me behind an armchair.
When he is seated in the chair and I appear from behind the back of
it at his right he does not know how to search for me on the left
after my disappearance. He will do the opposite at 0;11(22); see
obs. 105.

In the second place, by virtue of the fact that the "group"
does not transcend the level of simple reversible operations, the
child does not succeed in establishing complex relations among
objects. Of course he begins to make relationships among them,
since the behavior characteristic of the fourth stage, from the
point of view of the functioning of intelligence, consists in a
coordination of independent schemata and that coordination itself entails making relationships among objects as such (O.I.,
Chap. IV, §1-3). But this making of relationships remains elementary from the spatial point of view. For instance, when
the child pushes back an obstacle in order to reach the object,
or brings someone else's hand near an object on which he wishes
it to act, or even (O.I., obs. 130) drops an object over a basin so
that it may make a noise on striking it, etc., he confines himself

to utilizing simple relations such as "moving away from" or "moving near to." This is why the groups which result from such behavior patterns remain midway between subjective and objective groups and consist only in groups of reversible operations. A system of more complex relations among objects as such will appear only when the coordination of schemata is extended in precise accommodations through the mechanism of tertiary circular reactions and active experimentation, that is, during the fifth stage. For the time being, essential spatial relations are still lacking in the picture of the child's behavior, for all the groups enumerated earlier remain relative to the relations of objects with the behavior of the subject, and still do not apply to the interrelations of objects independently of the action.

A characteristic example of this situation is that of the relations of objects placed one upon another, in other words, the relation "placed upon." At first it seems as though the child at the fourth stage understands this relation, since he is capable of searching for an object under a screen and knows how to move objects toward or away from each other, consequently, to put them in contact or separate them. But in reality all the behavior patterns of this type which the child utilizes remain relative to the action in progress and none of them entails a real relationship of objects with each other independently of that action. In other words, the child who tries to get an object under a screen understands that the screen is placed "upon" the object but he understands it only to the extent that this relation is, so to speak, related to himself or to his action and not given for itself between two independent objects. Two correlative groups of facts make it possible to establish this. The first pertains to the difficulty, observed by Szuman and Baley, experienced by the child in grasping an object that is "upon" another when he perceives both objects at once. The second pertains to the child's inability at this stage to bring an object toward himself by utilizing as an intermediary the support on which the object is placed.

With regard to the first of these phenomena Szuman has shown[14] that seven-month-old children do not know how to grasp a small object placed on a support; when they try to put this ob-

[14] S. Szuman, "Observations on Syncretic Perception in Children," *Archiw. Psychol.*, Vol. II (1927), No. 1.

ject in the mouth they seize the support and try to swallow the object along with it. Following this interesting discovery, Baley[15] resumed these experiments with children, monkeys, and baboons and observed an equally interesting reaction which he has called the "negative reaction" in comparison to Szuman's "positive reaction": some children give up grasping the desired object as soon as it is placed on a support. Mr. Baley discovered this negative reaction in the lower monkeys and baboons such as the mangabeys and the mandrills, whereas the positive reaction is common in the lemurs. These two forms of behavior were revealed to be dependent on the size of the support: a small support is apt to invoke the positive reaction whereas a larger support leads rather to the negative reaction. In the case of the negative reaction the animal often presents curious behavior, "as though he were afraid."

We have found the same facts during the third stage and again throughout the present stage, and in analyzing them in relation to the other behavior patterns characteristic of these stages we have concluded that there is general difficulty in conceiving of the relations of objects among themselves (in contrast to the relations of objects with the subject himself). It is this general difficulty which prevents the child from realizing that two objects can be independent of each other when the first is placed upon the second.

OBS. 101. At 0;6 (22) Laurent tries to grasp a box of matches. When he is at the point of reaching it I place it on a book; he immediately withdraws his hand, then grasps the book itself. He remains puzzled until the box slides and thanks to this accident he dissociates it from its support.

Same reactions with a pencil, a penknife, etc. On the other hand, when I place upon the book a narrow and deep goblet which stands out from its support, Laurent takes possession of it directly. But this experiment does not teach him anything about the general problem and when I place the matchbox on the book again he still does not try to grasp it.

At 0;6 (27) I resume the experiment by placing the object (a matchbox, an eraser, a watch, etc.) sometimes on a notebook, some-

[15] "Behavior of Children and Animals when Confronted by Objects Placed on a Support," *Polsk. Archiw. Psychol.*, Vol. I (1932), No. 4.

times on the palm of my hand. Laurent does not once try to grasp the object directly even when his hand is already outstretched and touches it almost at the very moment I slide the support under it. Moreover, when Laurent grasps the support and I hold it, he does not return to the object but immediately strikes the whole thing without trying to dissociate the two objects.

At 0;7 (1) same reactions. I place the object sometimes on the back of my hand, sometimes on a small pillow; Laurent stretches out his hand to grasp the object (a little rubber lamb, a plush bear 10 centimeters long, etc.) as long as it is simply offered with my fingertips, but as soon as I put it on the support Laurent strikes the support and gives up the object.

At 0;7 (28), that is, in the middle of the fourth stage after he has learned to push back the obstacle interposed between his hands and the object, Laurent tries to grasp a small bell; at the very moment I place it on my upturned palm the child withdraws his hand, then grasps mine, and only when the bell begins to totter does he grasp it directly. The result is negative with a matchbox: he hits my hand and gives up the object.

At 0;8 (1) I resume the experiment systematically by placing a rubber lamb, a watch chain, etc., on a notebook; he grasps the support and not the object. On the other hand, when I place the same toys on a big cushion he grasps them at once; the disproportion between the dimensions of the cushion and those of the object evidently explains why the first is not considered a support in comparison with the second, but as a kind of neutral base.

From about 0;8 to 0;10 the latter reactions have been constant. The child tries directly to grasp the object on cushions, coverlets, etc., in short, supports which have a surface large enough to be likened to simple neutral bases. On very small bodies, on the contrary, the object ceases to be perceived as directly accessible and the child grasps the support itself.

Finally, at 0;10 (5) Laurent immediately grasps matchboxes, erasers, etc., placed on a notebook or on my hand; he therefore readily dissociates the object from the support.

Such facts substantiate the hypothesis of Szuman and Baley according to which the very manner in which the child perceives the object in relation to the substructure stands in the way of his dissociating it from the latter. But it must be added that this lack of perception pertains to a general characteristic of the spatial groups of this stage, which is that the movements and positions of moving objects are not yet conceived as interrelations of objects independently of the action, and thus the concept of one object placed upon another is not yet understood by the child. In effect, whatever practical relations the child may establish among objects in the coordination of schemata which characterizes the fourth stage, he does not yet study these relations for themselves, that is, truly experiment with objects as such by displacing them, for example, in relation to each other or, particularly, by placing some upon others in a series of diverse situations. This behavior pattern will first appear in the course of the tertiary circular reactions characteristic of the fifth stage.

To verify these statements it is sufficient to observe the difficulty the child experiences the first time he tries to balance one object on another: by virtue of the very fact that he does not imagine the interrelations of objects he is incapable of the simplest operations of rotation or even of displacement when they are not effectuated relative to himself but involve a relationship between the objects. Here is an example taken at the boundary of the fourth and fifth stages.

OBS. 102. At 0;11 (27) Jacqueline drops a thimble from a wooden box on which I placed it; she pushes it very gently but very methodically to the edge so that it will fall down. This is the beginning of experiments related to distant space which characterize the next stage.

But when it is a question of replacing the thimble correctly on the box she is unable to do so. She puts it upside down or on its side; the thimble slides instead of remaining in place. She tries to correct this; then I show her how I place the thimble on its open end (on the larger base). She tries to imitate me or to find for herself the position to balance it, but does not succeed. Everything takes place as though she did not know how to turn one object over systematically upon another whereas she well knows how to do this when it is in relation to herself alone.

But there is more. Proof that the relation "placed upon" is not understood during the present stage is that the child does not discover until the fifth stage what we have called the behavior pattern of the support with regard to the steps of intellectual functioning (*O.I.,* Chap. V, §2).

The behavior pattern of the support consists, as we have seen, in drawing toward oneself an object too distant to be grasped, by using as intermediary the support on which it is placed: for instance, pulling a coverlet or a cushion, etc., to reach a watch placed at the far end. But, curiously enough, the child at the fourth stage remains incapable of such behavior (except, of course, in the event of special training), whereas in the case of the supports of very limited dimensions (which were discussed earlier) he does not dissociate the object from the one on which it is placed. It is self-evident that this contradiction is only apparent, and on examining the child's difficulties we shall prove that they too stem from lack of comprehension of the relation "placed upon."

OBS. 103. I. At 0;7 (29) Laurent tries to grasp a box which I have placed on a large, flat, and light cushion 40 centimeters away from him. At first he tries to reach it directly by leaning forward, but misses it by about 10 centimeters. He then grabs the cushion for two reasons: first to keep his balance and then because, disappointed at not grasping the box, he grasps something else instead (as is almost the rule in such a case). But he does not perceive that in pulling the cushion he displaces the box; therefore he does not understand the relationship and gives up.

Second and third attempts: Same reactions with final failure.

Fourth attempt: Laurent still tries to grasp the box directly, then pulls the cushion, and seeing the box approach he lets go in order to grasp it. Afterward he again pulls the cushion, then again lets it go in order to reach the box directly. The same game is repeated a number of times and finally Laurent catches the box. At that time I had the impression that the behavior pattern of the support had been acquired, in other words, that the preceding attempts had been systematic, but the following counterproof shows that this first impression was false.

Fifth attempt: I place the cushion a little farther away than before but leave it accessible to the child's hand. The cushion itself is placed on a coverlet which covers Laurent's knees. Finally I place the box on the middle of the cushion. Laurent immediately tries to reach it. Not succeeding, he has the notion of pulling the cushion toward him; he simply grabs the coverlet and pulls it mechanically as he did previously with the cushion. Naturally this action is ineffective, and Laurent abandons any other attempt, not without having tried several times to grasp the box directly.

II. At 0;7 (30) I resume the experiment by reproducing the conditions of the fifth attempt. Laurent holds out his hand, leans forward, etc., but being unable to reach the box he catches hold of the coverlet under the cushion and pulls it. This behavior pattern is repeated a series of times but Laurent never tries to use the cushion itself as intermediary. He does not conceive of it then as a support. Concerning the coverlet, it is self-evident that he does not consider it, either, as a support or an intermediary: he pulls it either mechanically or as a substitute for the box (to abreact his need to grasp).

III. At 0;8 (1) I systematically resume the foregoing experiments. Laurent definitely reveals three distinct reactions.

1. When the cushion is near him and the box is placed at the far end of that support, Laurent tries to reach the box directly with his right hand while he grabs the cushion with his left and pulls it toward him. Then he manages to grasp the box and gives the impression of having the schema of the support (hence of using the cushion as intermediary).

2. But as soon as the cushion is farther removed and placed on a coverlet, Laurent grabs the coverlet only with his left hand, meanwhile trying to grasp the box with his right. He therefore pays no more attention to the cushion itself and thus reveals his lack of understanding of the situation.

3. Furthermore, when the cushion is again brought near and I keep the box 20 centimeters above its edge, Laurent extends his right hand toward the object while pulling the cushion toward him with his left! There is the proof that this last behavior pattern has as yet no connection with the schema of the support.

IV. At 0;8 (7) Laurent tries to reach my watch, placed on the same cushion. He extends his right hand toward it and pulls the cushion with his left. But this is only an effect of synkinesia and not a planned attempt to bring the watch to him; he never pulls the cushion toward him with both hands as he would do if he were using it as an intermediary.

Same experiment with a coverlet: Laurent pulls the coverlet with his left hand while trying to reach the watch with his right. But the coverlet, being more pliable than the cushion, yields at once and brings the watch with it.

I resume the experiment with the cushion: complete failure, as before.

v. Same negative reactions at 0;8 (8), at 0;8 (10), at 0;8 (28), at 0;9 (0), at 0;9 (20), etc.

vi. At 0;9 (24) I try a new apparatus. Laurent is seated in a double bed, facing a white quilt which is practically horizontal. I place a yellow cloth obliquely on the quilt, one end of it beside him, at his disposal, and the other end in front of him, beyond his grasp. I place a doll on the farther end. Laurent tries directly to grasp it but never tries to use the cloth as an intermediary. He finally pulls the sheet which is directly in front of him.

I resume the experiment on the following days without success. At 0;10 (12) none of the preceding attempts is yet successful.

At 0;10 (16), on the other hand, Laurent understands the relationship, as we have seen in *O.I.* (obs. 148). But on that date he is already in the fifth stage as judged by his various reactions.

This long observation seems to prove that throughout the fourth stage Laurent remains incapable of utilizing a support to bring the object to himself. Precisely during the same period, until about 0;10 (5), he does not succeed in grasping directly an object placed on a support of very limited dimensions (a notebook, a book, my hand, etc.). What does this mean if not that in both cases the child does not have the concept of one object "placed upon" another? When the support is very small the object is perceived or conceived as being at one with it; the object must be put in motion for the child to succeed in dissociating it. When the support has a large surface, on the contrary, it constitutes a sort of neutral base; the child does not understand that the object is "upon" it and that the movement of the first will therefore entail that of the second.

This example is such as to make us well understand the limitations of the behavior patterns of this stage. The child at the fourth stage succeeds in arranging his schemata, hence in forming practical interrelationships among objects. But these relations do not yet constitute a system of connections among objects as such. The complex groups characterizing "objective" space still remain to be constructed, only the groups of "reversible" movements being elaborated up to now.

In conclusion, the space of this stage represents a great advance over the preceding one in the direction of objectivity. If, as Mr. Brunschvicg says, to conceive of space consists first of all in furnishing it,[16] the child is beginning to conceive of it. He endows perceived images with permanence of substance, builds up the concept of objects of permanent shape and dimensions, and thus distinguishes between changes of position and changes of state. Moreover, through the discovery of reversible operations he develops a primary type of objective groups which go beyond the level of subjective groups. The subjective group is only a group of apparent movements which does not yet distinguish displacements of the subject himself from those of objects. The group of reversible operations is, on the contrary, an objective group, but limited to elementary relationships of subject and object. But, if he thus emerges from his solipsism, the subject at this stage remains egocentric, geometrically speaking; he does not yet recognize positions and displacements as being relative to one another, but only as relative to himself. He therefore still does not locate his whole body in a stationary field that includes other bodies as well as his own. He locates everything correctly in relation to himself but does not locate himself in a space common to himself and everything else.

§ 4. THE FIFTH STAGE: "OBJECTIVE" GROUPS

The fifth stage marks an essential advance in the construction of the spatial field: it is the acquisition of the concept of the relative displacement of objects, in other words, the elaboration of objective groups of displacements in the midst of a homogeneous environment.

In regard to object concept, the criterion of the appearance of the fifth stage is the child's success in noting the sequential displacements of the thing he seeks. Up to this point he has taken account only of a special displacement (he has systematically searched for the object where he found it the first time), that is, he has disregarded the order of the displacements even when they were all directly observed. From this arises the impossibility of arranging the movements of objects in a collective system

[16] Léon Brunschvicg, *Les Etapes de la philosophie mathématique and also L'Expérience humaine et la causalité physique* (Paris: Alcan). Those of our readers who are familiar with these excellent books will easily recognize all we owe them in these pages.

that insures the homogeneity of the spatial field. Henceforth, on the contrary, the child is aware of sequential displacements. He knows that when objects have gone from position A to position B or position C, it is useless to search for them in A. He is no longer bound to the memory of a special position but retains and combines in one objective group the totality of the displacements. Now for the first time he conceives of space as the homogeneous field in which objects are displaced in relation to each other.

Is it possible to find, apart from experimentation and simple observation, spontaneous behavior patterns proving the existence of this discovery and transcending the level of simple reversible operations? We shall demonstrate that it is. We must first note the interesting behavior which consists in throwing an object outside the visual field and in finding it again by a path different from the one that was followed in hiding it. It is no longer a matter of a simple reversibility of movements, but complementary movements linking one another. We are in the presence of the elaboration of objective groups discovered by the child himself.

OBS. 104. At 1;1 (7) Jacqueline is seated on the ground, holding a stick in her hands. She throws it behind her (putting her arm back), then turns to look for it. In the first attempts she searches in the direction in which she threw the stick, thus forming a simple group of reversible operations. But in later attempts she turns in the other direction; when she has thrown the stick by putting her left arm back she turns to the right to recover it, and vice versa. This behavior is repeated many times in the following weeks.

At 1;3 (6) same experiment with a doll: she puts it behind her with her left hand, then turns to the right to get it back. Same thing in the other direction.

At 1;3 (2) she is seated beside her mother who takes the doll from her hands to put it behind her back (passing in front); instead of following the same trajectory, Jacqueline searches directly behind her mother. She therefore applies to her mother the group discovered on herself at 1;1 (7).

At 1;3 (9) she holds a closed pin in her hands: with one hand she puts it as far away from her as possible, then recovers it with the other hand. She repeats this a number of times, constantly changing hands as well as the position of the object which she puts on the ground.

OBS. 104a. At 1;1 (18) Lucienne is seated on the ground; she puts a doll behind her with one hand and takes it with the other, turning to the opposite side.

At 1;3 (17) she drops a shoe behind her head over her shoulder; then turns, finds it, and begins again.

OBS. 105. In Laurent's case the same groups appeared toward the end of the first year and the beginning of the second, but instead of starting in connection with the body itself they began spontaneously in connection with objects.

At 0;11 (22) Laurent is behind the back of an armchair which masks me almost completely. I disappear: he leans to the left in order to see me, laughs, then leans to the right to find me again (see obs. 100).

At 1;1 (26) Laurent throws a box behind his back and immediately turns to look for it. Sometimes he turns toward the side where he threw it, and sometimes toward the opposite side.

At 1;2 (16), same observation with other objects. Again at 1;2 (25) he throws some toys behind him, either over his shoulder or at the level of his hips, and then searches for them on the other side.

At 1;2 (26) he applies the same group to my own person: I put a spoon behind me; he immediately goes around me and finds it.

We see that such behavior patterns consist in elaborating spontaneously a certain number of displacement groups. The simplest of these groups merely extends that of reversible operations, which appears in the fourth stage: hiding an object and finding it again by following the same route. Then the process becomes complicated: the operation of searching corresponds to that of hiding the object. But this latter group may still remain related to the body itself: the child hides behind himself the object to be found or he turns himself around to follow a moving object that passes behind him. Finally, there appears the objective group, which entails a system of relations established among things as such: Jacqueline, at 1;3 (2), sees an object disappear behind her mother on one side and searches for it on the other side.

This last type of groups demonstrates the chief advance accomplished in this stage as compared to the preceding stages: the discovery and utilization of the complex interrelations among objects themselves, and no longer only the relations between things and the subject's body, or relations that involve only the group of reversible displacements. The aggregate of behavior patterns that we shall now describe develops in every form the geometric relations established among objects.

The most typical and important behavior pattern in this regard consists in the child's experimental study of visible displacements: carrying objects from one place to another, moving them away and bringing them near, letting them drop or throwing them down to pick them up and begin again, making moving objects roll and slide along a slope, in short conducting every possible experiment with distant space as well as near space. We have already cited some of these observations in *O.I.* with regard to tertiary circular reaction and the discovery of new means through directed groping and apprenticeship, but it is necessary to review them here with regard to space.

OBS. 106. At 1;0 (19) Jacqueline's eyes follow a wooden horse and a postcard which she has thrown on the floor (*O.I.*, obs. 144): she studies the displacement of these objects as she herself sets them in motion, and particularly studies the displacement in depth.

Subsequently (see same obs.) she combines this examination of trajectories with the search for hidden objects which we have just described. Thus at 1;3 (27) she puts her hand on her shoulder and drops objects down her back, turning around immediately to pick them up; this is simultaneously a study of displacement in depth and an elaboration of a group. Similarly, at 1;4 (1) she throws objects under a table to search for them there, etc.

The attempts to "roll" (*O.I.*, obs. 145) are of the same kind. But the behavior patterns of which we have already spoken in connection with experiments in order to see appear from our present spatial point of view, as a simple particular case of an activity universal at that age—the study of any displacements whatever.

For example, at 1;3 (9) Jacqueline is sitting on her campstool before the two tiers of a table nearby (a narrow higher tier rests on a large tier). She plays with a doll whose displacements I observe for twenty minutes consecutively. She begins by putting it on the floor beside her, looks at it, then picks it up and begins again. Then she places it on the upper tier and pushes it gently with her finger.

She tries various balances, then puts it down flat and pushes it. She takes it up constantly, rests it on another part of the tier, and sometimes merely displaces it, sometimes tries to move it by pushing it. Then she puts it as far away as possible on the lower tier, to take it up with her other hand; afterward she brings it near her face until they touch. Then she presses it against the beads of an abacus near her stool (the whole procedure has lasted ten minutes). Several times in succession Jacqueline again moves the doll as far away from her as possible. She laughs, then puts it against the abacus again. Afterward she raises it above the table and brings it down suddenly on the tier (Jacqueline does not yet know how to let go of objects: she throws them or conducts them with her hand, as she does now). Then she puts the doll on the upper tier of the table and looks for it there; same reaction several times in succession. She puts it back on the tier and strikes it with her finger. After an interruption she replaces it under the upper tier and leans forward to look at it in this position. Another interruption, then she leans forward again to see it, pushes it farther in, brings it out again and pushes it in again, finally bringing it out. She rubs the edge of the table with it, puts it underneath, withdraws it, recommences and finally places it as far away as possible on the lower tier.

A moment later Jacqueline, in the same position, holds a beaded purse. Same play of displacements: she passes it from one tier to the other, slides it under the upper tier, then withdraws it in order to place it on top and looks at the space it occupied underneath, etc.

It is clear what interests the child in all these procedures: the displacements and positions of the object in relation to other bodies. The action of throwing or of hiding and finding intervenes here only as a simple particular case.

obs. 107. Lucienne also from 1;0 interests herself in displacements and produces them in order to study them in themselves. At 0;12 (30) she places my watch before her and spreads out the chain, first horizontally and perpendicularly to herself, then in other positions. After this she holds it vertically and shakes it. Finally she spreads it out on her bare legs, makes it slide and ends by grasping it in both hands and scraping her knee with it.

At 1;3 (3) she passes a pebble through the bars of her playpen and puts it inside. She does the same with three other pebbles that are in front of her. Then she places them 20 centimeters away from her on a rug and brings them closer to her.

At 1;3 (12) she holds a branch of foliage in her hand. She detaches the leaves and throws them to the ground one by one. Each time she very carefully examines the trajectory. The same day she alternately moves a strainer away from her and brings it toward her.

The next day, at 1;3 (13) she uses the same strainer to elaborate an original group of displacements; she pivots about, and at each new position displaces the strainer in a corresponding arc after having first put it as far from her as possible. The strainer thus describes a wide circular movement around her, following her in its own rotation.

At 1;3 (13) she puts a ball in a watering pot and searches for it with the same hand. When she cannot reach it immediately, she changes hands. At 1;3 (14) she puts a wooden cow in the watering can and looks for it there. When the toy gets caught, Lucienne moves it back and forth vertically inside the can, then puts it back in the bottom of the can, and finally brings it out. She does the same thing with various other objects: a necklace, metal molds, etc.

At 1;4 (8) her finger pushes blocks on a closed box and steers them to the edge until they fall.

At 1;4 (27) she studies the fall of a very light little feather which flutters as it falls. She repeats this experiment indefinitely.

At 1;4 (28) she carries a flower from one place to another (from a table to a sofa and vice versa). Lucienne prefaces this each time with a kind of dance step which she makes up herself.

OBS. 108. We have seen (*O.I.*, obs. 140 and 141) how Laurent at 0;10 (10) has begun to throw objects to the ground, no longer simply to analyze the act of letting go but to study the trajectories as such. In the following weeks he naturally multiplies these experiments. For example, at 0;11 (28) I note that for more than half an hour he drops everything he finds, examining very attentively the trajectory and the point of arrival.

From about 0;10 (15) this interest in movements of falling is on a par with a systematic interest in the displacement of objects in relation to each other. We recall (obs. 94) that from 0;9 Laurent has begun to displace new or even familiar toys at eye level, in order to explore them. But it is not yet possible to refer to displacements of bodies in relation to others. From the second half of the eleventh month, however, he seems to study such movements. When, for example, he is seated at his table, he amuses himself not only by making objects fall to the floor, but by transposing them, by picking them up to place them again, etc. That such gestures are intentional seems to be demonstrated by their later outcome.

At 0;11 (18) it is no longer possible to doubt this interpretation. Laurent is again seated at his table, beside a chair. He has various objects before him (plush toys, etc.). Instead of throwing them all to the floor he displaces several of them, sometimes a few centimeters from the spot where he picked them up, sometimes onto the chair itself.

At 0;11 (29) he grasps my hand in order to place it some distance from where it was and he repeats this several times in succession. He also displaces it in the air.

At 1;0 (23) he is seated before a table, next to a tray. He puts a block sequentially between his legs, on the table, between a cushion and the back of his chair, on the tray, on the floor, etc., and studies these displacements attentively.

At 1;3 (4) he still repeats what Lucienne did at almost exactly the same age—at 1;3 (13): he pivots on himself while displacing a pebble. More precisely, he is seated, places a pebble before him, then displaces it on the right, adjusts his own position to face the pebble again, displaces it once more to the right, and so on until he describes an almost complete circle.

There is no doubt that these behavior patterns simultaneously involve the elaboration of the relations among objects as such and consequently the elaboration of more or less complex objective groups of displacements.

Let us take as an example the displacement of an object perpendicularly to the child's glance, a displacement which the child follows with his eyes so as to keep the object constantly in view. We have already noted why this group, which seemed to Poincaré to be the most elementary possible, psychologically speaking, and as sufficing to insure the differentiation between changes of position and changes of state, has on the contrary seemed to us to remain for a long time in the state of a simple practical group or subjective group. On the one hand, the child who follows an object with his eyes does not know at first that he is displacing himself, and on the other hand, he does not establish relationships between the movements of that object and the movements or positions of surrounding objects. Besides, the child at first remains unaware of groups elaborated by his actions, such groups consisting in pure practical groups. When, during the third stage, he himself displaces objects by manipulating them, for instance, when he waves a rattle in the air, he locates his own displacements (those of his hand) in relation to those of the object. But he is still unaware of himself as the visual subject and above all he locates the object's displacements only in relation to himself and not yet in relation to other bodies. Moreover, the group he elaborates by manipulating things remains subjective because related to the action itself, although the child is unaware of that relativity. Finally, during the fourth stage, the child becomes capable of reversible operations (hiding the object and finding it again, etc.) but he does not generalize this discovery to the point of constructing more complex groups, since he does not yet note the sequential displacements of the thing sought. On the contrary, an operation like Lucienne's at 1;3 (13)—revolving while imparting to the object a corresponding circular movement—meets two psychological conditions of the objective group at the same time that it constitutes a typical geometric group. On the one hand, Lucienne well knows that she is turning herself around, and thus she clearly distinguishes between changes of position of the object and changes of state; moreover, the whole context reveals that, in displacing objects, Lucienne no longer tries merely to use them for the sake of the action itself (and so no longer confines herself to locating them in relation to herself), but that she studies their movements in relation to each other (she puts objects upon others, into others, etc.).

So also in all the other facts cited, there is at once awareness of displacements and awareness of the relations between objects as such; hence these are objective groups of displacements.

Another aggregate of facts which equally reveals the child's interest in the interrelations of objects is that of the behavior patterns relating to the *position* and *equilibrium* of bodies. Here are some examples.

OBS. 109. Lucienne, at 1;3 (4) and the next day, puts a metal bowl on a wooden pail (smaller than the bowl) and lets go of it. The bowl falls and she begins again, indefinitely. At 1;3 (6) she plays the same game but does not let go of the bowl until it is in equilibrium.

At 1;3 (19) she stacks three objects. She puts an iron mold upside down on the floor and upon it a box, and on the box a toy which falls down. She repeats this for a long time.

At 1;4 (25) she places a wooden cube on my leg; it remains in place but at an angle and insecurely balanced. Lucienne looks at it attentively but places a smaller cube upon it which of course makes the whole thing fall down.

Finally, at 1;6 (27) Lucienne stacks blocks in a column and succeeds in balancing as many as six large blocks. She adjusts them and corrects their position before letting them go, and is able to foresee when they will stand; this is surely an acquisition through directed groping and apprenticeship. She also tries to place a small wooden column on three stacked blocks; she puts it on the edge of the highest block, but in spite of this the column holds at first. Then she tries to put another one on top of the last, and the whole thing collapses.

obs. 109a. At 1;3 (6) Lucienne aligns four bowls very regularly side by side in a straight line. She then disarranges the series and begins again.

The following days she does the same thing with pebbles and blocks but keeps to a rectilinear alignment.

obs. 110. With respect to Laurent we have not limited ourselves as with Lucienne to observing spontaneous behavior patterns relating to positions and equilibrium, but have tried to determine by experimentation the age at which these relationships are understood. We have seen (obs. 101) how the relation "placed upon" appears only around 0;10 (5); hence it is only at the beginning of the present stage that Laurent has been able to understand the relation between an object and its support. Obs. 103 has shown us, moreover, that until 0;10 (20) he has not succeeded in using the support as an instrument or intermediary. It is therefore permissible to state that until about 0;11 the child has paid little attention to the relations of position and equilibrium. Only toward this date (obs. 108) has he systematically changed the position of objects in order to study their relative displacements.

But it is not until 1;0 (15) that Laurent systematically studies positions as such and the characteristics of equilibrium. At 1;0 (17) Laurent plays with a long box which he sets upright; he then pushes it and makes it fall. He immediately sets it up again, placing it a little further away, and resumes. He continues this game assiduously, varying the location but almost every time putting the box back upright; hence there is an intentional search for the vertical position.

At 1;1 (24) Laurent plays with little wooden pieces of furniture. He puts them on top of each other two by two, four times in succession. He begins again on the following days. At 1;2 (25) he does the same thing with the blocks.

Finally, at 1;4 (0) he tries to make a long block in the shape of a parallelepiped stand on one of its ends. He grows angry when he is unsuccessful but usually accomplishes his aim.

At 1;4 (1) he puts three cups on top of each other. The same day he stands a doll on its feet, then places it sequentially on three different round pieces of cardboard.

At 1;6 (0) he puts a block on a box and displaces the box in order to study the movements of the block thus produced. He ends by shaking the box faster and faster so as to make the block fall. He then replaces it and resumes the game, very much interested.

Unquestionably the child's searching with regard to the positions and characteristics of equilibrium of bodies presupposes or provokes an interest in the spatial interrelations of objects. When Lucienne places things on top of other things or beside them (obs. 109, 109a), she is establishing relationships among them, and when she studies the equilibrium of blocks or dolls, it is always a matter of equilibrium related to supports.

This interest in the interrelationship of position and of the displacement of objects is surely new in comparison to the interests of the fourth stage. The fourth stage initiates a behavior pattern involving the beginning of such relations: searching for objects under screens. But the special connection between the hidden object and the object-screen is far from implying a general establishing of interrelations among objects; proof of this is that the object found under screen A is then sought in that same position despite the displacements it undergoes later. The object-screen is therefore not considered by the child as something with which the hidden object is in relationship: the screen is still perceived as relative to the subject and not as relative to the object.

This leads us to examine a relationship which to us recalls that of the screen, but to the child seems connected with the relationships of the present stage, that is, with the discovery of the spatial interrelations of objects: the relation of *contents to container*. Only at the beginning of his second year does the child begin to put solid objects into hollow objects and to empty the latter to recover the former. Here are some examples.

OBS. 111. From 1;2 (28) to 1;3 (6) Lucienne systematically puts grass, earth, pebbles, etc., into all the hollow objects within reach: bowls, pails, boxes, etc.

At 1;3 (6) her finger explores the surface of a spade and discovers that the metal handle is hollow: she puts her finger inside and immediately looks for grass to put in the opening.

The same day she puts bowls (of identical dimensions) inside each other; she does it delicately, carefully examining the interrelations of objects.

At 1;3 (7) she has four or five pebbles before her. She puts them into a bowl one by one and takes them out in the same way. Then she empties them from one bowl into the other, still one by one.

At 1;3 (9), on the other hand, she discovers the possibility of emptying the entire contents of a receptacle at one stroke; she piles into a basket the metal molds she has at hand, some stones, blades of grass, etc., then turns the whole thing upside down.

At 1;3 (12) she puts her five molds into a big strainer and takes them out one by one. Sometimes she puts two or three in a pile, sometimes one, then she takes it out, puts in a second one, takes it out, etc.

Afterward she puts a little spade in the strainer, then lifts it up and turns it upside down until the spade falls out.

At 1;3 (14) she puts her molds in a watering can and empties the whole thing at once.

At 1;4 (11) for the first time she is presented with nested boxes. She immediately tries to take out those which are inside. Not succeeding, she purposely turns the whole thing upside down and the contents spread out on the floor. Then she tries to replace them, but hastily and naturally without order.

OBS. 112. At 1;3 (28) Jacqueline for the first time sees the same boxes to be nested but now scattered on the floor.[17] She takes one of them (I), turns it in all directions, and puts her index finger inside it. She rejects it and takes a second (II), same behavior (this time she puts her whole hand inside). In throwing aside the second cube she drops it accidentally into a much larger one (III); she immediately takes it out and puts it in again. Then she takes another (IV), which she also puts into the big one (III). She takes them out and puts them both in again, several times in succession.

After this she takes a big one (V), almost as large as the one she has heretofore used as a container (III), and immediately tries to

[17] Bühler and Hetzer, *Kleinkindertests* (Leipzig: Barth, 1932), Series X-XII.

put it inside. She does not succeed and merely places it askew across the opening of the other one. Then she manages to put it in but not to take it out. It does not occur to her to reverse the big one (III) in order to make the smaller one (V) fall out. Finally she discovers an adequate procedure by sliding her finger against the inside wall of the little one.

Then she chooses a much smaller cube (VI) and puts it into the big one (III). She takes it out and puts it in again about ten times. Then she takes the big one (V) which she puts back and takes out right away. Then she takes a little one (VII) which she puts in and takes out many times.

Then comes a curious experiment: she takes one of the largest cubes (VIII) which she tries to put into a smaller one (VI); she gropes a moment and then gives up quite soon. Same reaction a second time.

Then she picks up cubes V and III and tries to put the first into the second. She succeeds in putting it in but has great difficulty in getting it out again. As soon as she has achieved her goal she repeats the procedure ten times, through functional assimilation.

Finally, when cube V is in cube III, she grasps a smaller cube (IV) and puts it into V. She takes it out and puts it back in, sometimes performing this operation with her left hand, sometimes with her right.

OBS. 113. Around 1;2 (18) Laurent has begun to put pebbles, small apples, etc., into various pails, etc., and to turn them over. This behavior pattern becomes increasingly frequent during the following weeks. Between 1;3 and 1;6 the sight of a hollow object almost automatically arouses in Laurent a desire to fill it, to displace it, and to empty it shortly afterward. At 1;3 (17), for example, he fills a metal cup with grass and pebbles and empties it at a distance, etc.

These behavior patterns pertaining to the relations between container and contents demonstrate once again the child's interest in the spatial interrelations of objects. With regard to the groups thus elaborated, at first they are very crude and are constituted by merely reversible operations: putting one object into another and taking it out again. In this form they barely transcend the level of groups of the fourth stage, especially because, as we have seen in connection with object concept (obs. 60-63), it is enough to increase the number of displacements for the child to return to the concept of a special position. But then the group becomes complicated: emptying the container in order to pick up the contents on the floor, etc. Moreover, for instance, when Lucienne empties at one stroke the contents of a basket which she filled bit by bit she sums up in a single operation a possible series of detailed operations.

The procedure consisting in reversing the container to empty it leads us to the related groups of *rotations* or *reversals*. We recall that in the preceding stage the child became capable of reversing objects systematically. But he confined himself to turning them over in themselves, that is, in relation to himself. In the course of the present stage he adds to this by learning to turn objects over in relation to others.

OBS. 114. At 1;3 (9) Jacqueline plays with a doll and displaces it as in obs. 106. But besides the displacements she is interested in the doll's various positions in relation to surrounding objects. Thus she puts the doll on its feet, turns it over and puts it on its head; afterwards she tries various balances (leaning three-quarters over, etc.). Finally she turns it over, face down, then puts it on its back again. Here we see not only a study of positions and balance but also a series of reversals of the object in relation to others.

Similarly, when she has a beaded purse (obs. 106) she places it on one side, then turns it and places it on the other. Then she folds it in two and looks at the cleft thus formed; she looks at it from below, then from above, turning it over systematically.

OBS. 114a. At 1;3 (9) also, Lucienne opens and closes a watch case. At one moment she tries the hinge, then corrects this by turning the watch around on the table until the catch is in front of her.

We have seen that Lucienne also knows how to reverse cubes, bowls, boxes, etc., systematically to empty them of their contents.

OBS. 115. Laurent has already succeeded during the fourth stage (obs. 92 and 93) in turning objects over when they present two main surfaces, especially a reverse side and a right side. Two improvements are added to this during the fifth stage.

In the first place, the child becomes capable of turning over objects with several equivalent surfaces to find one of them. For instance, at 1;0 (20) Laurent immediately knows how to discover the lid of a box that is almost a cube. From 1;1 (24) he knows how to find one of the two sides which must be pressed in order to open an ordinary box of matches. At 1;3 (18) he turns an apple over in order to find the stem, etc. Each of these rotations seems to us to imply more than a simple group of reversible operations; in this they are superior to those of the fourth stage.

In the second place Laurent has become capable not only of turning objects over in relation to himself, even objects with several surfaces, but of imparting to them a rotation relative to other objects or their supports. When, for example, at 1;0 (17) Laurent (obs. 110) sets a box upright on the floor in order to make it fall down, it occurs to him after several trials that he must turn it over before placing it; this rotation is therefore related not only to himself but also to the horizontal plane of the floor.

The same is true when at 1;1 (24) he stacks small pieces of furniture and above all when at 1;4 (0) he balances a long block.

But here are some new facts. At 1;2 (25) he puts an apple into a small cup and presently turns this upside down. The same thing happens with a pail. At 1;5 (25) he turns a cover over and places it on a copper teapot, then reverses the teapot and makes the cover fall. The rotation of the cover is therefore related to its position on the teapot and the reversal of the latter is designed to make the cover fall; here two movements of rotation are related to each other.

Similarly at 1;6 (1), Laurent turns over a plush dog which had fallen on the floor, to place it on a cushion (balanced on its feet), then leans over for a full view of the dog. Not being entirely successful, he gives the cushion a slight rotation of about 15°. Here again is an aggregate of movements grouped according to the relations of the objects themselves.

These operations of reversal show us clearly what progress has been accomplished from the fourth to the fifth stage. We recall that at the fourth stage the child was able to turn an object over only by itself and without relation to other objects: thus Jacqueline (obs. 102) at 0;11 still does not succeed in putting a thimble into a box by failing to turn it the right way. By contrast, we have just seen that at 1;3 (9) she turns a doll in all directions, etc. The characteristic of this stage consists, therefore, in forming spatial interrelations among objects.

Finally, a last essential acquisition: by virtue of the fact that the child establishes relations of positions and displacements among objects he begins to gain awareness of *his own movements* as displacements of a whole. This does not yet mean that

he places himself in relation to other bodies in a system of reciprocal relationships, but that he purposely displaces himself in the
direction of desired objects and thus acquires the ability to elaborate groups more complex than before, especially with regard to
depth.

Here are some examples.

OBS. 116. From 1;1 (26) Jacqueline steers her own steps, still cling-
ing to her mother's arm, and goes toward the chairs, the sofa, etc.
At 1;3 (9) she walks around the room without preconceived plan,
but trying to get from the front of each piece of furniture to the next
one.

At 1;3 (12) she is in her playpen and I stand a clown on each of
the different sides in succession; each time Jacqueline gets to the desired spot by walking, still with some difficulty, along the sides of the
pen.

We have already seen (O.I., obs. 167) how on the same day—1;3
(16)—Jacqueline has shown herself capable of pushing her playpen
toward a distant object which she cannot otherwise reach.

At 1;4 (20) she watches me as I put her duck behind my back:
she rises and goes around me methodically to look for it.

OBS. 117. From 1;2 (15) Laurent has known how to construct, by
walking, true groups of displacements. Here are two examples.[18]

The first is related to a gate which attracted him every day during
his walk in the garden. To reach gate P, he was obliged either to
follow two paths, AB and BP, together describing a right angle at
point B, or to follow the rectilinear trajectory AP by going directly
through the grass. At the beginning of his daily outings, when Laurent arrived at A he looked from afar at gate P, but thought he had
to follow the trajectory ABP in order to reach it. Moreover he returned by the same path, extending line BA to reach another gate at
the opposite end of the garden. After a few days he began the return
trip by following line PA, whence the group AB, BP, and PA. Next
he followed the same itinerary in the opposite direction, AP, PB,
and BA. Thus it may be seen that an actual group is constituted by
the child's own displacements.

The second example is related to a square flower bed, DCIH.
The garden is formed of four juxtaposed squares (ABCD, EADF,
FDHG, and DCIH) together forming a big square EBIG. After

[18] See Fig. 1, p. 198.

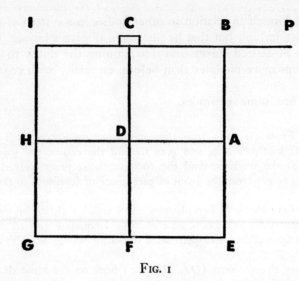

FIG. 1

departing from point H to go to the fountain at C by means of the itinerary HIC, Laurent knows how to return to H by following line CDH (thus he follows the sides of the square DCIH).

It is evident in both cases that the child, through his displacements, forms a group properly so called. A problem remains, it is true, to discover whether these groups are merely due to chance or are conscious and intentional. Both possibilities are equally likely. The first is that both groups are constituted by a simple coordination of signals, without preoccupation with the itinerary followed. For example, in order to reach gate P the child would know when he is at A that he must first pass by the bushes at B (he has discovered that itinerary by chance and has attributed a certain significance to the bushes at B). Inversely, when the child is at P he sees from far off certain signals at A which permit him to follow trajectory PA in a straight line, without knowing that he thus sums up, in a single operation, the two displacements PB and BA. In the other hypothesis, on the contrary, the child would be conscious of the spatial relations uniting the three points A, B, and P.

It is of course difficult to determine at first how such groups are formed and consequently which of the two hypotheses mentioned is the true one. It is even probable that, since these groups are not acquired in a single day but progressively, the first interpretation is the right one with respect to the formative phase. That is why we class these events in the fifth stage. With respect to the functioning of intelligence (see *O.I.*) this is the stage of the discovery of new means through directed groping and experimentation. But we believe that once Laurent has established a system of signs enabling him to recognize the meaning of the different right angles, he demonstrates his ability to combine displacements consciously and thereby form true groups. In this regard the decisive argument seems to us to be supplied by the child's expression: far from groping or appearing to act automatically, we see Laurent constantly examining the situation, then making his decision as though he were guided by perception of the spatial relationships themselves.

It is clear that the possibility of thus displacing himself consciously and of forming groups by his own comings and goings necessarily completes the groups elaborated by means of the interrelations of objects. On the whole the child thus succeeds in constructing really objective groups in every domain. Does this mean that everything ends in the development of group concept, apart from the question of the complexity of the different groups in comparison with one another? This is not the case, because the objective groups discovered during this stage remain limited to the displacements directly perceived and do not yet include any displacement simply imagined. In other words, the child does not yet know either how to take account of displacements produced outside the perceptual field (although he does perceive their result) or to locate himself in relation to objects (this operation presupposes that one pictures oneself as a moving object and is not merely aware of one's own movements). Let us examine these two kinds of gaps which still separate the objective group from the representative group.

Concerning the first point it can be maintained that the child, while knowing how to intercombine the sequential displacements of the objects he perceives, does not yet foresee the spatial relationships among these objects (except when this foresight springs from habitual actions) and he does not yet reconstruct invisible displacements; in short, he perceives space without being able to imagine it.

This results in a very general way from the observations discussed in *O.I.* under the heading "discovery of new means through active experimentation." When, for instance, the child uses supports in order to draw distant objects toward himself he sometimes, like Lucienne (*O.I.*, obs. 150), pulls the support up to him when the object is alongside it and not upon it. Or when the child uses a string attached to the object in order to grasp the latter, he does not pull the string taut (*O.I.*, obs. 154). As to the stick, at first he uses it only if instrument and object are perceived at the same time and if they are near each other; in other words, the child remains incapable of using a stick that is too far from the object and of imagining the relationship between the two. With regard to *O.I.*, obs. 162-166, they show us how the child who tries to pull a stick or a toy of some sort (a cardboard rooster, etc.) through the bars of his playpen needs a long apprenticeship to discover that the bars hold back an object which is too wide and that it must be turned over so as to enter it by its narrow side. Hence there is no anticipated representation of the relations of dimensions or even of the impenetrability of one solid by other solids. The latter characteristic is found in *O.I.*, obs. 174 when Lucienne, in order to put a ring around a stick, merely applies it against the stick as though the metal would cross through the wood to place itself at the desired spot. In short, in all these observations one sees that the spatial relationships among objects are a matter of apprenticeship and in no way give rise to images detached from the action. When the child directly perceives the objects in question he tries to form relationships among them; but he does not at all foresee the nature of these relationships and confines himself to organizing them after the event. During the next stage, on the contrary, it is possible to speak of spatial representation properly so called, because groups evoked mentally will be added to the objective groups merely perceived.

Here are a few examples of these difficulties of representation.

OBS. 118. At 1;2 (12) Lucienne puts over her head a hoop which comes down to her shoulders. She removes it, then tries to perform the same operation with a lid. She puts it on top of her head and pulls on the sides with both hands, very much surprised that the lid does not come down; obviously she hasn't the least idea that the bottom of the cover can be held back by her head.

At 1;6 (25) she is standing beside me. I stretch my watch chain along the floor and put my leg on top of it lengthwise, but so that the chain cannot come out on the side it went in. Lucienne looks for the chain in vain, and I draw it out from the other side. After the second attempt, Lucienne seems to have found the knack; as soon as I hide the chain at the left of my leg she looks for it at the right. But if I repeat the experiment under the other leg, Lucienne no longer understands; she searches for the chain systematically on the side where it entered and seems unable to understand that it could pass under the second leg. This is because in the first test I showed the child how to find the chain from the other side of the leg, whereas in the second attempt I remained passive.

OBS. 119. At 1;6 (8) Jacqueline puts a swan, a fish, and a frog down the neck of her rompers. Afterward she tries to get them back again but does not succeed, as the garment is too tight: she puts her hand as high as her chest and looks through the opening of her suit at the toys which have fallen much lower down. But it does not occur to her to take them out from below through the openings at the legs.

I myself take the three toys out one by one through the openings of the garment at the thighs. Jacqueline is astonished at the return of the toys, and immediately stretches the neck of the garment to look inside. It all takes place as though she wanted to verify the fact that the objects were no longer in her garment. She must, however, have felt the toys emerge from the bottom but obviously has no visual representation of their trajectory.

This observation is analogous to the one concerning Lucienne who, also at 1;6, does not yet represent to herself how one object can pass under another.

OBS. 120. At 1;3 (17) Laurent places a certain number of objects (pebbles and toys) on a small board, then decides he wishes to look at this sight from below. He seizes the board recklessly and turns it over. The objects spill onto the table. Laurent seems greatly surprised by their fall, then after looking at the scattered toys for a moment he puts them back on the board. It is as though he had not foreseen what would happen.

But is it through lack of representation that the child has not known how to foresee the phenomenon, although he clearly knows how to make objects fall by overturning their support (see obs. 115)? The matter could be interpreted more simply by invoking either distraction or the technical difficulty of keeping the board horizontal while looking under it. But the child's second attempt permits us to discard both solutions. Almost as soon as he has put the objects back on the board Laurent grasps it again in order to look under it. This time distraction is excluded. Moreover Laurent does not try to keep the support horizontal; he simply does not represent the situation to himself.

In short, the child perceives the spatial relationships among objects but still does not represent them to himself in the absence of direct contact. Naturally this applies also with respect to his own body. At this stage the child is already aware of the displacements of the whole of his organism, and in this he has made progress over the preceding stages, but he does not yet succeed in evoking his own movements by simple representation. When it is only a question of displacing himself to attain a distant object, the child knows how to steer his steps and thus is conscious of his own movement, distinguishing it from that of objects; but such behavior does not in the least imply that he represents his walking to himself from without and locates his displacements in the totality of the situation. In effect, when the problem which confronts the child presupposes this kind of representation we perceive that the subject always considers himself, if not as remaining outside space, at least as constituting a privileged center; he is not yet an object like others, whose displacements are relative to others.

OBS. 121. First we must recall the curious behavior described in *O.I.*, obs. 168 and 169, in which the child tries to grasp certain objects while he is on top of them and is thus immobilizing them; in such examples it seems evident that the child does not represent to himself the relations he sustains with the objects around him.

Here is an example of the same kind. At 1;4 (20) Jacqueline plays ball with me. I hide the ball under a cushion. Jacqueline hastens to find it having watched attentively what I was doing. But she puts her right foot on the cushion as she tries to lift it with both hands; the harder she tugs at the object-screen and the more firmly she presses it with her foot, the more obliged is she to remain in equilibrium. Finally she gives up trying to get the ball, through failure to realize what prevents her from raising the cushion!

OBS. 122. To support our interpretation, we may cite another observation. At 1;6 (13) Jacqueline descends into a deep and narrow ditch (she disappears into it to the middle of her thighs) and tries to get out. She puts her left foot on the edge but cannot hoist herself. Keeping her left foot on the bank, she bends over and grasps her right foot with both hands as though to bring it up to meet the first foot! She makes a series of real attempts and becomes red with effort. After this she gives up and climbs out on her stomach. But as soon as she emerges from the ditch she redescends and resumes her attempts. This time she places her right foot first and grasps the left one with both hands, obviously pulling.

It is to be noted that she went into the ditch alone and believed herself alone throughout the observation.

Surely the problem that is involved here transcends simple geometry; the child seems to be unacquainted with the aggregate of the physical relations, particularly gravity, that link him to the ground. But it seems probable to us that in order to try to move by leaning only on oneself one must be almost incapable of representation of the totality of one's own displacement; Jacqueline perceives very well the foot she is trying to pull out, but she represents to herself very poorly the total movement she would like to perform.

In conclusion, the fifth stage marks considerable progress with regard to the construction of space; with the elaboration of objective groups of displacements which define the beginning of this period one may say, in effect, that the concept of experimental space is established. Everything that enters into direct perception (apart from actual errors, of course) can therefore be organized in a common space or in a homogeneous environment of displacements. Furthermore, the subject becomes aware of his own displacements and thus locates them in relation to others. But the intellectual construction which made possible this elaboration of spatial perceptions does not yet transcend perception itself, to give rise to true representation of displacements. On the one hand, the child does not take account of the displacements which occur outside the visual field. On the other, the subject does not represent to himself his own total movements, outside his direct perception of them.

§ 5. THE SIXTH STAGE: "REPRESENTATIVE" GROUPS

As we have seen in connection with object concept, during the sixth stage the child becomes capable of rediscovering a hidden object after several sequential displacements, even if some of these are effected outside the visual field. Hence there is representation of movements, whatever the method of production of these representations may be. A new factor of this kind seems at first to add nothing essential to the formation of spatial relations. But in reality the representation of space is necessary to its completion for two reasons.

The first is that without representation of invisible displacements the perceptual universe remains incoherent or at least incomprehensible. Objects change position behind one another and on different planes of depth; to arrange their various displacements among themselves it is necessary to correct simple perception by representation of movements not perceived or of real displacements masked by apparent movements.

The second reason is that, to place himself in space and thus to attain the relativity constitutive of homogeneous space, the child needs representation of himself and his own displacements as if he saw them from the outside. Lacking this capacity the subject would be able only to perceive directly the movements he performs, without placing them from the outside in a space common to objects and to himself; from this is derived a spatial egocentrism, which tends to disappear from the moment he locates himself in space as such, instead of perceiving space as a function of himself.

It is precisely these two factors that mark the progress of the sixth stage: representation of spatial interrelations and representation of displacements of the body itself.

From this dual point of view, in addition to the representative groups described in the preceding chapter in connection with the sixth stage of object concept (Chap. I, §5), we may cite the acts of invention of new means through mental combination analyzed in *O.I.* For example, when the child rolls a watch chain into a ball before introducing it into a narrow opening (*O.I.* obs. 179) or tilts up a stick before pushing it through bars (*O.I.*, obs. 178), etc., he mentally combines the spatial relationships of objects. This capacity for spatial representation has the immediate effect of inducing the child to invent detours, that is, itineraries that allow for obstacles. This pattern of the detour seems to us the most typical behavior pattern acquired during the present stage. On the one hand, it presupposes representation of the spatial interrelations of objects as well as that of displacements of the body. On the other, it leads to the elaboration of actual groups which are not only objective but representative.

Here are some examples of these behavior patterns.

OBS. 123. At 1;6 (8) Jacqueline throws a ball under a sofa. But instead of bending down at once and searching for it on the floor she looks at the place, realizes that the ball must have crossed under the sofa, and sets out to go behind it. But there is a table at her right and the sofa is backed against a bed on the left; therefore she begins by turning her back on the place where the ball disappeared, goes around the table, and finally arrives behind the sofa at the right place. Thus she has closed the circle by an itinerary different from that of the object and has thereby elaborated a group through representation of the invisible displacement of the ball and of the detour to be made in order to find it again.

At 1;6 (11) also, Jacqueline loses the ball under a double bed. She bends down and sees that the ball is far under. Jacqueline gets up and goes around the bed and also around a bedside table. The next day, in the garden, she makes an analogous detour to meet me at the other side of a taut cord (but in this latter case the whole path was visible in advance).

The following weeks I observe many detours about the furniture in my office. The most definite is this one, at 1;10 (21): I put a doll on the back of a sofa placed in the window embrasure; Jacqueline, realizing that it would be too difficult to reach the doll from in front, does not even try, but slips adroitly between sofa and window, then rises and grasps the object.

OBS. 124. Lucienne also reveals the behavior pattern of detours from about 1;6. We have already noted (O.I., obs. 181) how, playing with a doll carriage for the first time, she has pushed it against the wall of her room and is unable to pull it back; she releases the handle of the carriage and goes to the other side, between the wall and the forward end, and begins pushing in the new position. The detour is here all the more distinct since it is accompanied by a reversal of direction in the traction of the object.

At 1;6 (28) Lucienne, who still does not like to launch out alone across open spaces, tries to meet me at her right in a corner of the room. But she is afraid of the two meters she must cross without support; then she inspects the whole room and goes off on the left to a chair, from which she reaches a table, and from this she crosses 1.5

meters without support to get to a sofa; here she changes direction to set out toward me and reaches me after having leaned against another chair and my work table. The whole journey is made without looking at me.

OBS. 125. With Laurent, the first obvious detour was observed at 1;3 (4). The child is standing in a garden. He clings to his father with his left hand and with his right tries to pull an iron gate toward him (the gate is solid and without any grillwork). He succeeds to a slight degree but does not succeed in opening it wide. He stops, then suddenly leads me to the other side of the wall; there, without any hesitation or false move, he pushes the gate with both hands and thus succeeds in opening it. Hence he has gone around the object, representing to himself ahead of time the path to follow since the gate is not transparent; see also below obs. 159 at 1;4 (4).

Another example. We recall (obs. 117) the square garden IBEG formed by four juxtaposed flower beds.[19] At 1;4 (10) and the days following, Laurent succeeds in executing, in the garden walks, a certain number of detours that clearly indicate representation. Thus, setting out at G, he directs himself without hesitation toward gate P by following the itinerary GFDCBP. Inversely, when he is at P, if one says to him "maman" (his mother is seated at G throughout), he returns without hesitation, following path PBADFG.

It may be seen how these detours differ from the simple displacements of oneself observed in the course of the fifth stage. They presuppose representation that anticipates the steps to follow and an itinerary which either is not visible in its entirety (obs. 123 and beginning of obs. 124) or else entails a play of complex relations (end of obs. 124). During the fifth stage, on the contrary, the child limits himself to following the path that is directly perceived (obs. 116-117), or, if he goes around an obstacle, like Jacqueline at 1;4 (20) when she looks for a duck behind my back, he confines himself to adopting the path already followed by the object which has just disappeared.

Such detours therefore involve representation of spatial relationships among objects. Moreover they involve the representation of movements of the whole of the body proper; when Jacqueline goes around a sofa or a bed or Lucienne goes around a doll carriage, they know not only that they are displacing

[19] See Fig. 1, p. 198.

themselves but also that their displacements are in relation to the surrounding objects. The child finally imagines himself as being *in* space instead of considering himself a privileged center whose displacements remain absolute (see obs. 121).

This dual representation of the spatial relationships between objects and one's own displacements is manifested in the acts of orientation which merely extend the behavior pattern of detours. Here are two examples.

OBS. 126. At 1;7 (27) Jacqueline follows me about a hundred meters away from a mountain chalet on a path descending to the plain, a path which her grandfather took on his departure three days earlier. I ask Jacqueline: "Where is mother?"; "Where is grandpa?" etc., alternately naming members of the family who remain in the chalet and those who have gone down to the plain. Each time Jacqueline points in the right direction.

At 1;11 (10) we follow a straight road at about 1 kilometer from the house. I ask Jacqueline where the house is; she turns around and points in the right direction. On the return trip I repeat my question; Jacqueline begins by pointing behind her systematically (which is wrong). But after a few meters she changes her mind and points in front. Now, this correction does not come from seeing the house in the distance but only from noticing that she is on the return trip.

OBS. 127. In the garden which we have already mentioned (obs. 117 and 125), from 1;4-1;5 Laurent is sufficiently oriented not to be fooled by the false moves we try to make him take.

For instance, going from G to gate P, passing points G, F, and D, Laurent, at my instigation (I hold his right hand) sets out on trajectory DH. But he has taken only a very few steps when he turns around and resumes itinerary DCB. At C, a new attempt; I steer him along route CI. But he turns around at once and finds his path again.

At 1;5 (21) he knows how to point his finger toward various members of the family who are no longer in sight but whose location he assumes according to their respective whereabouts more than an hour ago or according to their habitual occupations; thus he points out the back of the house where he knows his sisters play, the point in space toward which his grandfather was walking, etc.

These last behavior patterns are important. They show how the child, having become capable of representation, tends to arrange different spatial aggregates in relationship to each other.

When Jacqueline, following a path, no longer sees either her mountain chalet or her house she nevertheless knows they are behind her. Without having seen her grandfather for three days she knows in which direction he went. In short, the displacements of her own body do not prevent her from constantly placing herself in a universe which has become stationary and which includes herself.

Of course something still remains of absolute space centered around the subject. Jacqueline's mistake at 1;11 (10) in locating her house behind her on the return trip reveals that even without landmarks there is still an absolute "in front of" and "behind," and our previously published studies show that until the age of eight years a left and a right still persist on the verbal plane.[20] But with regard to "in front of" and "behind," the child, instead of merely turning around, is oriented on his homeward way when he recognizes the landmarks along his route.

Acts of orientation, even more than simple detours, attest to the dual acquisition peculiar to this stage. On the one hand, it is evident that in his representation the child puts into relationship not only objects but the spatial totalities among them. On the other hand, he surely represents his own displacements, because otherwise it would be impossible to form the relationships of which we have just spoken.

In short, through spatial representation and the capacity to elaborate representative groups, space is constituted for the first time as a motionless environment in which the subject himself is located. This final acquisition insures the objectivity of the groups perceived and the possibility of extending these groups to displacements which do not fall directly in the perceptual field. Hereafter, the initial egocentric space is in some way turned around; the universe is no longer centered on a self, ignorant of itself, but contains the personal body aware of its displacements in the unlimited series of permanent solids which have movements independent of the subject.

[20] Piaget, *Judgment and Reasoning in the Child* (New York: Humanities Press, 1928).

§ 6. THE MAIN PROCESSES OF THE CONSTRUCTION OF SPACE

As Stern has well said apropos of the child's psychology and
Brunschvicg with respect to "stages of mathematical phi-
losophy," the problem of empiricism and nativism is badly stated;
the reality of space is in its construction and not in the extended
or unextended character of sensations envisaged as such. But
once this has been established, it remains true that a construction may be interpreted from one point of view or another, depending on whether it is more or less directed from without or
from within.

In wishing to reduce to the minimum the innate realities which
serve as the point of departure for the construction of space, one
cannot deny the existence of two fundamental facts: first, the
very functioning of biological and psychological assimilation
entails *a priori* an organization by groups; and, second, from the
beginning of their activity the organs of perception apply this
organization to the displacements they perceive.

The concept of group goes far beyond the construction of
space. Every self-enclosed system of operations constitutes a
group, that is, it is possible to return to the point of departure
through an operation which forms part of the system. In a very
general sense one may say that every living or especially psychological organization contains in germ the characteristic operations of the group, since the nature of organization is precisely
to constitute a totality of interdependent processes; the concept
of group thus forms the principle of this system of operations
which logicians have called the "logic of relations," since the
product of two relations is still a relation. The logic of relations
is immanent in all intellectual activity; every perception and
every conception are the making of relationships. If the logic
of relations is only tardily reflected as a normative system, it is
virtually preformed in the functioning of every act of intelligence. We may say that the group is immanent in intelligence
itself. We may even go so far as to say that every act of assimilation, that is, every relation between the organization of the subject
and the external environment, presupposes a system of operations
arranged in groups. In effect, assimilation is always reproduction,

that is, it involves a reversibility, or a possible return to the point of departure, which precisely defines the group.

These considerations, applied to the perception and execution of movements, make clear how the formation of space is outlined from the time the apparatus of sight or of balance begins to function. From the sixth day of life, Preyer's child turns his head toward the window as he is carried away from it, and does so in order to recover the agreeable sensation of light; this single act of seeking an aliment that is functional to his looking constitutes, independently of any precise coordination, a group of displacements immanent in reflex activity. The construction of space is therefore directed from within by the very laws of assimilatory functioning. Does this mean that spatial organization is innate to the extent that it is a structure? It would be absurd to draw this conclusion. Doubtless the conformation of our perceptual organs influences the nature of our spatial intuition, since the geometry of common sense rests upon a three-dimensional Euclidean space. But this influence is only limiting, restraining the possibilities of intuition among all the geometries rationally possible. As to finding out how the space characteristic of that intuition, as well as space in general, is constructed, the organization of groups peculiar to the functioning of assimilation would not be adequate to explain it, for this constitutes only a functional organization and not a concrete structure. It merely explains why reflex movements are already organized in space, but nothing can be drawn from the structure of the movements as such with regard to spatial perceptions or representation. The problem to be resolved is that of the transition from physiological space to perceived and conceived space or, to put it differently, the transition from the functional *a priori* to the structural *a posteriori*.

We have described the stages in this evolution: the development from practical groups to subjective groups, and from the latter to objective groups. The essential problem raised by such a description is to understand how the child, starting from a space completely centered on his own activity, manages to locate himself in an ordered environment which includes himself as an element. Two processes are distinguishable here, each of which requires a special explanation, although they are closely interconnected: the progressive structuring of the spatial field and the desubjectification or consolidation of its elements.

First the *structuring*. During the first stage the behavior patterns of sucking, sight, etc., reveal an hereditary coordination of movements in space but without spatial intercoordination. The stages of progress peculiar to the second stage, connected with the acquisition of primary circular reaction, permit the child, in each of the buccal, visual, tactile, kinesthetic, etc., spheres, to follow or even to rediscover the habitual perceptual images by means of movements grouped in coherent systems superposed on the reflex systems. The perception of space is therefore still reduced to that of certain movements of bodies in the respective fields of various sensory organs, and the child imagines neither displacements external to those fields nor movements of the body itself, not even coordinating in a single environment the various spaces thus sketched. With the advent of secondary circular reaction, that is, the coordination of sight and prehension, the structuring of space achieves two notable advances: first, the coordination in a single system of the different practical spaces previously constituted; second, the formation of groups in the field of perception. In effect, through the intervention of prehension the child becomes capable of displacing objects in the visual field and thus of making them describe trajectories that return periodically to the point of departure. But coordination does not go beyond the limits of the perceptual field and, lacking representation, this field does not include the body itself as such, but only manual activity. With the advent of the fourth stage which is that of the intercoordination of secondary shemata, the structuring of space begins to go beyond the field of immediate perception, since the child becomes capable of searching for vanished objects. But by failing sufficiently to detach the object from personal activity this structuring extends only to the reversible groups and does not yet concern either the free movements of bodies in motion or the body itself conceived as an object. In the fifth and sixth stages, owing to new conditions of directed searching and the mental combination of schemata, the structuring extends to the aggregate of displacements which have been perceived sequentially and then to those which the intelligence is able to reconstitute deductively without having seen them. Reciprocal relations are thus established among bodies in motion, whatever they may be, and between them and the body itself conceived on the same plane as other objects.

From the point of view of simple behavior, this gradual structuring, or more precisely this construction of spatial relations, is explained by the progress of intelligence. To the extent that activity is regulated by global schemata, spatial coordination operates only between the subject's movements and objects which are in their immediate extension. To the extent, on the contrary, that the schemata become sufficiently mobile to combine among themselves in many ways, spatial relations are established among objects on the one hand, and affect the body *in toto* on the other. This means that the true nature of space does not reside in the more or less extended character of sensations as such but in the intelligence which interconnects these sensations. But as sensations do not constitute primary elements and exist only as a function of perceptions of the totality linked with mental assimilation, one might affirm the existence of spatial perceptions *sui generis*. But, as we have seen in *O.I.*, perceptions are not primary elements independent of intelligence. They are the result of intellectual activity, and from that point of view space cannot be conceived as a reality separate from the whole of the work of the mind. Space is therefore the very activity of the intelligence, in so far as the latter intercoordinates external images. Doubtless such a definition includes externality, that is, the specific character of space itself, but the essential thing is to conceive of this datum of extension as existing not in itself but only in relation to the intelligence which supplied it with a progressive structure. This situation is comprehensible only after the second process of the evolution of space has been examined.

The structuring of space can be described from the point of view of behavior. Spatial *desubjectification* and *consolidation* are, on the contrary, essentially related to the acquisition of consciousness. True, we know the baby's consciousness only through his behavior, but it is possible to reconstruct it by starting from that behavior, for without this mental translation of the construction of primitive space the child's behavior would be incomprehensible.

If we assume that reflex activity, alone at work during the first stage, is accompanied by consciousness and that, as nativism would have it, elementary sensations are extended from the outset, it is nevertheless true that sensory images are originally uncoordinated with each other from the point of view of space. Only the movements which accompany such perceptions are, each in its own realm, hereditarily organized in mechanisms constituting so many practical spaces. But if consciousness is not through certain global acts (because regulated in advance) completely unaware of these various groups of displacements, it is reduced to the feeling of being able to rediscover certain perceptual images some of which are doubtless already external to others but which do not have any stable relationship either among themselves or with the subject. At first there is neither external nor internal world but a universe of "presentations" whose images are endowed with emotional, cenesthetic, and sensorimotor qualities as well as physical ones. This primitive universe constitutes thenceforth the child's self as well as the objective of his actions. Hence there are as yet neither substances nor individualized objects nor even displacements, since without objects changes of position cannot be distinguished from changes of state; there are only global events connected with movements of the body proper, hence with kinesthetic and postural impressions.

But gradually as space develops the situation is exactly reversed. Instead of remaining immanent in each of these heterogeneous images which correspond to the various classes of sensations, space encompasses them in a single environment. Moreover, these images are detached from the activity itself, and are externalized and interrelated. A series of planes in depth thus transform the shape of the universe to the extent that qualitative images are consolidated into permanent and substantial objects. Above all, the child discovers his own body and locates it in space with other objects, establishing a totality of reciprocal relations between its own movements and those outside.

On the whole, the correlative desubjectification and consolidation of space consist in a gradual elimination of the initial unconscious egocentrism and in the elaboration of a universe in the midst of which the subject will, in the end, place himself.

Such an evolution could only be explained by the operations

which form the object and those which permit the structuring of groups. So long as the child does not admit the existence of substantial objects the extension inherent in the various perceptions could not be that of a space external to the self. On the contrary, to the extent that the coordination of schemata simultaneously entails the elaboration of subjective, and then objective, groups and the formation of permanent substances, extension becomes the property of the objects themselves and of their mutual relations; thus space ceases to be centered on the activity itself but encompasses it, in turn, in a system of the totality. We understand, therefore, why extension is not given in itself but always remains related to intellectual activity: it is in so far as groups are organized and the subject places himself in the midst of a universe of substantial objects that the concept of externality is really formed.

We are now ready to discuss the questions raised by the classic debate of empiricism versus nativism. If one acknowledges the close connection between the development of space and that of intelligence, the problem seems to escape such a simple alternative, each of the two presenting terms being revealed as equivocal. Nativism limits itself to presenting to us space or certain aspects of space as congenital, whereas empiricism considers the same realities to be acquired by experience. But the real question is to ascertain how spatial schemata are acquired and, if some are hereditary, what their meaning is, considering the relations between the organism and the external environment. As we have seen in *O.I.* (Introduction and Conclusions) there exist, both on the plane of acquired experience and on that of inherited characteristics, at least five different interpretations of the genetic mechanism.

If we assume that hereditary spatial characteristics exist, as nativism declares, they may be interpreted by the following hypotheses, of which at least the first contains nothing contradictory to the idea of an empirical origin of space. According to this first point of view, local signs, etc., would constitute hereditary characteristics acquired under the influence of the environment, space thus being considered a property of things implanted in our organism under pressure of ancestral experiences. According to a second hypothesis, hereditary spatial data would only be potentialities preadapted by an organizing vital power and made real by contact with things. A third point of view, that of pure apriority, would consider space innate because it constitutes the necessary mode of perception peculiar to the sensory organs; knowledge of space would therefore owe nothing to the environment, space being merely projected by the mind onto things without belonging to them. A fourth interpretation, that of mutationism, would add to the preceding one the reservation that our space, instead of constituting the necessary form of every adapted perception, might be only the product of a chance variation, the human species having sensory organs different from those of most other animals. Finally, in the fifth place, spatial adaptation can be conceived as due to an interaction between the organism and the environment, the structure of our organs implying certain hereditary relations between the things perceived and the assimilatory function.

But before choosing from among those different possible interpretations of nativism, it is essential to understand that the same five points of view are found again on the plane of so-called "empiricism," inasmuch as the latter confines itself to denying that space is given from birth and in affirming that, in all its aspects, it requires for its formation contact with experience.

First there is pure empiricism, for which the discovery of space consists in a simple progressive perusal of the properties of experimental space. But, near such an interpretation linked to one or another of the forms of associationism, one can conceive of a vitalistic empiricism which would refuse to acknowledge an hereditary space but would conceive of spatial adaptation as proceeding simply from the faculty which the intelligence possesses of understanding the nature of things. In the third place, it is even possible to conceive of an apriority negating, with empiricism, the existence of a space given from birth; preformed structures would then be considered as arising in accord with the subject's needs in his contacts with experience. In the fourth place, the hypothesis of chance variations with selection after the event, which in the realm of hereditary adaptations has given rise to mutationism, inspires, in the realm of individual adaptations, pragmatic interpretations of intelligence and consequently what has been called by Poincaré spatial "conventionalism." One can, in effect, conceive of the space of our ordinary perception as not resulting from the nature of things, as not being at all necessary from the subject's point of view, but as merely constituting a convenient instrument of adaptation among many other possible ones. Finally, in the fifth place, one can consider space as being due to an intellectual activity, elaborating between subject and objects a totality of relations simultaneously taking account of experience and the conditions of intellectual assimilation.

An exact parallel therefore exists between the different possible forms of nativism and the interpretations which may be given to spatial elements learned in the course of individual experience. The real question for us is not to choose between nativism and empiricism, both of which undoubtedly express aspects of reality, but among the five explanatory systems found on both planes.

To proceed from the more known to the less known, let us begin by directing ourselves to the field of individual spatial acquisitions. In this respect the processes of progressive structuring and of desubjectification or consolidation which we have just described may serve as a touchstone for the necessary choice.

First of all, it is impossible to interpret—as does pure empiricism—the evolution of space as the result of a simple perusal of the properties of the thing perceived. It is clear from the functional point of view that the group as the organization of displacements is not a product of experience but, as Poincaré has demonstrated, a condition of the perception of movements. If no group is innate as structure, the functioning of the perceptual organs necessarily entails the elaboration of groups. With regard to the structuring of groups, the very fact that it results in a total change in perspective, proceeding from egocentric phenomenalism to the constitution of a universe formed of permanent objects with ordered displacements, shows that this is a question of a construction of intellectual relations and not of the discovery of ready-made properties.

Moreover the objections already raised to vitalism and preformism in the realm of intelligence (*O.I.*, Conclusions) also obtain with regard to space. In particular, the transition from practical to subjective groups and from the latter to objective groups attests to a continuous and increasingly experimental searching which contradicts the hypothesis of preformed structures, imposed in proportion to the subject's needs. The construction of spatial relations, still more than that of particular perceptual schemata, attests to the primacy of intellectual activity over ready-made structures, a primacy which Gestalt psychology seems to us to neglect.

In the fourth place, the system of increasingly coherent relations between perceptions and movements, which space thus presupposes and which are formative of perceptions themselves, could not be reduced to a totality of mere practical conventions, since it is the very structure of objects and their substantial permanence which are elaborated in correlation with the groups.

Hence, in the last analysis, it is the functioning of intelligence which explains the construction of space. Space is an organization of movements such as to impress upon the perceptions shapes that are increasingly coherent. The basis of these shapes derives from the very conditions of assimilation that entail the elaboration of groups. But it is the progressive equilibrium of this assimilation with the accommodation of the motor schemata to the diversity of objects which accounts for the formation of sequential structures. Space is therefore the product of an interaction between the organism and the environment in which it is impossible to dissociate the organization of the universe perceived from that of the activity itself.

What role can hereditary spatial elements play in such an organization? As we have noted, it is necessary to distinguish "group" organization in general from the particular spatial intuition of the organs of perception. The first of these elements acts upon the elaboration of space only indirectly by impressing on every spatial construction a shape permitting the formation of groups, the latter not being predetermined as completed structures. As such, this first element may be conceived as emerging from the "general heredity" common to every living organization. With regard to the perceptual organs it can be asserted, we think, that they involve a certain geometric structure in contrast to others (Euclidean three-dimensional space). This would present simultaneously an adaptation and a limitation. As to limitation, this structure would doubtless constitute an heredity peculiar to man or the higher animals. But how shall we account for its acquisition? To the extent that it is adapted, such a structure could only be explained according to the five solutions we have just classified. But if the first four of these cannot be justified on the plane of individual adaptation, they are all the more difficult to apply to the past of the species. How is it possible to conceive that ancestral experience has imposed on us, by means of the inheritance of acquired characteristics, Euclidean three-dimensional geometry, when we are not sure either that such an hereditary process is possible or that the universe obeys the laws of that geometry? On the other hand, according to the solutions offered by vitalism, preformism, and mutationism, the eventual hereditary data of space were constituted independently of the environment. How can we believe this when, from the child's earliest sensorimotor intelligence to the most recent discoveries of physics, we constantly witness the prodigious adaptation of the human mind which constitutes the accord between geometric schemata and experience? All that remains is to acknowledge that this interaction of things and the intelligence, whose genetic progress demonstrates existence on the plane of individual acquisitions, is prepared by an earlier interaction of the environment and hereditary biological processes, although no positive analysis can yet account for its mechanism.

CHAPTER III

The Development of Causality

The nursling's psychic activity is at first only simple assimilation of the external environment to the functioning of the organs. Through the medium of assimilatory schemata, at first fixed, then mobile, the child proceeds from this elementary assimilation to putting means and ends into relationships such that the assimilation of things to personal activity and the accommodation of schemata to the external environment find an increasingly stable balance. The undifferentiated and chaotic assimilation and accommodation which characterize the first months of life are superseded by assimilation and accommodation simultaneously dissociated and complementary.

Corresponding to this process of evolution related to intellectual behavior is a sort of law of development of knowledge, as we have seen through the analysis of the concept of object and of space. The initial state is that of a universe which is neither substantial nor extended in depth, whose entirely practical permanence and spatiality remain related to a subject ignorant of himself and perceiving reality only through his own activity. The final stage is, on the contrary, that of a solid and vast world obeying physical laws of conservation (objects) and kinematic ones (groups), in which the subject places himself consciously as an element. From egocentrism to objective relativism seems to be the formula of this law of evolution.

If this is the case we must now expect to find, with regard to causality, a completely analogous process of formation. As we shall try to establish, at first there is no causality for the child other than his own actions; the initial universe is not a web of causal sequences but a mere collection of events arising in extension of activity itself. Efficacy and phenomenalism are the two poles of this elementary causality, from which both physical spatiality and the feeling of a self acting as internal cause are absent. At the other end of sensorimotor development the universe becomes a coherent whole in which effects follow causes which are independent of the subject and in the midst of which the activity itself must, in order to intervene in the structure of things, submit to objective laws that are both spatial and temporal. Just as object and space, at first centered on a self ignorant of itself, finally transcend the self by encompassing it as an element, so also causality and time, at first dependent on internal operations unaware of their subjectivity, are at last conceived as interconnecting external events or objects and as governing the subject who has become conscious of himself.

But is it possible to speak of causality to describe the behavior patterns characteristic of the first two years of mental life? It is apparent that this expression would be incorrect if it led to attributing to the child a need for "explanation" with regard to the phenomena which surround him. It is clear that on the level of sensorimotor intelligence to the analysis of which we confine this study, the child only tries to act, that is, to achieve a practical result and, even if for this purpose he uses mental "images" and constructions, his aim is never to understand for the sake of understanding, but merely to modify reality to suit his action. In such behavior there is no room for concern about "explanation" or for abstract and theoretical causality. On the other hand, even at the level of practical intelligence it is impossible for the child to perceive the realities on which his action bears without relating them to this action or to each other; hence it is as legitimate to speak of causality from the first months of life as to speak of objects and spatial connections. There is a causality in acts just as there exists space or practical objects, and in relation to causal images this causality is as precocious as is space or the active object in relation to geometric concepts and the idea of matter. Furthermore, the formation of these elementary connections peculiar to causality in the act is inseparable from that of the objects themselves, just as the elaboration of time is inseparable from that of space. The term "groups of displacements" means, in effect, ordination of movements in time, and the term "permanence of objects" necessarily implies causal connection between events; the causal and temporal series we shall now study constitute merely the other face of the objective and spatial series envisaged hitherto. If we think of causality as a sensorimotor schema before conceiving it as a concept, or as a practical category before it becomes a noetic category, the language we use will raise no difficulties.

Moreover it is very possible that the evolution of causality on the sensorimotor plane obeys the same laws as its development on the plane of reflective and verbal thought. The object of primitive physics and geometric space reflect, respectively, phenomena peculiar to the practical object and to practical space; similarly, it is possible that noetic causality may consist in the acquisition of awareness of practical causality. But this acquisition is not limited to extending the last stage to which sensorimotor intelligence leads: through an aggregate of temporal displacements, it repeats stages analogous to those observed on the initial plane. This parallelism without synchronism certainly complicates the description of causality, but renders all the more necessary the use of a common terminology which can be applied to all phases of this complicated history.

§ I. THE FIRST TWO STAGES: MAKING CONTACT BETWEEN
INTERNAL ACTIVITY AND THE EXTERNAL ENVIRONMENT,
AND THE CAUSALITY PECULIAR TO THE PRIMARY
SCHEMATA

As with regard to space and objects, the first stages of causality are chiefly remarkable for their negative characteristics. Consequently, analysis of this initial state cannot be made except by a method of recurrence, which consists in extending in the opposite direction the lines of the genetic process revealed by the study of the last stages. The ground for interpretations relating to the point of departure of a concept can only be shown *a posteriori* by the probability of the explanation based on the total evolution of that concept. Nevertheless, one is forced to begin with the description of the initial stages, at the risk of leaving the reader in a state of indecision until the examination of the following ones.

We shall call the first and second stages the period of pure reflexes and of the acquisition of elementary habits before the coordination of prehension and sight, that is, before the appearance of secondary circular reactions. During these two stages the child learns how to suck, to look, to grasp what he touches, etc., through reflex exercise and then through primary circular reactions. Moreover he does not reveal any behavior pattern related to vanished objects, and his space remains spread out in purely practical and heterogeneous groups. If there is relatively early coordination of hearing with sight and of prehension with sucking, there do not yet exist systematic connections between the visual and tactile universes or between visual and buccal spaces. What, then, is the causality of this period?

Without wishing to discuss for their own sake the classic interpretations of Hume and of Maine de Biran, it is, however, necessary to ask two questions concerning the point of departure of practical causality: that of the role of habit or external association and that of the influence of the feeling of effort.

Primary circular reaction, which characterizes the second stage, constitutes the point of departure for habit and acquired association. By the practice of sucking and by constructing various schemata suitable to this activity, the child succeeds in forming relationships between the position in which he finds himself and the approach of food, or between the contact of the cheeks with the nipple and the nursing which follows, etc. (see *O.I.*, obs. 25-26). By the practice of looking he discovers that a certain face announces a certain event or corresponds to a certain voice. (*O.I.*, obs. 37: sight of the nurse or his mother makes Laurent smile as though he foresaw everything that this image involves.) By the practice of hearing, the child associates visual sounds and images and he begins to try systematically to see what he has heard. By the practice of prehension the child finally learns to associate certain contacts with certain properties (the things grasped are for sucking, etc.). Would it not be possible to assert, therefore, that the connections stemming from assimilatory schemata and consolidated by primary circular reactions constitute the first forms of causality? For instance, having associated the tactile perception of the nipple with the gustatory impression of food, the child would come to consider the object furnished by the first perception as the cause of the second, that is, the mother's breast or the bottle as the causes of food. Or else having associated a certain image with a certain sound, the child would understand that the object seen is the cause of the noise or that the person looked at is the cause of the voice, etc. If such connections could be established at the outset, causality would seem to be completely formed as early as this first stage; through habit and association a coherent universe would be impressed on the child's mind.

But three fundamental reasons prevent us from considering things as being so simple. The first is that, if our foregoing interpretations are correct, the nursling's primitive universe does not yet consist in objects. Once the bottle, the sound-making object, or the interesting person has disappeared the child behaves as though they had reentered the void. Such realities are aggregates of qualities perceived simultaneously, rather than substantial objects; how then can it be asserted that the child attributes a causal value to them? It would surely be possible to suppose that in the absence of substantiality the child begins by interconnecting simple qualities, and the essence of the phenomenalistic solution consists precisely in considering these purely qualitative connections, by virtue of their repetition, as laying the foundation of causality and substantiality combined. But if one takes strictly the point of view of the phenomenon, which is that of the first months of life, it is noteworthy that the qualities most striking for the subject must not be those which through longstanding habit we attribute only to the object; besides tactile, gustatory, auditory, and visual qualities the child must perceive, closely united to them, his impressions of pleasure and pain, of success and failure, of effort and expectation, etc. In such complex qualitative aggregates which constitute the whole universe of primitive perception, how is it possible to isolate associative series sufficiently regular so that certain elements are conceived as causes and others as effects?

The second remark to be made reinforces the foregoing one: the qualities perceived by the child are not located in a common space. Buccal, visual, auditory, tactile, and kinesthetic spaces are so many procedures of coordination of movements related to sucking, sight, hearing, etc., but are not yet environments enclosing in the capacity of contents objects located on the same plane. All the more reason that they do not form among themselves a single and homogeneous environment enclosing such contents. How, then, is it possible to conceive that the qualitative aggregates described above can give rise in themselves to causal series if they are not yet arranged in space, and when their spatiality remains wholly relative to their use by the subject's action?

Finally, it is fitting to observe that such qualitative aggregates, not yet realized in the form of objects nor placed "in" space, could not be deployed in regular associations forming causality for the third reason that they are not yet differentiated from personal action. This statement merely sums up the two preceding ones: if the qualitative aggregates discovered by the child are not yet realized in the form of objects it is because they remain related to personal activity, and if they are not yet placed in a common space it is because spatial groups still depend entirely upon the subject's movements. We have just seen that this lack of differentiation between the qualitative aggregates and the action apparently results in the fact that the subject always unwittingly associates certain qualities of the external environment with others pertaining to himself, and does not confine himself to associating purely external qualities. For example, contact with food will appear to him as the extension not only of the tactile contacts, etc., which have preceded it, but also of the efforts accomplished, of sensorimotor searching, of postural and kinesthetic impressions, of emotions of expectation and recognition, etc. In short, the qualitative aggregate on which the child's action bears forms a global and indissociable whole in which internal and external elements are closely intermingled.

It is therefore impossible to consider primitive sensorimotor assimilations and primary circular reactions as giving rise to associations sufficiently simple and regular to engender relationships of causality. Seen from without, the subject seems to put one element of the external environment into constant relationship with another, and we might be tempted to believe that he considers the first as cause of the second; from the point of view of behavior, it thus might seem as though the child understood that the breast or the bottle are causes of food and the rattle or the person seen are causes of the sound or the voice. But a more careful analysis of the totality of the child's behavior patterns shows, on the contrary, that these simple associations do not exist for him and that the relations he attains are functions of global and undifferentiated schemata in which there is no room either for objects or for a space related to things themselves, or, consequently, for causes external to the subject's action.

Is it necessary, from this point on, to look for the point of departure of causality in the child's activity, as some people do? Since the external environment is not yet organized or even dissociated from the action itself, could it not be said that the only cause available to the subject's consciousness is located at the heart of this action? The most definite conclusion from our analysis of the beginnings of mental assimilation (*O.I.*, Chap. I) is that ever since the first contacts with the external environment, the child is active. The sucking reflexes, however well established they may be in the individual's hereditary structure, give rise from birth to practice, to searching, in short to a truly sensorimotor functional assimilation, and this psychic assimilation is continuously extended in the form of acquired schemata and secondary circular reactions. Sight and hearing are not at all passive: the child practices looking or hearing, and visual or auditory images are less external realities exerting pressure on him than they are nourishment sought in order to maintain a constantly growing activity. Prehension develops in the same way, through assimilations that are reproductive, recognitory, and generalizing. Nothing is further removed from psychological truth than the image proposed by classical empiricism of a ready-made universe gradually impressing itself on the sensory organs to engender fixed associations and thus to constitute causality. Would it not be true that the only cause perceptible to the child is to be sought in the very activity which characterizes each of his acquisitions? Does not the reality of sensorimotor assimilation imply the conclusion that the little child, ever since the beginnings of his mental life, conceives of his own effort as the cause of every phenomenon?

Here a meticulous criticism of the mechanism of assimilation must put us on guard against a realism which is as unpsychological when it deals with internal experience as when it deals with external experience. If the subject constantly absorbs into his own activity the data of the external environment, this does not mean at all that there is awareness of the activity prior to the act of assimilation or independent of it. Moreover it does not mean at all that the impressions of effort, expectation, satisfaction, etc., which may intervene in the course of the actions, should be attributed to an internal substantial subject located in the consciousness any more than other perceived qualities should be attributed to permanent external objects located in space. To the extent that the subject organizes the external world he will discover himself and will conceive of his actions in relation to that universe. But so long as this organization is not realized from without, there is no reason to assert that it is realized from within. The term mental assimilation means the interdependence of the assimilator and the assimilated, for this assimilation could not from the outset be the identification of a datum to an internal reality already completely formed. Assimilation is only one pole of the adaptational process; accommodation is the other. Consequently, far from constituting a substantial and permanent force which would present itself to the consciousness as an immediate datum, assimilation is an activity in the formation of relationships which unites the external world with the internal world but excludes any direct experience common to both.

From this time, when the nursling finds his food after having made an effort to obtain it or discovers with his eyes the object whose sound he has heard, one cannot say that he perceives his effort as a cause of which the result would be the effect, or still less that he distinguishes in this result that which is due to his own activity and that which comes from a submissive or unyielding external world. His impressions of effort, expectation, success or disappointment, etc., cannot, from the outset, appear to the little child to emanate from a self separate from the qualitative aggregates given in immediate perception; these internal qualities are welded with the external qualities into a mass which is as yet indissociable. Consequently, neither the self nor any reality conceived as being "internal" is capable of constituting a "cause"

to the child of this stage, for the whole process of the action itself is placed by the subject on the single plane of an experience which has not as yet been dissociated, neither truly external nor truly internal.

In conclusion, a simple point of departure for causality cannot
be supplied by the feeling of effort or of internal activity, any
more than by external associations or habits. Nevertheless, on
seeing how, from the third stage, that is, from the time he is able
to use his hands, the child can exercise power over things and
construct a thousand causal relations among the data entering his
perceptual field, one must admit that as early as the first stage,
the subject must introduce some concept of cause into his awareness of the results of his assimilatory activity. What, then, can
this initial causality be?

In interpreting by recurrence the lines of the evolutional process which we see emerge from the third stage on, we think it is
possible to assume the following. On the one hand, the child perceives nothing, whether in the realm of sucking, sight, or prehension, etc., unless the perceived data extend a simultaneously
assimilatory and accommodating activity of the child himself. On
the other hand, since the data perceived are neither conceived
as objects nor placed in a space independent of the action, their
connection with the activity itself can be only the more impressed on the child's consciousness. Thereafter, in perceiving
some reality which he has succeeded in attaining through his
own action, the subject must experience a feeling which might
be translated thus: "Something is happening." But the cause of
this something cannot be sought in a "self" conceived as such,
since no internal world has been distinguished. It cannot be
placed in the external world either, since there is not yet a solid
and permanent universe. The production of interesting results
must therefore be experienced as merely extending the sensations of desire, effort, expectation, etc., which precede their appearance. In other words, the food obtained must be perceived
as extending the act of sucking, and visual images as extending
that of seeing, etc. Primitive causality may therefore be conceived as a sort of feeling of efficiency or of efficacy linked with
acts as such, always with the reservation that such feelings are
not considered by the subject as coming from himself but are

localized in perceptual aggregates constituting the point of departure for objects in general or for the body itself. The universe of the first stages would therefore be a collection of centers of creation or reproduction in which the child localizes his own impressions of effort and activity, but one cannot say that he conceives of these centers as either external or internal to himself.

Primitive causality thus assumes a dual aspect. On the one hand, it is dynamic (feeling of efficacy) and expresses consciousness of the activity itself. But on the other hand, it is phenomenalistic and formed only with respect to an external datum perceived by the subject. It is this indissoluble union of dynamism and phenomenalism which, on the plane of causality, seems to us to result most directly from the lower forms of assimilation and accommodation. To the extent that the nursling absorbs objects into his activity he can conceive of them only by endowing them with some of the dynamism or the feeling of efficacy under the influence of which he becomes aware of that activity. Moreover, to the extent that primitive assimilation is undifferentiated from a crude and elementary accommodation to things, this dynamism will arise only with respect to the phenomenalistic connections perceived among objects. A causality resting on the union of phenomenalism and efficacy is therefore that which expresses most simply the acquisition of awareness characteristic of the elementary intellectual mechanisms. It is this union we shall find again in the succeeding stages and chiefly in the third stage; little by little, the two poles of external or physical causality and internal or psychological causality are detached from one another, and by virtue of this very fact lose their mixed character of phenomenalism and dynamism, the one to become spatial, the other intentional.

In conclusion, the point of departure of causality should, it seems to us, be sought in a diffuse feeling of efficacy which would accompany the activity itself but would be localized by the child, not in a self, but in the point of culmination of the action. This efficacy would therefore fill the little child's whole universe or rather would be localized in each familiar center of perception, whether it concerned objects perceived in the environment or the subject's own body. Whether the nursling at the age of one or two months succeeds in sucking his thumb after having attempted to put it into his mouth or whether his eyes follow a moving object, he must experience, though in different degrees, the same impression: namely that, without his knowing how a certain action leads to a certain result, in other words, that a certain complex of efforts, tension, expectation, desire, etc., is charged with efficacy.

§ 2. THE THIRD STAGE: MAGICO-PHENOMENALISTIC CAUSALITY

We define the third stage as that which begins with secondary circular reactions, that is, with the systematic coordination of prehension and sight. From the point of view of space, this third stage is that of the formation of subjective groups and of the coordination of practical groups with them. From the point of view of object concept, it is the stage of elementary permanence attributed to things as a function of the action. We must therefore expect that this triple acquisition of secondary schemata, of subjective groups, and of permanence related to the action entails essential progress in regard to causality.

In the child's behavior patterns, it is from this stage on that we may establish with certainty the existence of a systematic interest in causal relations; from the earliest secondary circular reactions the child examines the result of the activity of his hands or feet and places into relationship certain movements and a certain result. Thus he knows how to shake the hood of his bassinet or the objects hanging from it, how to shake his rattles, swing them, make them sound, rub them against the sides of his bassinet, etc. How does he represent to himself the relations he discovers and establishes? And in a general way, what causality does he attribute to his universe?

To try to solve such a difficult problem it will be convenient to analyze separately the three kinds of connections which come into the child's visual field at this stage: movements of the body, movements which depend on these, and entirely independent movements. Here are three examples which seem to justify this distinction: 1) The child sees his hands and feet move in his visual field. He is already in control of the movements of his hands and is gradually learning to control those of his feet. 2) The child discovers that by striking hanging objects with his hand or by kicking them he can make them swing indefinitely (see *O.I.*, obs. 103, etc.). 3) The child turns his head when he hears a familiar voice and stops looking when he sees the person to whom the voice belongs, as if he understands that this is the cause of the sound. At the outset it seems as though the first two of these sequences must constitute, in the eyes of the child, causal relations depending on his body, and that the third must constitute an independent relation. But such an hypothesis has value only from the point of view of the observer, and the problem is to discover how these three kinds of causal connection appear from the child's point of view.

With regard to body movements, the following suppositions may be made. The first time the child has attentively watched his hands emerge in the visual field (this happens toward the middle of the preceding stage: *O.I.*, Chap. II, §4), and above all the first time he has been able to influence their trajectory while looking at them (obs. 63-66) he must experience a dual impression. On the one hand, his hands evidently seem to him to be bodies of some sort, like objects observed in the environment. On the other hand, the feeling of efficacy which, in connection with the first stage, we have supposed he attached to all perception extending a real action must have been all the more keen because, in the particular case, desire or effort constantly leads to an effective result. The hands and later the feet must constitute, from the first stages, particularly lively centers of causality through efficacy. Now, what will happen when, toward the end of the second stage, the hand becomes not only a spectacle which one can preserve and almost direct, but an actual instrument for prehension and consequently subject to conscious intentions on the child's part?

It is at this precise moment of development that the initial causality begins to be differentiated and to take on the form which will characterize it during the third stage. The nature of causality will not yet change, and the union of efficacy and phenomenalism will always define it in each of its aspects. But the difference will doubtless be that because with prehension and the handling of objects the child's behavior becomes more systematic and consequently more intentional (see *O.I.*, Chap. III, Introduction), he will better dissociate the purpose or the desire preceding the result from the action and the result itself. Hitherto cause and effect were, so to speak, condensed into a single mass centered around the effect perceived; the feeling of efficacy was merely one with the result of the act (the action being too global to be analyzed in two phases: the search and its result). Henceforth, on the contrary, as a result of the greater complexity of acts and consequently of their greater purposefulness, cause reveals a tendency to be internalized and effect to be externalized.

Before pursuing this analysis let us try to illustrate it by an example. During the present stage there are fairly frequent instances in which the child makes his hand perform all sorts of movements which he examines most attentively. This is no longer a question of actual experimentation, since prehension has already been learned, but rather, so to speak, an act of taking possession. True, the child sometimes performs these examinations for the sake of imitation or to evaluate distances and construct his space in depth. But often he seems to act through purely causal interest: it is his power over the hand that he seems to study. Furthermore, even when it is a question of imitations or of space, this causal aspect of the phenomenon must not be excluded. Here are some clear-cut cases in which interest in causality seems to us to be paramount.

OBS. 128. At 0;3 (12) that is to say, several days after he revealed his capacity to grasp objects seen, Laurent is confronted by a rattle hanging from his bassinet top; a watch chain hangs from the rattle (see *O.I.*, obs. 98). From the point of view of the relationships between the chain and the rattle the result of the experiment is wholly negative: Laurent does not pull the chain by himself and when I place it in his hands and he happens to shake it and hears the noise, he waves his hand but drops the chain. On the other hand, he seems immediately to establish a connection between the movements of his hand and those of the rattle, for having shaken his hand by chance and heard the sound of the rattle he waves his empty hand again, while looking at the rattle, and even waves it harder and harder (he has already executed behavior of this type during the preceding days: see *O.I.*, obs. 97).

Observing that the rattle no longer moves—and this is what we wanted to come to—or rather, no longer seeing anything of interest in it, Laurent looks again at his hands, which he is still waving. He then examines most attentively his right hand, which he is swinging, meanwhile retaining exactly the same facial expression he had when watching the rattle. It is as though he were studying his own power over it (just as he has already seen his power over the rattle).

OBS. 129. At 0;8 (7), that is at the end of this stage, Laurent looks at his hands most attentively, as if he did not know them. He is alone in his bassinet, his hands motionless, but he constantly moves his fingers and examines them. After this he moves his hands slowly, looking at them with the same interested expression. Then he joins them and separates them more slowly while continuing to study the phenomenon; he ends by scratching his covers, striking them, etc., but watching his hands the whole time.

It is noteworthy that each of these behavior patterns is very primitive and familiar to the child. It cannot therefore be their results as such which excite his momentary interest. It is as if Laurent were merely struck by the subjection of his hands to his intentions, that is, by the strange behavior of these objects which depend more than any others on the power to continue, to stop, or to alter the spectacle perceived.

OBS. 130. At 0;7 (21), 0;7 (28), etc., I observe that Jacqueline still looks at her hands with surprise when she separates them and brings them together again.

The same day she looks attentively at her right hand as she moves the fingers.

At 0;8 (9) she takes her thumb from her mouth and looks for a long time at her fingers as she moves them more or less systematically.

At 0;8 (13) she looks at her right hand which she alternately opens and closes.

All this behavior is familiar to Jacqueline and has been observed by her throughout the whole acquisition of prehension. Why, then, does she return to it until about 0;8 (15)? (It is only from this date on that Jacqueline stops looking at her hands for their own sake.) We see only one explanation for this; it is not the sights as such which are new and interesting to the child, it is his progressive awareness of his power over the particular objects that are his hands. In other words, Jacqueline's persistent interest in the movements of her hands, considerably after the coordination of sight and prehension, comes from a sort of reflection on the purposefulness of those movements.

Same observations on Lucienne, until toward 0;8.

How shall we interpret the causality which the child must attribute to these movements of his body, especially of his hands and feet? On the one hand it seems that, during this third stage, the subject becomes conscious of their purposefulness. When Laurent, at 0;3 (12), having tried in vain to reproduce the movement of a rattle, consoles himself by looking at the hand he is moving, or when Jacqueline at 0;7 and 0;8 still contemplates the activity of her fingers, there is little doubt that they sense their power and experience a more or less clear awareness of their desire to continue and reproduce those movements. But, on the other hand, it would certainly be rash to attribute to the child of that age a consciousness of self. The self is constituted only by comparison and by contrast with other selves and with the external environment. During the present stage, another person barely begins to be analyzed through imitation, and action on the material environment is so faintly outlined that it does not yet give rise to any precise feeling of resistance. The child is therefore still very far from being able to attribute his intentions and his powers to a "self" conceived as different from a "non-self" and opposed to the external world; the self and the universe still make up only one and the same totality.

If the child becomes conscious of the purposefulness of his movements and of the reality of his power over his hands and feet, he still merely places his effectual purpose and power in an absolute identified with the perceptual world. Awareness of purpose results merely in the dissociation between cause and effect, the cause being identified with the effectual purpose and the effect with the phenomenon perceived. By virtue of this fact, doubtless cause reveals a tendency to become internalized, but it still is not internalized in a self; it is immanent in immediate reality. As to effect, this is naturally placed in the same universe as the other phenomena; it is only to the observer that the child's hands and feet belong to his body for, to the child himself, they are on the same plane of reality as other objects.

But this beginning of differentiation between cause and effect has considerable importance in the structure of causality. At least with regard to his body movements—but we shall see that the same applies to other causal sequences—the child henceforth becomes conscious of the existence of a general cause: the efficacy of desire, of purpose, of effort, etc., in short, the whole dynamism of conscious action. But of course it is never when some phenomenon has been fortuitously observed (the appearance of the hands or of an object to be grasped, etc.) that this causality is made manifest; the union of efficacy and phenomenalism therefore remains complete and, if the first tends to be distinguished from the second, it nevertheless remains immanent in it.

Let us now proceed to the second type of causal relations: the relations between the movements of objects and those of the body itself (the relations characteristic of secondary circular reaction). At first it would seem as though, from the child's point of view, these second relations must be essentially different from the first. In the case of the hand which moves intentionally there could not be any intelligible connection in the subject's mind between his intentions and the movement perceived; the child does not yet know himself as the subject endowed with sight, intentionality, etc. The relation of cause and effect which unites his desires with his body movements can therefore only be the type of causality achieved by efficacy and phenomenalism combined. On the contrary, when the child pulls a string and thereby shakes the rattles hanging from the top, it seems that all the elements of the problem were presented to immediate perception: the child sees the hand which is pulling the string, he sees the string attached to the rattles or to the hood, and needs only to establish the relationship between these various parts of the same perceived totality. But in reality, analysis of the process of secondary circular reaction and, above all, of its generalizations in the form of procedures to make interesting spectacles last (see *O.I.*, Chap. III, §4) shows that, from the point of view of causality, such relations hardly differ to the child from the relations concerning his body only. All the transitions are given between these two types of relations, and thus secondary circular reaction is completely contained in causality achieved by efficacy and phenomenalism combined.

If the child undoubtedly begins (around 0;2-0;3) by examining his empty hand, he quickly becomes accustomed to looking at it when it holds an object. Furthermore, the coordinations between sight and prehension which mark the beginning of the present stage and give rise to the discovery of the purposefulness of hand movements occur only in behavior related to the objects themselves. The child perceives simultaneously that his hand obeys his desires and that it has become capable of taking possession of desired objects. The efficacy of intentions therefore applies both to visible aspects of the body and to objects. That being the case, it goes without saying that the child immediately undertakes the conquest of the world, without placing any limit in advance on the act of taking possession. A conquest undertaken in these circumstances is not causal, in the physical and spatial sense of the word. It is a mere extension of the magico-phenomenalistic "efficacy" which explains the causal relations established by the child in the course of his secondary circular reactions.

To be convinced of this it is enough to examine how secondary circular reactions are acquired. When the child has by chance obtained an interesting result which he will immediately try to reproduce, to accomplish this he does not try at all to insure physical and spatial contact between the different elements which come into play; he simply forces himself to repeat his gesture exactly, as if the gesture itself were charged with all the necessary efficacy. From this point of view let us take up again the acts described in *O.I.* (Chap. III, §1).

OBS. 131. When Lucienne, from 0;3 (5) on, shakes herself in her bassinet in order to make the hood sway (*O.I.*, obs. 94), it is apparent that to her no intermediary exists serving as a physical link between the movements of her body and those of the top; the latter directly extend, in her mind, the muscular sensations through which she is aware of her own movements.

It is true that from 0;4 (27) she makes sure of a contact between her feet and the hanging dolls (obs. 95) so as to swing them. But this contact is not visual. It is merely tactile, and the experiment made on Jacqueline in this connection (*O.I.*, obs. 96) shows that even so it is not considered necessary: Jacqueline shakes her legs as soon as she sees the doll in the distance, as though the empty movement alone were charged with efficacy.

In the same way when Laurent (*O.I.*, obs. 97 and 98) shakes strings and chains in order to shake the rattles, he establishes a relationship only between the act of grasping the end of the chain and the movement of the rattles, not seeing the chain as a necessary intermediary between his movements and the rattles. The chain is simply something to be grasped and shaken when one wants to act upon the rattle; it is not yet the physical and spatial extension of the rattle. Certainly, concerning this last point, it is impossible to prove at once that the connection is phenomenalistic. On the contrary, the child seems to act as though he understood the necessity for the contacts, and one can be fooled by this for a long time. But in order to interpret the subject's behavior correctly it suffices to see how it is acquired and above all how it is corrected in the event of failure.

In both cases, observation reveals that the child places all emphasis on his gesture as such and none at all on the physical interrelations of objects. The child learns to perform the correct movements simply by repeating those which succeed. For instance (beginning of obs. 98), having fortuitously shaken a chain and heard the sound of the rattles thus shaken, Laurent waves his empty hand as if this movement were the sole cause of the effect perceived. Then little by little he discovers that the chain is necessary; but we may still say it is the tactile and kinesthetic impressions connected with the chain grasped and swung that are put in relationship to the movement of the rattles, and not the chain as a spatial and physical object. At 0;3 (14) Laurent, having dropped the chain, continues for five minutes to swing his fist while looking at the rattle, without trying to control his gesture to insert it correctly in the series of necessary intermediaries!

But we have seen that, besides the secondary circular reactions related to the movements of the bassinet, from the beginning of the coordination of sight and prehension all sorts of reactions of the same type are constituted in connection with the child's familiar objects: shaking, swinging, rubbing, etc. (*O.I.*, obs. 102-104). Here it seems that we transcend mere efficacy to enter the realm of causality through spatial and mechanical contact. But nothing is less sure. So long as the child's hand acts directly on object A, and not on A through the intermediary of object B coming in contact with A, one cannot speak of a truly physical causality. It is through simple extension of the efficacy of gestures of prehension that the subject discovers the various properties at issue.

In short, in the acquisition of secondary circular reactions nothing indicates that the child transcends the level of efficacy and phenomenalism. Just as, in actions related to his own body, the child puts his intentions and his impressions of effort into direct relationship with the image of his limbs, as though the former acted magically and without intermediaries upon the latter, so also in his actions upon external objects he seems to establish an immediate link between his movements as experienced from within and their final result, without paying attention to the necessary connections between them. Doubtless through a progressive differentiation of his movements he very soon can pull, push, tap, swing, shake, rub, etc., according to circumstances and the desired effect, but these actions are not yet controlled from without. They are controlled from within, that is, the child, relying upon his various sensory impressions (usually kinesthetic and tactile and, much more rarely, visual), simply tries to reproduce the movement which proved to be efficacious. But whatever this differentiation of his movements may be, the child does not yet succeed—and this is the essential point—in establishing among the perceived objects a relation other than a phenomenalistic one. He has as yet no knowledge of the spatial and physical relations on which objective causality is based. For instance, the string which connects his hand with the bassinet hood is still only a thing to be grasped and shaken in order to obtain a certain movement of the hood; it is not yet the substantial intermediary necessary for contact between hand and hood. From this point of view the true cause of the results obtained in the course of the secondary circular reactions must be, to the child, the efficacy of his desires, of his efforts, of his actions experienced from within, just as though it were a question of the first type of causal relations, that is, movements of the body only. But this general cause is not yet conceived as emanating from a "self" since, precisely because he feels omnipotent, the child cannot yet contrast his own self with the external world. Finally, it is always when a result has been obtained fortuitously that such causal connections are established. Phenomenalism remains indissolubly united with efficacy.

Such interpretations may seem arbitrary so long as we remain, as heretofore, within the narrow confines of strictly secondary circular reaction. But they acquire a certain circumstantial strength as soon as one envisages these behavior patterns in a broader form and remembers the generalizations to which they give rise. As soon as the child finds himself in possession of a gesture whose efficacy is revealed in the course of a typical circular reaction he applies it to everything. Thus Laurent, having learned to shake the string attached to his hand in order to shake the bassinet top, waves his empty hand in order to continue the movement of a rattle (*O.I.*, obs. 112). Similarly, Jacqueline pulls the string hanging from the top to continue the movement of a book or a bottle, etc., which I swing at a distance (*O.I.*, obs. 113). Or again, gestures such as shaking the hand (gesture of farewell), tapping the edge of the bassinet, shaking the head from side to side, shaking the legs, arching oneself up, etc., are used to make some interesting sight last (objects which are moved in front of the child, noises and sounds, etc.; see *O.I.*, obs. 114-118).

It is clear that causality of this kind can be interpreted only through the union of efficacy and phenomenalism. On the one hand, the child endows his own gesture with efficacy, independently of any physical or spatial contact. But on the other hand, it is always when this gesture coincides with an internal effect that the subject endows his own action with efficacy. Here it is necessary to discuss a particular case, especially interesting from the point of view of causality, in order to justify this interpretation.

OBS. 132. I. At 0;8 (9) Jacqueline is lying down looking at a saucer which I swing about 50 centimeters in front of her eyes. She reveals a lively interest and expresses her pleasure by the well-known behavior of arching herself upward, with her weight on her feet and shoulder blades, and then letting herself fall in a heap. I pass the saucer before her again. She watches it smiling, then stares at it seriously and attentively and arches upward a second time. When Jacqueline has fallen back again I pass the object before her once more; the same play three more times. After this I hold the object motionless before her; she arches herself again two or three times, then proceeds to something else. I resume twice; as soon as the saucer is motionless Jacqueline arches upward again. I then definitely pause in my game; Jacqueline nevertheless draws herself up five or six times more, while looking at the object, then tires of it. Every time the child's gesture has been followed by the saucer's movement, Jacqueline has manifested great satisfaction; otherwise, an expression of disappointment and expectation.

At 0;8 (13) Jacqueline is still lying down in her bassinet but its top is up and the child looks at it above her. I manage to make the top shake by means of a long ribbon without having Jacqueline see me or know I am there. After a few frightened little movements she reveals a lively interest. I stop. She waits a few moments, then arches herself while staring at the top. I again make it shake; as soon as I stop she arches herself (same play six or seven times). A continuous smile. Pleasure at succeeding. Five minutes later, same reactions, as well as at 0;8 (15).

At 0;8 (16) I give Jacqueline different new objects (cigarette case, etc.) which she explores carefully (see *O.I.*, obs. 136). Part of this exploratory behavior characteristic of the fourth stage of the development of sensorimotor intelligence is the movement of arching upward. This is particularly the case with a tin box; Jacqueline has struck it many times against the wicker of her bassinet while laughing at the noise, then has arched upward several times while looking at it.

The same day, she arches herself in order to oscillate a leather case attached to the strings hanging from the top.

At 0;8 (16) Jacqueline looks at me while I put my index finger in my mouth and remove it at regular intervals (to study imitation); instead of imitating me, Jacqueline arches herself up while looking at my mouth very attentively. I put my index finger back into it; as soon as I withdraw it she arches herself again, etc.

II. After this last experiment I decide henceforth to thwart all Jacqueline's attempts to utilize the movement of arching herself up, in other words, no longer to repeat the movements she tries to prolong by means of that procedure. Thus I shake the top without her seeing me; Jacqueline immediately draws herself up, but unsuccessfully, then recommences five or six times with an air of constant surprise.

Same day. I make a sort of mewing sound by letting air escape between my teeth and lips. Jacqueline begins by imitating it vaguely, then, when I pause, she arches upward three or four times. A few minutes later she does it once more after I have repeated the sound or after I have put a finger back into my mouth.

The next day, at 0;8 (17) and at 0;9 (19) Jacqueline continues to draw herself up following movements of the top, despite the ineffectiveness of the gesture. At 0;8 (20) she arches herself twice after I have stuck out my tongue, swung my watch, said "coucou" behind a hat, etc.

At 0;9 (3) she repeats the arching movement three or four times when faced with an object which I have placed too high for her to grasp. Same reaction at 0;9 (8). At 0;9 (13) she draws herself up when I stop clapping my hands.

Thus we see how the coincidence between an attitude of pleasure (arching upward) and sights such as a saucer which I swing or an oscillating hood suffices to give the child the impression that his gesture is efficacious. Above all it is evident that this procedure, fixed after several apparently successful efforts, has lasted from 0;8 (16) to 0;9 (13) despite a month of repeated frustrations! Nothing about these behavior patterns can have been intelligible to the child; only the union of the most external phenomenalism and the feeling of efficacy attributed to the activity itself can account for the origin and persistency of such behavior which, although it appeared during the third stage, has been extended, in Jacqueline's case, throughout the fourth.

In short, these procedures to make an interesting sight last wholly confirm, from the point of view of causality, our interpretation of secondary circular reactions. His own movements, which in the course of the secondary circular reactions are revealed to the child as able to engender a certain definite result, are immediately utilized outside that particular context and outside any material and spatial contact; here then is proof that the causality attributed to the gesture is not yet a physical causality, based on the external qualities of the action, but a causality through mere efficacy.

In conclusion, what is this efficacy? In the case of secondary circular reactions and of procedures to make an interesting sight last we cannot say that it is a purely internal dynamism, as when the child realizes that he is acting upon his own hands and feet but does not know at all how he does it. Besides his impressions of desire, effort, expectation, satisfaction, etc., the child experiences kinesthetic, tactile, and even visual sensations which give to each of his gestures a physiognomy all its own. It would thus seem that the action, in so far as it is global, is understood to be the cause in the type of relations now under consideration. This is not action conceived solely in an external and material aspect, precisely because the child is not at all concerned with physical contacts or connections. Neither is it action conceived as emanating from a self, since we have just seen that the subject still considers himself capable of everything and is consequently ignorant of the contrast between internal and external worlds.

Hence it is action experienced as a whole and placed in reality midway between the internal and the external.

Because this is so, efficacy is always phenomenalistic. If the child were conscious of a self independent of things and attributed his various powers to it, he would doubtless try to use this omnipotence and try to produce some effect or other outside the immediate stimuli of the environment. But precisely because efficacy is experienced only on the occasion of a fortuitous conquest (secondary circular reaction) or a situation presenting some analogy to situations in which the act is successful (interesting sights which recall the conquests of circular reaction), it has always a phenomenalistic connection. Therein, this kind of causality, though based on the dynamism of action, deviates from the absolute cause envisioned in the Biranian theory of effort;[1] efficacy is not first located in a self and later projected into things; on the contrary, it is first located in external phenomenalism and later progressively detached from it and moved closer to the action itself. During the first stage efficacy and phenomenalism remain a unit. Thereafter they begin to be dissociated, as action is more conscious of itself and its purposefulness. But they always remain indissociable so long as activity is not attributed to an inner self and phenomenalism is not replaced by a system of connections that are truly external, that is, spatial and objective.

Let us now come to the third type of causal relations represented in the course of this stage: those which, to the observer, seem independent of the child's body and his activity. Thus, from the second stage on, the child tries to look at the things he hears, as if he considered them the cause of the noise. Or again, he studies with very lively interest the actions performed before him, as though he knew his mother were the cause of the advent of the bottle or his father the cause of the various sights arousing his curiosity.

How does the child interpret such relations? Three solutions seem possible to us. The first would consist in asserting that these

[1] Translator's note: Reference is to Maine de Biran (1766-1824) who wrote on habit and the influence of physical characteristics on mental faculties. His psychology is based on consciousness of self perceived in voluntary effort.

relations are not in the least causal from the subject's point of view: when the child sees the object he has heard or watches a person who shakes a toy he is only able to perceive more or less coherent totalities or to establish more or less stable connections; he cannot conceive of the existence of objective centers of action that would make him regard the object or the person as causes of the noise or the movements. The second solution would consist, on the contrary, in endowing the child with the power to associate causally any one perception with any other: thus if the child has regularly associated the sound of the rattle with the sight of it or the movement of toys with those of the person who holds them, the rattle or the person will be conceived as causes.[2] Finally, in the third place, we might say that relationships independent of the body remain divorced from causality so long as they are external to the subject's activity and that they become causal to the extent that they are incorporated in that activity. This incorporation may be conceived in two different ways: either the child can intervene in the context of these relations (for example by inducing the rattle to reproduce the usual sound or the person to repeat what he was doing), or else he can conceive of objects by analogy with his own activity and thus invest them with a causal power derived from his own.

How to choose from among these three hypotheses? It is obviously impossible to analyze directly the behavior of the child relative to the sequences independent of his action. At most we may affirm that the child foresees certain sequences and thus establishes a constant relation between an antecedent A (a sound, for example) and the consequent B (the corresponding visual image). But does this involve causality? There is nothing to prove that it does; such a relationship may be a mere linking of signifier to signified, based upon the concept of sign or indication and not at all on that of causality. With regard to actions the child witnesses but does not participate in (when, for instance, a person shakes a rattle before him), these may be a matter of mere sequence or of complex perception and may not at all involve the relationship of cause and effect.

However, there is a way of interpreting such relations. We

[2] This is the classical solution of Hume and of associationism: habit engenders causality.

may do so by analyzing the child's behavior at the moment when he intervenes in causal sequences already organized before his intervention. For example, assume object A which, for the observer, is the cause of effect B. The child who is interested in B looks at the aggregate AxB up to the moment that A ceases to produce B. How will the child go about making the phenomenon last? Will he try to act on A simply by setting it in motion (touching or pushing it slightly, for instance)? If so, we may assume that in all probability A is conceived by the subject as a causal center independent of his body, which would be tantamount to confirming the second of the three solutions proposed above. Will he, on the contrary, act directly on B or try to act on the complex AxB, as though it constituted an inseparable whole? In this case the first solution will probably be the correct one (the relations independent of the action are not considered causal), or the third, in one form or another.

We shall now undertake the analysis. But in studying these behavior patterns we must be careful not to confuse them with simpler ones in which the child does not discern the duality of A and B. For example, in a circular reaction such as shaking a rattle to make it sound, it would be impossible to maintain, without being arbitrary, that the child distinguishes as separate items the rattle's visual image and its product, in other words, the rattle as cause and the sound as effect; the rattle is merely a unit regarded as dependent on the subject's own activity. The same is true of all circular reactions, whatever may be their complexity from the observer's point of view, if one concedes the interpretation we have given of them from the point of view of causality, With regard to procedures to make an interesting sight last it would be impossible to find in them, either, a favorable analytic field for the goal we propose to reach. True, at first it might seem that, when the child sees a person move an object and arches himself up in order to make the sight continue, he is witnessing the development of a causal sequence independent of himself and is trying to act upon that sequence. But as the sight is produced outside the field of prehension it is impossible to determine on which precise factor the child is trying to act: is it the person who moves the object or the object itself? In reality, everything happens as though the child does not analyze the phenomenon at all in detail and merely tries to reproduce it as a whole; hence for him it is not a question of a causal sequence between the person A and the effect B, but only of a causal relation between his own action and the complex AxB.

Let us therefore examine the situations in which the causal sequence presented to the child develops in his field of prehension and thereafter is open to analysis by the subject himself: to make the sight before his eyes continue, the child may either employ global procedures or try to put the cause observed into relationship with the effect he wishes to see renewed.

OBS. 133. At 0;7 (7) Laurent looks at my hand while I snap my middle finger against the base of my thumb, and he bursts into peals of laughter. When I do this at a distance of 50 centimeters or one meter from him, in order to make me continue he employs the usual magico-phenomenalistic procedures: he arches himself, waves his hands, shakes his head from side to side, etc. But what will he do when my hand comes into his field of prehension? Will he merely push my hand lightly in order to start a repetition of the movement, that is, put it in motion as though it constituted an autonomous center of causality (this is what the child will do during the fourth stage), or will he try himself to reproduce the desired effect?

The result obtained is very definite: Laurent grasps my hand between his, strikes it, shakes it, etc. He therefore treats it like a rattle whose properties depend on his own action, and not at all like an independent source of activity.

When I place my hand at a distance of 30 centimeters from him he draws himself up, etc., then when I bring it to 10 centimeters he begins again to strike it, shake it, etc.

OBS. 134. At 0;7 (7) Laurent looks at me very attentively when I drum with my finger tips on a tin box of 15x20 centimeters. The box lies on a cushion before him and is just two centimeters beyond his reach. On the other hand, as soon as I pause in my game I place my hand five centimeters from his, while he watches, and leave it there motionless. So long as I drum Laurent smiles delightedly but when I pause he looks for a moment at my hand, then proceeds very rapidly to examine the box and then, while looking at it, claps his hands, waves goodbye with both hands, shakes his head, arches upward, etc. In short, he uses the whole collection of his usual magico-phenomenalistic procedures. With regard to my hand, placed before his eyes, he grasps it for a moment twice in succession, shakes it, strikes it, etc.

But he does not lead it back to the box, although that would be easy, nor does he try to discover a specific procedure to set its activity in motion.

A moment later I grasp a tin bird with movable wings. I hold the bird up in the air 40 centimeters from Laurent and move its wings with my hand. Then I put my hand in front of him. The child's reaction is very definite: he immediately tries to act upon the bird by arching himself, shaking his head, hands, etc. But he pays no attention to my hand. However, every time it leaves the bird and comes back in front of the child, Laurent's eyes follow it and watch it for a moment. But he immediately tries to exercise his power over the bird without trying to push my hand toward the object (let us note once more that this last behavior pattern is that which the child will adopt during the next stage).

At 0;7 (8) Laurent is seated and I place a large cushion within his reach. I scratch the cushion. He laughs. Afterward I move my hand five centimeters from the cushion, between it and his own hands, in such a way that if he pushed it slightly it would press against the cushion. As soon as I pause, Laurent strikes the cushion, arches, swings his head, etc. True, subsequently he does sometimes grasp my hand. But it is only in order to strike it, shake it, etc., and he does not once try to move it forward or put it in contact with the cushion.

At a certain moment he scratches my hand; on the other hand, he does not scratch the cushion although this behavior is familiar to him.

At 0;7 (11) I repeat the experiment with the cushion. Laurent begins by arching himself, etc., looking sometimes at my hand, sometimes at the cushion, and finally scratches the latter. But he never tries to push my hand. At 0;7 (12), in the same circumstances, he hardly looks at my hand which I offer him near the cushion; he strikes the cushion, tries to shake it, etc. But it does not occur to him, as it did yesterday, to scratch it himself, for today his hands were not placed on the cushion at the beginning of the experiment. Laurent ends by grasping my hand in both his hands and shaking it, but he does not move it near the cushion. A moment later I again scratch the cushion while Laurent's left hand is on it: he scratches it immediately.

Then, still at 0;7 (12), I resume the experiment with the tin box on which I drum and then leave my hand five centimeters from it. Laurent takes the box, strikes it, etc., but pays no attention to my hand. I recommence, moving the box out of reach and, after drumming on it, place my hand between it and the child; Laurent draws himself up while watching the box, claps his hands, etc., and finally scratches the cushion which is still beside him.

OBS. 135. At 0;7 (22) Laurent is facing a hanging rattle and watches what I do with it. I slowly approach my hand to the rattle and when I am two centimeters away from the object I shake it hard by snapping my index finger against my thumb. I immediately withdraw my hand but leave it in the air at a distance of ten centimeters from the rattle, at the child's disposal and ready to be pushed toward the object. Laurent bursts out laughing and immediately arches himself, shakes his head, his hand, etc., while looking at the object. But at first he looks only at the rattle and pays no attention to my hand. As the desired effect is not reproduced, Laurent finally examines my hand three times in succession but without doing anything (without even arching himself). On the other hand, as soon as he again looks at the rattle he arches himself, etc., apparently wishing to see again the phenomenon of shaking it (this is new to him).

At 0;7 (23) same reactions, as well as in the experiment of the metal bird (he tries to act on the bird only, and not on my hand). The same is true with the rattle and the bird at 0;7 (29).

At 0;8 (1) I swing a chain and then offer him my hand; he still tries to act on the object only, and not on my hand.

OBS. 136. From 0;8 (7) Laurent's behavior changes and reveals patterns belonging to the next stage: instead of acting only on the object or being satisfied to strike or shake my hand, Laurent pushes it toward the object, thus counting on my activity and not on his to secure the desired result.

On the other hand, at 0;8 (25) he relapses momentarily into the behavior patterns of this stage, given the difficulty of the problem posed. He looks at my foot which I direct toward a table to knock a tier of it gently, thereby shaking a flower pot placed upon it. Then when he sees me move my foot toward the table or hears the sound this suffices to make him look at the flowers immediately. He therefore understands that there is a relationship between the movement of my foot and that of the flowers. But is it an objectively causal relation or a mere phenomenalistic sequence? When I put my foot on his lap he does not steer it toward the table but handles my shoe, mainly tapping it on top, producing a sound similar to the first one; then twice in succession he looks at the flowers as though the act of striking my foot were enough to set them in motion.

This behavior is therefore intermediate between the behavior of this stage and that of the next.

Such observations seem to us significant. The child finds himself confronted by a relation which to the observer is causal and in which cause A (the adult's hand) is clearly distinct from effect B (the sound produced by snapping the finger, drumming on a box, shaking a metal bird, or scratching a cushion). The child sees hand A engender effect B, but he sees the hand move away and can observe that, as it does so, the phenomenon ceases. If the child considered hand A an independent and sufficient cause of the phenomenon it would be very easy for him either to bring it nearer to the point of application or simply to set it in motion without wanting to substitute himself for it. Can it be said that the child acts as though he considered hand A an autonomous center of causality?

We think not. The child's whole behavior seems to indicate that at the time the interesting sight is interrupted he has recourse to a single causal agent only—his own activity. Sometimes he tries to reproduce the observed effect B directly by himself, but he always goes about it by procedures depending on efficacy and phenomenalism. Sometimes he tries to act on hand A; but he behaves toward it not as though it were a real motive power to be released but as though it remained subordinate to his own activity, the activity of another person being similarly conceived as depending on his own.

Concerning the first point we notice that, to reproduce effect B, Laurent tries to act directly on the object: he arches himself, etc., while looking at the tin box, the mechanical bird, and the cushion, or he strikes and shakes the object when it is within his reach. Now some of these procedures are merely those we have discussed above in connection with efficacy (arching, shaking the head, waving the hands, etc.). As to the others, they are the usual movements inherent in secondary circular reaction (striking, shaking, etc.) and not imitations of what hand A had done or of procedures adapted to effect B. The child therefore considers effect B as one of the many phenomena which extend his own action and not as the product of a process independent of that activity.

The actions performed on cause A are equally significant. The child makes no attempt, as he will do later, to push toward object B the hand which he has just seen in action, or even to put it in motion by touching it. Are we to say that by striking or shaking hand A the child really wishes to put it in action? It is evident that he is trying to make it do something (he wants to induce it to drum again, or swing the bird, or scratch the cushion). But the question is whether he considers the hand as a causal center independent of his own activity or as the extension of that activity. Does he consider hand A as being a reality analogous to his own hand but autonomous in relation to it, or does he regard it as something comparable to a rattle, for instance, which, to the child, does not exist or act except when grasped or manipulated by him? Stated thus, the question seems easy to answer. When he tries to put hand A in motion the child confines himself to striking it, shaking it, etc.: he treats it as a kind of appendage to his own action, an appendage whose properties are manifested as a function of his own movements, and not at all as an independent object of autonomous activity.

This interpretation must, it seems to us, lead to the third of the three solutions indicated above: the sequences independent of the activity become causal only in so far as they enter into the sphere of that activity. At first they are nothing more than simple sights or "presentations" without real causality. But does this mean that all causality is absent from them? We do not believe so, because all perception, as we have seen in connection with the first stage, involves an effort of assimilation and accommodation. It is therefore very possible that, to the extent he follows an object with his eyes, turns in order to see it, or simply concentrates his attention and his interest on it, the child has the impression that the object is connected with his pleasure, his expectation, etc., in short, with the more or less conscious dynamism of his activity. The causality of independent sequences would therefore remain that of the first stages, as long as prehension and intentional action do not intervene in their context. On the other hand, once they do intervene, the sequences are brought back to those of the second type, that of relations depending on the movements themselves (secondary circular reactions and procedures to make an interesting sight last).

The only difference that can be established between the second and third types of causal relations is a difference in degree. When the child acts directly and repeats his action the causal relation he establishes between it and the result obtained is purely a relation of efficacy and phenomenalism: the effect produced merely extends the dynamism of the act. When, on the contrary, the child intervenes in a sequence of events already under way (obs. 133-136) he must experience a slightly stronger impression of objectivity or externality. But it is a matter of degree and not of real contrast.

Of the two above-mentioned possibilities regarding the third solution, only the first is fulfilled at this stage. The child does not yet attribute, by analogy with his own action, causal power to the objects he perceives; he is limited to including them in his habitual schemata of causality and to subjecting them to the magico-phenomenalistic efficacy of his own movements.

In short, the three types of causal relations we have delineated in connection with this stage—actions brought to bear on the body itself, actions of the body on external objects, and interactions of objects—actually constitute only one type: in these three cases it is to the dynamism of his own activity that the child attributes all causal efficacy, and the phenomenon perceived outside, however removed it may be from his own body, is conceived only as a simple result of his own action. In the first case this result is perhaps felt to be more intimate and familiar, in the third more external, but that is only a difference in degree. Moreover, to the extent the externality of the result is established, phenomenalism becomes dissociated from efficacy and tends to be transformed into physical causality, but the dissociation is still not completed and the totality of the causal connections belonging to this third stage thus remains based on the union of phenomenalism and efficacy.

A final point remains to be examined. This is causality "by imitation," a causality which overlaps the three types of relations hitherto kept distinct and which has therefore been saved until last. The phenomenon is, in a word, as follows: from the time the child learns how to imitate systematically, that is, from 0;6-0;7, he uses this new power to try to make others repeat the various movements they have initiated. It is thus apparent that such a form of causality partakes of the three types enumerated earlier. First there is the child's action on his own body, since the child imitates behavior external to himself and, in imitating it, incorporates it into himself in the strict sense of the term. Later there is the child's action on an external object, since he tries to act on another person. Finally, there is a relation independent of the self, since, before he begins imitating, the child is simply a spectator, and since the question arises as to how he conceives of an action which, from the observer's point of view, is independent of himself. Let us now ask ourselves what this behavior means in relation to causality.

OBS. 137. At 0;7 (27) Jacqueline is seated in front of a big quilt. Her mother strikes the quilt with her hand and Jacqueline immediately imitates her amid peals of laughter. For a brief moment both of them strike together and this unison seems to delight Jacqueline. Jacqueline stops striking the quilt to look at her mother's hand. The hand continues to strike for a few more seconds and then stops. Then Jacqueline, while staring at her mother's hand (and without looking at her own once during the observation), begins to strike the quilt, at first gently and then harder and harder, exactly as if she were trying to force her mother to recommence. Her mother yields, Jacqueline stops (which shows that the imitation was entirely inherent in causal procedure), then when her mother's hand is again motionless, Jacqueline resumes tapping while looking at it.

Five hours later I strike the quilt with my hand. Jacqueline watches me, then imitates when I stop. When I recommence she stops and so on: obviously she is only trying to make me continue.

At 0;8 (8) in the same way, Jacqueline looks at a bottle I am swinging. When I pause she pulls a string hanging from the top to make it continue (although the bottle is 50 centimeters away). Hence this is a procedure analogous to the procedures in observation 113 (*O.I.*). Then, realizing her failure, she makes a movement of imitation with her hand while looking at the bottle and without trying to grasp it. I again move it; Jacqueline then imitates the movement ten to twelve times while staring at it, the object remaining motionless.

At 0;8 (10) Jacqueline coughs, I cough in response, and she laughs at my imitation. To make me continue she then coughs again, at first normally, then harder and harder and faster and faster. The manner in which she looks at me with an expression of desire and expectation, and the way she regulates her coughing in proportion to my silence, leaves little doubt as to the purpose of this behavior.

This causality by imitation is extended by Jacqueline through all the following stages, as we shall see.

OBS. 138. Around 0;7 I observed in Lucienne the first definite examples of causality by imitation.

At 0;7 (1) for instance, when she sees me open and shut my hand, sometimes she shakes her legs (one of her procedures to make interesting sights last), sometimes she moves her fingers to copy my gesture. In both cases she wears the same expression of expectation and seems to try to act on my hand.

At 0;7 (20) imitation of the same kind definitely plays the role of causal procedure: she regulates her movement by beginning slowly and accelerating until I resume mine.

Same observation at 0;7 (27). The next day she opens and closes her hands while looking at a chandelier, as though to swing it.

At 0;7 (29) she imitates the gesture of goodby and that of shaking the head from side to side, regulating her efforts until I resume; this is definitely a causal feeling.

These reactions become increasingly frequent on the following days.

At 0;8 (17) she cries out and I imitate her. Then she imitates me to make me begin again, etc. At 0;8 (18) I cry out in the same way, first: she begins by shaking her hands (usual causal procedure) and by shaking her head harder and harder, then she imitates me, at first gently, then increasingly violently and fast, until I resume.

OBS. 139. At 0;3 (29) Laurent already imitates my farewell gesture in order to make me continue (he regulates his attempts until I resume). He uses this gesture currently as a causal procedure and has known how to imitate it since 0;3 (23).

At 0;4 (23) he imitates me when I shake my head until I recommence. He also uses this gesture as a causal procedure on other occasions.

During the following months he also uses his nascent or consolidated imitations as procedures of a causal kind.

At 0;7 (11) he imitates a sound I make with my glottis until I recommence, etc.

Causality by imitation is prolonged in his case as in his sisters' until much later, in the next stages.

The question raised in connection with these observations is to ascertain whether the use of imitation as a causal procedure emerges from the general rule of the union of efficacy and phenomenalism or whether the child attributes to the person he imitates a causality independent of that of the activity itself. At first it seems that such behavior patterns mark progress over the preceding ones and transcend the level of mere efficacy. By virtue of the very fact that the child imitates someone else, one is tempted to believe that he attributes to the person imitated a causal activity separate from his own, and that causality thus begins to be objectified. But does this apparent truth correspond to reality?

We must recognize that to the child at this stage another person constitutes a more lively center of actions than any object whatever. It is enough to observe the subject's expression to realize this difference. On the one hand, in the presence of a person the child seems to await events rather than to bring them about as he does in the presence of things. When a person appears, the child is reserved for a moment, ready to follow in the direction indicated and thus attributing to the person a certain a certain spontaneity. On the other hand, the child unquestionably smiles and laughs more often in the presence of persons than of things —proof that the former excite him more than the latter and that in his eyes they are invested with a greater vitality. It is therefore very probable, as we have glimpsed several times, that contact with persons plays an essential role in the processes of objectification and externalization: the person constitutes the primary object and the most external of the objects in motion through space. Now, a remarkable parallel exists between the development of objects and spatial frames and that of causality: evidently it is to the extent that the object is externalized and becomes substantial that causality is detached from the action and is crystallized into independent centers. Thereafter it is probable that another person represents the first of these centers and contributes more than anything else to dissociating causality from the movements of the child himself and objectifying it in the external world.

But such an evolution does not take place in a single day, from the moment at which, through imitation, the child begins to analyze the acts of another person. If the child endows others with a certain spontaneity he is far from submitting to it at once and may believe it to be, like the spontaneity of things, in the main subservient to his own activity. If the child cries, sooner or later someone comes to his rescue; if he is hungry, he is provided for; if he takes pleasure in displays of affection, they are repeated to his full satisfaction. In short, another person cannot assume the privilege of being from the outset independent of efficacy and phenomenalism; he is perhaps the most externalized of the centers of production which animate the universe at this stage, but as yet nothing contrasts him in principle with the rest of that universe.

The proof is that all the procedures used by the child to act on things are applied to persons themselves. Thus, the procedures to make an interesting sight last are without exception utilized to make persons repeat their amusing actions: if one whistles, sings, snaps the fingers, etc., the child arches upward, shakes his head, waves his hands, rubs them against the edge of the bassinet, moves his legs, and sometimes even pulls strings in order to make someone else's activities last. In this way he brings the activities of others into the cluster of phenomena subject to control by the efficacy of his own movements. Of course another person does not give rise to secondary circular reactions as do rattles hanging from the bassinet hood or toys of one kind or another. Nevertheless every time someone yields to the child's entreaties true cycles are at once elaborated. We believe that the reciprocal imitation which evokes the attempts at causal utilization of which we have just spoken forms such phenomena. The child who imitates someone else with the sole aim of making him continue his acts is behaving no differently from the child who tries constantly to reproduce a certain result with the first object at hand. The only difference is that in the case of the object the child uses any means that chance reveals to him, whereas in the case of persons causality takes a precise form prescribed by the convergence of another person's body and his own—the form of imitation. But what is imitation, at this elementary level, if not mere extension of that circular reaction which Baldwin has so aptly called "imitation of oneself"? (During the third stage the child imitates only the behavior patterns he already knows how to perform himself.)

In short, the first times the child tries to act on someone else by imitating him and thereby forces him to repeat his interesting acts the behavior pattern is not much more complicated than when the child exerts effort on his own body. Therefore, someone else's person does not yet constitute an independent causal center; in a sense, it is still only the extension of the activity itself. Causality through imitation is thus connected with the three types of causal relations previously defined. It is related to activity brought to bear on the body itself. Moreover it belongs in the group of actions applied directly to external bodies. Finally, to the extent that the other person does something by himself before being imitated, there is present a relationship independent of the subject which the subject renders causal by intervening after the event. Precisely because causality by imitation combines in itself the three forms of causality, it does not bring about decisive progress by itself alone, and does not entail externalization and objectification of relations of a causal kind.

On the whole it may be said that, without at the outset marking any noteworthy innovation in the objectification of causality, causality through imitation leads the child toward this externalization and thus forms a transition between the behavior patterns of the third stage and those of the fourth. Another transition from the causal behavior patterns of the third stage to those of the fourth is furnished by certain behavior intermediate between secondary circular reaction and the application of familiar schemata to new situations. From the point of view of causality this behavior is, in effect, exactly midway between the efficacy characteristic of circular movements and spatialized causality. When, for example, without having himself produced a certain result, the child perceives the effects on his own body or in his field of prehension, he sometimes tries to reproduce the phenomenon as a whole merely by acting on one of its parts: there follows an incipient spatial analysis of causality. Such acts certainly belong in the same group as the secondary circular reactions and the procedures to make an interesting sight last, since it is still a question of a result to be prolonged or reproduced and not, as in the higher behavior patterns, of new relationships to be formed. Nevertheless, the present behavior patterns foretell those of the next group since the child is already trying to dissociate the relationships.

Here is an example.

OBS. 140. At 0;8 (17) Jacqueline holds a cloth bell (silent) which hangs from the bassinet top. I shake the top lightly, though she does not understand how, and the shaking reacts on the bell, which the child is holding firmly. When I stop, Jacqueline shakes her bell while watching the top. She does not pull the hanging string and thus shows that a familiar procedure is not involved. She confines herself to moving the object lightly from side to side; when I shake the top at the same time, she laughs, convinced of the efficacy of her procedure. We may account for this behavior pattern by saying that one part of the phenomenon has been used to reproduce all of it. This is the *pars pro toto* in its most elementary form.

That evening Jacqueline holds a rag doll also connected with the hood of the bassinet. I repeat the experiment and shake the top; the result is the same and Jacqueline waves the doll. But a half hour later the doll is abandoned within reach. I shake the hood. Jacqueline then arches herself up (see obs. 132) but once only. Noting the failure (she still watches the hood) she then looks for the doll. She grasps it at the exact place (near the head) where it is attached to the suspension string so that in grasping it she shakes the hood; she pulls several times, laughing at her success. Afterward she arches herself again and then pulls the doll. At the first pause I shake the hood myself; Jacqueline pulls the doll again, at the same time making the arching movement. Thus two procedures are used together, the second one tending to be no more than a helpful symbol.

It is evident that, without as yet involving causal relations other than those included in secondary circular reaction, such behavior patterns nevertheless proclaim imminent progress in the spatialization of causality. As the schemata in play here are not initiated haphazardly by the child, he can no longer be satisfied merely to repeat the global action which has led him to success (as, after having fortuitously pulled the strings hanging from his bassinet hood, he confines himself to pulling them again to rediscover the interesting result). He must grope and approach the complex totality of the phenomena, beginning by reproducing the most accessible, that is, the one which directly concerns the body itself. From this arises the apparent causal analysis and spatialization of causality presented by this behavior pattern. However, the very fact that the child believes he can attain the whole by means of a part and that he can reconstitute all of the observed causal process merely by reproducing its effects on his body shows that this is no true analysis but simply circular reaction applied to a schema which is not yet constructed and is in process of elaboration.

In short, despite the progress proclaimed by the imitation of persons and by these linkages of the part with the whole, causality at this stage remains impregnated with efficacy and phenomenalism and does not yet arrive at real objectification or spatialization.

§ 3. THE FOURTH STAGE: THE ELEMENTARY EXTERNALIZATION AND OBJECTIFICATION OF CAUSALITY

Causality through efficacy, characteristic of the third stage and the remains of which are observable well beyond the first seven or eight months of life, is a form of causal relation foreign to objective and spatial connection. When he acts or believes he acts on the external world, the child at the third stage has no clear awareness of his body movements as objective displacements producing the effects perceived, and he has still less awareness of the intermediaries linking these body movements to the effects perceived. In the presence of an interesting sight which he has produced or which he desires to prolong, the baby reacts with a global attitude projected in differentiated movements, but the causal connection is not, for him, established between these movements, the series of intermediaries, and the final result; it merely links the global attitude, above all experienced from within, and the effect produced. Beginning with the fifth stage, on the contrary, we shall witness a progressive spatialization of the causal connection in the sense that the child increasingly will notice and utilize the intermediaries between his own movements and the culminating point of his acts. For the same reason causality will succeed in becoming objectified, that is to say it will be detached from the activity itself to be formed into independent centers.

But during the intermediate stage which we are about to study and which in the main extends from 0;9 to 0;11, neither the spatialization nor the objectification of causes leads to a complete dissociation of these causes in relation to the action itself: objects begin to acquire causality in themselves instead of being conceived as wholly subject to activity, but they acquire this intrinsic causality only in situations in which activity itself is involved. In other words, the causality of objects henceforth constitutes a pole opposite to that of the action itself, but these two poles are opposed only to the degree in which they appear simultaneously. The external world is not yet conceived as a system of actions among which a particular activity may be inserted, but whose existence and efficiency do not depend on this activity.

The fourth stage of causality is therefore wholly comparable to the fourth stages of the evolution of object concept and of the development of groups of displacements. Between the time when the permanence of the object merely extends the activity itself (second and third stages) and the time when the object constitutes a substance independent of the self and capable of changing position without changing state (fifth stage), we have recognized the existence of an intermediate stage in the course of which the object acquires a certain permanence but in special positions only, these positions themselves depending on earlier successes of the activity itself. Hence this fourth stage corresponds, logically and chronologically, to the period in which causality becomes detached from the child's action without, however, being attributed once for all to objects independent of the self. So also, from the point of view of space, between the subjective groups characteristic of a third stage during which the groups depend wholly on the activity itself, and the objective groups characteristic of a fifth stage during which the displacements of objects are themselves arranged in groups, we can recognize the existence of intermediate groups or groups of reversible operations which denote the presence of objective groups while still depending on the actions of the body itself. This fourth stage of the development of space also corresponds to the fourth stage of causality: a space which tends to be externalized without however being detached from the self is entirely comparable to a causality which tends to be spatialized without yet being dissociated from the efficacy of gestures.

Furthermore, this aggregate of intermediate processes comprising a spatial, an objective, and a causal aspect, itself depends on an essential level of the evolution of intelligence—the level characterized by the application of familiar schemata to new situations. This application, which begins at about 0;8 at the advent of the present stage, consists in an adjustment of means to ends, that is, in an operation directly involving the formation of series simultaneously causal, objective, and spatial. But even if it is when this interadjustment of schemata occurs that the objectification and spatialization of causality are set in motion, these processes go beyond a mere application of familiar means to new situations. They are observable in all sorts of situations which may consist both in simple reactions (for example, certain secondary circular reactions of a higher order and of tardy advent such as swinging objects, etc.) and in complex acts of intelligence (subordination of schemata serving as means to schemata assigning a goal to the action).

It is, roughly speaking, beginning with the first application of familiar means to new circumstances that we must date this fourth stage related to causality. Unfortunately it is very difficult to find a precise criterion permitting us to assert that, from a given moment, the child conceives spatial contact as necessary to the causal action of one body on another. All one can do is follow the child's behavior step by step and note the cases in which he renounces his desire when the spatial connection seems to him insufficient.

In this respect, the first forms of spatial and objective causality are forms directly connected with manual activity: drawing to oneself or pushing away. From the beginning of the third stage (for this is the criterion of the advent of the stage) the child learns how to grasp; he knows, therefore, that on seeing an object he needs only to stretch out his hand and take the object to bring it nearer to his eyes or mouth. This elementary experiment would constitute the point of departure of spatial causality if the hand were conceived from the outside as an intermediary between the object and the body itself. But as we have seen, the act of grasping is, on the contrary, apprehended by consciousness only globally and in the form of magico-phenomenalistic efficacy. At the very least it accustoms the child to the necessity of contacts: no prehension is possible without contact between hand and object, and even before it is causal this fundamental relation may accustom the mind to the schemata of the action by the contiguity necessary to the development of spatial causality. When will such a schema give rise to that causality? We think from the time when the relation of hand and object are perceived from

the outside, objectively, and the existence of this external perception can be definitely established only from the moment the
child perceives this relation with respect to someone else. One
of the first forms of spatial causality will therefore be the behavior
pattern which we have also cited as the simplest example of the
application of familiar means to new situations: removing someone else's hand when it retains a desired object or is about to
take possession of it.

OBS. 141. We have already described (*O.I.*, obs. 124) the elementary
operations by means of which Jacqueline removed obstacles. At 0;8
(8) she pushes away my hand which grasps her duck at the same
time she does, and at 0;8 (17) she pushes away the hand which
offers her unpleasant medicine. Hence she endows the hand or the
person of another with a spatialized causality distinct from her own.
  Furthermore, simple acts have given way quite soon to more complex series during which the child incontestably attributes causality
to someone else's hands and arms. At 0;11 (19) for instance I hold
with my hand Jacqueline's feet which are hidden under a coverlet.
She sees neither her feet nor my hand. First she tries to disengage
herself, but not succeeding she leans over and pushes back the part of
my arm that is visible. It is not necessary to refer here to an image of
contacts because they are experienced tactually, but we may definitely
conclude that my arm is conceived by Jacqueline as the cause of the
retention of her foot.

  Behavior of this kind seems to indicate that the images perceived as external to the body itself are considered independent
centers of action: someone else's hand or arm is therefore endowed with causality and to prevent it from performing its action the child grasps it and displaces it intentionally. But in such
observations, we may ask just how far the causality attributed
to someone else's body extends. The action the child recognizes
in the latter remains essentially negative: the subject is removing an obstacle rather than utilizing an active instrument. The
following observations demonstrate, on the contrary, that very
early, at about the same period as the preceding behavior patterns,
the child attributes a particular activity to someone else.

OBS. 142. We have already seen (*O.I.*, obs. 127) how, from 0;8
(13) Jacqueline has used her mother's hand to make her repeat what

she was doing shortly before: Jacqueline grasps the hand, places it in front of a flounce and pushes it to make it swing the flounce again.

This behavior immediately becomes generalized. Thus at 0;8 (17) Jacqueline and her mother imitate each other in singing the same chant. At a certain moment Jacqueline stops, then, instead of making her mother continue by using the procedures characteristic of causality through efficacy (arching, waving her hands, etc.), she delicately touches her mother's lower lip with her right finger. Her mother then begins to sing again. New interruption; Jacqueline once more touches the lip. She continues thus for a moment after which, when her mother stops the procedure, Jacqueline presses her lip harder and harder.

At 0;8 (19) Jacqueline watches me as I alternately spread my index finger and thumb apart and bring them together again. When I pause she lightly pushes either the finger or the thumb to make me continue. Her movement is brisk and rapid; it is simply a starting impulse and not a continuous pressure.

Finally, and most important, as we have already noted (*O.I.*, obs. 127) at 0;10 (30) Jacqueline takes my hand, places it against a singing doll which she is unable to activate herself, and exerts pressure on my index finger to make me do what is necessary. This last observation reveals to what extent, to Jacqueline, my hand has become an independent source of action by contact.

OBS. 143. With Lucienne, also, we witness such acts from about 0;9. In particular, at 0;10 (7) I carry her in my arms and every 15-20 seconds give her a little shake which makes her laugh. When I stop she shakes her arm in space to make me continue (this is a form of causality based on the efficacy of movement of which we have spoken before). As I resist, she does it harder and harder, then taps me on the shoulder and the cheeks. The next times she confines herself to a slight pressure on the shoulder.

The same day I make my lower lip vibrate with my index finger. She laughs, then shakes her arm to make me continue. I resist. She touches my cheeks. I still resist. She touches my lips and finally imitates my movement herself.

At 0;11 (7) she is seated, I tickle her belly and place my hand on the edge of the bassinet. She laughs, waves her hand while watching mine, then touches my hand, tries to push it and ends by grasping it and bringing it to her belly. Next attempts: same reactions, each step lasting a while, but when I resist she always grasps my hand to bring it to her.

OBS. 144. With respect to Laurent this new form of causality appears at 0;8 (7) in the following circumstances. I tap my cheek with my left middle finger, then drum on my eyeglasses (he laughs). Afterward I place my left hand halfway between his eyes and my face but without blocking his view. He looks at my glasses, then at my hand. Then instead of trying to act on my glasses, he grasps my hand and pushes it toward my face. Again I drum on my glasses and then put my hand in the previous position; he pushes it back more decisively each time. Finally I remain motionless; he grasps my hand and with it hits, not my face, which he cannot reach, but the top of my chest.

A moment later I lower my hand very slowly, starting very high up and directing it toward his feet, finally tickling him for a moment. He bursts out laughing. When I stop midway, he grasps my hand or arm and pushes it toward his feet.

At 0;8 (25) there is a momentary recession to the behavior patterns of the fourth stage, because of the difficulties of the problem (obs. 136). At 0;8 (29), on the other hand, Laurent looks at me when I drum on a box and then hold out my hand to him (cf. obs. 134); he begins by trying to grasp the box, then tries to act on it from a distance (he shakes his head while looking at it, shakes himself, etc.), then, after these behavior patterns inherited from the third stage, he gently pushes my hand toward the box, only directing it a little too low.

The same day he pushes my hand toward a little bell which I have just shaken with my index finger; this time the spatial adjustment is accurate and his purpose is undoubtedly to make me continue to swing it.

At 0;9 (0) he grasps my hand and places it against his belly which I have just tickled; he thus merely sets my hand in motion and does not strike it as before and as though my activity depended entirely on his. Same reactions at 0;9 (15), 0;10 (8), etc.

At 0;9 (6) similarly, when he is in bed he directs my hand to the bars to urge me to scratch them as I was doing just before.

At 0;9 (13) Laurent is in his baby swing which I shake three or four times by pulling a cord; he grasps my hand and presses it against the cord.

Such facts seem to us to indicate that during this fourth stage the child ceases to consider his own action as the sole source of causality and attributes to someone else's body an aggregate of particular powers. On the one hand the child, not succeeding in reproducing by himself the results which interest him, uses the hand, shoulders, or lips of someone else as necessary intermediaries. On the other hand, he acts on someone else's body not as upon inert matter merely extending his own action, but by releasing the activity of the other body through a discreet pressure, a mere touch, etc.

There is in these behavior patterns proof of a simultaneous objectification and spatialization of causality. Objectification occurs precisely to the extent that someone else's body becomes, in the child's eyes, an autonomous center of causal activity. But spatialization of causality is also present in the sense that to secure the repetition of an interesting phenomenon, the child is no longer limited to acting through efficacy on someone else's hand as if this hand, also through efficacy, would set in motion the expected phenomenon. He pushes the hand and if it does not go to the desired place he takes it there himself and puts it in contact with the object on which it is supposed to perform its action.

Let us note that logically it is not at all necessary that spatialization be on a par with objectification. In other words, the phenomena of objectification do not, as such, involve a spatialization of causality.[3] Thus Lucienne, at 0;11 (7) begins by simply waving her hand while watching mine when I have tickled her and have withdrawn my hand to the edge of the bassinet (end of obs. 143). There is here an objectification of causality on my own hand but without spatialization of the causal relation (when Lucienne touches my hand and finally pulls it to her to make me continue, it is possible to speak of spatial contact). But the observation shows that at the same period when the first acts of causal observation appear the first examples of spatialization also appear. Psychologically the two processes are equal. To the extent that the child endows objects (including someone else's body) with a certain causal power he becomes interested in spatial contacts, and, inversely, to the extent that he inserts intermediaries between his body and the desired results he endows these intermediaries with an objective causality.

[3] On the other hand, inversely, the spatialization of causality does not involve its objectification, either. It is possible to conceive that the child may establish a series of intermediaries between his hand and the desired effect without endowing any of these intermediaries or the terminal object with actual causality.

These remarks enable us to understand how these behavior patterns differ from those of the preceding stage. At first one might consider the difference minimal. When the child waves a rattle to produce a sound he seems to endow the rattle with as much causal power as when he touches someone else's lips to cause the other person to make them vibrate again. Or again, when he pulls a string to shake his bassinet top he seems to spatialize causality and objectify it in the string or the top as much as when he grasps an adult's hand and steers it to a flounce in order to swing it. But if one concedes our interpretation of the causality characteristic of the earliest secondary circular reactions and the procedures to make an interesting sight last, an essential difference nevertheless contrasts that causality with the one we are now studying. In the present case the child no longer tries to produce the desired result himself; he merely sets in motion an intermediary conceived as capable of producing that result. In the third stage, on the contrary, the intermediary is always considered as being a mere extension of the child's movement; it is passive, and the movement alone is efficacious. Doubtless the child already is aware of the necessity for certain contacts: he knows how to pull the string of the top in order to shake it, etc. But to the extent that he utilizes the intermediaries as extensions of his limbs instead of merely setting in motion an activity latent in them, one can only interpret this search for contacts as the product of a differentiation of the schemata of the action and not as the indication of a spatialization of causality. Undoubtedly the child at the third stage is also often limited to actions of setting in motion (as when he merely arches himself to induce someone else to repeat an act or to make an object reproduce an interesting effect). But nothing proves, in such circumstances, that he really attributes efficacy to the person or the object on which he is trying to act. Everything takes place as though only his own movement were considered causal, the rest flowing from it, globally and necessarily. On the contrary, in the present behavior patterns the child analyzes the particulars of the observed sequences instead of confining himself to a global action and puts the various elements in contact (the adult's hand and the flounce or the singing doll, etc.), if the initial operation of setting in motion fails to produce the desired result. Certainly the differences we mention are matters of proportion and all the intermediaries exist between the extremes, but they are nonetheless the indication of opposite orientations in the elaboration of the causal series: efficacy, originally concentrated in the movement itself, becomes decentralized, objectified, and spatialized by being transferred to the intermediaries.

Once these contrasts have been defined, we must now reestablish continuity by showing that, if the present behavior patterns differ from those of the third stage, they also differ from those of the fifth, which involve a causality entirely attributed to objects. In other words, if the causality of the fourth stage presupposes an incipient objectification and spatialization, it is not necessarily freed from the efficacy of the second stage and thus is transitional between the subjective and objective forms of causality. We have no information about the causality the child attributes to persons apart from his own action. It is possible that he already attributes to them an activity entirely independent of himself. In this hypothesis, he would consider his mother or father as being capable of performing certain acts at all times and places, whether or not he witnesses them. But it is possible, on the contrary, that the activity of persons appears to him as being set in motion only in his presence and consequently under his influence, this activity being conceived simultaneously as the cause of certain external results and as depending to some extent on efficacy. How shall we choose between these two interpretations?

First we must recall that the development of causality is one with that of object and of space. A truly objectified and spatialized causality presupposes beyond any doubt the existence of permanent objects whose displacements are arranged in groups independent of the self. To be conceived by the child as a cause really detached from the activity, someone else's person must form a substantial object having constant properties and subject to displacements that do not alter its nature. It is precisely this objective and spatial formation which the child at this stage does not yet seem able to attribute to his universe, if one believes the results of the last two chapters: the object of the fourth stage remains midway between permanence dependent on the action and true permanence, and the corresponding groups remain intermediate between subjective and objective groups. These are important presumptions in favor of the second of the two interpretations just proposed: the causality attributed to persons must still be conceived by the child as linked to his own activity.

But can we go further and find arguments in favor of this interpretation without leaving the realm of causality? It seems so. On the one hand, if the child at this stage acts upon persons through contact and spatial causality (by touching or pushing their hands, their lips, etc.) he still tries constantly to act upon them through procedures pertaining to simple efficacy: he arches himself up, waves his hand, etc., as though someone else's acts depended merely on his own desires and movements. On the other hand, it is noteworthy that during this fourth stage one does not yet observe behavior patterns such as the tertiary circular reactions which attest to a permanent causality attributed to objects by the child. The tertiary circular reaction is a sort of search for novelty or an experiment in order to see, which rests on the implicit postulate that there is something unknown to be discovered in each new object. On the contrary, the behavior patterns we have called secondary circular reactions and applications of familiar means to new situations are limited to reproducing interesting effects observed on the object or transposing these procedures of reproduction to new circumstances. Tertiary circular reaction therefore seems to us to involve attributing permanent causality to things and persons (since the child tries to discover the properties of objects as though they were necessarily new and consequently not due to his own activity), whereas the behavior patterns of the third and fourth stages can be interpreted as though causality arose with respect to objects only at the moment the subject acts upon them (since he confines himself merely to reproducing the effects he observes on them at the time they are exposed to his activity).

In short, the child's action on persons during this fourth stage seems to reveal an intermediate causality, already partly objectified and spatialized (since the persons already constitute external centers of particular activity) but not yet freed from the efficacy of the child's own movement (since these centers of activity are conceived as always depending on his personal procedures).

How does this apply to material objects? The following observations show that they also are endowed with an activity conceived as being partly autonomous and partly subordinated to the action.

OBS. 145. At 0;8 (21) Jacqueline holds the cloth bell mentioned in obs. 140. Without her knowledge I have kept the end of the string attached to the bell. I shake the bell and pull it toward me. Jacqueline immediately lets it go in alarm and looks at it with curiosity. After some hesitation she brings her hand forward with great delicacy and touches the bell, pushing it gently as though to see what will happen. At each repetition of the experiment she does the same thing with more assurance.

At 0;9 (14) she manifests the same reaction to my watch which is new in comparison with the one of the preceding months. At 0;8 (20) for example, I offer her my watch which she immediately grasps with both hands and examines with lively interest. She feels it, turns it over, says *apff*, etc. I pull the chain and she feels the tug; she grips it forcibly and smiles at this game. I end by shaking the chain and she lets go the watch, but at once searches for it with her hands, catches it again, and replaces it before her eyes. I pull again; she laughs at the watch's resistance and searches for it as soon as she lets it go, etc. (See the whole of obs. 13, Chap. I.)

At 0;9 (14) I repeat exactly the same experiment. But, curiously enough, although Jacqueline knows the object well (she often plays with this watch), because she experiences a slight anxiety she no longer tries to catch it when it escapes from her hands; she looks at the watch in a daze, as though the object's movements were entirely spontaneous. Jacqueline tries to touch it and even advances her index finger to set it in motion, but at the first movement of the watch she withdraws her hand abruptly.

Jacqueline's reactions to an object which is very familiar to her seem to show that she is beginning to attribute to it a causality independent of personal activity.

OBS. 146. At 0;9 (9) Jacqueline has already manifested a reaction of the same kind to an equally familiar object but in slightly different circumstances, in the sense that it was she herself who gave the object its first movements.

Jacqueline is seated on a sofa and I place her celluloid parrot beside her. Doubtless never having seen it in that position she touches it very prudently, immediately withdrawing her hand, so that the parrot jumps slightly. She repeats this many times, displacing it a little at each attempt. She pushes it on the one hand, but on the other she behaves toward it as if face to face with a being endowed with life and spontaneous movement.

This behavior pattern should be compared to the reactions, slightly earlier and then contemporaneous, which consist in making hanging objects swing and in letting them come and go by themselves and putting them in motion again. We have described these secondary circular reactions of a higher order in *O.I.* (obs. 138-140): relinquishing and recapturing a necktie, a hanging cloth, swinging a lampshade, etc. These behavior patterns also reveal the beginning of spontaneous movement attributed to objects but still subordinate to the movements of the body itself.

At 0;9 (9) also, without being able to see me, Jacqueline watches the parrot which I swing vertically before her. When I stop she imitates this movement with her hand, stops, then begins again obviously to make it continue. Noting failure, she gives the parrot a sharp blow with her right hand to make it move again.

OBS. 147. So also Lucienne, at 0;9 (8) manifests toward a familiar doll (a rubber doll hanging from her bassinet top) a reaction which is new as compared to those of the preceding stage. She is sucking the doll which is attached to a string as taut as possible. Without revealing myself and without letting Lucienne see me beforehand I give the doll several strong tugs by means of the string. Lucienne immediately smiles at her doll without letting it go, and even ends by laughing uproariously to it, as to a person. She does not look for any cause external to the movement and looks only at the doll, fixedly, ready to laugh at each new movement. Then when I stop shaking it Lucienne tries to make it continue, first by moving her own head from side to side, then by arching herself up, waving her own feet, and finally by pushing the doll itself which she has not ceased to hold!

These last movements would be of no interest without the reaction at the beginning. But the aggregate of these patterns is characteristic of the behavior of this stage.

These reactions to objects seem to confirm what we assumed earlier with regard to reactions to people. They reveal simultaneously a relative objectification of causality and a spatialization intervening to the extent the child continues to consider his own actions as necessary to those of the object.

The objectification of causality seems undeniable. The child behaves toward the object in an entirely new way in comparison with the behavior patterns of the third stage. When, in the presence of multiple movements of his bassinet hood, of the toys which are hanging or held in the hand, of objects manipulated by an adult, etc., the child examines each sight and tries to make it last (either through circular reaction or action at a distance, that is, in both cases, through efficacy mixed with phenomenalism), he does not give the impression of placing in each image perceived an autonomous center of causality. First of all, as we have tried to establish in the preceding chapters, the child does not yet substantiate these images in individualized and permanent objects and does not yet arrange the displacements, even the visible ones, of bodies in objective groups. He would therefore be very much at a loss in attributing to things as such a causal power which he must rather feel as diffused throughout the whole sight. Moreover, from the point of view of our present analysis, the very fact that the child tries to make these sights last through a global procedure not resting upon a reaction of intermediaries but on the mere efficacy of more or less differentiated movements shows that the external image and the child's own activity (the attitude inherent in perception, the feelings of pleasure, expectation, effort, etc., and the action performed on the thing perceived) still constitute, from the subject's point of view, a single, hardly dissociable, whole. Thenceforth it seems very probable that during the third stage the most striking events of the external world are not conceived as emanating from discrete centers of causality; they must be experienced as extensions of activity itself in the widest sense of the term. On the contrary, the observations we have just described reveal an entirely different attitude: instead of participating at the outset in the sight he is watching the child seems to wait to let things act. Instead of seeming to anticipate and enjoy the movements he observes he seems to consider them as unpredictable and even alarming, and consequently as spontaneous. The difference betweeen Jacqueline's reactions at 0;8 and 0;9 in the presence of the same phenomenon is extremely instructive. Whereas at 0;8 she tries at once to catch hold of my watch which was slipping from her hands, at 0;9, on the contrary, she looks at it with great astonishment. In short, the child now clearly reveals by his attitude that he locates in the moving object an autonomous center of forces, whereas up to this point he seemed to see in the movements of things only events in which he himself participated.

But if causality is thus objectified we still cannot maintain that it is radically detached from the activity itself. In other words, during this stage it is impossible to prove that to the child objects move or act upon each other entirely independently of his own actions. Without recapitulating our reasons for thinking thus, given the concepts of object and space formed by the child up to about 1;0, we must at least note how common the procedures based on efficacy remain until the end of the first year of life. So Lucienne at 0;9 (8), after seeing her doll move spontaneously (obs. 147), still tries to make it continue by arching herself up, shaking her head, etc., using all the methods that date from the third stage. This persistence of efficacy up to the end of the first year of life shows that the beginnings of causal objectification do not exclude the feeling of being able to act directly upon things. Moreover, in the three observations we have just mentioned, we see that as soon as the child has observed the spontaneous activity of the objects perceived he believes himself able to maintain the continuity by intervening himself. He does not, therefore, locate the causes of such events outside his own sphere of action.

But from this point on how does he conceive of his action upon things? It is this which marks the second advance characteristic of the fourth stage: the spatialization of causality. If numerous traces of causality through efficacy linger until the end of the first year, it is nevertheless obvious that from about 0;9 the child comes to act upon things (as we have noted above) as he has acted upon persons: through physical contact, pressures, attempts to set things in motion, etc. Thus Jacqueline, on seeing my watch jump about, pushes it lightly with her index finger (obs. 145), and in the same way by brief contacts shakes the parrot lying beside her (obs. 146); so too, Lucienne finally acts to put her rubber doll in motion again (obs. 147). Each of these acts constitutes an action by setting things in motion analogous to the actions of the child who touches the hands or lips of the adult to make him reproduce an interesting gesture (obs. 142-144). True, here again the difference between such acts and those of the preceding stage may seem minimal. When, for example, a child four to six months old taps on a hanging rattle, grasps it to shake it, or rubs it against the edge of the bassinet, does it not seem as though his causality were as spatialized as when he touches a watch, a parrot, or a doll to make them move forward, as we have just seen him do? Nevertheless, there seems to be a considerable difference between these two kinds of reactions. As we have emphasized apropos of action upon persons, the causality whose advent characterizes this stage is a causality through setting things in motion, whereas the only form of causality represented during the third stage merely extends that of the action itself. In other words, when the child of four to six months strikes, shakes, rubs, etc., he is not dissociating the various elements of his perceptual field from the point of view of causality. The action forms a unit even if it becomes differentiated by following the variations of obstacles in a manner which, to the observer, resembles a utilization of causality by spatial contact. On the contrary, when the child of 0;9-0;11 cautiously pushes a watch, a parrot, or a doll to set it in motion, he conceives of these things as moving objects partly independent of himself and acts upon them by contact. Here, too, objectification therefore entails a beginning of real spatialization of causality.

If one has doubts concerning these distinctions, let him refer once more to our analyses of space and object. They alone can make us understand how an action which is apparently similar to our own actions may be different from the subject's point of view, since the objective and spatial structure of the universe is not the same for the observer and the child.

In a general way, this fourth stage is therefore a stage of transition. It marks the decline of causality through efficacy and the beginning of causality through objective contacts, but the behavior patterns which characterize it actually partake of both of these types of connection. With regard to objectification, the child begins to endow objects with true activity and consequently to center in them a causality previously reserved for the activity itself. But as objects are not yet conceived as truly permanent substances and still exist only as a function of the action regardless of the solidity they are in the process of acquiring, it cannot be said that this objectification results yet in a complete detachment. With regard to spatialization, the child begins intentionally to establish the contacts necessary for spatial connections, but as he does not renounce causality through efficacy and still does not elaborate objective groups of displacements it is impossible to conclude that there is a radical transformation of causality. In short, the universe and the activity itself still form a symbiosis or a global whole in which two poles are in the process of differentiation, but personal actions are not yet conceived as simple causal series among the totality of the others.

§ 4. THE FIFTH STAGE: THE REAL OBJECTIFICATION AND SPATIALIZATION OF CAUSALITY

Toward the end of the first year of life, as we have seen in the preceding chapters, a series of essential stages of progress is established from the point of view of space and object concept. The object acquires a real permanence and a physical identity independently of its movements in the field of prehension or in depth. Space is constituted in a parallel way and is regulated as a function of these objective groups of displacements. It is self-evident that these transformations will profoundly influence the structure of causality, the evolution of which is correlative to that of the static categories just discussed. In other words, causality will be really objectified and spatialized, thus becoming detached from the action itself to be externalized in the universe of perception, free to be applied in return to the visible aspects of the action itself.

The totality of these transformations is, on the other hand, the function of two new and fundamental aspects of the development of intelligence as such. At about the age of one year, two types of very characteristic behavior patterns appear: "tertiary circular reaction" and the "invention of new means through active experimentation." Both these behavior patterns involve a certain organization of space and the formation of objects properly so called. It would be difficult to conceive of the development of behavior patterns that no longer consist only in reproducing results obtained by chance or in applying efficacious gestures to everything, but in truly testing objects, if the purely phenomenalistic universe of the first stages were not progressively solidified by these experimentations. Thenceforth it is self-evident that these same behavior patterns, sources of spatialization and objectification in general, will transform causality in an analogous sense and finally construct it in the external universe.

We shall now try to demonstrate this. We shall see that the tertiary circular reactions are sources of objectification of causality and that the apprenticeship through active experimentation consolidates the spatialization of causal series. But to understand this mechanism it is important to remember that objectification and spatialization are two processes which, though correlative, remain essentially independent of each other. Thus apprenticeship through active experimentation essentially results in spatializing the causal series related to the action of the body itself upon things. This behavior pattern teaches the child the necessity for contacts and intermediaries between himself and objects but does not teach him the causal interrelations of objects. Tertiary circular reaction, on the contrary, has as its principal effect initiating the child into these interrelations and confronting him with a system of causes independent of himself. It happens that these two kinds of transformations of causality, although not always resulting from the same experiments, reinforce each other and lead to the same result: the formation of a universe in which the child's action is located among other causes and obeys the same laws.

Before showing how the invention of new means through active experimentation leads to the spatialization of causality, let us first examine the way in which tertiary circular reactions achieve the objectification of the causal series begun during the preceding stage.

First, here are some facts.

OBS. 148. The first definite example of completely objectified causality seems to us to be the behavior patterns consisting in placing an object in such a position that it puts itself in motion.

Let us recall as applied to this subject what we have already stated concerning the tertiary reactions (*O.I.*, obs. 144), namely, that if toward 0;11 (15) the child begins to throw objects to the floor he has at first no concept of gravity; he throws an object instead of dropping it. So long as the subject proceeds thus—until about 1;3 (20) in Jacqueline's case—it is impossible to speak with certainty of objectified causality. The action of throwing seems to the child necessary to the fall; consequently such acts still belong to the type of behavior patterns of the fourth stage.

On the other hand, when it is a matter of sliding the moving object along an inclined plane, it seems that from the end of the first year the child learns to let the object act; he simply puts it in the right position and attributes to it the power to act by itself (see *O.I.*, obs. 145).

Thus at 0;11 (19) Jacqueline places her wooden horse on the edge of her table and pushes it gently until the moment when she lets it fall. At 0;11 (20) she slides a series of objects down a sloping coverlet, etc. (see *O.I.*).

But most important, at 1;0 (3) she grasps a plush toy and places it on a sofa, obviously in expectation of a movement, then she changes its location a series of times, always as though it were going to move by itself. The child's behavior is very interesting from the point of view of causality. Jacqueline, instead of pushing the object or even giving it a shake by a simple touch, makes every effort to put it down as rapidly as possible and to let go of it immediately, as though her intervention would impede the toy's spontaneous movements instead of aiding them! After several fruitless attempts she changes method, lets it go a few millimeters above the sofa or pushes it slightly. Finally she places it on a sloping cushion until it rolls.

The same causal attitudes are found again at 1;1 (19): Jacqueline places a red ball on the floor and waits for it to roll. Only after five or six attempts does she push it slightly. The ball, like the plush toy, has therefore become an autonomous center of forces, causality thus being detached from the action of pushing to be transferred onto the object itself.

OBS. 149. At 1;0 (29) for the first time Jacqueline is in the presence of the well-known toy consisting of chickens set in motion by a weight. A certain number of chickens are arranged in a circle on a wooden ring and the front of each chicken is connected by a string to a heavy ball placed on a lower plane than the ring: thus the slightest movement of the ball sets the chickens in motion, and they knock with their beaks against the edge of the ring.

Jacqueline, after examining for a moment the toy which I put into action by displacing it gently, first touches the ball and notes the concomitant movement of the chickens. She then systematically moves the ball as she watches the chickens. Thus convinced of the existence of a relationship which she obviously does not understand in detail, she pushes the ball very delicately with her right index finger each time the swinging stops completely.

In this example Jacqueline therefore does not attribute spontaneous movements to the ball (as she did in the preceding example of the ball or the plush toy), but she definitely conceives the activity of the ball as causing that of the chickens. Therefore from this point of view there is objectification of causality. Moreover the ball is not, to her, a mere extension of her manual action (like the strings hanging from the bassinet hood, etc.); she makes it active simply by releasing it.

OBS. 150. Here is an observation made on Jacqueline at 1;3 (9) in which she does not succeed, as in the preceding observation, in finding the cause sought but in the course of which the same attitudes of objectification may be found.

I present the child with a clown whose arms move and activate cymbals as soon as one presses his chest. I put him in motion, then offer him to Jacqueline. She grasps him, looks him all over, evidently trying to understand. Then she tries to move the cymbals directly, each in turn. After this she touches the clown's feet and tries to move them. Same effort with the buttons attached to the chest. She gives up, sighs, and looks at him. I put him in action once more: Jacqueline cries *pou* quite loudly (causality through imitation of the sound) then touches the buttons again. After a new stimulus from me Jacqueline once more shakes the cymbals, crying "pou, tou," etc. (imitation of the totality observed), then she again tries to shake the buttons and gives up the project.

Thus we see that, besides an attempt at direct action (activating the cymbals) and action through the efficacy of imitation, Jacqueline searches on the very body of the clown (feet, buttons, etc.) for the cause of the movement observed.

OBS. 151. Similarly, at the end of his first year Laurent attributes an entirely objectified causality to objects.

At 1;0 (0) for example, he takes possession of a new ball which he has just received for his birthday and places it on top of a sloping cushion to let it go and roll by itself. He even tries to make it go by merely placing it on the floor, and, as no movement is produced, he limits himself to a gentle push.

At 1;0 (9) Laurent is standing near a panel of the open French window against which is the back of a chair. I move the window by pushing the chair slightly with my foot. Laurent, who has not noticed the movement of my foot, is surprised by the sudden displacement of the window and tries to understand it. He moves the window panel against the back of the chair, then gives the chair a little shake to make sure it was the cause of the movement. He is satisfied only after having reproduced the phenomenon exactly. Such a causal sequence is therefore simultaneously objectified and spatialized.

We must add to these observations the facts of objectification of causality in people. This objectification, outlined in the course of the preceding stage, becomes complete from the beginning of the second year as the following examples reveal.

OBS. 152. At 1;0 (3) Jacqueline is before me and I blow into her hair. When she wants the game to continue she does not try to act through efficacious gestures nor even, as formerly, to push my arms or lips; she merely places herself in position, head tilted, sure that I will do the rest by myself. At 1;0 (6) same reaction when I murmur something in her ear: she puts her ear against my mouth when she wishes me to repeat my gesture.

At 1;3 (30) Jacqueline holds in her right hand a box she cannot open. She holds it out to her mother, who pretends not to notice. Then she transfers the box from her right hand to her left, with her free hand grasps her mother's hand, opens it, and puts the box in it. The whole thing has occurred without a sound. This type of behavior pattern is common around 1;4.

So also, during the next days, Jacqueline makes the adult intervene in the particulars of her games, whenever an object is too remote, etc.: she calls, cries, points to objects with her finger, etc. In short, she well knows that she depends on the adult for satisfaction; the person of someone else becomes her best procedure for realization. Furthermore, her grandfather being the most faithful of her servants, she says "Panama" (grandpapa) as soon as her projects fail and she needs a causal instrument which is not defined or present as such in the context of her field of action.

OBS. 153. Similarly, from as early as 0;10 (3) Laurent reacts to the action of persons simply by assuming an expectant attitude. For instance, his mother rubs her forehead against his; he then puts himself against her and merely waits for her to do it again.

At 0;10 (30) he holds out to me a box I have just thrown so that I may throw it again in the same way.

At 0;11 (2) when I stop his swing from behind him at a certain height he looks above him for the cause of this immobility. At 0;9 (9), on the contrary, he did not seek any external cause of the phenomenon and when I interrupted my experiment merely shook himself to make it last.

At 0;11 (17) he replaces in or on my hand a toy I have just thrown, to make me do it again.

Analogous reactions at 0;11 (28), etc.

OBS. 153a. Lucienne, also, at 1;1 (18) returns to my hand a doll I have just thrown at her feet, whereas up to then she has brought my hand near the toy to set my activity going.

From 1;3 (2), like Jacqueline, she holds out to her parents boxes she cannot open or toys she cannot operate, or else she points with her finger to objects that are too far away, so that they will be brought to her.

Such behavior patterns seem very different from those of the preceding stage. With regard to persons, for example, the child no longer limits himself to starting their activity by pushing their arms, lips, etc.; he places himself in front of them in the position in which they can act upon him or he places in their hands the object upon which he expects them to act, etc. (obs. 152). Behavior of this kind indicates the existence of a new attitude: from this time on, the child considers the person of another as an entirely autonomous source of actions and no longer as a center partly independent, but also partly dependent on the activity. True, by acting thus the child seems merely to return to a behavior pattern the use of which is manifested very early. When the child cries for his meal, which he has known how to do from the first months of life, or cries particularly in his mother's presence, it may seem that he considers the adult an autonomous cause and that he expects everything from this external power. Moreover, when the baby, in his mother's arms, grows calm because he knows his food is coming, one has the impression he represents things to himself exactly as would a child of two to three years of age, and that in respect to the person of his parents causality is from the outset objectified and externalized. What does the behavior of which we are now speaking (obs. 152) add to these behavior patterns? Does not the difference pertain merely to a technical or motor progress, the child now knowing how to put himself in a position of expectation or how to place in someone else's hands the object on which he wishes him to act, whereas formerly he was satisfied to weep or cry out, causality being the same in both cases? Let us beware, however, of the "psychologist's fallacy"; if from the observer's point of view the situation is the same in these different cases, nothing proves that it is so from the point of view of the child. When the child at the second and third stages cries to make another person act or calms down on seeing his mother put him in a position to eat, he does not consider the other person as a permanent object with displacements arranged in space and acting by himself on objects such as the bottle, the body itself, etc. On the contrary, everything occurs as though the universe consisted of moving pictures merely extending each other and extending *en bloc* the desires, efforts, cries, and gestures which characterize the activity itself. Primitive action performed on someone else therefore arises from causality through efficacy and phenomenalism combined, and not yet from physical causality simultaneously objectified and spatialized. When, during the fourth stage, the child adds to this the use of contacts (starting someone else's activity by touching his hands, lips, shoulders, etc.), he surely begins to dissociate two terms in such connections: the person of someone else is thus conceived as a center of action itself dependent on the action. But this concept, perfectly correct so long as it is applied to the data of direct perception, is not necessarily accompanied by the idea that someone else constitutes a permanent object always capable of spontaneous actions. The object still exists only when it is perceived or located in a special position, and it comes into action only when impelled by the activity itself. On the contrary, with the behavior patterns of the present stage it seems that another person finally assumes these characteristics of externalized and objectified causality. By limiting himself, in order to make the adult act, to placing himself before him in position to undergo the action, or to placing in his hands the object on which the action will be performed, the child seems definitely to attribute to the adult the qualities of an autonomous and objective cause.

Progress is the same with regard to material objects: from this time on, the child at the present stage considers these objects permanent and independent sources of actions. Obs. 148 shows us, for example, that Jacqueline behaves with respect to her plush toy at 1;0 or to her ball at 1;1 exactly as she does toward persons: she places these objects in position to act and waits for them to put themselves into action. If this behavior is compared with that of the fourth stage (obs. 145-147), it is impossible not to recognize an essential difference: the patterns of the fourth stage consist in determining the action of objects, whereas the present pattern consists in considering the action spontaneous and objectively necessary. In the case of obs. 149 to 151 the progress achieved is still more remarkable: the child conceives object A (or part A of the total object) as cause of the movements of object B (or of part B of the total object). In this way he starts the activity of ball A (obs. 149) to put in motion chickens B; he tries to find in the buttons, feet, etc., of clown A (obs. 150) the cause of the movements of cymbals B, which are attached to the arms of the clown; or again (obs. 151) he seeks in the movements of chair A the cause of those of door panel B. We claim that this is a new and important behavior pattern in regard to the objectification of causality.

It is new because up to now the child has never, despite appearances, dissociated the elements of a global schema of action to arrange them in a causal series. When in the course of the secondary circular reactions the child utilizes object A to produce result B (when he pulls a string, for instance, to shake a rattle or the bassinet hood), he does not consider the activity of object A as causing result B: the true cause is the gesture itself (pulling the string), and object A (the string) is only the extension of the gesture or of the hand. The proof is that this gesture is applied to everything and is endowed with an efficacy that greatly transcends the situations in which its action is really performed; the child pulls the string to achieve the most varied results. (See O.I., obs. 113.) True, object A is conceived as necessary to result

B (the child pulls the string to produce result B instead of performing an empty gesture of pulling). But this does not prove at all that the movements of A are conceived as causes of result B; that is explained merely by the fact that the schema of the action itself is constituted and differentiated as a function of object A. Just as the agreeable result obtained by thumb-sucking necessitates a contact and coordination between hand and mouth, although the child does not conceive either of his fingers or his lips as causes of this result, so also the swinging of the toys hanging from the hood presupposes a connection between the hand and string A, though the child does not conceive of the string as an independent cause of the activity. On the contrary, when, in obs. 149-151, the child sets the ball in motion to act upon the chickens, or gently pushes a chair to move the door panel touching it, his attitude is quite different. The ball of obs. 149 is not a mere extension of the movement itself or the mere element in a global schema of action; it constitutes an independent cause sought as such, on which the child acts simply by setting it in motion It is a cause of the same kind the subject seeks in obs. 150-151. Does this mean that thereafter such causes are reduced to those of the fourth stage and thus consist in centers of force which are partly autonomous and partly subordinated to the action? No, because result B (the movement of chickens or door panel) is conceived as depending entirely on A; hence for the first time a causal series is detached from the action itself, in other words, a relation of cause to effect between one external object and another equally external object. The formation of these series is thus comparable, in the realm of causality, to that of real permanence and of objective groups of displacements with regard to the elaboration of objects and of space itself.

The innovation characteristic of these behavior patterns is therefore none other than the true objectification of causality. For the first time the child recognizes the existence of causes completely external to his activity, and for the first time he establishes among the events perceived links of causality independent of the action itself. By virtue of the fact that objects are henceforth detached from the action and considered permanent substances and that their movements are arranged in space in truly objective groups, they become capable of forming autonomous centers of activity and thus serving as the *substratum* of a system of external causal relations.

In a general way, in the development of the mechanism of intelligence, such progress is expressed by the transition from the secondary circular reaction to the tertiary circular reaction. The secondary reaction, which consists in a simple repetition and generalization of movements that have fortuitously given rise to interesting results, does not comprise any causal structure other than that of efficacy and phenomenalism combined. When the schemata thus acquired are intelligently adapted to certain problems through application of familiar schemata to new situations (fourth stage), a beginning of objectification and spatialization channels this efficacy without, however, eliminating it entirely. With the tertiary circular reaction, on the contrary, a reversal of direction occurs: such a behavior pattern consists in experiments in order to see intended to discover the unknown properties and particular activities that each new object comprises. The mental orientation which characterizes such behavior is the same as that which marks the objectification of causality: interest is brought to bear on the objects themselves and no longer on the movement intended to utilize them, and objects acquire, for the first time, a solidity forcing the subject to accommodate himself to it and expressed in the form of causality independent of and external to the self.

Let us now come to the second basic advance which distinguishes this fifth stage: the spatialization of causality. We have already observed that this second aspect of causality does not stem analytically from the preceding one. One conceives of a universe such that the centers of action are considered by the subject to be external to himself and thus entirely objectified in things, but these centers are not linked with one another spatially and the subject does not try to enter into spatial contact with them; this would be, so to speak, a universe of monads acting upon each other at a distance and not a world of physically interdependent objects. But such a conception, to the extent that the child has it,[4] only appears, in fact, on a much higher plane than that of sensorimotor intelligence: it is the product of thought, doubtless incomplete and distorted by the egocentrism peculiar to

[4] Traces of it may be discerned in animism and infantile magic.

the initial forms of thought, but thought of a much higher quality than the schematism of practical intelligence, and presupposing all the work of conceptualization.

On the sensorimotor plane to which we limit our investigations here, it happens, on the contrary, that the objectification of causality is always on a par with its spatialization. The spatialization of causality begins with a spatialization of the action itself practiced upon things. To the extent that he discovers the need for intermediaries and spatial contacts in order to act, the child renounces causality through efficacy and substitutes for it a truly physical causality. This tendency, the beginnings of which we have analyzed apropos of the fourth stage, is definitely established in the behavior patterns we have called "discovery of new means through active experimentation" (*O.I.*, Chap. V). True, such progress does not in itself necessarily lead to the objectification of causality. It is possible to conceive of a universe in which the subject intervenes in events only through spatial contact with things, but attributing to his own action the totality of phenomena (thus there would be spatialization of efficacy, but the individual would not emerge from his solipsism or recognize the existence of interactions between individualized and independent objects). But it happens that the spatialization of the action itself entails psychologically the objectification of causality, for it is the same mental attitude of interest in objects and of accommodation to their physical and spatial peculiarities which animates the search for new means through active experimentation and which sets the tertiary circular reaction in motion. In other words, the act of multiplying the intermediaries between the action itself and its external result involves the same process of externalization as does experimentation with the properties of objects; in both cases the subject learns how to dissociate, if not as yet his own self from the external world, at least an internal pole of effort and an external pole of objective resistance; in both cases, causality tends to be objectified in spatialized connections, while causality through efficacy tends to be internalized and no longer applied only to the connections uniting intention to the movement of the body itself.

Let us now examine how the invention of new means through active experimentation results in spatialization of the causal connections which characterize the action of the body upon things. Let us recall the various examples we have given of these behavior patterns and try to find out how each of them concerns causality and synchronizes with the preceding examples of causal objectification.

The behavior pattern of the supports is the first interesting case: drawing some bulky object (cushion, coverlet, etc.) toward oneself to reach the objects placed upon it. As we have seen (*O.I.*, obs. 148-152), this behavior is at first purely phenomenalistic. In grasping the support the child sees the object move. Thus he establishes a link of cause and effect between the movements of the support and those of the object. But at its point of departure this link is spatialized so little that the child even draws the support toward him when the desired object is placed beside it (obs. 150). Up to then causality remains characteristic of the fourth stage—intermediate between phenomenalistic efficacy and truly spatialized causality. On the contrary, to the extent that the behavior pattern of the support has become systematic it is spatialized, and from the beginning of the second year of life it gives rise to connections typical of the fifth stage. For example when Lucienne (*O.I.*, obs. 152) at 1;0 (5) turns a box around in order to get an object on its far side, there is no longer any doubt that the causal relations established by her between the movements of the support and those of the object are of an objective and truly spatial type.

The behavior pattern of the string would give rise to analogous remarks.

The interpretation regarding the use of the stick is a little more subtle. In the main its development is the same; the causal relations it involves, at first merely phenomenalistic, are spatialized little by little. Thus the child begins by discovering fortuitously that by hitting an object the stick can put it in motion (*O.I.*, obs. 157-158); he then perceives he can direct this movement (obs. 158), and finally draws to himself the object of his desires. By truly becoming an instrument, which occurs only between 1;2 and 1;4, the stick therefore becomes simultaneously an objective causal center and an organ of spatial connection between the movements of the arm and those of the objects. Because such a behavior pattern is more complex than that of the support or that of the string, the transitional factors it puts to work between mere efficacy and the spatial forms of causality are more numerous and raise the question of structural transformation of the concept of cause in a more precise way. To understand this, let us try to distinguish among the various types of causal connection revealed by analysis of the behavior pattern of the stick.

OBS. 154. We shall designate by letters A, B, C, and D the four types of connection observed in Jacqueline.

A. At 1;0 (28) Jacqueline, after seeing me use a stick to make a cork drop, imitates my gesture and uses the stick, either when she happens to see it or when she looks for it for that purpose (obs. 159 and 160). We think that from the causal point of view, these first reactions may be classified in the type characteristic of the fourth stage—the forms intermediate between phenomenalistic efficacy and objectified and spatialized causality.

B. At 1;1 (0) Jacqueline manifests a behavior pattern which may be viewed as a regression or as a product of dissociation of the preceding behavior patterns in the direction of pure efficacy. About two hours after using a stick (to which I pointed with my finger) to draw to herself a toy placed on the edge of her bassinet (see *O.I.*, beginning of obs. 161), Jacqueline holds a celluloid doll trimmed with a rattle which sounds at the slightest movement. I take it from her hands and hide it behind the edge of the bassinet, at a different place from where it was two hours earlier; Jacqueline then tries to see the vanished doll, leans over and looks for a moment, then, as if an idea occurred to her, picks up the stick lying at her feet and strikes the edge of the bassinet with it at the exact place where the doll disappeared. After a few minutes I return the doll to her and repeat the experiment at several other places. Each time, Jacqueline takes the stick to tap on the edge of the bassinet at the point where the desired object disappeared. It is difficult not to see in such movements a procedure to make the doll return; the causality inherent in the stick therefore regresses, in such a case, toward pure efficacy.

C. In the following act there is, on the contrary, a spatialized and objective causality typical of the fifth stage. At 1;1 (28) Jacqueline (*O.I.*, obs. 161) touches with her stick a plush cat placed on the floor, but does not know how to pull it to her. The spatial and optical contact between the stick and the cat seem to her sufficient to displace the object. Causality is therefore spatialized but without yet making allowance for the mechanical and physical laws that experience will reveal (need for pressure of the stick in certain directions, etc., resistance of the moving object, etc.)

D. Finally, at 1;3 (12) Jacqueline utilizes the stick correctly (*O.I.,* obs. 161); objective and spatialized causality is therefore applied to the physical conditions of the problem.

Such a sequence of causal varieties (forms A to D) raises no new question concerning the objectification of causality. At first a mere extension of the hand (this is the case from the third stage when the child holds a stick by chance and fortuitously discovers his power over things), the stick becomes an object capable of particular semi-autonomous actions (forms A and B), then an object whose activity is subordinated to laws (forms C and D). On the other hand, with respect to spatialization the sequence of these forms raises a subtle problem, which is to find out how the child conceives of the contacts necessary to the causal action of the stick on the object, and how this concept of contacts evolves. In this regard let us examine forms A and D separately.

Form A seems at first to indicate in the child's mind a definite spatial contact between the stick and the object whose movement it sets going. But this is apparent only, and for that reason we consider form A as residual from the preceding stages; in reality, the stick is still only an extension of the hand, and its power is always conceived as participating in the efficacy of the movement as much as necessitating a physical contact. The object upon which the stick acts is in unstable equilibrium and falls at the slightest blow, which maintains the illusion, peculiar to secondary circular reaction, that the movement engenders certain results. True, the gesture requires a more or less fine accommodation, but does not necessarily involve a perception of intermediaries or a definite concept of contacts. This also occurs when the child discovers the stick's powers, not like Jacqueline by making a moving object fall, but by striking objects placed on the floor. The movements of the object immediately seem linked to those of the stick, but without precise perception of the contacts.

Proof of this is the facility with which form B is constituted through dissociation of behavior patterns of type A. Form B brings us back to the most characteristic and primitive manifestations of causality through efficacy and phenomenalism combined; because use of the stick has resulted in drawing to him the desired object, the child concludes that striking with a stick the place where the object disappeared will make the object come back. The complete absence of spatial contact demonstrated by such a behavior pattern shows the extent to which form A (earlier than form B) has remained intermediate between efficacy and spatialized causality. It is noteworthy that this is a general phenomenon. We shall see below (§5 of this chapter) how every acquisition on the order of spatial causality may give rise at its beginnings to the return of efficacy and phenomenalism—proof that spatialization is a slow and subtle process and that its initial manifestations are more frail in reality than in appearance. The behavior pattern of supports has just furnished us with an example of the same kind; as soon as the child discovers the possibility of drawing an object to him by pulling the support on which it rests (for example, a toy on a cushion) he pulls the support, even if the object is obviously alongside it, the movement thus being immediately endowed with efficacy.

With forms C and D, on the contrary, an entirely different causality appears: the child learns that to move the object by means of the stick, the stick must touch and push the object. The subject is no longer satisfied to strike or knock; he insures a real contact between object and stick, intentionally and accurately. The stick is, therefore, no longer the mere extension of the hand; it becomes the spatial intermediary indispensable to the hand's action on the object.

A considerable difference separates type C from type D and it is precisely the discrepancy between these two types which makes it possible not only to measure the effort necessary for spatialization but also to make clear the progress achieved as compared to the preceding types. When the child limits himself to touching the object by means of the stick as though this contact sufficed to move the object, he does something analogous to that which we have seen above concerning his behavior with respect to moving objects. Just as he places a ball or toy on the floor as though it were going to put itself in motion, so also he places the stick in contact with the objects as though it would start up their displacements by itself. In both cases there is complete objectification of causality, the child transferring the efficacy of his movements to the bodies themselves; but in the second case there is also spatialization, the stick being conceived as having to touch the object in order to act upon it. As to form D, it indicates not a return to the efficacy of the gesture but, on the contrary, an advance in the application of spatial causality to the actual conditions of the phenomenon itself.

This last point evokes some remarks because the analogue of this evolution from type C to type D is found in all the other cases of spatialization of causality. We even touch upon the most important question raised by the behavior patterns of this fifth stage. At the time when the spatialization of causality begins, to the child objects are still merely images without substance or permanence in their spatial qualities; true, from the beginning of the fifth stage they acquire the quality of real objects, and their displacements are arranged in actual groups, but it is clear that these acquisitions merely constitute frames in which the particular properties of each image remain to be discovered and placed in relation to each other. This is precisely what happens in the case of the stick. Once it has been promoted simultaneously to the rank of a substantial object with displacements arranged in space and to the rank of an autonomous causal center, it acquires the capacity of being put into relationship with other similar objects; but the relations the child thus contructs for the first time (up to now the stick has been only an extension of the hand, arising from other types of causal relations) remain completely external and purely optical, that is, governed by immediate perception and not yet analyzed intellectually. But by virtue of the fact that the child begins simultaneously to concern himself with spatial contacts and to make the stick an objective cause obedient to laws, he discovers these laws and learns little by little to displace objects while taking into account the physical data of the problem. Type D thus merely extends type C.

In a general way, the causality which enters into the relations of simple optical contact constitutes the point of departure of true spatialization. As the behavior patterns insuring the development of these contacts are on a par with the tertiary circular reactions which entail the objectification of causality, we witness during this third stage the formation of causal series external to the self which for the first time permit the child really to arrange his universe. It behooves us, however, to mark the limits of this spatialization and correlative objectification: these processes as yet only reach the data of perception and are not accompanied by representation. We have emphasized in *O.I.* the fact that the directed gropings and experimentations peculiar to this stage operate through dynamic and not yet representative schemata. When the child tries in vain to pass an object through the bars of a playpen (*O.I.*, obs. 162-166) or a ring through a wooden rod (*O.I.*, obs. 174), he is limited to regarding these bars or the rod for what they are in immediate perception—mere optical images which offer no *a priori* proof that they cannot be traversed through and through—and to making relationships among these perceptual data without representing the events to himself in advance or mentally combining the experiments instead of actually performing them. It is only in the sixth stage that we shall see causality become representative and transcend the level of mere spatialization of perceived data.

A final point remains to be discussed in connection with this stage: the way in which the child conceives of his own causality. But two problems must be distinguished here: that of the relations which, from the subject's point of view, unite the intention with the act, and that of the relations established by the child between the action of his body and the causal sequences characteristic of the external world.

Concerning the first, we may limit ourselves to saying that the two poles of efficacy and phenomenalism of which we have spoken in connection with the second and third stages are progressively dissociated during the fourth and most of all during the present stage. To the extent the child renounces considering external phenomena as the mere extension of his own action and confers upon them, along with ojectivity and spatiality, a causal structure which is truly physical and independent of the self, it is very probable that he becomes aware of his own activity as direct power exerted by his intentions upon his organism. In other words, just as phenomenalism is transformed into spatial causality by being differentiated from efficacy, efficacy, in turn, does not disappear but is confined to the realm of the activity itself and changes into simply psychological causality.

If our hypotheses are correct, the evolutionary process with which the causality of the first five stages complies is that of a gradual dissociation starting from an initial state of undifferentiation in which efficacy and phenomenalism are indissolubly united. The primitive universe (of the earliest stages) is a confused totality of sensory images each of which seems to the subject simultaneously to obey certain given regulations (phenomenalism) and to extend certain attitudes of desire and effort (efficacy). When during the third stage the child begins to act upon things through the intermediary of prehension, the situation remains the same, except that two poles begin to stand out in opposition to one another among the causal sequences of which the subject becomes aware; efficacy is revealed at its maximum in the relations directly concerning the body itself, and phenomenalism in the relations between things. But this is still a question of two indissociable poles, since every sequence partakes of both efficacy and phenomenalism; to the child, sequences related to his body seem more dependent on his own purposefulness and remote sequences less dependent on it, but in either case they are conceived as linked with it. On the other hand, from the fourth stage on, and above all during the fifth, a break of equilibrium occurs. Certain causal sequences begin to be dissociated from purposefulness, either partially (fourth stage) or completely (fifth stage), since causality is simultaneously objectified and spatialized. Thereafter phenomenalism is differentiated from efficacy and is consequently transformed into physical causality. Does this mean that efficacy is forced to disappear completely? Not at all; it is merely confined to the realm of the connections which the child now recognizes between his intentions and the movements of his body and doubtless also between these movements and those of someone else's body. Causality through efficacy thus becomes psychological causality, the latter existing only in contrast to physical causality. To the extent that the subject discovers that certain relations are formed among objects independently of himself, he becomes the more clearly aware of the particular powers that his intentions, desires, or efforts have over the central and perpetually present body which is his own body. All efficacy previously attributed to his activity is thus limited and, by being limited, is fixed and confirmed in the sphere of movements perceived on the organism.

Moreover it is interesting to note that it is precisely during the fourth and fifth stages that the child learns to imitate new models when they correspond to visible parts of his body or to imitate familiar gestures performed by invisible parts.[5] These two kinds of progress naturally help him the better to know himself and to analyze his own movements by analogy with what he observes concerning the body of someone else. These factors, together with what we have seen concerning the objectification and spatialization of external causality, converge to reinforce the dissociation of the outer world from the self and, thenceforth, the dissociation of the causality belonging to the sequences independent of the organism from internal or psychological causality.

A second question arises here: that of the causal relations established by the child between his own body and the objects in the environment. If it is true that henceforth the child distinguishes two types of causality—an objectified and spatialized causality affecting the interrelations of things and, on the other hand, a causality through efficacy or psychological causality uniting intention with acts—how will the subject conceive of the relations between his own body and the actions of things?

It is this point which shows most clearly the reversal of direction peculiar to the behavior patterns of the present stage as compared to those of the preceding stages. As we have already seen, not only does the child spatialize the causal relations which characterize his action upon things but also, as we shall now try to establish, he conceives of his action as partly depending on the laws of the external world. This last point is fundamental. Up to this time the child's own activity—to the extent that he has remained incapable of attributing it to a self separate from the external world—has been conceived as the center of production of the movements of the universe. But now, that activity is not only established as limited in power by a totality of actions independent of the self, but is also recognized as subject to pressures

[5] See Piaget, *Play, Dreams and Imitation in Childhood* (New York: Norton, 1951).

emanating from an external universe. More precisely, the child ceases to place his own activity in the center of the world and instead conceives of it as maintaining relations of mutual dependence with objects. Instead of monopolizing the only causality possible, he becomes a mere cause among other causes. Now, let us note, such a transformation is exactly on a par with that which, in the course of the same stage, characterizes the evolution of objects and of space as a whole. The child at 11 to 12 months of age begins to discover the essential fact that he is only an object among other objects and occupies only a point in the middle of a space that goes beyond him on every side, whereas previously the universe consisted in moving pictures existing in space and spatially organized only as a function of his own action. The evolution of causality is identical, the child feeling himself to be dependent as well as active, with respect to the external world, to the precise extent that the world is formed into real objects and into space that includes his own body.

But how can we prove that the child at this stage conceives of his action only as a cause among other causes and thus feels his dependence on the external world as well as his power over it? All the spatialization of his action of which we have spoken in connection with the "invention of new means through directed groping and apprenticeship" is an indication of this attitude and involves a renunciation of efficacy in favor of making relations between the body and things. But a certain number of situations make it possible to isolate this new attitude. Here are one or two examples which, without presenting anything particularly interesting from the point of view of the intelligence exercised by the child, are nevertheless representative of the causal links established by him between his action and the objects on which it depends.

OBS. 155. Since 1;0 (10) Jacqueline has known how to utilize the laws of swinging. Seated in her baby swing she gives it an increasing momentum, then turns backward, raises her legs and lets herself swing, remaining perfectly quiet until the movement stops. The difference between this attitude and the attitudes that have previously characterized her play is this: up to now she has been constantly active when in her swing, as though her movements were necessary to make the phenomenon last, whereas now she knows that the action itself is controlled by and can be referred to the laws of the swing's activity.

So also at 1;3 (10) Jacqueline, in her playpen, discovers the possibility of letting herself fall down in a sitting position; she holds the bar and lowers herself gently to within a few centimeters of the floor, then lets go of her support. Before this she has not released the bar until she was suitably placed, but from now on she lets herself go, foreseeing the trajectory her movement of falling will follow independently of any activity on her part.

Let us again note that at 1;3 (12) she knows how to step backward when her dress catches on a nail and try to detach herself instead of simply pulling to overcome the resistance; her attitude reveals awareness of the relations of dependency existing between her movements and external objects.

These few facts of the most commonplace kind converge to show how the child henceforth considers himself dependent on laws external to himself or as submitting to the effect of causes independent of himself. Until toward the end of his first year, the child is constantly active when he is not sleepy or bored. Either he succeeds in bending reality to his desires or else he yields to the actions of someone else, but under the impression that they prolong his own. It is striking to observe, for example, how the nursling, when his mother is getting him ready for his meal, counts very little on her for obtaining the object of his desires; he makes a great fuss, becomes impatient, tries to grasp the bottle or cries with disappointment, but is not at all content to await the natural course of events. It all happens as though he depended only on himself to attain his goal. Jacqueline, on the contrary, when she abandons herself to the motion of the baby swing and to the fall which will seat her on the floor, or when she goes backward to disengage her dress, behaves as though her actions depended on a series of external causal relations. Whereas up to now the child has commanded nature, he now begins to do so only by "obeying it."

This application of causality to actions which the body submits to instead of performing remains limited to the data of perception: as we have already noted concerning the spatialization of causality, the child still conceives of causes as merely a function of perceived objects, since he is incapable of imagining absent causes of a present effect. From this time, with regard to the body, the displacements of the totality not directly perceived are detached from the concept of a dependency on the subject and always give rise to causal interpretations bordering on efficacy. We have cited apropos of space (Chap. II, obs. 122) the case of Jacqueline, who at 1;6 (13) tries to emerge from a ditch by pulling her feet with her hands. Inversely, we have cited (*O.I.*, obs. 168 and 169) the cases in which the child tries to grasp a handkerchief or a coverlet on which he is standing without having the idea of moving away from it. (See also obs. 121 of this volume.) In all these examples the body is still detached from the causality of the external world and placed on a privileged plane; but this is through lack of representation and because the formation of the causal series does not yet transcend the level of perception.

In a general way, we may draw the following conclusions from our analysis of the facts pertaining to this stage. Whereas the fourth stage was a period of transitions, during which the nascent objectification and spatialization of causality remained tinged with the residue of primitive causal egocentrism, these processes of externalization seem henceforth freed, in exact parallel to what happens at the same ages in the construction of substantial objects and the spatial field. The child's behavior toward people, who from now on are conceived as autonomous centers of independent actions, and his behavior relating to things, to which are attributed series of external powers, both attest to this objectification. Spatialization results from similar progress made by the intelligence, since the most advanced coordination of schemata entails a proportionate making of relationships among objects. Finally, except with regard to the realm of representations which transcend the field of immediate perception, the child henceforth conceives of his own body as being inserted in the external causal series, that is, as subject to the action of things as well as a source of actions which operate upon them.

§ 5. THE SIXTH STAGE: REPRESENTATIVE CAUSALITY AND THE RESIDUES OF THE CAUSALITY OF PRECEDING TYPES

In the course of the preceding stage the universe has become to the child an independent system of causes and effects among which the sequences characterizing his own action come to be placed as elements in a totality which transcends them. Just as he ends by considering himself an object among other objects after having conceived of the images of the external world as extending his own activity, and just as he will end by locating himself in a common space after having believed himself to be at the center of the universe, so also the child at the fifth stage discovers that he is only one cause among other causes and that his acts constantly depend on external factors, whereas up to then he had regarded all causality as linked to his own action. Hence one might regard the evolution of causality as completed with the results thus obtained. But this is not true, for two reasons. First, the causes recognized by the child at the fifth stage are solely those within his perceptual field and not those outside of immediate sensation which require representation or evocation through thought. Second, the child does not succeed in representing to himself his own activity when it goes beyond the data of direct perception. Both of these restrictions mean that at the fifth stage the child is not yet capable of a representation of causality; he perceives causes but does not yet know how to evoke them when only their effects are given.

It is this essential acquisition which defines the advent of a sixth stage and thus marks the conclusion of sensorimotor causality. Just as during the sensorimotor development of objects and the spatial field the child becomes capable of evoking absent objects and of representing to himself displacements not given as such in the perceptual field, so also at the sixth stage the child becomes capable of reconstructing causes in the presence of their effects alone, and without having perceived the action of those causes. Inversely, given a certain perceived object as the source of potential actions, he becomes capable of foreseeing and representing to himself its future effects. This representation of causes and effects which has just been superimposed on mere perception is itself necessary for the completion of this perception. The universe cannot be perceived as a coherent system of causes and effects encompassing activity itself unless it is a universe which endures and not a sequence of creations and annihilations. This duration presupposes a representation of causality and not merely a perception of it. Just as the permanence of the object is thus necessarily extended in representation of absent objects, so also the objectification and spatialization of physical causality sooner or later entail the representation of sequences not directly given in the sensory field.

From the theoretical point of view such considerations seem self-evident. From the point of view of practical observation, on the other hand, it is very difficult to know exactly when there begins to be true representation of causes and effects. We must, for example, make careful distinction between this representation and a mere anticipation due to the working of signals. For instance, when the child of seven to eight months old expects to see his mother on hearing the door open, there is nothing to prove that he considers the movement of the door as an effect having as cause his mother's action; there is only "legality," that is, a regular sequence, and not yet causality, that is, understanding of this relation. On the other hand, there is in all perception of causes and effects a beginning of representation. When in the fifth stage the child puts a ball on the floor, expecting to see it roll, there is in this expectation a sketchy representation. Where is the boundary between perceptual anticipation and representation? We believe the only sure facts of representation of causality are those related to new sequences regardless of whether they were recently discovered by the child or are in process of elaboration. In such cases the signal no longer plays a role and perception cannot give rise to pre-representative sensorimotor anticipations. Either, as is the case during the last stages, the child clings to the data of perception alone, or else he truly represents to himself causes not perceived and effects not yet produced.

The first type of these behavior patterns is that of mental reconstructions of the cause, from a perceived effect. The child perceives effect B; to interpret it he evokes an absent cause A, this evocation being made manifest to the observer either by the subject's attitude of searching or by his language (this stage is contemporaneous with the first systematic formulations). Here are examples.

OBS. 156. Let us first give an observation which is transitional between the observations of the fifth stage and those of the sixth. At 1;6 (6) Jacqueline watches me as I place a little lamb on top of a quilt and make it run faster and faster toward her (I go "tch, tch, tch" while making the toy descend and she bursts out laughing). After this I place the lamb on top of the quilt, withdraw my hand, and remain motionless. Jacqueline waits a moment, without trying to act upon the lamb herself. Then when I go "tch, tch, tch" she looks at the animal but seeing it without my hand she immediately looks at my arm, remaining fixed in that position. Jacqueline therefore knows that the lamb will not put itself in motion but that my hand alone is cause of the movement—this is objectified and spatialized causality—and she is expecting to see my hand move in the direction of the object. This is a beginning of representation of causality but, as Jacqueline has just perceived my hand in contact with the lamb, it is still only anticipation based on immediate experience; such behavior by itself cannot mark the transition from the fifth stage to the sixth.

But the next day, at 1;6 (7) Jacqueline is examining the arm of an old armchair, unfamiliar to her, with an extension leaf used for trays, which I operate from behind. This time Jacqueline has not seen me do this and does not see my arm when I push the leaf. Nevertheless when it stops Jacqueline immediately turns to me, looks at my hand, and definitely shows by her behavior that she considers me the cause of the object's movement. Hence this involves mental reconstruction of the causes of a perceived effect.

OBS. 157. At 1;6 (8) Jacqueline sits on a bed beside her mother. I am at the foot of the bed on the side opposite Jacqueline, and she neither sees me nor knows I am in the room. I brandish over the bed a cane to which a brush is attached at one end and I swing the whole thing. Jacqueline is very much interested in this sight: she says "cane, cane" and examines the swinging most attentively. At a certain moment she stops looking at the end of the cane and obviously tries to understand. Then she tries to perceive the other end of the cane, and to do so, leans in front of her mother, then behind her, until she has seen me. She expresses no surprise, as though she knew I was the cause of the sight.

A moment later, while Jacqueline is hidden under the covers to distract her attention, I go to the foot of the bed and resume my game.

Jacqueline laughs, says "Papa," looks for me in the place where she saw me the first time, then tries to find me in the room, while the cane is still moving. She does not think of finding me at the foot of the bed (I am hidden by the footboard), but she has no doubt that I am the cause of the phenomenon.

OBS. 158. At 1;8 (11) Jacqueline, observing from her window the mists on the side of the mountains, says, "Mist smoke papa." The next day, confronted by the same sight, she says, "Mist papa." The following days, on seeing me smoke my pipe she says, "Smoke papa." It would seem to me difficult not to interpret the first of these circumstances by a causal relation which can be formulated as follows: "It is papa who has made those mists with his pipe," or more cautiously, "There is in those mists something connected with the smoke papa makes with his pipe." Because on the following days, until toward 1;9 (10), Jacqueline has constantly repeated, "Clouds papa," on seeing the clouds, the first interpretation seems to us the most probable. But whatever may be true of this artificialism which we need not emphasize here, it seems apparent that such talk involves an attempt at causal representation, that is, mental reconstruction of a causality not immediately given in the perceptual field. It is only this point we wish to emphasize.

OBS. 159. Lucienne and Laurent have presented analogous behavior patterns at the same ages. Here are just two examples.

At 1;1 (4) Laurent is seated in his carriage and I am on a chair beside him. While reading and without seeming to pay any attention to him, I put my foot under the carriage and move it slowly. Without hesitation Laurent leans over the edge and looks for the cause in the direction of the wheels. As soon as he perceives the position of my foot he is satisfied and smiles.

At 1;4 (4), a month after obs. 125, Laurent tries to open a garden gate but cannot push it forward because it is held back by a piece of furniture. He cannot account either visually or by any sound for the cause that prevents the gate from opening, but after having tried to force it he suddenly seems to understand; he goes around the wall, arrives at the other side of the gate, moves the armchair which holds it firm, and opens it with a triumphant expression.

We shall see how such behavior differs from that of the fifth stage, even while completing it. In the observations characteristic of this last stage, either the cause and the effect are given in the same perceptual field and it is simply a matter of putting them into relationship with one another, or else one of the two terms is not directly perceived, but since it is linked to the other by customary or newly operative schemata, its evocation involves no representation. In the preceding observations, on the contrary, the causal link on which the child's searching bears is new, as long as the cause is not given in the perceptual field; the child must therefore reconstruct, or simply search for, the cause of an observed phenomenon when that cause is neither known nor perceived directly. The difference between the behavior patterns of the sixth stage and those of the fifth is therefore of the same kind as that subsisting between representative groups and the merely perceived objective groups. In both cases mental construction takes the place of direct contact, even though in the current examples comprehension rather than invention is involved.

A second group of acts included in the present stage is made up of inverse steps which proceed from cause to effect and no longer from effect to cause. Instead of reconstructing the causes by starting from a given effect, the child is led to foresee effects by starting from a considered cause. But, of course, in order that such a behavior pattern may truly spring from causality and not merely constitute an act of sensorimotor anticipation on the basis of signals or indications, the situation defining the causal link must be relatively new to the child and not merely give rise to application of familiar relations.

OBS. 160. At 1;4 (12) Jacqueline has just been wrested from a game she wants to continue and placed in her playpen from which she wants to get out. She calls, but in vain. Then she clearly expresses a certain need, although the events of the last ten minutes prove that she no longer experiences it. No sooner has she left the playpen than she indicates the game she wishes to resume!

Thus we see how Jacqueline, knowing that a mere appeal would not free her from her confinement, has imagined a more efficacious means, foreseeing more or less clearly the sequence of actions that would result from it.

In a general way, therefore, at the sixth stage the child is now capable of causal deduction and is no longer restricted to perception or sensorimotor utilization of the relations of cause to effect. If the objectification and spatialization of causality begin with the fourth stage and are consolidated with the fifth, the sixth stage marks the completion of these processes. This is true because representation is necessary to the concept of the universe as a lasting system of causal connections (without representations the perceptual field is constantly made incomprehensible by events whose source remains beyond its narrow confines) and because the action of the body itself is unintelligible without representation of its total activity. With the causal deduction characteristic of this stage the child becomes accessible both to an extension in time of the data of perception and to an application to himself of the causal connections observed on someone else. For the first time the subject can really place himself as an element, at once both cause and effect, in the context of a universe which transcends him everywhere. This making of relationships, supplanting the radical egocentrism of primitive efficacy, has certainly been prepared by the acquisitions of the preceding stages and particularly by those of the fifth; it becomes effective only with the beginnings of representation peculiar to the present stage.

It now behooves us to correct this summary picture by some remarks which we might have made in the course of the foregoing paragraphs but which we have saved for this one in order to avoid repetition. The acquisitions peculiar to a given stage do not immediately abolish the manifestations characteristic of the preceding stages. The problem of evolution of the forms of causality is therefore not resolved by the earlier analyses, which are limited to defining the innovations at the advent of each stage and not to explaining the method of succession of these different steps.

The unfolding of the stages in the development of a concept such as causality may be considered in two ways. In the first place, it can be stated that each stage introduces a complete transformation, whose manifestations are almost simultaneous in the child's mind. According to this hypothesis if the child became capable of the objectification and spatialization of causality, he would renounce all efficacy and all phenomenalism. The discovery of the new form of causality, occurring in connection with a precise problem presented to the child and with a particular, delimited phenomenon, would thus give rise to an immediate generalization, so that the early forms would be forced back by it. According to a second conception, on the contrary, the advent of each stage would merely be marked by the differentiation of a nucleus whose formation would not directly influence the totality of the strata constituted by the acquisitions of preceding stages. The new stage would thus be defined by the fact that the child becomes capable of certain behavior patterns of which he was up to then incapable; it is not the fact that he renounces the behavior patterns of the preceding stages, even if they are contrary to the new ones or contradictory to them from the observer's point of view. The sequence of stages would thus be conceived as a series of sequential differentiations or neoformations taking shape in the midst of the old formations, though the latter are not immediately abolished.

The facts seems to us very clearly to substantiate this second solution. This is true first, of course, when old acquisitions do not lose their objective value in the presence of new ones. Thus the behavior patterns characteristic of the sixth stage (representation of causal relations) do not exclude those of the fifth (perception of those same relations) but complete and presuppose them. But it remains partly true when the old acquisitions are stripped of objective value as compared to the new ones. It would seem, for example, that at the fourth or fifth stage the child who has discovered the need for spatial contacts in the course of certain of his actions must have renounced belief in the efficacy of gesture; in other words, belief in the action, at a distance, of movements of hand or head on objects neither in contact with the body nor connected with it by any intermediary. This is not so; we still find, in the middle of the sixth stage, behavior patterns identical to those of the first stages.

First let us try to describe the different residues of the primitive stages which continue in the present stage and then try to draw theoretical conclusions which accord with these observations.

First of all, up to the very middle of the sixth stage we encounter numerous examples of causality through imitation.

OBS. 161. At 0;10 (30) Jacqueline, as we have seen in obs. 142, above, and in *O.I.*, obs. 127, tries to reproduce the sound of a singing doll which I have just activated. She begins by pushing my hand to make me continue (the reaction of the fourth stage), then after a series of fruitless maneuvers makes little sharp cries which resemble the sound of the doll, while she stares at it.

Moreover we recall analogous behavior patterns she revealed at 1;3 (9) in order to activate a clown (obs. 150); she imitated the sound, lacking the ability to discover the mechanism.

At 1;3 (10) I hang a little monkey before her, at her height, and show her how to swing it with a stick. When it has stopped swinging Jacqueline, instead of using the stick, makes an imitative gesture with her hand (the movement of to and fro), while watching the object. The same thing happens many times in succession, after which I again demonstrate the use of the stick. Then, noting the failure of her procedure, she takes possession of the stick and succeeds after the first attempt (cf. obs. 154, D). But as soon as the monkey is stationary again, Jacqueline again imitates with her hand the movement she desires to give it!

At 1;6 (16) Jacqueline is in bed and I go to and fro from her right to her left. She laughs, then as soon as I stop, shakes her head (gesture of negation, but more rapid), obviously to make me continue.

At 1;6 (17) she has a newspaper on her head and shakes herself to make it fall down. An hour or two later she watches me when I place a postcard on my head. She immediately shakes her own head, evidently to make the postcard drop. But does she hope that I will imitate her gesture and thus let the object fall or does she want to act directly upon the postcard? It is an interesting fact that Jacqueline has constantly watched the postcard and not my face, which speaks in favor of the second interpretation. Furthermore, after having touched the card with her index finger but without succeeding in making it fall from my head, she immediately resumes shaking herself while watching the object. This seems to be, as on the day before, a residue of causality through imitation.

OBS. 161a. Similarly, Laurent at 1;0 (10) shakes his head while watching a matchbox which I have placed on top of my head and which he cannot reach with his hand.

At 1;0 (12) he is seated in his bassinet and imitates the to and fro movement of the hood bending slightly, straightening up, and beginning again. But is this a mere representative imitation analogous to those he has manifested the day before with regard to a window[6] or is it an attempt at causal action?

[6] J. Piaget, Play, *Dreams and Imitation in Childhood*, obs. 58.

At 1;1 (2) at a distance of several meters he watches me activate a mechanism which forces me constantly to bend over and straighten up. As soon as I stop, Laurent bows his head and lifts it again (gesture of greeting), this time with the obvious intention of making me continue.

OBS. 162. With regard to Lucienne we have observed in her second year, in addition to the behavior patterns analogous to the preceding ones—for instance, at 1;1 (25) she swings herself while looking at my bicycle as soon as I pause in moving it backward and forward —the following interesting behavior.

At 1;3 (6) after having with great pleasure heard her mother sing, Lucienne tries to make her continue. She begins by touching her mother's lips with her index finger and pressing lightly (reaction intermediate between those of the fourth stage and those of the fifth), then, this method being inadequate, she stares at her mother's mouth while slowly opening and closing her own.

A moment later I take her right hand and shake it, which entertains her very much. To make me repeat, she extends her hand. This is a reaction typical of the fifth stage. Lucienne counts on my initiative for the game's continuation and not on the efficacy of her imitative gestures or her magico-phenomenalistic procedures. But as I remain motionless, she shakes her head while watching my hand!

Here is a totality of behavior patterns observed after the first year of life, in which are found clear manifestations of the combined efficacy and phenomenalism peculiar to the initial forms of causality.

OBS. 163. First, here are some of Jacqueline's residual behavior patterns relating to things and not to people.

At 1;6 (8) she is seated in a double bed facing a quilt rolled up to make a hill. I place on top of it a little wooden lamb and strike the bottom of the quilt so that at each shake the lamb comes nearer the child and finally rolls into her hands. Then I put the lamb back on top of the quilt; Jacqueline immediately imitates successfully what she has just learned and makes the lamb roll to her two or three times in succession.

Then I place the lamb on a bedside table at a distance of about one meter from Jacqueline and at the same height as herself but separated from the bed by a space about 80 centimeters wide. Jacqueline strikes the quilt as before, while looking at the lamb and striking harder and harder as though the failure of this procedure were due to the weakness of the blows.

Fifteen minutes later: same behavior with a fish which she has made fall from the quilt and which she seems to want to reach by the same procedure after I have put it on the bedside table.

When I put the lamb or the fish on the window sill, that is, farther away and a little higher, she looks at it without reacting, but as soon as I put it back on the table she begins again to strike the quilt.

At 1;6 (13), five days later, Jacqueline is in the same bed. I take the lamb from her but instead of placing it on the quilt I put it on the table and push it lightly with my finger. As soon as I stop, Jacqueline strikes the quilt while watching the toy!

At 1;6 (20) she is in another bed. I put my watch chain on top of the quilt. She immediately strikes the quilt and the chain slides to her. Jacqueline laughs and does it again. Then I take the object and place it on a chair, one meter from the bed; Jacqueline hits the quilt two or three times, but weakly and without conviction, as though "to see if" perhaps the procedure would succeed notwithstanding. Then I put the chain on the back of the chair; Jacqueline looks at it but no longer reacts.

OBS. 164. If the foregoing behavior patterns were elicited by our experimentation, here, on the contrary, is an analogous example of spontaneous behavior.

At 1;6 (5) Jacqueline walks into a room and moves a chair whose back touches one of the panels of an open French window. The window stands slightly open and Jacqueline notices the movement imparted to it indirectly. Then she grasps the chair with both hands and shakes it, this time intentionally, while watching the window and the shaking thus produced. Afterward Jacqueline continues her walk in the room without seeming to pay any further attention to the phenomenon. But on knocking against another chair two meters away, she grasps it, shakes it as before and looks at the window. She sees that a wide empty space separates her from the window and that no contact exists between it and the new chair; nevertheless, despite failure, for a while she continues to shake the chair while watching the window.

OBS. 165. Let us now take up Jacqueline's residual procedures relating to people.

At 1;9 (28) Jacqueline comes and goes in a dimly lighted room. I am lying on a sofa with a cape over my legs, which are bent. Jacqueline notices the hill thus formed and comes and puts her head on it. I move slightly; she lifts her head abruptly, smiles, puts it back again, and I recommence. When I definitely stop, she shakes her head harder and harder while watching the hill. This movement, evidently designed to make me continue, is not directed at me but at my knees which are covered with a cape. Jacqueline does not look at my face which is barely visible in the growing darkness and perhaps does not even know that the legs under the cape are mine.

At 1;10 (16) Jacqueline plays in a room in which I have been in bed since morning, as I am ill. She does not see me and is behind the wood of the bed, my keys in her hand. She encounters the waste-paper basket and strikes its empty bottom with the keys. Then I cry out: "Oh. . . .": she starts, then laughs, knowing it is I, and without turning around, starts to strike again. I cry out again, and so on for six or seven times. Then I pause and look at her without her seeing me. She increases her blows and, noting failure, withdraws her keys with her right hand, with her left slowly pushes the basket about 10 centimeters farther away, as though to adjust it, and begins striking again. I cry out once more, and she bursts out laughing. But I remain silent when she resumes striking. Then the whole maneuver is repeated. She increases the blows, withdraws the keys, readjusts the basket a few centimeters farther away, and strikes again. Jacqueline thus seems to believe that my cries depend on the way she strikes and the position of the basket, as though they were substantially governed by these factors and not solely by my wish to amuse her. Jacqueline does not try to look at me or to exchange a word with me.

obs. 166. At 1;0 (14) Lucienne is seated in a carriage which I shake by the handle. At a certain moment I put my hand near the handle but without touching it. Lucienne looks at my hand without paying attention to the rest of me, and while watching it, shakes herself, then waves her own hand. Hence she tries to act upon my hand through direct procedures, just as Jacqueline, in the previous observation, wished to force me to cry out by means of a purely physical procedure.

At 1;1 (23) in the course of the attempts she is making to fit a ring into a case (O.I., obs. 174), Lucienne makes the ring roll too far to recapture it. For a moment she extends her hand toward the object, then gives up. But then she looks for the case from which the ring has emerged—she no longer holds the case—and, after having found it again, holds it out toward the ring as though the case would attract it or go to meet it!

At 1;10 (2) she tries unsuccessfully to open a closed phonograph. Not succeeding, she begins to sing.

OBS. 167. At 1;4 (20) Lucienne is standing in the middle of a room. I turn the light out three times in succession to make her laugh. When I turn it on for the third time she closes her eyes either to make me continue, or to imitate darkness, or else not to be dazzled by the sudden changes of light. Then I go to a distance of one meter from the light switch; Lucienne, opening her eyes again, looks at me and then looks attentively at the switch button from a distance. She approaches it after a moment and then, opposite the switch button and without paying any more attention to me, she closes her eyes for a long time. When she reopens them she looks at the lamp for a moment, then at the switch button again. I turn out the light once more and relight it two or three times; then I go away.

When I reenter on tiptoe a few minutes later, Lucienne is in the act of making the experiment alone, facing the light switch. Her eyes are closed and then she opens them while looking at the lamp.

She manifests the same reactions at 1;6 (22).

OBS. 167a. At 1;4 (2) Laurent manifests a completely analogous reaction. He is in a half-darkened room which I light up suddenly, completely dazzling him. When he has recovered he blinks his eyes in front of the lamp, then blinks his eyes in front of the light switch, turns around immediately and looks at the lamp!

OBS. 168. Laurent's behavior is identical to that of little G., about whom Dr. Raymond de Saussure has been kind enough to furnish me with this observation.

At 0;11 G. cries at night and a hanging lamp is lighted by pulling a certain cord with which G. is very familiar. The light dazzles G., who blinks. Several times in succession, apparently wanting to see the lamp relit or to see the dazzling light again (the lamp, once lighted, is less striking), G. looks at the cord while intentionally blinking his eyes.

After an interruption of four months, according to Dr. de Saussure's account, we looked for G. (then aged 1;3) and placed him 50 centimeters away from the cord in daylight. We lit the lamp; G. blinked involuntarily, then after a few seconds, noticing that nothing more was happening, he blinked several times, this time intentionally, while looking at the cord.

These residual behavior patterns, along with those we have already had the opportunity to observe in passing (for example, obs. 154, B) are of great interest in understanding the causality peculiar to the child's sensorimotor intelligence. They make us comprehend with what deep motive powers the earliest forms of causality comply, since these elementary forms reappear through a sort of continuous temporal displacement during the sixth stage, when the problems confronting the child are too new and too difficult for him.

It is very difficult to question the analogy between these acts observed during the second year of life and those characterizing the earliest stages of causality. For example, when Jacqueline in obs. 163 imitates the way in which I make a toy descend from the top of a quilt, and then applies this procedure from a distance when the same toy is placed on a table separated from her bed, it is impossible not to translate the matter in terms of efficacy and phenomenalism. Jacqueline knows how to imitate my gesture but does not understand the physical conditions well enough to avoid applying it to a new situation independently of any contact. In this example the relation between the gesture of striking the quilt and the fall of the object has remained phenomenalistic through lack of understanding (the role of the shaking imparted to the quilt and that of the disarrangement of the surface doubtless escape the subject), and by that very fact the gesture has been invested with an efficacy which is independent of the surrounding conditions. So also in obs. 164, the contact between the chair and the window not having been understood, the relation remains phenomenalistic and the act of shaking the chairs is conceived as comprising a general causality relative to the window. In obs. 166 the phenomenalistic relation established between the case and the ring is all the more curious because it involves a mere relation of contiguity which the child considers causal, as in the magical operations based on belief in action of remote objects which were once in contact. In observations 167 and 168 the child, naturally not yet understanding anything about the mechanics of illumination, merely notes the action of the switch button or the cord, the lighting up of the lamp, and his own dazzlement. This phenomenalistic relation is accompanied by such a belief in the interconnection among the three presenting terms that the subject considers his own blinking to be charged with an efficacy sufficient to act upon the switch button and the lamp! In obs. 165 and the beginning of obs. 166 the phenomenalism of the relations observed (between my outcry and the blows of the key, for instance) is also powerful enough— given the weak power of social adaptation which the child has during his second year of life—to make him forget he is trying to act upon persons and not upon things. Besides, the way in which the subject tries to force adults to do what he wishes still results from the laws of efficacy and phenomenalism combined. Let it be said in passing that this confusion of the physical and the psychic revealed by obs. 165 is extremely instructive and shows the exaggeration in asserting, as do certain child psychologists, that the ability to distinguish between people and things is given from the beginning of mental life and particularly from the first smiles! With regard to obs. 161 and 162, that is, causality through imitation, they raise a question of the same kind. We can ask ourselves whether the child, when he wants to force adults to continue interesting actions and with this purpose in mind imitates their gestures, is not simply trying to be imitated by them in return, which would lead to the desired result. In that case causality through imitation should be interpreted as a simple language without speech, that is, as a causal action of a psychic and not a physical kind. But though causality through imitation leads to acts of this kind later on, we do not believe that obs. 161 and 162 can be interpreted thus; it is noteworthy that in these observations the child does not look at the person on whom he tries to act, in other words, he looks not at his face but only at the exact region of his body on which the action should bear (hands, mouth, etc.) or at the object toward which the adult's activity is directed (clown, postcard, matchbox, bicycle, etc.). Finally, this causality through imitation is exerted on things (the monkey in obs. 161) as well as on people.

In short, obs. 161-168 confront us with forms of causality analogous to those of the first stages of the development of this fundamental category. How can this paradoxical retrogression be explained? To state that the primitive stages we have described constitute steps necessary to the formation of causality is sufficient to understand how these elementary forms can reappear through temporal displacement every time problems which are too new and too difficult arise in the course of the child's activity. All the situations described in obs. 161-168 except those in obs. 161a at 1;0 (12)—and precisely on this point it is doubtful whether the reaction is of a causal nature and, if it is, whether it can be interpreted as mere automatism—constitute situations which are new and hard to understand. From obs. 161 to 162 adults' actions, hitherto unfamiliar, are involved; obs. 163 and 164 and the end of obs. 166 to 168 deal with physical phenomena incomprehensible during the second year of life; and obs. 165 to the beginning of 166 describe unforeseen or new personal actions. In every case, therefore, the unadapted child can only remain on the surface of experience and rely, like the baby a few months old, upon the mere phenomenalistic bringing together of the covariant elements of reality. It is interesting that in the context of this compulsory phenomenalism, so to speak, efficacy reappears at the outset; from the point when, through the very novelty of the problems which arise and the incomprehensible character of the observed phenomena, the child can no longer structure reality by placing his own action among causes and effects arranged in a system external to it, he again confers on efficacy an unwarranted power. This obviously indicates how painful the progressive reduction of egocentrism becomes in the conversion into reality, and how hard the self seeks to escape from this submission, once the facts seem to permit spatialized and objectified causality to relax and to lay itself open to an intervention of personal action.

In conclusion, despite the progress of objectification and spatialization due to the work peculiar to the fourth and fifth stages, and despite the progress of the causal representation which characterizes the sixth stage, with each new obstacle there is a reappearance of phenomenalism and efficacy combined. Moreover, beside these "temporal displacements in extension" it is noteworthy that even on the plane of representation the activity due to the subject's egocentrism is found again through a "temporal displacement in comprehension," in the way in which the child conceives of causes. Thus as soon as the child attributes wholly to others the actions he can no longer consider as emanating from himself (obs. 156 and 157), he thereby invests another person with an exaggerated power over the universe, a sort of artificialism due to the projection of personal activity onto those new centers of forces constituted by the other "selves." Thus in obs. 158 and in analogous observations which could be multiplied, "Papa" is believed to produce the mists and clouds. But this temporal displacement in comprehension raises the whole question of the child's transition from sensorimotor intelligence to verbal thought. Moreover it is outside the scope of the present discussion and should be taken up in the systematization we shall try to make in the general conclusions of this work.

§ 6. THE ORIGINS OF CAUSALITY

The construction of schemata of a causal kind is completely interconnected with that of space, of objects, and of temporal series. If the child succeeds in forming causal series independent of the self, in which his own body intervenes in the same capacity as other causes and without any sort of privilege, this is because a spatio-temporal field is being organized and the images perceived acquire the permanence of objects. On the other hand, to the extent that causality remains connected with the activity of the self, space, time, and objects remain in the same situation. It is therefore useless to revert to the source of the evolutionary processes of objectification and spatialization of causality which are obviously parallel to the mechanisms already analyzed apropos of the object and of space. It is, however, fitting to account for them by taking up again, from the point of view of causality, the five tendencies among which the various theories of intelligence oscillate. Classification of the famous hypotheses of the origin of causality reveals the extent to which the contrast between these tendencies is found in every realm; the symmetry of these findings is real and not artificial.

In the first place, associational empiricism inspired Hume to an interpretation of causality which retains all its interest; the foregoing facts permit a discussion of it in the same field chosen by the philosopher: that of the origin of habits. In the second place the equally famous interpretation by Maine de Biran must be described as vitalistic. According to this, causality results from awareness of voluntary activity conceived as a primary datum. It is in this doctrine of the self and of personal causality that Biran's vitalism deviates most definitely from ordinary rationalism. In the third place, the *a priori* interpretation of causality implies a psychological hypothesis according to which the concept of cause constitutes a necessary structure inherent in every intellectual act and present, consequently, from the first contacts of the mind with reality. In the fourth place, in the pragmatic theory of trial and error, causal relations constitute so many constructions destined to insure the prevision of phenomena and the adaptation of personal action to the external world, but these constructions are based neither on the nature of things nor on any necessary structure of the mind. Finally, in relativity, causality is the totality of the relations elaborated by sensorimotor intelligence and later by thought in order to understand things, and its growing deductive success shows that these relations correspond to a real interaction between subject and object.

Now Hume's interpretation, quite outmoded as regards the higher forms of causality, retains all its probability in the realm of inchoate forms. It is perfectly true that from the time when, transcending the purely reflex level, the child elaborates his schemata by experience, he begins by associating any one thing to any other thing. Thus from the second stage on, the baby turns his head in the direction of the sound to find the corresponding visual image. It is apparent that the child at this level does not know how to establish any rational connection between the sound and the image and that the association remains purely phenomenalistic. So also when in the course of the third stage the child pulls a string to shake his bassinet hood, no comprehensible relation exists for him between the movement of the string and that of the hood. Furthermore, to the extent that the universe of the earliest stages consists only in moving pictures without substantial permanence, causality necessarily remains phenomenalistic. Finally, with regard to the actions performed by the child on his own body, Hume is obviously right: the baby discovers little by little that his desires govern the movements of his hands or legs but he does not at all understand the "how" of this operation. But must we, like Hume, draw from this self-evident and general phenomenalism of the earliest stages of causality the conclusion that causal connection stems from the force of habit? We do not think so.

To be sure, as we have just recalled, the elementary causal relations are all due to the mechanism of circular reaction, first primary, then secondary, and if circular reaction could be reduced to the simple concept of habit, Hume would be right. But circular reaction involves an element of organization or active repetition which transcends habit. Hume says: "For wherever the repetition of any particular act or operation produces a propensity to renew the same act or operation, without being impelled by any reasoning or process of the understanding, we always say, that this propensity is the effect of *Custom*." [7] But can one say that the motive power of circular reaction does not involve any "process of the understanding" when this motive power consists in an act of assimilation tending to reproduce an interesting result, that is, tending to rediscover an effect identical to that which was just perceived or felt? Obviously one cannot. Assimilation, which is at the point of departure of all schemata, is the source of classifications and the making of relationships which transcend the frames of simple habit and which therefore involve a more complex concept of causality. It is this we shall try to demonstrate.

First we must recall what we have already said about the theories of intelligence (*O.I.*, Conclusions) which consider habit a primary fact, called either conditioned reflex, associative transfer or simple association. The mechanisms upon which these doctrines rely are never autonomous but are always supported by more complex processes which make them possible. The conditioned reflex is thus explained only by an assimilation of certain signals to the reflex schemata, and the associative transfer by an analogous assimilation of signals to the schemata of the various stages. It would therefore be most improbable that a concept as fundamental to the mind as the concept of causality should result from non-autonomous processes merely attached to the existence of deeper mechanisms. As habit, in any of its forms, does not constitute a primary act, it cannot account for causality.

[7] D. Hume, *An Enquiry Concerning Human Understanding* ("Harvard Classics," New York: Collier & Sons, 1910), Chap. V, par. 5.

On the other hand, causal relations can be traced back to reproductive assimilation which itself explains the origins of habit. When, having fortuitously set an interesting phenomenon in motion, the child immediately tries to reproduce his gesture and recapture the desired result, we may say that this effort, which will subsequently engender a habit, constitutes the most elementary form of causal relation. But the formation of this schema presupposes that from the very beginning the subject establishes a connection between the result perceived (whether this result is located in the external world or remains inherent in his own body is of little importance) and a certain aspect, more or less analyzed, of the activity itself. Hence it is this connection, and not its automatization into habits, which defines causality. Such a connection presupposes, of course, an experimental sanction, and on this point empiricism is right, but it does not result from experimentation alone: it involves also the ability to establish relationships, in which reproductive and generalizing assimilation consists, and, in general, the organization of schemata. The relations thus established are not, of course, rational from the outset, since they are partly phenomenalistic and make personal activity play a role which it does not fill in reality. We must therefore avoid the belief that causality is an identification from the outset or that it constitutes from its inception a category of ne varietur structure. But the organization of schemata which constitutes causality is capable of a progressive structuring in the direction of reversibility and geometric connection and thus presages from the beginning the possibility of a later rationalism.

Finally, to the extent that causality appears as reproductive assimilation it is always, during the earliest stages, on the occasion of personal activity that causal connections are established. Never, therefore, does the subject at first elaborate a relation between an external cause and effect. Such a situation reveals once again the objections to Hume's schema, which excludes from the outset the existence of purely external empirical connections. With regard to the statement that a simple associative transfer can account for the relation thus established between the external results on the one hand, and the personal activity on the other, the latter being conceived as the sole cause of phenomena, Hume himself has shown (thereby criticizing in advance the thesis of Maine de Biran) that action by the self could not give rise to a direct intuition; this, it seems to us, would render impossible any pure association between this action and the images perceived in the external world. The way in which the child conceives of himself as cause therefore depends, according to Hume, on his progressive awareness of his activity: at first diffuse sensations of effort and desire, then more and more precise awareness of movements and intentions. Consequently, cause and effect cannot, at the outset, be placed on the same plane; contrary to the empiricist intepretation, causality involves a formation of relationships which surpasses in depth the awareness of cause. Morever when, under the influence of the progressive spatialization and objectification of causality, cause and effect are gradually placed on the same plane, this homogeneity is acquired only through an increasingly complex elaboration of schemata and here again it is the organization of these schemata which constitutes causality, and not experience alone.

This necessary intervention of personal activity in the origins of causality leads us to discussion of the famous theory of Maine de Biran on the internal sources of causality from the point of view of vitalism. The phenomena we have just emphasized seem to favor Biran's hypothesis, according to which the prototype of causality is to be sought in action by the self; during this effort to obtain a certain result, regardless of whether this result is merely repetition of a fortuitous event or involves a goal set beforehand, causal connection appears. But as a result of the works of J. M. Baldwin, we know today how hard it is to attribute to the baby a direct intuition of the self and even a delimitation between the objective and the subjective. At most what is given at the point of departure is the connection between a certain result and a feeling of effort which fills the subject's whole universe. But far from constituting the intuition of personal will or of action by the self, that is, the intuition of a current of energy bearing upon the object, this connection constitutes only an acquisition of awareness after the event, and so to speak centripetal, of the assimilatory activity which incorporates the object with the personal action. That is not intuition of subjective causality but, as we have just seen apropos of Hume, a progressive consciousness of the relations constituted by the assimilatory schemata prior to any distinction between the internal and the external. In other words, consciousness arises through contact with things, as Biran says, but far from merely contrasting an object and a subject already perceived, it depends on their mutual relations in order to form them; at the time it appears, action is already engaged in a construction which consciousness only extends. Causality is therefore essentially an intellectual elaboration inherent in the organization of the schemata and of the concomitant organization of the universe. Just as Hume did not persuade us to reduce causality to pure phenomenalism, so also Maine de Biran does not persuade us to identify it with the feeling of efficacy: arising from the relations between personal activity and the external world, at first it partakes of efficacy mixed with phenomenalism but later breaks loose from both this subjectivism and this empiricism and is incorporated into a system of pure relations.[8]

From the fact that causality necessarily remains a relation between object and subject, must we conclude according to a possible third point of view that causality constitutes an *a priori* form in the mind, that is to say, a category with a permanent and necessary structure? The difficulty of apriority is the structural invariance with which it is obliged to endow the categories of intelligence. In fact, if causality remains in the state of virtual relationship which the mind apprehends bit by bit without quite understanding it immediately by direct intuition, such a notion, inasmuch as its structure is imposed necessarily by the mind, should present permanent content. But it is precisely this hypothesis of structural invariance which the genetic analysis of causality upsets. In considering only the sensorimotor stages, those which have been reported in this work, it is possible to establish the existence of obvious structural transformations. At first simply a relation between the efficacy of personal action and the phenomenalism of immediate experience, causality is progressively objectified and spatialized so that it unites, no longer only muscular impressions with external sensory images, but also objective displacements with one another; such a transformation

[8] J. Piaget, in collaboration with H. Krafft, "De quelques formes primitives de causalité chez l'enfant," *Année psychol.*, XXVI (1925), 31-71.

presupposes the elimination of a solipsistic universe in favor of a system of temporal, spatial, and objective series. True, one might say that the relation of cause to effect remains invariant in the course of this process, as only the interconnected factors vary. But how is it possible to conceive of a relation independently of the factors it unites? Moreover the nature of primitive connections is to locate the cause (the impressions of efficacy attached to personal action) and the effect (the sensory images furnished by phenomenalistic experimentation) on heterogeneous planes, whereas the nature of the evolved forms of causality is to establish a more and more highly developed homogeneity, to say nothing of necessary identification, between cause and effect. How is it possible to separate relations of causality from relations which are spatial and temporal and which pertain to the formation of the objects themselves? The elaboration of causality is closely linked with that of the universe and from this point of view it seems impossible to acknowledge a progressive transformation of the perception or the representation of the world without recognizing the existence of a structural evolution of the relation which unites causes with effects. To be sure, there exists one invariant whose manifestations are visible throughout the history of causality. But that invariant is functional and not structural in nature. It consists in this: at every level the subject assimilates actions and their results into a system of coherent schemata; at first actions of the body, then actions attributed to increasingly externalized and spatialized objects. Hence it is the functional permanence of assimilation which is the source of causality, to the extent that the assimilatory schemata are accommodated to the sequence of events and not only to their static and classificatory aspect. Will it be said that assimilation leads to causality only on condition that it first presupposes time? But the perception of sequence, which must not be confused with the sequence of perceptions, is itself formed only as the function, if not of causality as such, at least of the organization of actions, that is, of the assimilatory process envisaged in its totality. The roots of causality and of time are therefore to be sought in the functioning of action, and the different structures with which these categories are endowed are not given *a priori* but constitute sequential structures owing to this functioning which alone is invariant.

But, from a possible fourth point of view, we may interpret these constructions as simple practical adaptations having only provisional value and emanating neither from internal necessities nor the nature of the external world. Of course the first forms of causality which we have discerned seem to conform to such a conception through their inadequacy and their empirical character. But if primitive phenomenalism remains on the surface of things and if the feeling of efficacy which seems to characterize the beginnings of awareness of causal relations remains on the surface of the work of the mind, nevertheless, envisaged in its progress, the evolution of causality leads to the construction of schemata which attest to an increasingly close union of experience and deduction. The objective and spatialized causality of our last stages is therefore simultaneously closer to the physical characteristics of the object and the spatial schemata due to the activity of the subject.

Only the fifth point of view seems to us to be justified. Causality consists in an organization of the universe caused by the totality of relations established by action and then by representation between objects as well as between object and subject. Hence causality presupposes at all levels an interaction between the self and things, but if the radical egocentrism of the beginnings first leads the subject to attribute all external events to personal activity, the formation of a permanent universe subsequently enables the self to be located among things and to understand the totality of the sequences which it sees or in which it is engaged as cause or effect. Such an elaboration presupposes an invariant functioning, as we have just seen, but a structuring which is progressive and not *a priori*. How do we account for this?

It is obvious that the progress of such a structuring stems from that of intelligence, and that causality must definitively be conceived as intelligence itself to the extent that the latter is applied to temporal relations and organizes a lasting universe. That is why, to the extent that the assimilatory and accommodating activity which comprises the intellectual mechanisms is not yet disentangled from the reflex schemata or primary or secondary circular reactions, causality is reduced, from the structural point of view, to an indissociable mixture of efficacy and phenomenalism. Efficacy is the assimilation of events to personal activity, and phenomenalism is accommodation to the empirical data inseparable from that activity. Assimilation and accommodation are dissociated to form increasingly complex systems, first through simple coordination of the schemata, then through active experimentation, and finally through mental combination. To the extent that this occurs, the causal nucleus—personal activity—is broken down into a series of centers by the progressive objectification of causality, and the relations between those centers are spatialized correlatively. In this sense the development of causality is correlative to that of space and object: it is not that the objectification and spatialization of causality are determined from without by the progress of these categories, but that these various structures are interdependent, each one constituting one of the aspects of the elaboration of intelligence.

It is useless to return at length to the explanation of the beginnings of causality. We have just seen, in discussing the hypotheses of Hume and Biran, that if causality springs from the reproductive effort characterizing reflex activity and the origins of the earliest habits, it involves simultaneously and from the outset indissociable assimilation and accommodation. If these mechanisms constitute the point of departure for all later intellectual activity (that is, in the realm now under consideration, the point of departure for the union of deduction and experience which constitutes rational causality) nevertheless, during the phase of radical undifferentiation characteristic of the beginnings of mental life they are systematic illusions of perspective which explain the primitive forms of the concept of cause. Assimilation of events to personal activity necessarily entails belief in the efficacy of the activity, to the extent that actions are still governed only by global schemata and pure reproduction (first three stages, that is, reflex schemata, primary and secondary). As long as accommodation of these schemata to the conditions of experience does not yet lead to behavior patterns of search and experimentation properly so called (tertiary reactions, etc.) it can entail only a phenomenalism inseparable from efficacy and not a real adaptation to objective sequences. The union of phenomenalism and efficacy characteristic of the beginnings of causality therefore results merely from the initial forms of accommodation and assimilation.

At the fourth stage, however, as soon as the schemata begin to intercoordinate in intentional series in which it becomes possible to distinguish means from ends, things change. On the one hand, through the very fact that the subject's action is dissociated into discrete elements and that relations are established among factors up to then intermingled within the global schemata, these factors tend to acquire a certain autonomy and consequently a causality separate from that of personal activity. Thus in our examples of coordination of schemata (*O.I.*, obs. 120-130), the obstacle the child removes to reach an object is experienced as having an action independent of the self and negating its intentions (*O.I.*, obs. 120-126), whereas objects serving as intermediaries or means are experienced as having a positive action (*O.I.*, obs. 127-130). One may therefore say that the intercoordination of secondary schemata leads to the objectification of causality, just as it entails an incipient formation of the objects themselves and of objective groups of displacements in space. Moreover this same coordination presupposes a progressive adjustment of means to ends, that is, of objects to one another; from this comes the spatialization of causality, along with its objectification.

With regard to the innovations of the fifth stage in the realm of intelligence, that is. "tertiary circular reaction" and the "discovery of new means through active experimentation," we have already seen, in §4, how essential they are in the formation of causality, the first leading to an objectification and the second to a spatialization both of which are more advanced than those of the fourth stage. Finally, it is apparent that the representative causality which appears during the sixth stage owes its particular characteristics to the development of the practical deduction or mental combination of the schemata which is the innovation at this period from the point of view of intelligence.

But if it is clear that the progress of sensorimotor causality is due to that of intelligence itself, we must not overlook one circumstance which, though it does not spring from the realm of intellectual mechanisms, certainly accelerates that progress. Just as people doubtless constitute the first permanent objects recognized by the baby, so also they are very probably the first objectified sources of causality because, through imitating someone else, the subject rapidly succeeds in attributing to his models' action an efficacy analogous to his own. Imitating someone else, as Baldwin has shown, is the source of both *alter* and *ego*. One may probably go so far as to say that it represents one of the principal occasions for distinguishing between the external world and the self and consequently a factor in the substantiation and spatialization of the world.

It is striking to note how the child, in proportion as he learns to imitate, attributes objective causality to the people around him. True, as soon as it is acquired imitation engenders a causality through imitation which constitutes one of the varieties of efficacy (obs. 137-139). The people imitated are at first conceived, in the manner of various inert bodies that can be moved, swung, etc., as being centers of movement upon which it is possible to act directly and which thus extend personal activity. But as soon as the child begins to imitate unfamiliar models, or gestures known but executed by means of movements which he cannot see (fourth stage), by virtue of that very fact he endows someone else's body with an activity at once distinct from his own and similar to it. Thus causality is necessarily objectified. It is precisely this period that witnesses the appearance of the acts of causality by instigating starting motion that we have discussed apropos of people (obs. 142-144). It is essential to note that this attribution of causality, being on a par with the progress of imitation, does not consist in simple foresight based on habit or transfer, but in a real objectification. From the first months of life the baby knows what his mother will do in the day's events: nursing, bath, etc. But this does not yet imply any objectified causality, for it is not a matter of causality; these are images which succeed each other with regularity and which make possible the formation of habits. For causality to exist there must be a kind of fixation on or delegation of efficacy to external and autonomous centers. This is precisely what imitation brings about.

But, let us repeat, we do not thus leave the realm of intelligence, since it is its development which governs imitation, and since the coordinations of schemata explain the imitation of new gestures and alone account for the objectification and spatialization of causality.

CHAPTER IV

The Temporal Field

In adult thought, or at least in scientific thought, any relation of causality presupposes a temporal relation. Whether one agrees with E. Meyerson that causality is identity in time, or with H. Hoeffding, L. Brunschvicg, and the Kantian tradition that it is an analogic application of the relation of reason to consequence in temporal series, in any case the cause is considered anterior to the effect. It is only in certain magical connections that effect and cause appear simultaneously, but here again distinction must be made between the moment when the relation is automatized and the moment it arises in the course of the behavior patterns in which awareness of duration certainly plays a role. How does this apply to sensorimotor causality, whose evolution we have just traced?

In a sense it can be said of time, as of space, that it is already given in every elementary perception; every perception lasts, just as every perception is extended. But this first duration is as removed from time properly so called as is the extension of sensation in organized space. Time, like space, is constructed little by little and involves the elaboration of a system of relations. These two constructions are correlative. Poincaré has maintained that time precedes space, since the concept of displacement presupposes before and after. But one may also say that time presupposes space, for time is nothing other than the forming of relationships between the events which fill it and those which require for their formation the concept of object and spatial organization.

It is this interconnection among the four fundamental categories of object, space, causality, and time which makes possible an analysis of time on the sensorimotor level of infantile intelligence. Without the relations of time with the other forms of organization of the universe it would be useless to try to reconstruct the temporal series which the child's mind elaborates, since consciousness of time is not externalized in the form of separable behavior as is the consciousness of spatial relations. But if what we have thus far established with regard to objects, space, and causality has a temporal aspect, this may be disentangled by comparing the results obtained in each of those categories.

Can it be said that consciousness of time is made manifest merely by the progress of memory? But memory itself—which is the best of the "reagents" of the temporal organization—is not revealed in a direct way in the child's behavior. It is in connection with the displacement of objects and the causal series that we best succeed in discerning its elementary forms. But if we have thus been forced to repeat the facts already analyzed from other points of view, the new perspective from which we shall now examine the sequence of stages seems to us, like the preceding ones, necessary to understanding the beginnings of mental life.

In a general way, the formation of time is then parallel to that of space and complementary to that of objects and causality. In other words, it proceeds equally from the immediacy characteristic of radical egocentrism to a forming of relationships such that the mind is freed from its personal point of view and located in a coherent universe. At its point of departure time is intermingled with the impressions of psychological duration inherent in attitudes of expectation, effort, and satisfaction, in short, with the activity of the subject himself. This duration is subsequently put into closer and closer relations with the events of the external world. At its point of arrival, time is promoted to the rank of an objective structure of the universe as such. The sequence of the subject's acts is thus inserted, as a lived sequence, in the series of remembered events constituting the history of the environment; this history does not remain incoherent, as before, with its fragments attached to current action conceived as the sole reality.

Beginning with sensorimotor intelligence, time necessarily transcends pure duration, and, if this duration is indeed at the source of time, it would never become truly temporal without a spatialization and an objectification inseparable from the entire intellectual activity. Hence it is unquestionable that, to describe the steps in the formation of the temporal field and of memory, we may use the already prepared frame of the stages characteristic of the evolution of space, objects, and causality itself.

§ 1. THE FIRST TWO STAGES: TIME ITSELF AND THE PRACTICAL SERIES

The only question that can be asked in connection with the reflex stage and the stage of primary circular reactions is whether these primitive behavior patterns fulfill the conditions which the remaining observations will show to be necessary for the arrangement of moments in time and for measuring duration. No direct analysis of the initial forms of time being possible, we must be satisfied to compare what the child at the first two stages does or does not do with what the child of the subsequent stages is capable of performing, from the temporal point of view.

As early as his reflex activity and the formation of his first habits, the nursling shows himself capable of two operations which concern the elaboration of the temporal series. In the first place, he knows how to coordinate his movements in time and to perform certain acts before others in regular order. For instance, he knows how to open his mouth and seek contact before sucking, how to steer his hand to his mouth and even his mouth to his thumb before putting the thumb between his lips, etc. In the second place, from the third stage, he knows how to coordinate his perceptions in time and even how to utilize one perception as signal for another. Thus from 0;1 (22) to 0;2 (12) (*O.I.*, obs. 44-49) the child knows how to turn his head when he hears a sound and to try to see what he has heard: in such cases auditory perception regularly precedes visual perception and even commands it by signaling. What do these behavior patterns imply from the point of view of consciousness of time?

It is self-evident that the first precaution to be taken in attempting this interpretation is to dissociate the point of view of the observer and that of the subject. For the observer, not only are the child's acts arranged in time but it is easy to establish that they are made with regard to the sequence of events. But that does not prove that the sequence as such is perceived by the subject, that is, that it gives rise to a consciousness of sequence. Or if this consciousness exists, nothing proves that it is related to the sequence of external events (gestures as physical displacements or movements of things) and is not solely related to the development of internal states, objectified and conceived as filling the universe of perception. To separate the point of view of the observer from that of the subject we must compare the facts with those of the later stages and those presented by the evolution of the concept of space.

Concerning space, we have seen that instead of locating himself as well as objects in a common environment, the nursling is confined to coordinating his own movements spatially without conceiving of them as spreading out into groups, externalized and related to things. The practical group of the first two stages is precisely this space in action. Thus it precedes all perception and all representation of groups which define space as a relation between objects and as a common, homogeneous, and external environment. From this point, everything leads us to believe that the initial groups of displacements which remain purely practical from the point of view of space remain so also from the point of view of time. In other words, the child can manage to regulate his acts in time without either perceiving or representing to himself any sequence or temporal series regulating the events themselves.

If we now compare these practical series (to designate the temporal sequences by analogy with the corresponding spatial groups) with the more complex series which study of the later stages will reveal, a marked difference engages our attention. From the secondary circular reaction, that is, from the advent of the third stage, the child becomes capable, in the presence of spectacle (R) on which he wishes to act, of first trying to produce an external effect conceived as causal condition (C) of the result. Thus in order to shake a rattle hanging from the top (R) from 0;3 (13) Laurent is able (O.I., obs. 98) to seek with his hand a chain attached to the rattle and to pull it (C). Therefore in the presence of sight R (the rattle) the child is able to reconstruct the series $C \to R$. On the contrary, in the series of the first two stages, things are never thus: either the series of gestures remains purely practical, that is, without perception of sequential events, or else there is a sequence of perceptions but of the type $R_1 \to R_2$, etc., and not of the recurrent type $C \to R$.

In the case of the practical series, for example, when the child directs his thumb to his mouth to suck it, the sequence of movements cannot be compared to the series $C \to R$, for two reasons. First, a sequence of coordinated gestures constitutes a single act, a global schema, so long as the movements do not encounter resistance from the external environment, whereas in secondary circular reaction the intervention of things differentiates the sequential moments of the act and, in particular, means and ends. That is why we have considered the behavior patterns of the third stage "intentional" in contrast to the "primary reactions": from the point of view of time, this means that the two terms C and R of the series $C \to R$ are differentiated, whereas in the practical series they still form an undissociated whole. Moreover, in the case of the practical series (putting thumb in mouth to suck it) there is no perception of external sights (the child does not look first at his thumb, then at his mouth), whereas in the series $C \to R$ there is a separate perception of two things or distinct events (the chain and the rattle). Consequently nothing proves that in the practical series the child becomes aware of two sequential moments in time, whereas in the series $C \to R$ there is this distinction: starting from the perception of R the child must himself reconstruct the sequence $C \to R$. In short the practical series, although regulated in time from the point of view of the observer, remains global and undifferentiated from the point of view of the subject, whereas the series inherent in the secondary circular reactions necessarily tend to be differentiated.

Regarding the sequences of perceptions due to the intersensory coordinations of the second stage (hearing a sound, then perceiving the visual image thus announced) or to observation of someone else's activity (expecting the bottle after seeing the door open), we claim that they are never of type $C \to R$ but only of type $R_1 \to R_2$, etc. In other words the child, when confronted by a perceptual image R_1, expects by means of signalment to see image R_2 etc., whereas in the case of series $C \rightarrow R$ the child seeing image R reconstructs, through a recurrent process, the sequence $C \rightarrow R$ to act upon R. That is why in the latter case it is very likely the sequence $C \rightarrow R$ is perceived as such. On the contrary, in the case of the sequence $R_1 \rightarrow R_2$ we may ask whether or not the child is aware of the sequence. We have often noticed that a sequence of perceptions does not necessarily entail a perception of sequence. Furthermore, the remainder of our analysis will show that the child does not take account of the order of a sequence of events unless he himself has imposed that order or has intervened in its formation. On the other hand, when he passively witnesses a sequence of events with which he has nothing to do the child cannot remember or utilize this order until he is 11 or 12 months old. (We have already seen this in Chap. III in connection with object concept; the order of the sequence of displacements is of no concern to the child until the fifth stage.) Thenceforth, in the case of the sequence $R_1 \rightarrow R_2$ etc., everything takes place as though the child experienced sequentially a series of perceptions but without perceiving the sequence as such.

Shall we say, however, that, in the latter case, signalment entails an expectation which is equivalent to an awareness of sequence? In a general way may we not assert that in the whole practical series there is effort, desire, hence expectation, feeling of dissatisfaction, then of satisfaction, in short, awareness of duration and of a sequence of states? This, we believe, is the crux of the matter. The preceding considerations do not in any way demonstrate that awareness of time is absent in the first two stages of intellectual evolution. All that we say is that there are not yet concepts of time applying to external phenomena nor is there a temporal field encompassing the development of events in themselves independently of personal action. But just as space begins as the simple practical coordination of body movements before it is constituted as a relationship between permanent objects and the body itself, so also time begins as simple duration immanent in the practical series before it is established as an instrument of ordination interconnecting external events with the subject's acts. Hence primitive time is not time perceived from without, but duration experienced in the course of the action itself.

What is this duration? It is mingled with impressions of expectation and effort, with the very development of the act, experienced internally. As such it certainly fills the child's whole universe, since no distinction is yet given between an internal world and the external universe. But it does not comprise either a real "before" or "after," which are always relative to events regulated in themselves, or a measure of intervals, which also depends on the formation of relationships between the actions and the guidemarks of the external world. It is therefore time itself, in its immediacy as well as its imprecision: simply the feeling of a development and of sequential directions immanent in the states of consciousness.

From the point of view of memory, of this "perception of time" as Delacroix calls it, such a situation requires this result: the only form of memory evidenced by the behavior patterns of the first two stages is the memory of recognition in contradistinction to the memory of localization or of evocation. The child, from the first weeks of his life, knows how to recognize perceptual images (as we have emphasized in *O.I.* apropos of recognitory assimilation). But this does not prove either that he knows how to evoke these images when he does not see them or that he is able, when he does see them, to localize in the past the memory of having seen them before. True, according to Delacroix, every recognition entails a localization. But though it is true that to the adult the impression of "déjà vu," inseparable from recognition, implies a distinction between past and present, hence the beginning of localization, it is not proved that, during the stage in which no guidemark yet makes it possible to establish a seriation of events in the external world, recognition transcends a global sensation of the familiar which does not entail any clear differentiation between past and present but only the qualitative extension of the past into the present.

§ 2. THE THIRD STAGE: THE SUBJECTIVE SERIES

The time characteristic of the first two stages is a practical time, interconnecting the sequential movements of the same schema but unconscious of its own unfolding and at most giving rise to the sensations of expectation, effort, arrival at a goal, etc., that are characteristic of purely psychological duration. Beginning with the third stage, on the contrary, this situation is modified to the extent that the child begins to act upon things and to make use of their interrelations through prehension of visual objectives. The temporal series thus transcend the purely practical relations subsisting between personal acts and gestures and are henceforth applied to external events. But this extension of time to the movements of things remains subordinate to one essential condition: it takes place only to the extent that these movements depend on personal action. In other words, time begins to be applied to the sequence of phenomena but in proportion as that sequence is due to the intervention of the child himself. It is this type of series we shall call subjective series.

To understand the nature of these subjective series it is necessary to compare them to the subjective groups characterizing the third stage of the development of space, as well as to the behavior patterns of the corresponding stages of the object and of causality. We recall that during the first two stages after having evidenced an almost complete indifference to images that disappear from the perceptual field, in the third stage the child begins to attribute to them an incipient permanence. But this nascent objective consistency remains wholly related to personal action, since it is only by extending sketchy movements of accommodation that the child reveals himself capable of searching for vanished objects. The object begins to be formed, but only to the extent that it emanates from the activity of the subject. So also causality, which at first is intermingled with the inner relationships of the act (those uniting desire with satisfaction), begins, from the third stage on, to be applied to things. But it is applied without being detached from personal activity. To the exact contrary, the causality of the third stage consists in a confused relationship of efficacy and phenomenalism such that personal action is conceived as sole cause, not only of the results which experience shows it is actually capable of producing, but also of any effect that emerges without objective contact with the subject. In these conditions the space of the third stage consists in a projection of practical groups into the perceptual field, but a field circumscribed by personal action alone. In other words, the child does not yet establish spatial interrelations among objects as such and does not take into account the displacements of his own body in its totality. The space he perceives remains immanent in the action exerted upon things, and the subjective groups thus defined remain intermediate between practical groups and objective groups. With regard to time, the following is true: the subjective series constitute an application of time to things, but to the extent that the sequence of events which occurs in the midst of things is governed by the subject. In other words, the child does not yet perceive the sequence of events which are independent of himself, that is, he is not yet capable of forming objective series. But he has transcended the level of merely experienced time; the subjective series thus form the transition between the practical series and the objective series.

It is in the field of secondary circular reactions that the subjective series are made manifest, just as it is deferred circular reaction which constitutes the first definite example of memory of localization. But one may ask if any circular reaction whatever gives rise to subjective temporal series, and for this reason a discussion of the observations from this new point of view is necessary to define the series in question.

At the time secondary circular reaction begins it is not certain that it immediately necessitates an orderly arrangement of perceptions in time. The child is limited to seeing that this gesture produces that result and to reproducing the efficacious gesture as precisely as possible. The temporal arrangement required by such a behavior pattern begins, therefore, by being practical and does not at the outset presuppose a seriation of the perceptions themselves, in other words, an elaboration of subjective series. For instance when, between 0;3 and 0;4 (*O.I.*, obs. 94 and 94a), Lucienne discovers that by shaking her legs she moves her bassinet top, it goes without saying that she regulates her movements in time. It does not occur to her to look at the top to see it shake or to expect it to move *before* she has shaken her legs. Hence this is a definite practical series; she shakes first and only then awaits the movements of the top, however short the interval separating the first factor from the second may be. But does this practical arrangement involve from the outset the more complex action of perceiving the seriation as such and of discovering that one of the factors of the series is necessarily anterior to the other? We ourselves would find it almost impossible, for example, to reconstruct the exact sequence of the movements we perform in swimming, diving from a height, etc., although we know very well how to form the series in practice. It is therefore difficult to prove that the subjective series are already constructed in such instances. Once these elementary schemata of secondary circular reaction have been formed (and they are elaborated partly by chance), there is no need, in order to make them work, to perceive the seriations which each of them comprises. Thus, if the child looks at his bassinet hood again this is enough to reactivate the schema we have just discussed; to the child, the movement of his legs does not necessarily precede the movement of the hood they are shaking, since the whole phenomenon is still conceived as an indissociable and almost immediate connection.

On the other hand, the situation is without doubt differently presented when perception of image R, within which the desired effect will be produced, sets in motion not a gesture capable of being produced immediately (such as the movement of the legs, of which we have just spoken), but a complex gesture necessitating search for and use of a perceived intermediary object C. Take, for example, a rattle (R) which the child knows he can swing by means of shaking the chain (C) attached to it; the perception of R will not directly start the action of pulling but rather that of searching for the chain and only then pulling it. In such a case, though the child knows nothing about the contacts between chain and rattle (here causality remains of the type of mixed efficacy and phenomenalism), he is probably led to perceive the seriation of his own procedure: the sight of R sets in motion series $C \rightarrow R$, and, as this series gives rise simultaneously to true searching (condition C not being fulfilled automatically) and to an external perception of the movements executed (those movements being related to material objects), the seriation ceases to be purely practical and enters the sphere of subjective series.

Of course in attempting a hypothetical reconstruction of the inner reactions peculiar to these behavior patterns it is difficult to say with certainty when the purely practical series end and when the subjective series really begin. But if as heretofore we simply try either to describe things in terms of behavior patterns or to find in behavior the criterion of operations which may be conceived in terms of consciousness, we may believe that the subjective series are formed when secondary circular reaction bears upon two objects at once, and not solely upon one. The presence of two separate objects one of which conditions the activity of the other makes possible a perception of sequence in addition to a mere practical arrangement of sequential movements. It is fitting to note that such circular reactions bearing upon two objects are as early as the others. Only chance determines whether the child will begin with one type or the other.

Here are examples.

OBS. 169. At 0;3 (13) Laurent, already accustomed for several hours to shake a hanging rattle by pulling the chain attached to it (*O.I.*, obs. 98), is attracted by the sound of the rattle (which I have just shaken) and looks simultaneously at the rattle and the hanging chain. Then, while staring at the rattle (R), he drops from his right hand a sheet he was sucking, in order to reach with the same hand for the lower end of the hanging chain (C). As soon as he touches the chain he grasps and pulls it, thus reconstructing series C → R.

Same observation at 0;3 (23), 0;5 (25) etc., apropos of a hanging string (C) and the top (R) of the bassinet (see *O.I.*, obs. 99).

Same observation at 0;4 (30) apropos of a doll (C) hanging from rattles (R) attached to the top: first he looks at the rattles and only then shakes the doll (*O.I.*, obs. 99).

Same observations on Jacqueline at 0;7 (23) in connection with hood R and string C (*O.I.*, obs. 100) and on Lucienne at 0;6 (5) (*O.I.*, obs. 100 repeated).

We must interpret subjective series of this kind from the point of view of the understanding of time, that is, contrast them with the more complex behavior patterns of the fourth stage. It seems that the subject capable of the current behavior patterns utilizes only the concepts of before and after but is not yet capable of an orderly arrangement of the events themselves. It must be remembered that the temporal field is correlative to the elaboration of the causal series. Secondary circular reaction, even when it bears upon two objects at once, still distinctly differs from the application of familiar means to new situations. In the first of these two behavior patterns, it is not the activity of object A which is conceived as cause of the movements of object B but rather the global movement which utilizes A, whereas in the second behavior pattern causality is spatialized and objectified in A, so that B is regarded as depending on A. From the point of view of time, this means that the child able to execute the first of these behavior patterns is thereby capable of discerning a before and after in the results of his own acts, whereas only the use of the second behavior pattern will teach him to arrange events in order, that is, in so far as they are related to objects as such.

This distinction may seem subtle. But by examining the mnemonic progress in this third stage we shall prove that it corresponds to real facts and is not merely an intellectual view. We recall that memory peculiar to the second stage is essentially recognitory, presupposing the formation of sensorimotor habits and an assimilation of familiar objects to these practical schemata. It has therefore seemed to us that neither the localization in time nor, even less, the evocation of memories was accessible to this elementary kind of memory, except perhaps with regard to a completely internal localization translated by the impression of the familiar and, precisely, of the known. With the third stage and its subjective series there appears a beginning of localization of memories in time, but as we shall see this localization remains linked with the action itself and is not yet extended in an orderly arrangement related to events as such. Hence we shall rediscover on the plane of memory the distinction just established in connection with causality.

The first form of localization of memories seems to us to be furnished by the behavior pattern we have already emphasized in connection with objects: the deferred circular reaction (Chap. I, §2). This has to do with interrupted actions which the sub-

ject resumes soon after the interruption and without the renewed intervention of the habitual excitant. For instance, the
child looks at an object (primary circular reaction) or exerts his
own activity upon it (secondary circular reaction), and after
having been distracted for a moment by another source of interest, he returns at one swoop to his first position of contempla-
tion or of action. We have cited (obs. 18-20) examples of deferred secondary reactions. Here are some examples of primary
reactions equally deferred and just as interesting as the latter
from the point of view of memory.

OBS. 170. At 0;8 (7) Laurent sees his mother enter the room and
watches her until she seats herself behind him. Then he resumes playing but turns around several times in succession to look at her again.
However there is no sound or noise to remind him of her presence.

Hence this is a beginning of object formation analogous to what we
have cited in connection with the third stage of objectification; this
process is on a par with a beginning of memory or localization in
time.

OBS. 170a. At 0;9 (18) Jacqueline plays with a glass box, which she
grasps, sets before her, etc. Several times in succession she lets go the
object to look at her mother, who is beside her, and to smile at her.
But every time she returns to the box, immediately directing her
glance and her hand in the right direction.

At 0;9 (20) also, when she is sitting in her bassinet playing with
various objects, she perceives my hand above her, placed on the semi-
transparent top. She smiles, then resumes playing, but several times in
succession lifts her head to look at my hand again.

Unquestionably such behavior patterns presuppose, besides the
commencement of permanence and spatial localization mentioned in regard to objects and space, the beginning of localization in time. For example, when Laurent watches his mother sit
down behind him, then returns to the objects which I present
to him and then turns around several times, it is apparent that
he is capable not only of recognizing her (recognitory memory)
but also of locating her in memory at the place she has just
occupied in a recent past, in contradistinction to the other
places where she was seen previously (localization in time).

Like the secondary reactions relating to two objects which are joined, such a behavior pattern presupposes an elementary concept of before and after: at the time Laurent looks at the toys I extend to him he remembers that just beforehand his mother was seated behind him. To be sure, this is not yet evocation and it is by virtue of the movement of turning around in order to see that the child forms his nascent memory, but however greatly "motor" and however little "representative" this memory may be, it nevertheless presupposes the beginning of localization.

But may we conclude from this that there is an orderly arrangement of memories relating to external events as such? There the distinction reappears which we have just established between the subjective series and the beginnings of objective arrangement. If the events on which this elementary memory bears develop independently of the child's action (the movement of turning around) or presuppose a sequence of identical actions and not a coordination of separate schemata, the subject ceases to preserve the memory of the sequence. It is this that we have constantly affirmed in connection with the concept of object and space; the child does not take note of sequential positions occupied by the object, as if he forgot them successively or as if the object had for him no spatial permanence (we have stated before that these two explanations amount to the same thing; see Chap. I, §2 and §3).

Let us cite an example to complete obs. 170.

OBS. 171. At 0;8 (7) Laurent, immediately after the behavior patterns of obs. 170, reveals a reaction which clarifies their meaning. His mother having risen and left the room, Laurent watches her until she reaches the door, then, as soon as she disappears, again looks for her behind him in the place where she was first!

True, a prejudicial question arises in connection with these facts: to ascertain whether they really concern memory and time and not only the structure of the object and the spatial field. In other words, when Laurent, having seen his mother leave the room, looks for her behind him where she had been, is it because he has lost the memory of the object's sequential displacements or merely because these displacements are not yet arranged either in a coherent space or in a universe of permanent substances? This question will arise again in more precise form in connection with the fourth stage, but we must take a position now. Let us suppose that neither time nor memory intervenes in the explanation of these behavior patterns; according to this hypothesis if the child, while remembering that his mother, after being seated behind him, has left the room, nevertheless looks for her in her initial place, that is because his mother is not to him a permanent object whose displacements are arranged in space but merely a sensory image capable of reappearing where it was previously perceived. Precisely because we affirm the latter theses with regard to space and the object (we have tried to demonstrate them in Chaps. I and II), we believe they entail parallel interpretations with regard to memory and time. In other words, if Laurent remembered his mother's sequential displacements, by applying that capacity to all perceptual images of interest to him he would be able to construct a coherent space and a world of substantial objects and would not look for his mother behind him when she disappeared elsewhere. Inversely, if he looks for his mother where he saw her first without taking into account her displacement in an opposite direction in space, it is because his memory—hence his perception of time—remains entirely subjected to his practical movements, as when I look for my watch in a pocket after I have put it on the table. If our memory always functioned as in this last example, we would possess neither organized space nor objects; the universe would remain for us what it is for the child at the present stage, a world of polarized reactions and not of events arranged in space and in time.

In short, at the third stage the child is able to perceive a sequence of events when he himself has engendered that sequence or when the before and after are related to his own activity, but if the perceived phenomena succeed each other independently of himself he disregards the order of occurrence. We do not thereby mean to maintain that he systematically upsets that order or is incapable of grasping some of its features. We merely claim that in such circumstances practical memory, connected with personal movements, takes precedence over every operation directed by external facts, and thus the objective structuring of time remains impossible.

The analysis of facts relating to memory of positions confirms that of the behavior concerning causality. If the third stage marks progress over the preceding stages in that it seems to include for the first time a consciousness of time or a perception of before and after, everything concurs to show that this perception remains related to personal activity. Hence the series formed remain subjective in the sense in which we have spoken of subjective groups, the objectification of time taking form only after the next stage. In other words, the child at the present stage is not yet capable of reconstructing the history of external phenomena themselves, or of locating his own duration in that of things or of measuring the length of intervals, but only of perceiving the elementary sequence of his already organized actions.

§ 3. THE FOURTH STAGE: THE BEGINNINGS OF THE OBJECTIFICATION OF TIME

To understand how the fourth stage differs from the preceding stages we must once more put the evolution of time into relationship with that of objects, space, causality, and intelligence in its total mechanism. It is only in the light of these relationships that the details of facts acquire some meaning.

Starting from the fourth stage the schemata acquired by means of the secondary circular reactions give rise to the kind of behavior patterns we have called application of familiar means to new situations. After having merely reproduced the movements leading to interesting results the child becomes capable of intercombining the schemata and of subordinating them to one another in the capacity of means and ends. Such progress brings about important results with regard to the development of time. A seriation of means and ends is possible only to the extent that the subject is able to arrange events in time; thus the subjective series peculiar to secondary circular reaction begin to be objectified.

This supposition acquires still more probability on examination of the behavior patterns pertaining to the object, space, and casuality. With regard to object concept we have stated that at this stage the child begins to look for things which have disappeared behind screens. The concepts of before and after, therefore, apply henceforth to displacements of the object itself and no longer only to the child's movements in the course of these actions. So also with regard to space, the formation of reversible groups denotes an incipient objectification of groups of displacements and consequently an objectification of the corresponding temporal series. With respect to causality, the outlines of spatialization and objectification which mark its evolution during this stage bring about the same results from the point of view of time; the temporal series begin to be applied to things themselves, that is, to the objective and spatial connections uniting an external cause to its particular effect.

In short, the various behavior patterns characteristic of this stage converge and show how time, at first inherent in personal action alone, begins to be applied to events external to the self and thus to constitute objective series. But they converge and also show how limited this objectification still is. In the various realms to which we have just referred the objectification peculiar to the fourth stage remains relative and does not yet succeed in freeing itself from the primacy of personal activity. Thus the application of familiar means to new situations only constitutes a term of transition between simple circular reaction and the more complex behavior patterns that use the interrelationships of objects freely. Thus throughout the stage search for the vanished object remains falsified by the concept of a special position, a concept which, as we have seen, derives from the illusions inherent in personal activity. The same remarks apply to space itself. Finally causality, while beginning to be objectified and spatialized, remains intermediate between subjective efficacy and physical causality. The aggregate of these circumstances is of weight in the fate of the temporal series. We shall now see in studying the particulars to how great an extent the objectification of these series remains inchoate as compared to the progress of the subsequent stages.

The clearest examples of temporal arrangement characteristic of this fourth stage are those revealed by analysis of object concept. As we have seen in obs. 36-38 (Chap. I), at this stage the child is capable of searching for the vanished object when he has seen it hidden under a screen or when the screen has just been interposed between the object and his eyes. From the point of view of memory or the seriation of perceptions in time, this is an important behavior pattern for, we think for the first time, the child retains a series of events in which he plays no role. Up to then the child has sought the vanished object only if at the moment of its disappearance a gesture of prehension has already been sketched, thus enabling the memory to extend the action in progress. Or again, at the time of deferred circular reactions the child rediscovered the interrupted action or perception by merely resuming his initial attitude or position, which was another form of active memory. The behavior patterns of which we now speak, on the contrary, consist in arranging in time the events that are independent of personal action. The child perceives an object (image O), then a screen coming to mask that object (image P), but, while perceiving P, he keeps the memory of image O and acts accordingly. For the first time the child reveals the ability to recall events and not actions.

Of course, there are all the transitions between such behavior patterns and simple deferred circular reactions. When at the preceding stage the child looks at object O, then is distracted by P and finally returns to O, it seems as if he both recalls events as such and arranges them in time. We have not, however, been able to interpret things thus. We think the child does not so much set in order the objective existence or the position of O as the action or position of his own body relative to O. On the contrary when, without acting himself, the child sees O disappear behind P and then remembers the presence of O, we believe that it is the external facts, independent of the action, that give rise to the seriation. But it goes without saying that such a distinction is a matter of nuances which are very difficult to state precisely. The only certainty is that the memory and construction of time do not merely proceed from a physical and objective time to an internal duration, but on the contrary, from a duration which is not set in order and is at first purely practical (at once internal and external) to a time which is set in order and whose physical aspect is progressively differentiated from its psychological aspect. It is only in relation to such a law of evolution that an attempt at differential analysis of sequential behavior patterns acquires some meaning. In this respect, search for the object hidden by a screen seems to us to mark progress in the objectification of the temporal series in comparison with the act of rediscovering an object lost from sight; but if it were necessary to homologize these two behavior patterns we would say that practical memory still predominates in the search for the hidden object, rather than admit the primacy of objective memory in either of the behavior patterns.

Proof that practical memory and the subjective series subsist in the search for the vanished object is not very difficult to furnish. Complicating the object's displacements only slightly is enough to prove how unstable the objectification of the temporal series still is. In this respect the time has come to discuss from the point of view of the concept of time the facts presented in Chapter I, §3, in connection with object concept (obs. 39-45 and 46-52).

A toy is hidden in A. The child looks for it and finds it. Afterward the same object is hidden in B. Now, this is what happens in the fourth stage: the child sometimes directs himself toward A where his search was previously crowned with success (the typical reaction, obs. 39-45, of the beginnings of the stage), and sometimes toward B; but if he does not immediately succeed in seeing the objective he returns to A (residual reaction of the end of the stage; obs. 46-52). How shall we interpret these facts from the point of view of memory and the concept of time?

First we might assume that such observations have no relation to the temporal series. In this hypothesis the child who searches in A for the object he saw disappear in B would know how to set in correct order in his memory the positions of the object in A, then in B; but having seen the annihilation of the object in B he would acknowledge that by one procedure or another the same object would be capable of reappearing in A. If this were the case the objective structure of the universe would be different to the subject from what it is to us, but this difference would not necessarily imply a lack of orderly arrangement in time.

But if such an interpretation remains plausible from the logical point of view, it is not so from the genetic. As we have already tried to show apropos of the object, the construction of objects, space, and time is closely interconnected. Of what use would it be to the child to remember, that is, to set in order in time, the series of displacements or positions of an object, so long as the object's permanence is conceived as linked to a special position? And inversely, if the child were capable of this objective seriation, why would he not conceive of the permanence of objects precisely as linked to the law of their displacements? If this is not the case it is because, as we have seen, the permanence conferred by personal action still takes precedence over that of objective structures. From the point of view of time, such an interpretation would seem to us to produce the following results: when the child searches in A for the object he has just seen disappear in B, the practical memory of the action linked with position A still prevails over all memory of the sequence of the displacements. In other words, the series again becomes subjective as soon as consideration of past actions exerted upon the object reappears, whereas the series marking the beginnings of this stage remain objective before intervention of the action. From the point of view of memory, this explains the paradox of residual reactions. The child sees the object disappear in A, looks for it and finds it, sees it disappear in B, explores position B for a moment and finally returns to A! What does this mean if not that the subject begins to elaborate an objective temporal series, this time involving two sequential displacements, but at the first practical obstacle the series again becomes subjective, that is, governed by the memory of actions which succeeded? In other words, the child acts here like the adult who takes his watch from his pocket, puts it on the table and who, later hunting for it under his papers, very briefly recalls having placed it in front of himself, then is no longer very sure about it and looks again in its usual place. Practical memory thus finally dominates that of real displacements.

In short, the behavior patterns of the fourth stage relating to the object show that the child becomes capable of elaborating objective series and thus of arranging events in order of time, but that this acquisition remains unstable and subordinate to practical memory, in other words, to subjective series.

Examination of the behavior patterns relating to space leads to the same conclusions. In his analysis of group concept Poincaré maintained that the formation of time precedes that of space, since the group of displacements presupposes a temporal ordination of movements. But how is it possible to conceive of a seriation of events without a spatial and causal elaboration of them? It seems that if we distinguish between subjective and objective series, the elaboration of the latter could not occur independently of space; in this regard the consitution of time is nothing other than its spatialization. The groups of the fourth stage, like the permanence of objects, remain intermediate between the subjective state and the objective state. It is enough to say that the temporal structure which they share also manifests the form of transition of which we have spoken apropos of the time in which objects move.

With regard to the causality peculiar to the fourth stage it is this, we believe, which makes it possible to state most precisely the nature of the temporal series we are now trying to analyze.

The main difference between the causality of the fourth stage and that of the third may be characterized as follows: when the child utilizes object A to act upon object B he no longer considers as cause of the movements of B the global movement he himself executes by utilizing A, but rather the activity of A as the center of relatively separate forces. For instance (obs. 142-144), the child utilizes someone else's hand by simply placing it in the proper position (in contact with B), thus showing he attributes to the hand an autonomous and spontaneous power. This is simultaneously the beginning of the objectification of causality and of spatialization of causal connections. It goes without saying that such behavior patterns reveal from the point of view of time an ability to arrange events in objective series. For instance, the activity of someone else's hands is necessarily conceived by the subject as "anterior" to its effects, since before trying to achieve these effects the child endeavors to activate the hands as indispensable means. Hence there is an objective series in the temporal order which defines causal connections of this kind.

But if time applies to things as such in proportion as causality is objectified and spatialized, the same reservation should be made apropos of such facts as apropos of observations relating to the object and to space. The behavior patterns of the fourth stage mark only one phase of transition, and if causality begins to be externalized it still remains impregnated with the efficacy

characteristic of personal activity. Thereafter if the first objective series are observable during this period, the before and
after they introduce into events do not give rise to systematic
and connected arrangements. Time is not yet a common environment encompassing the totality of phenomena including
personal action. It is only an extension into events of the subjective duration inherent in the activity of the child. In other
words, the child's memory begins to enable him to reconstruct
short sequences of events independent of the self, but it cannot
yet retrace the entire chronology of the phenomena perceived in
the external world nor, much less, permit an evaluation of the
duration of intervals.

§ 4. THE FIFTH STAGE: THE OBJECTIVE SERIES

With the advent of the behavior patterns of the fifth stage,
most of which appear at about the age of one, time definitively
transcends the duration inherent in personal activity, to be applied to things themselves and to form the continuous and systematic link which unites the events of the external world to
one another. In other words, time ceases to be merely the
necessary schema of every action connecting subject with object
and becomes the general environment encompassing the subject in the same capacity as the object. At the moment when
objects cease to be mere displays at the subject's disposition and
are organized into a substantial and permanent universe, when
space is freed from the perspective peculiar to individual action
and becomes established as the structure of that universe, and
when causality transcends the efficacy of subjective activity and
intercoordinates external phenomena, it is natural that time should
obey an analogous evolutionary law and be constituted as objective reality, interconnected with physical causality, space, and
permanence, and that it should incorporate the sequences emanating from personal action to which it had up to then been
subordinate.

This decisive advance in the elaboration of time is made manifest in the course of each of the behavior patterns previously
studied apropos of object, space, and causality.

With regard to the first of these, we recall that the behavior patterns characteristic of this fifth stage consist in a systematic search for the vanished object by taking into account the sequence of its displacements. Thus when the child has found the object hidden in A, then sees it disappear in B, he no longer looks for it in A, as he did in the course of the preceding stage, but directly in B. From the point of view of time, this surely means that the child remembers the sequential displacements of the object and sets them in proper order. True, it might be assumed that the subject forgets position A and looks for the object in B simply because that position is the last one observed. But because during the fourth stage it is precisely toward A that the child first turns, such an objection cannot be substantiated; position A takes precedence in the memory over position B because it is connected with practical success. Hence it is possible to conclude that for the first time the child is capable of elaborating an objective series, that is, of arranging in temporal order external events and no longer only personal actions or their extensions.

True, the objective series thus formed remain limited by a condition common to all the behavior patterns of this stage: they concern only events directly perceived and not yet displacements merely represented. As we have seen in obs. 55-57, Chapter I, if certain displacements of the object remain invisible, this is enough to make the child relapse into the habits peculiar to the fourth stage. But this stems from the difficulties of representation and not from those of arrangement in time. But could one not answer that representation is already included in the temporal arrangement of the past and the mnemonic operations necessitated thereby? When the child remembers that the object has been placed in A and has been rediscovered and finally hidden in B is he not yielding, thanks to his memory, to an evocation properly so called, which constitutes representation? That is possible while memory still consists in classifying acts (the act of having grasped the object in A and the potential act outlined by perception of the object's departure into B) and leads to an orderly arrangement of events without necessitating representation of these events. But even if there is evocation, that is, representation of past events, it is one thing merely to reproduce the past and another mentally to combine representation of displacements which have never been directly perceived. Our interpretation of the behavior patterns of the fifth stage, from the point of view of the concept of time, is therefore not contradictory to the one we have given from the point of view of object concept.

With regard to the behavior patterns of the present stage relating to space, they converge with the preceding ones to show how the child has become capable of elaborating objective series. Like the groups just discussed in connection with experiments bearing upon the permanence of the object, the spontaneous groups arising in the course of the present stage reveal an arrangement in time of events themselves.

OBS. 172. At 1;0 (20) Jacqueline throws over the edge of her bassinet a doll which is usually attached to a string above her and which she often plays with by grasping or swinging it in that position. For a brief moment she examines the place where it fell (study of trajectory). Then, after she has played at something else, I pull the string at the place where the doll usually hangs; Jacqueline at once directs herself to the side where she threw it and looks at it over the edge of the bassinet. She has therefore kept an exact memory of the displacement.

At 1;3 (12) she plays with an eyeglass case at the moment when I am putting a book on the other side of the bars of the playpen in which she is seated. As she wants to reach the book she puts behind her the case which is in her way. For at least five minutes she tries unsuccessfully to pass the book through the bars. Each time the book slides out of her hands. Then, tired, she searches unhesitatingly for the case which she no longer sees; turning halfway around she extends her hand behind her back until she touches it.

But when the actions are too far separated in time and thus necessitate an exact representative memory to be arranged in order, the child relapses into the earlier difficulties. Thus as late as 1;6 (27) Jacqueline hides a key under a balustrade, at A. Then she plays in a meadow for ten minutes and goes back to the balustrade at B (eight meters from A and at the other side of a staircase). She says "key, key" and runs to search for it directly at A. Then she takes the key and places it on a coverlet. Fifteen minutes later Jacqueline, coming back to the balustrade, again says "key, key" and returns to look for it at A, long and carefully. Hence this is a residue of the behavior patterns of the fourth stage, caused by the complication of the problem and the intermediate actions.

The behavior patterns of the present stage relating to causality support the same interpretations. It is apparent that a causality which is entirely objectified and spatialized presupposes or entails an orderly arrangement of events in time. For example Jacqueline, at 1;0 (29), obs. 149, is watching the toy with the ball and chickens. When I activate the chickens by revolving the toy very slowly, she sees only the concomitant movement of the ball and the chickens and does not directly perceive any seriation implying a before and after; however since she tries to understand the relation of the ball and the chickens this is enough to make her arrange the causal relation in time. Thus in touching the ball she looks at the chickens beforehand, or once the chickens have been stopped she returns to the ball. Therefore she reveals the concept of a regular sequence between the causal activity of the ball and the induced activity of the chickens. The same is true whenever causality is objectified and spatialized, even when it gives rise to reversible connections. What we have just said about the chickens would remain true if the child had utilized them to set the ball in motion. The essential thing is not the direction taken by the causal action; it is that an order exists, that is, a sequence of separate movements occurring according to an understandable principle. In this respect, the chief difference between causality through efficacy and spatialized causality is that the first is immediate and unanalyzable and the second is spread out in moments that are distinct and capable of objective ordination.

In a general way, the type of behavior patterns which characterizes the present stage from the point of view of intellectual functioning, that is, the discovery of new means through active experimentation, involves the elaboration of these objective series. Whether it is a matter of using the supports on which the object is placed, the strings that extend from it, or real instruments such as the stick, or whether it is a matter of imparting to an object certain movements to bring it to the desired goal, the behavior patterns in question presuppose a subordination of means and ends of a new type as compared to the behavior patterns of the preceding stages. In the course of the secondary circular reactions it is the personal actions as such that are subordinated to each other and not the movements of things; the

act of pulling a cord and not the activity of the cord itself is considered the means necessary for reaching the goal, and from this
arises the misjudgment of the conditions of spatial contact and
of objective temporal seriation. On the contrary, the behavior
patterns of the present stage (for which the acts of application
of familiar means to new circumstances pave the way, in the
capacity of transitional behavior) are characterized by the fact
that they subordinate external phenomena to each other. The
supports, the strings, the sticks, etc., are no longer only symbols
of personal activity but objects whose objective activity comes
to be inserted into the web of events themselves and is thus subordinated to precise conditions of time and place. From this
stems the formation of objective series properly so called. For example, when Lucienne (*O.I.*, obs. 152), in trying to reach an
object outside her field of prehension, revolves the box serving as
its support, there is no doubt that the concepts of before and
after are no longer limited to her acts but are henceforth applied to the phenomena, that is, to the displacements which are
perceived, foreseen, or remembered.

§ 5. THE SIXTH STAGE: THE REPRESENTATIVE SERIES

The elaboration of the temporal series, of which we have just
retraced the main steps, is an attempt to go beyond the present
for the sake of the immediate past and future. Consequently it
is one attempt among others to free the mind from direct perception in favor of an intellectual activity capable of placing the
data of that perception in a stable and coherent universe. But
still more than the construction of objects, space, and causality,
the elaboration of the temporal field requires the development
of images. If it is possible to postulate the permanence of things,
to form real groups of displacements and to join to them objects
or movements by causal connections without systematically
leaving the perceptual field, every attempt at reconstruction of
the past or deduction of the future presupposes or engenders
representation. If we concede the results of our foregoing analyses concerning the functioning of intelligence (*O.I.*) or the development of real categories, representation as evocation by
image or by a system of signs of absent objects scarcely appears

except in a sixth and final stage, which is contemporaneous with the progress of language and whose manifestations we shall now study from the point of view of time. That is why the temporal series just described are revealed as so short and so dependent on the constructions characteristic of object, space, and causality; it is why, for lack of representations properly so called, the time developed by the series necessarily remained linked with present perceptions, with practical memories derived from recent action, and anticipations in accord with the action in progress. But as soon as mental assimilation has been liberated from direct perception and is capable of functioning without external support, the objective series formed by the totality of the intellectual work which made that liberation possible are themselves extended into the future and the past in the form of representative series. The representative series are therefore only objective series extended by the intellectual operations peculiar to this sixth stage, and these operations, to the extent that they engender representations relating to time, are nothing other than evocative memory. Hence the latter does not in any way constitute a special faculty; it is only psychic assimilation and especially reproductive assimilation to the extent that it reconstructs mentally, and no longer in reality, a more and more extensive past.

OBS. 173. The first definite examples that can be given of the representative series, apart from those which pertain to the groups of displacements already cited in regard to the object and to space, are those which result from the progress of language and the beginning of narration.

At 1;7 (25) Jacqueline picks up a blade of grass which she puts in a pail as if it were one of the grasshoppers a little cousin brought her a few days before. She says, "Totelle [*sauterelle*, or grasshopper], totelle, jump, boy [her cousin]." In other words, perception of an object which reminds her symbolically of a grasshopper enables her to evoke past events and reconstruct them in sequence.

So also, at 1;7 (27) Jacqueline, on the terrace of a mountain chalet, locates the people I name, taking into account their recent displacements. "Where is Mother?" She points to the chalet. "Where is Grandpa?" She points down to the plain where her grandfather went two days before. "Where is the boy?" She points to the chalet. "Where is Vivianne?" She points to the woods where Vivianne went for a walk. And so on.

Let us note, moreover, that such representative series relating to external events encompass at the outset the memory of personal activity, no longer the purely practical memory of the primitive series but an evocation properly so called, making it possible to locate in time the action of the self amidst other events.

OBS. 173a. At 1;6 (15) Jacqueline weeps while calling her mother. I imitate her, repeating, "Mama, Mama," in a tearful tone, and she laughs. Two days later, at 1;6 (17); we play at reproducing the sounds of animals and Jacqueline inserts this memory into the game: "How does the goat go?" "Meh." "And the cow?" "Moo." "And the dog?" "Voovoo." "And Jacqueline?" "Mama." This final answer is given by imitating exactly the tone of the other day and with a meaningful smile, which demonstrates clearly that Jacqueline is alluding to a past behavior pattern and is not making up a new game.

It is useless to emphasize such commonplace facts. It is important to recall them only in order to conclude our analysis of the beginnings of the construction of time.

By comparing these last reactions—which thus mark the beginning of reflective and conceptual ideas relating to the temporal categories in contradistinction to the schemata of sensorimotor intelligence—with the behavior patterns of the five sequential stages previously studied, we reach the conclusions which follow. The development of time, parallel to that of space, of object, and of causality, proceeds from an initial practical egocentrism such that events are set in order by a personal action immobilized in a continuous present, to an objectification such that events are linked together in an order which ends by encompassing personal duration and memories as particular episodes in this real history. Thus, during the first two stages, everything takes place as though time were completely reduced to impressions of expectation, desire, success, or failure. There is here the beginning of sequence linked with the development of different phases of the same act. But each sequence forms a whole isolated from the others, and nothing yet enables the subject to reconstruct his own history and to consider his acts as succeeding one another. Furthermore, each sequence consists in a gliding from the preliminary phase of desire or effort into the terminal phase of success or failure, experienced as a present without a past. Finally and most important, this completely psychological duration is not accompanied by a seriation of events as external and independent of the self, since no boundary yet exists between personal activity and things. During the third stage, on the other hand, external events begin to be set in order as a function of secondary circular reactions, that is, of the beginnings of action upon things. But as the child still perceives the order of phenomena only when he himself has been the cause, he remains incapable of conceiving the chronology of his universe independently of his own action. In effect, a universe without permanent objects, without objective groups of displacements in space, and without causality externalized in things could not comprise temporal series other than those relating to the acts of the subject. But by virtue of that very fact, this personal duration, while related to the realities on which the actions bear as well as to the actions, could not be inserted in the general duration of the environment and still less be exposed to a quantitative evaluation of moments in time: therefore, to the child, objective time still does not exist. With the advent of the fourth stage this objectification progresses to the degree that the adjustment of means to ends in the intelligent behavior patterns entails a permanence of objects, an organization of groups of displacements, and a spatialization of causality which force the child to begin to arrange events in order, and no longer only his personal actions. With the coming of the fifth stage this orderly arrangement of time no longer applies only to some privileged events but in principle to the whole perceptual field, without yet being extended to a more distant memory of the past, that is, to the evocation of moments of a time which elapsed without leaving a perceptible trace in the present. Finally, with the sixth stage, the objectification of the temporal series extends to representation, that is, the child, becoming capable of evoking memories not linked to direct perception, succeeds by that very fact in locating them in a time which includes the whole chronology of his universe. This does not in the least imply that this chronology is as yet well seriated or that the evaluation of duration is correct, but apart from the interpersonal relations these operations become possible because hereafter personal duration is placed in relation to that of things, and this makes possible both the orderly arrangement of moments in time and their measurement in relation to external points of reference.

The Elaboration of
the Universe

In our first study of the beginnings of mental life we analyzed the origins of intelligence in children and tried to show how the forms of intellectual activity are constructed on the sensorimotor level. In the current work we have tried, on the other hand, to understand how the real categories of sensorimotor intelligence are organized, that is, how the world is constructed by means of this instrument. In conclusion, the time has come to show the unity of these various processes and their relations with those of the child's thought, envisaged in their most general aspect.

§ 1. ASSIMILATION AND ACCOMMODATION

The successive study of concepts of object, space, causality, and time has led us to the same conclusions: the elaboration of the universe by sensorimotor intelligence constitutes the transition from a state in which objects are centered about a self which believes it directs them, although completely unaware of itself as subject, to a state in which the self is placed, at least practically, in a stable world conceived as independent of personal activity. How is this evolution possible?

It can be explained only by the development of intelligence. Intelligence progresses from a state in which accommodation to the environment is undifferentiated from the assimilation of things to the subject's schemata to a state in which the accommodation of multiple schemata is distinguished from their respective and reciprocal assimilation. To understand this process, which sums up the whole evolution of sensorimotor intelligence, let us recall its steps, starting with the development of assimilation itself.

In its beginnings, assimilation is essentially the utilization of the external environment by the subject to nourish his hereditary or acquired schemata. It goes without saying that schemata such as those of sucking, sight, prehension, etc., constantly need to be accommodated to things, and that the necessities of this accommodation often thwart the assimilatory effort. But this accommodation remains so undifferentiated from the assimilatory processes that it does not give rise to any special active behavior pattern but merely consists in an adjustment of the pattern to the details of the things assimilated. Hence it is natural that at this developmental level the external world does not seem formed by permanent objects, that neither space nor time is yet organized in groups and objective series, and that causality is not spatialized or located in things. In other words, at first the universe consists in mobile and plastic perceptual images centered about personal activity. But it is self-evident that to the extent that this activity is undifferentiated from the things it constantly assimilates to itself it remains unaware of its own subjectivity; the external world therefore begins by being confused with the sensations of a self unaware of itself, before the two factors become detached from one another and are organized correlatively.

On the other hand, in proportion as the schemata are multiplied and differentiated by their reciprocal assimilations as well as their progressive accommodation to the diversities of reality, the accommodation is dissociated from assimilation little by little and at the same time insures a gradual delimitation of the external environment and of the subject. Hence assimilation ceases merely to incorporate things in personal activity and establishes, through the progress of that activity, an increasingly tight web of coordinations among the schemata which define it and consequently among the objects to which these schemata are applied. In terms of reflective intelligence this would mean that deduction is organized and applied to an experience conceived as external. From this time on, the universe is built up into an aggregate of permanent objects connected by causal relations that are independent of the subject and are placed in objective space and time. Such a universe, instead of depending on personal activity, is on the contrary imposed upon the self to the extent that it comprises the organism as a part in a whole. The self thus becomes aware of itself, at least in its practical action, and discovers itself as a cause among other causes and as an object subject to the same laws as other objects.

In exact proportion to the progress of intelligence in the direction of differentiation of schemata and their reciprocal assimilation, the universe proceeds from the integral and unconscious egocentrism of the beginnings to an increasing solidification and objectification. During the earliest stages the child perceives things like a solipsist who is unaware of himself as subject and is familiar only with his own actions. But step by step with the coordination of his intellectual instruments he discovers himself in placing himself as an active object among the other active objects in a universe external to himself.

These global transformations of the objects of perception, and of the very intelligence which makes them, gradually denote the existence of a sort of law of evolution which can be phrased as follows: assimilation and accommodation proceed from a state of chaotic undifferentiation to a state of differentiation with correlative coordination.

In their initial directions, assimilation and accommodation are obviously opposed to one another, since assimilation is conservative and tends to subordinate the environment to the organism as it is, whereas accommodation is the source of changes and bends the organism to the successive constraints of the environment. But if in their rudiment these two functions are antagonistic, it is precisely the role of mental life in general and of intelligence in particular to intercoordinate them.

First let us remember that this coordination presupposes no special force of organization, since from the beginning assimilation and accommodation are indissociable from each other. Accommodation of mental structures to reality implies the existence of assimilatory schemata apart from which any structure would be impossible. Inversely, the formation of schemata through assimilation entails the utilization of external realities to which the former must accommodate, however crudely. Assimilation and accommodation are therefore the two poles of an interaction between the organism and the environment, which is the condition for all biological and intellectual operation, and such an interaction presupposes from the point of departure an equilibrium between the two tendencies of opposite poles. The question is to ascertain what forms are successively taken by this equilibrium which is being constituted.

If the assimilation of reality to the subject's schemata involves their continuous accommodation, assimilation is no less opposed to any new accommodation, that is, to any differentiation of schemata by environmental conditions not encountered up to then. On the other hand, if accommodation prevails, that is, if the schema is differentiated, it marks the start of new assimilations. Every acquisition of accommodation becomes material for assimilation, but assimilation always resists new accommodations. It is this situation which explains the diversity of form of equlibrium between the two processes, according to whether one envisages the point of departure or the destiny of their development.

At their point of departure they are relatively undifferentiated in relation to each other, since they are both included in the interaction which unites the organism to the environment and which, in its initial form, is so close and direct that it does not comprise any specialized operation of accommodation, such as the tertiary circular reactions, behavior patterns of active experimentation, etc., will subsequently be. But they are none the less antagonistic, since, though each assimilatory schema is accommodated to the usual circumstances, it resists every new accommodation, precisely through lack of specialized accommodative technique. It is therefore possible to speak of chaotic undifferentiation. It is at this level that the external world and the self remain undissociated to such a point that neither objects nor spatial, temporal, or causal objectifications are possible.

To the extent that new accommodations multiply because of the demands of the environment on the one hand and of the coordinations between schemata on the other, accommodation is differentiated from assimilation and by virtue of that very fact becomes complementary to it. It is differentiated, because, in addition to the accommodation necessary for the usual circumstances, the subject becomes interested in novelty and pursues it for its own sake. The more the schemata are differentiated, the smaller the gap between the new and the familiar becomes, so that novelty, instead of constituting an annoyance avoided by the subject, becomes a problem and invites searching. Thereafter and to the same extent, assimilation and accommodation enter into relations of mutual dependence. On the one hand, the reciprocal assimilation of the schemata and the multiple accommodations which stem from them favor their differentiation and consequently their accommodation; on the other hand, the accommodation to novelties is extended sooner or later into assimilation, because, interest in the new being simultaneously the function of resemblances and of differences in relation to the familiar, it is a matter of conserving new acquisitions and of reconciling them with the old ones. An increasingly close interconnection thus tends to be established between the two functions which are constantly being better differentiated, and by extending the lines this interaction ends, as we have seen, on the plane of reflective thought, in the mutual dependency of assimilatory deduction and experimental techniques.

Thus it may be seen that intellectual activity begins with confusion of experience and of awareness of the self, by virtue of the chaotic undifferentiation of accommodation and assimilation. In other words, knowledge of the external world begins with an immediate utilization of things, whereas knowledge of self is stopped by this purely practical and utilitarian contact. Hence there is simply interaction between the most superficial zone of external reality and the wholly corporal periphery of the self. On the contrary, gradually as the differentiation and coordination of assimilation and accommodation occur, experimental and accommodative activity penetrates to the interior of things, while assimilatory activity becomes enriched and organized. Hence there is a progressive formation of relationships between zones that are increasingly deep and removed from reality and the increasingly intimate operations of personal activity. Intelligence thus begins neither with knowledge of the self nor of things as such but with knowledge of their interaction, and it is by orienting itself simultaneously toward the two poles of

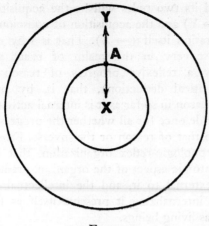

FIG. 2

that interaction that intelligence organizes the world by organizing itself.

A diagram will make the thing comprehensible. Let the organism be represented by a small circle inscribed in a large circle which corresponds to the surrounding universe. The meeting between the organism and the environment takes place at point A and at all analogous points, which are simultaneously the most external to the organism and to the environment itself. In other words, the first knowledge of the universe or of himself that the subject can acquire is knowledge relating to the most immediate appearance of things or to the most external and material aspect of his being. From the point of view of consciousness, this primitive relation between subject and object is a relation of undifferentiation, corresponding to the protoplasmic consciousness of the first weeks of life when no distinction is made between the self and the non-self. From the point of view of behavior this relation constitutes the morphologic-reflex organization, in so far as it is a necessary condition of primitive consciousness. But from this point of junction and undifferentiation A, knowledge proceeds along two complementary roads. By virtue of the very fact that all knowledge is simultaneously accommodation to the object and assimilation to the subject, the progress of intelligence works in the dual direction of externalization and internalization, and its two poles will be the acquisition of physical experience ($\rightarrow Y$) and the acquisition of consciousness of the intellectual operation itself ($\rightarrow X$). That is why every great experimental discovery in the realm of exact sciences is accompanied by a reflexive progress of reason on itself (of logico-mathematical deduction), that is, by progress in the formation of reason in so far as it is internal activity, and it is impossible to decide once for all whether the progress of the experiment is due to that of reason or the inverse. From this point of view the morphologic-reflex organization, that is, the physiological and anatomic aspect of the organism, gradually appears to the mind as external to it, and the intellectual activity which extends it by internalizing it presents itself as the essential of our existence as living beings.

In the last analysis, it is this process of forming relationships between a universe constantly becoming more external to the self and an intellectual activity progressing internally which explains the evolution of the real categories, that is, of the concepts of object, space, causality, and time. So long as the interaction between subject and object is revealed in the form of exchanges of slight amplitude in a zone of undifferentiation, the universe has the appearance of depending on the subject's personal activity, although the latter is not known in its subjective aspect. To the extent, on the contrary, that the interaction increases, the progress of knowledge in the two complementary directions of object and subject enables the subject to place himself among objects as a part in a coherent and permanent whole. Consequently, to the extent that assimilation and accommodation transcend the initial state of "false equilibrium" between the subject's needs and the resistance of things to attain a true equilibrium, that is, a harmony between internal organization and external experience, the subject's perspective of the universe is radically transformed; from integral egocentrism to objectivity is the law of that evolution. The relations of assimilation and accommodation thus constitute, from the time of the sensorimotor level, a formative process analogous to that which, on the plane of verbal and reflective intelligence, is represented by the relations of individual thought and socialization. Just as accommodation to the point of view of others enables individual thought to be located in a totality of perspectives that insures its objectivity and reduces its egocentrism, so also the coordination of sensorimotor assimilation and accommodation leads the subject to go outside himself to solidify and objectify his universe to the point where he is able to include himself in it while continuing to assimilate it to himself.

§ 2. THE TRANSITION FROM SENSORIMOTOR INTELLIGENCE TO CONCEPTUAL THOUGHT

This last remark leads us to examine briefly, in conclusion, the relations between the practical universe elaborated by the sensorimotor intelligence and the representation of the world brought about by later reflective thought.

In the course of the first two years of childhood the evolution of sensorimotor intelligence, and also the correlative elaboration of the universe, seem, as we have tried to analyze them, to lead to a state of equilibrium bordering on rational thought. Thus, starting with the use of reflexes and the first acquired association, the child succeeds within a few months in constructing a system of schemata capable of unlimited combinations which presages that of logical concepts and relations. During the last stage of their development these schemata even become capable of certain spontaneous and internal regroupings which are equivalent to mental deduction and construction. Moreover, gradually as objects, causality, space, and time are elaborated, a coherent universe follows the chaos of the initial egocentric perceptions. When in the second year of life representation completes action by means of the progressive internalization of behavior patterns, one might therefore expect that the totality of sensorimotor operations would merely pass from the plane of action to that of language and thought and that the organization of schemata would thus be directly extended in a system of rational concepts.

In reality, things are far from being so simple. In the first place, on the plane of practical intelligence alone, the excellent studies of André Rey[1] show that not all the problems are solved by the child by the end of his second year. As soon as the data of problems become complicated and the subjects are obliged to attain

[1] A. Rey, L'Intelligence pratique chez l'enfant (Paris: Alcan, 1934).

their ends by means of complex contacts or displacements, in the solution of these new problems through a sort of temporal displacement in extension we rediscover all the obstacles analyzed in this volume apropos of the elementary stages of the first two years of life. Furthermore, and this is valuable to the theory of temporal displacements, these obstacles reappear in the same order despite the gap which separates the ages of birth to 2 years, studied here, from the ages of three to eight years studied by André Rey. Thus in Rey's experiments the child begins by revealing a sort of "dynamic realism," "in the course of which the movement (pulling, pushing, etc.) would possess a quality independent of any adaptation to the particular data of the environment." [2] Then he goes through a phase of "optical realism" analogous to that which we observe among chimpanzees, in which he substitutes for the physical relations of bodies the visual relations corresponding to the apparent data of perception. How is it possible not to compare these two preliminary steps to those which characterize the beginnings of sensorimotor intelligence and of the practical universe resulting from them? Dynamic realism is the residue of the assimilation of things to actions that accounts for practical groups and series, for the magico-phenomenalistic causality and the object-less universe peculiar to our elementary stages. Before being able to structure a complex situation, the child from three to four years of age, like the baby a few months old who is confronted by a situation that is simpler but from his point of view obscure, is limited to assimilating it to the act which should be performed. Because of a residual belief in the power of his personal activity, he still confers upon his gestures a sort of absolute value, which is tantamount to forgetting momentarily that things are permanent substances grouped spatially, seriated temporally, and sustaining among themselves objective causal relations. With regard to optical realism it seems clear that it constitutes a residue of behavior patterns which are intermediate between the primitive egocentric stages and the stages of objectification, behavior patterns characterized by subjective groups and series or by transitional behavior relating to the beginnings of the object and of spatialized causality. Optical realism, too, consists in considering

[2] *Ibid.*, p. 203.

things as being what they appear to be in immediate perception and not what they will become once they have been inserted in a system of rational relations transcending the visual field. Thus the child imagines that a stick can draw an object because it is beside it or touches it, as though optical contact were equivalent to a causal link. It is precisely this confusion of immediate visual perceptions with physical realities that characterizes the subjective groups or series, for example, when the baby does not know how to turn over a nursing bottle because he cannot conceive of the object's reverse side, or when he imagines himself able to rediscover objects where he saw them the first time, regardless of their actual trajectory.

Hence, between the sensorimotor intelligence which precedes the advent of speech and the later practical intelligence which subsists under verbal and conceptual realities, there is not only a linear continuity but also there are temporal displacements in extension, so that in the presence of every truly new problem the same primitive processes of adaptation reappear, although diminishing in importance with age.

But above all, even if these obstacles encountered in action by the two- to seven-year-old child are destined to be overcome finally, through the instruments prepared by the sensorimotor intelligence during the first two years of life, the transition from the merely practical plane to that of speech and conceptual and socialized thought brings with it, by nature, obstacles that singularly complicate the progress of intelligence.

At the outset, two innovations place conceptual thought in opposition to sensorimotor intelligence and explain the difficulty of transition from one of these two forms of intellectual activity to the other. In the first place, sensorimotor intelligence seeks only practical adaptation, that is, it aims only at success or utilization, whereas conceptual thought leads to knowledge as such and therefore yields to norms of truth. Even when the child explores a new object or studies the displacements he provokes by a sort of "experiment in order to see," there is always in these kinds of sensorimotor assimilations, however precise the accommodation they evidence, the concept of a practical result to be obtained. By virtue of the very fact that the child cannot translate his observations into a system of verbal judgments and reflexive concepts but can simply register them by means of sensorimotor schemata, that is, by outlining possible actions, there can be no question of attributing to him the capacity of arriving at pure proofs or judgments properly so called, but it must be said that these judgments, if they were expressed in words, would be equivalent to something like, "one can do this with this object," "one could achieve this result," etc. In the behavior patterns oriented by an actual goal, such as the discovery of new means through active experimentation or the invention of new means through mental combinations, the sole problem is to reach the desired goal, hence the only values involved are success or failure, and to the child it is not a matter of seeking a truth for itself or reflecting upon the relations which made it possible to obtain the desired result. It is therefore no exaggeration to say that sensorimotor intelligence is limited to desiring success or practical adaptation, whereas the function of verbal or conceptual thought is to know and state truths.

There is a second difference between these two types of activity: sensorimotor intelligence is an adaptation of the individual to things or to the body of another person but without socialization of the intellect as such; whereas conceptual thought is collective thought obeying common laws. Even when the baby imitates an intelligent act performed by someone else or understands, from a smile or an expression of displeasure, the intentions of another person, we still may not call this an exchange of thoughts leading to modification of those intentions. On the contrary, after speech has been acquired the socialization of thought is revealed by the elaboration of concepts, of relations, and by the formation of rules, that is, there is a structural evolution. It is precisely to the extent that verbal-conceptual thought is transformed by its collective nature that it becomes capable of proof and search for truth, in contradistinction to the practical character of the acts of sensorimotor intelligence and their search for success or satisfaction. It is by cooperation with another person that the mind arrives at verifying judgments, verification implying a presentation or an exchange and having in itself no meaning as regards individual activity. Whether conceptual thought is rational because it is social or vice versa, the interdependence of the search for truth and of socialization seems to us undeniable.

The adaptation of intelligence to these new realities, when speech and conceptual thought are superimposed on the sensori-motor plane, entails the reappearance of all the obstacles already overcome in the realm of action. That is why, despite the level reached by the intelligence in the fifth and sixth stages of its sensorimotor development, it does not appear to be rational at the outset, when it begins to be organized on the verbal-conceptual plane. On the contrary, it manifests a series of tem-poral displacements in comprehension and no longer only in ex-tension, since in view of corresponding operations the child of a given age is less advanced on the verbal-conceptual plane than on the plane of action. In simpler terms, the child does not at first succeed in reflecting in words and concepts the procedures that he already knows how to carry out in acts, and if he cannot reflect them it is because, in order to adapt himself to the col-lective and conceptual plane on which his thought will hence-forth move, he is obliged to repeat the work of coordination be-tween assimilation and accommodation already accomplished in his sensorimotor adaptation anterior to the physical and practi-cal universe.

It is easy to prove: (1) that the assimilation and accommoda-tion of the individual from the time of the beginnings of speech present a balance less well developed in relation to the social group than in the realm of sensorimotor intelligence; and (2) that to make possible the adaptation of the mind to the group these functions must proceed again over the same steps, and in the same order, as during the first months of life. From the social point of view, accommodation is nothing other than imi-tation and the totality of the operations enabling the individual to subordinate himself to the precepts and the demands of the group. With regard to assimilation it consists as before in in-corporating reality into the activity and perspectives of the self. Just as on the plane of adaptation to the sensorimotor uni-verse the subject, while submitting to the constraints of the environment from the very beginning, starts by considering things as dependent on his actions and succeeds only little by little in placing himself as an element in a totality which is coherent and independent of himself, so also on the social plane the child, while at first obeying someone else's suggestions, for a long time remains enclosed in his personal point of view before placing it among other points of view. The self and the group therefore begin by remaining undissociated in a mixture of egocentrism and submission to environmental constraints, and subsequently are differentiated and give rise to a cooperation between personalities which have become autonomous. In other words, at the time when assimilation and accommodation are already dissociated on the plane of sensorimotor adaptation, they are not yet dissociated on the social plane, and thus they reproduce there an evolution analogous to that which has already occurred on the former plane.

From this arises a series of consequences very important in the structure of the child's thought at its beginnings. Just as sensorimotor intelligence starts as the assimilation of objects to the schemata of personal activity with necessary accommodation but of inverse tendency to the preceding accommodation, and subsequently arrives at a precise adaptation to reality through the coordination of assimilation with accommodation, so also thought, at its advent, begins by being the assimilation of reality to the self with accommodation to the thought of others but without synthesis of these two tendencies, and only later acquires the rational unity which reconciles personal perspective with reciprocity.

In the first place, just as practical intelligence seeks success before truth, egocentric thought, to the extent that it is assimilation to the self, leads to satisfaction and not to objectivity. The extreme form of this assimilation to personal desires and interests is symbolic or imaginative play in which reality is transformed by the needs of the self to the point where the meanings of thought may remain strictly individual and incommunicable. But between this ultimate region of egocentric thought (a region in which the symbolic imagination makes it possible to increase tenfold the possibilities of satisfacton offered to the action and consequently to reinforce the tendencies of assimilation to personal activity previously manifested by sensorimotor intelligence) and thought adapted to another person is found an important zone of thought which, while presenting no quality of play, presents analogous characteristics of anomia and egocentrism. To account for this it is enough to demonstrate the difficulty experienced by little children from two to six years of age in participating in a conversation or a discussion, in narrating or explaining, in short, in emerging from personal thought to adapt themselves to the thought of others. In all the social behavior patterns of thought it is easy to see how much more easily the child is led to satisfy his desires and to judge from his own personal point of view than to enter into that of others to arrive at an objective view. But in contrast to this powerful assimilation of reality to the self we witness during the earliest stages of individual thought the child's astonishing docility with respect to the suggestions and statements of another person; the little child constantly repeats what he hears, imitates the attitudes he observes, and thus yields as readily to training by the group as he resists rational intercourse. In short, assimilation to the self and accommodation to others begins with a compromise without profound synthesis, and at first the subject wavers between these two tendencies without being able to control or organize them.

In the second place, there arises a series of intellectual structures peculiar to these beginnings of infantile thought and which reproduce through temporal displacement the initial sensorimotor structures. Thus the first concepts the child uses are not at the outset logical classes capable of operations of addition, multiplication, subtraction, etc., which characterize the logic of classes in its normal functioning, but rather kinds of preconcepts proceeding by syncretic assimilations. So also the child who succeeds in handling relationships on the sensorimotor plane begins on the verbal and reflexive plane by substituting for relationships absolute qualities for lack of ability to coordinate the different perspectives and to emerge from the personal point of view to which he assimilates everything. Thereafter the primitive infantile reasoning seems to return to the sensorimotor coordinations of the fifth and sixth stages: not yet familiar with classes or relations properly so called, it consists in simple fusions, in transductions proceeding by syncretic assimilations. It is only in the course of a laborious development which transforms egocentric assimilation into true deduction, and accommodation into a real adjustment to experience and to perspectives surpassing the personal point of view, that the child's reasoning becomes rational and thus extends, on the plane of thought, the acquisitions of sensorimotor intelligence.

Thus we see the extent to which the developmental pattern of assimilation and of accommodation characterizing sensorimotor intelligence constitutes a general phenomenon capable of being reproduced on this new plane of conceptual thought before accommodation actually extends assimilation. In order better to understand this evolutionary process and this temporal displacement it is fitting to examine more closely a few concrete examples drawn from the facts analyzed in this book.

§ 3. FROM SENSORIMOTOR UNIVERSE TO REPRESENTATION OF THE CHILD'S WORLD

1. *Space and Object*

The understanding of spatial relations is a particularly clear first example of the parallelism with temporal displacement between the sensorimotor acquisitions and those of representative thought.

We recall how, starting with purely practical and quasi-physiological groups, the child begins by elaborating subjective groups, then arrives at objective groups, and only then becomes capable of representative groups. But the groups of this last type, if they constitute the culminating point of practical space and thus insert in sensorimotor spatial relations the representation of displacements not occurring within the direct perceptual field, are far from marking the beginning of a complete representation of space, that is, a representation completely detached from action. What will happen when the child is called upon, apart from any current action, to represent to himself a group of displacements or a system of coherent perspectives? It is from this decisive moment that we witness, on the plane of thought properly so called, a repetition of the evolution already accomplished on the sensorimotor plane.

Take, for example, the following problem.[3] The child is presented with a model, about one square meter in size, representing three mountains in relief; he is to reconstruct the different perspectives in which a little doll views them in varying positions that follow a given order. No technical or verbal difficulty impedes the child, for he may simply point with his finger to what the doll sees, or choose from among several pictures showing the possible perspectives, or construct with boxes symbolizing mountains the photograph the doll could take from a given point of view. Moreover, the problem posed to the child consists in representing to himself the simplest of all the spatial relations which transcend direct action and perception, that is, to represent to himself what he would see if he were in the successive positions suggested to him. At first it would seem as though the child's answers would merely extend the acquisitions of the sixth stage of sensorimotor space and arrive immediately at the correct representations.

But interestingly enough the youngest of the children capable of understanding the problem of the mountains and of responding without difficulties of a verbal or technical kind reveal an attitude which, instead of extending the objective and representative groups of our sixth stage, on the contrary, regresses to the integral egocentrism of the subjective groups. Far from representing the various scenes which the doll contemplates from different viewpoints, the child always considers his own perspective as absolute and thus attributes it to the doll without suspecting this confusion. In other words, when he is asked what the doll sees from a particular position the child describes what he himself sees from his own position without taking into account the obstacles which prevent the doll from seeing the same view. When he is shown several pictures from among which he is to choose the one which corresponds to the doll's perspective, he chooses the one which represents his own. Finally, when he is to reconstruct with boxes the photograph the doll might

[3] This problem was studied at our request by our assistant, Miss E. Meyer; see E. Meyer, "La Représentation des relations spatiales chez l'enfant"; *Cahiers de Péd. exp. et de Psych. de l'Enfant de l'Institut des Sciences de l'Education*, No. 8 (1935).

take from its place, the child again reproduces his own view of things.

Then, when the child disengages himself from this initial egocentrism and masters the relationships involved in these problems, we witness a totality of transitional phases. Either the child who begins to understand that the perspective differs according to the doll's position effects various mixtures between those perspectives and his own perspective ("pre-relations"), or else he takes into account only one relation at a time (left-right or before-behind, etc.) and does not succeed in multiplying the interrelations. These transitions correspond to the limited groups of displacements belonging to the fourth of the sensorimotor stages. Finally, complete relativity is attained, corresponding to stages V-VI of the same series.

How then can this temporal displacement be explained, as well as this return to the phases which have already been transcended on the plane of sensorimotor space? To act in space the child is certainly obliged to understand little by little that the things which surround him have a trajectory independent of himself and that their displacements are thus grouped in objective systems. From a purely practical point of view the child is therefore led to emerge from an initial egocentrism, in which things are considered to depend solely on his personal activity, and to master a relativity which is established between displacements successively perceived or even between certain perceived moments and others which have simply been represented. But the egocentrism and objective relativity in question here concern only the relationships between the child and things, and nothing in sensorimotor action forces him to leave this narrow realm. So long as the problem is not to represent to himself reality in itself, but simply to use it or to exert an influence upon it, there is no need to go beyond the system of relations established between objects and self or among objects as such in the field of personal perspective; there is no need to assume the existence of other perspectives and to interconnect them in including his own among them. To be sure, the act by which one confers an objectivity on the displacements of things already implies an enlargement of the initial egocentric perspective and it is in this sense that, apropos of the fifth and sixth sensorimotor stages, we have been able to speak of a change in perspective and the mastery of a universe in which the subject locates himself instead of bringing the universe illusively to him. But this is only the first step, and even in this objective, practical universe, everything is related to a single frame of reference which is that of the subject and not that of other possible subjects. Hence there is objectivity and even relativity, but within the limits of a realm which is always considered absolute, because nothing yet induces the subject to transcend it. If we may be permitted to make a somewhat daring comparison, the completion of the objective practical universe resembles Newton's achievements as compared to the egocentrism of Aristotelian physics, but the absolute Newtonian time and space themselves remain egocentric from the point of view of Einstein's relativity because they envisage only one perspective on the universe among many other perspectives which are equally possible and real. On the contrary, from the time when the child seeks no longer merely to act upon things, but to represent them to himself in themselves and independently of the immediate action, this single perspective, in the midst of which he had succeeded in introducing objectivity and relativity, no longer suffices and has to be coordinated with the others.

This is true for two reasons, one relating to the subject's intention in his attempt at representation, the other to the requirements of representation. Why at a given moment in his mental evolution does the subject try to represent spatial relations to himself instead of simply acting upon them? Obviously in order to communicate to someone else or to obtain from someone else some information on a fact concerning space. Outside of this social relation there is no apparent reason why pure representation should follow action. The existence of multiple perspectives relating to various individuals is therefore already involved in the child's effort to represent space to himself. Moreover, to represent to himself space or objects in space is necessarily to reconcile in a single act the different possible perspectives on reality and no longer to be satisfied to adopt them successively. Take, for example, a box or some object upon which the child acts. At the end of his sensorimotor evolution he becomes perfectly capable of turning the box over in all directions, of representing to himself its reverse side as well as its visible parts, its contents as well as its exterior. But do these representations connected with practical activity, with the "concrete active behavior" of which Gelb and Goldstein have spoken in their fine studies on space, suffice to constitute a total representation of the box, a pattern of "formal conceptive behavior?" Surely not, for to achieve that the box must be seen from all sides at once, that is, it must be located in a system of perspectives in which one can represent it to oneself from any point of view whatever and transfer it from one to the other point of view without recourse to action. Now, if it is possible for the child to imagine himself as occupying several positions at one time, it is obvious that it is rather by representing to himself the perspective of another person and by coordinating it with his own that he will solve such a problem in concrete reality. In this sense one can maintain that pure representation detached from personal activity presupposes adaptation to others and social coordination.

Therefore we understand why, in the problem of the mountains which is typical in this respect, the child four to six years of age still reveals an egocentrism reminiscent of the beginnings of sensorimotor intelligence and the most elementary subjective groups; it is because, on the plane of pure representation to which this experiment pertains, the subject must compare various points of view with his own, and as yet nothing has prepared him for this operation. Besides, the attitudes which have already been transcended in the relations between things and himself reappear when connections are established with other persons. Social egocentrism follows sensorimotor egocentrism and reproduces its phases, but as the social and the representative are interdependent there appears to be regression here, whereas the mind simply wages the same battles on a new plane to make new conquests.

Moreover, this temporal displacement in comprehension, which arises when there is transition of thought from a lower to a higher plane, may combine with the temporal displacements in extension (of which we have spoken earlier), which arise when problems located on the same plane present increasing complexity. Thus, on the occasion of movements near at hand, after having constructed the groups of displacements studied above, the child finds himself confronted by analogous problems raised by the observation of more distant movements: displacements relating to bodies situated on the horizon or to celestial movements. For many years we have observed the child's attitude toward the moon and often toward clouds, stars, etc.; until he is about seven years old he believes that he is followed by these bodies and considers their apparent movements real. From the point of view of space, this is only an extension of the behavior patterns relating to nearby objects observed during the first sensorimotor stages. The child, by taking appearance for reality, links all displacements to himself, instead of locating them in an objective system that includes his own body without being centered on it. Similarly, we have observed in our children analogous illustrations relating to mountains, on an excursion in the Alps or in an automobile going up and down the hills. At four or five years of age the mountains still seem to be displaced and actually to change shape in connection with our own movements, exactly like the nearby objects in the subjective groups of the baby.

These last remnants of primitive space in the child of school age lead us to the temporal displacements of processes relating to the object. It is self-evident that in proportion as the groups of displacements require new constructive work on the plane of representation or of conceptual thought to complete them, the object, in its turn, cannot be considered as entirely elaborated once it has been formed on the sensorimotor plane. At the time of displacements in extension, of which we have spoken apropos of the moon and the mountains, the matter is clear. The mountains which move and change shape with our movements are not objects, since they lack permanence of form and mass. So also a moon which follows us is not "the" moon as object of simultaneous or successive perceptions of different possible observers. The proof is that at the period in which the child believes he is being followed by the stars he believes in the existence of several moons rising over and over again and capable of occupying different regions of space simultaneously.

But this difficulty in attributing substantial identity to distant objects is not the most interesting residue of the processes of objecification peculiar to the stages of sensorimotor intelligence. Or rather, it constitutes only a residue explainable by the simple mechanism of temporal displacements in extension, whereas, because of the temporal displacements in comprehension that condition the transition from the sensorimotor plane to the plane of reflective thought, the construction of the object seems to be not only a continuous process unremittingly pursued throughout the evolution of reason and still found in the most elaborate forms of scientific thought, but also a process constantly passing through phases analogous to those of the initial sensorimotor series. Thus the different principles of conservation whose progressive formation occupies the whole development of the child's physics are only successive aspects of the objectification of the universe. For example, the conservation of matter does not seem necessary to the child three to six years old in cases of changes of state or even changes of form. Sugar melting in water is believed to be returning to the void, only taste (that is, a pure quality) being supposed to subsist and that only for a few days. So also, when one offers the child two pellets of the same weight and mass and then molds one of them into a long cylinder, this one is considered to have lost both weight and mass. When one empties the contents of a large bottle of water into small bottles or tubes, the quantity of liquid is conceived as having been changed,[4] etc. On the contrary, the child subsequently arrives at the concept of a necessary conservation of matter, independently of changes of form or of state. But having arrived at this level, he nevertheless continues to believe that the weight of bodies can change with their form; thus the pellet by becoming elongated loses weight while conserving the same quantity of matter. Around eleven or twelve years of age, on the other hand, the child is so convinced of the conservation of weight that he attributes to the particles of sugar dissolved in water the same total weight as to the initial lump.[5]

Thus we see that, from the point of view of conservation of matter and weight, the child again, this time on the plane of

[4] This excellent experiment is thanks to our assistant, Miss A. Szeminska; (see A. Szeminska, "Essai d'analyse psychologique du raisonnement mathématique," *Cahiers de Ped. Exp. et de Psych. de l'Enfant*, No. 7 (1935).
[5] See B. Inhelder, "Observations sur le principe de conservation dans la physique de l'enfant," *Cahiers de Ped. Exp. et de Psych. de l'Enfant*, No. 9 (1936).

conceptual and reflective thought, passes through stages analogous to those he traverses on the sensorimotor plane from the point of view of conservation of the object itself. Just as the baby begins by believing that objects return to the void when they are no longer perceived and emerge from it when they re-enter the perceptual field, so also the six-year-old child still thinks the quantity of matter augments or diminishes according to the form the object takes, and that a substance which dissolves is completely annihilated. Then, just as numerous intermediate stages exist between the level on which the baby is the victim of appearances and that on which he constructs a permanence sufficient to make him believe in objects, so also the child who talks passes over a series of steps before he is able to postulate, independently of any direct experience, the constancy of weight itself despite changes in form, and before he forms, with this objective in view, a sort of crude atomism which reconciles quantitative invariance with qualitative variations.

How then can we explain this temporal displacement; how can we explain why thought, at the moment it gathers up the work of sensorimotor intelligence and in particular the belief in permanent objects, does not at the outset attribute to objects constancy of matter and of weight? As we have seen, it is because three formative processes are necessary to the elaboration of object concept: the accommodation of the organs which makes it possible to foresee the reappearance of bodies; the coordination of schemata which makes it possible to endow each of these bodies with a multiplicity of interconnected qualities; and the deduction peculiar to sensorimotor reasoning which makes it possible to understand displacements of bodies and to reconcile their permanence with their apparent variations. These three functional factors—foresight, coordination, and deduction—change entirely in structure when they pass from the sensorimotor plane to that of speech and conceptual operations, and when systems of classes and thoughtful relations are substituted for simple practical schemata. Whereas the substantial object is a mere product of action or practical intelligence, the concepts of quantity of matter and conservation of weight presuppose on the contrary a very subtle rational elaboration. In practical object concept there is nothing more than the idea of a permanence of qualities (form, consistency, color, etc.) independent of immediate perception. There is, however, in the concept of the conservation of matter such as sugar, the clay pellet which changes shape, or the liquid poured from a large receptacle into several small ones, a quantitative relation which as soon as it is perceived seems essential; this is the idea that despite changes of state or of form (real form and no longer merely apparent form) something is conserved. This something is not at the outset weight, but it is volume, occupied space, and only later is it weight, that is, a quality that is quantified in so far as it is considered invariant. But for their construction these qualitative relationships do not solely involve a foresight which remains practical in kind (foresight of the water level when the sugar is dissolved, of the weight of the pellet made into a cylinder, etc.); they involve primarily a coordination of classes and of logical relations as well as true deduction, for on the plane of thought foresight gradually becomes the function of deduction instead of preceding it.

In the case of the sugar which dissolves in water, how does the child succeed in postulating the permanence of matter and even in making the atomic hypothesis of invisible particles of sugar permeating the liquid, particles whose total volume equals that of the initial lump, to the point of explaining that the water level remains above the original level? From all the evidence this is not a simple lesson of experience or, as in the case of the permanence of the practical object, an intelligent structuring of experience, but rather a deduction which is primarily due to thought and in which a complex series of concepts and relations intervenes. So also, the idea that the pellet conserves its weight while becoming a cylinder is a deductive construction which experience does not suffice to explain, for the child has neither the means to perform the delicate weighing that verification of such a hypothesis would necessitate nor, above all, the curiosity to attempt such a verification, because its affirmation seems to him self-evident and because as a general rule the problem does not arise for him. What is most interesting in the child's reaction is the fact that, having doubtless never thought about the problem, he solves it at once *a priori* and with such certainty that he is surprised it was raised, whereas a year or two earlier he would have solved it in precisely the opposite direction and would not have had recourse to the idea of conservation!

In short, the development of the principles of conservation can only be explained as the function of an internal progress in the child's logic in its triple aspect of an elaboration of deductive structures, of relations, and of classes, forming a corporate system. This is the explanation of the temporal displacement under discussion here. Through speech the child arrives on the plane of representative thought, which at the same time is the plane of socialized thought; to the extent that he must now adapt himself to other persons, his spontaneous egocentrism, already overcome on the sensorimotor plane, reappears in the course of this adaptation, as we have shown with the examples concerning space. From this arises a series of consequences with regard to the structure of thought, as we have emphasized in §2. On the one hand, in proportion as the child does not succeed in coordinating with his own perspective the perspectives peculiar to different individuals, he cannot master the logic of relationships, although he knows how to handle practical relations on the sensorimotor plane. Thus the concepts of heavy and light which directly concern the conservation of weight are conceived as absolute qualities long before they are understood as purely relative ones, because, once they have been detached from any personal frame of reference, they are applied to the egocentric point of view of immediate perception before being transformed into relations among different subjects and different objects and into relations among objects themselves. Moreover, and by virtue of this fact, the child begins by utilizing only syncretic pseudo-concepts before elaborating true logical classes, because the operations formative of classes (logical addition and multiplication) require a system of definitions whose stability and generality transcend the personal point of view and its subjective attachments (definitions by usage, syncretic classifications, etc.). From this stems the conclusion that a deductive structure on the plane of reflective thought presupposes a mind freed from the personal point of view by methods of reciprocity inherent in cooperation or intellectual exchange, and that reason, dominated by egocentrism on the verbal and social plane, can only be "transductive," that is, proceeding through the fusion of preconcepts located midway between particular cases and true generality.

If the conquest of the object on the sensorimotor plane is not at once extended on the conceptual plane through an objectification capable of insuring rational permanence, it is because the egocentrism reappearing on this new plane prevents thought from attaining at the outset the logical structures necessary for this elaboration. Let us try again to define this mechanism by analyzing some examples chosen from the periods of the beginning of speech and of reflective thought; these will show us both how difficult it is at first for the child to form true logical classes and how those pseudo-concepts and primitive transductions lead us back to a stage which, from the point of view of the object, seemed to be surpassed by sensorimotor intelligence and which reappears on the conceptual plane.

First of all it is currently observed that the first generic concepts utilized by the child, when they do not designate certain ordinary objects related to daily activity but totalities properly so called, remain midway between the individual and the general. For a long time, for instance, one of my children, to whom I showed slugs on successive walks, called each new specimen encountered "the slug"; I was unable to ascertain whether he meant "the same individual" or "a new individual of the slug species." While it is impossible to furnish definitive proof, in such a case everything seems to indicate that the child himself neither succeeds in answering nor tries to answer the question and that "Slug" is for him a sort of semi-individual and semi-generic type shared by different individuals. It is the same when the child encounters "Lamb," "Dog," etc.; we are confronted by neither the individual nor the generic in the sense of the logical class but by an intermediate state which is precisely comparable on the conceptual plane to the primitive state of the sensorimotor object floating between the unsubstantial perceptual image and permanent substance.

Interpretation may seem hazardous when observations of this kind are involved because one can always attribute them to mere mistakes by the subject, but it becomes more certain when these pseudo-concepts come into operation in transductions properly so called, that is, in the analytical or classificatory reasoning proceeding by fusion of analogous cases. Let us refer, for example, to the explanations given us by the youngest of our subjects concerning the phenomenon of the shadow or the draft:[6] the shadow produced on a table before their eyes comes, according to them, from "under the trees" or other possible sources of darkness, just as the draft from a fan emanates from the north wind which blows outside the room. The child thus likens, as we do ourselves, the shadow from a notebook to that of the trees, the draft to the wind, etc., but instead of simply placing the two analogous phenomena in the same logical class and explaining them by the same physical law, he considers the two compared terms as participants of each other from a distance and without any intelligible physical link. Consequently, here again the child's thought wavers between the individual and the generic. The shadow of the notebook is not a pure singular object since it emanates from that of the trees, it "is" really that of trees arising in a new context. But an abstract class does not exist either, precisely since the relation between the two shadows compared is not a relation of simple comparison and common appurtenance to the same totality, but of substantial participation. The shadow perceived on the table is therefore no more an isolable object than is, on the sensorimotor plane, the watch which disappears under one cushion and which the child expects to see appear under another. But if there is thus an apparent return to the past it is for an opposite reason to that which obstructs objectification in sensorimotor intelligence; in the latter case the object is difficult to form in proportion as the child has difficulty in intercoordinating perceptual images, whereas on the plane of conceptual thought the object, already elaborated, again loses its identity to the extent that it is coordinated with other objects to construct a class or a relation.

In conclusion, in the case of the object as in that of space, from the very beginnings of verbal reflection there is a return of the difficulties already overcome on the plane of action, and there is repetition, with temporal displacements, of the stages and process of adaptation defined by the transition from egocentrism to objectivity. And in both cases the phenomenon is due to the

[6] J. Piaget, *The Child's Conception of Causality* (New York: Humanities Press, 1930).

difficulties experienced by the child, after he has reached the social plane, in inserting his sensorimotor acquisitions in a framework of relationships of logical classes and deductive structures admitting of true generalization, that is, taking into account the point of view of others and all possible points of view as well as his own.

§ 4. FROM SENSORIMOTOR UNIVERSE TO REPRESENTATION OF THE CHILD'S WORLD

II. *Causality and Time*

The development of causality from the first months of life to the eleventh or twelfth year reveals the same graphic curve as that of space or object. The acquisition of causality seems to be completed with the formation of sensorimotor intelligence; in the measure that objectification and spatialization of relations of cause and effect succeed the magico-phenomenalistic egocentrism of the primitive connections, a whole evolution resumes with the advent of speech and representative thought which seems to reproduce the preceding evolution before really extending it.

But among the displacements to which this history of the concept of cause gives rise, distinction must again be made between the simple temporal displacements in extension due to the repetition of primitive processes on the occasion of new problems analogous to old ones, and the temporal displacements in comprehension due to the transition from one plane of activity to another; that is, from the plane of action to that of representation. It seems useless to us to emphasize the former. Nothing is more natural than the fact that belief in the efficacy of personal activity, a belief encouraged by chance comparisons through immediate or phenomenalistic experience, is again found throughout childhood in those moments of anxiety or of desire which characterize infantile magic. The second type of temporal displacements, however, raises questions which it is useful to mention here.

During the first months of life the child does not dissociate the external world from his own activity. Perceptual images, not yet consolidated into objects or coordinated in a coherent space, seem to him to be governed by his desires and efforts, though these are not attributed to a self which is separate from the universe. Then gradually, as progress is made in the intelligence which elaborates objects and space by spinning a tight web of relations among these images, the child attributes an autonomous causality to things and persons and conceives of the existence of causal relations independent of himself, his own body becoming a source among other sources of effects integrated in this total system. What will happen when, through speech and representative thought, the subject succeeds not only in foreseeing the development of phenomena and in acting upon them but in evoking them apart from any action in order to try to explain them? It is here that the paradox of displacement in comprehension appears.

By virtue of the "why" obsessing the child's mind, as soon as his representation of the world can be detached without too much risk of error, one perceives that this universe, centered on the self, which seemed abolished because it was eliminated from practical action relating to the immediate environment, reappears on the plane of thought and impresses itself on the little child as the sole understandable conception of totality. Undoubtedly the child no longer behaves, as did the baby, as though he commanded everything and everybody. He knows that adults have their own will, that the rain, wind, clouds, stars, and all things are characterized by movements and effects he undergoes but cannot control. In short, on the practical plane, the objectification and spatialization of causality remain acquired. But this does not at all prevent the child from representing the universe to himself as a large machine, organized exactly by whom he does not know, but organized with the help of adults and for the sake of the well-being of men and particularly of children. Just as in a house everything is arranged according to a plan, despite imperfections and partial failures, so also the *raison d'être* for everything in the physical universe is the function of a sort of order in the world, an order both material and moral, of which the child is the center. Adults are there "to take care of us," animals to do us service, the stars to warm us and give us light, plants to nourish us, rain to make the gardens grow, clouds to "make night," mountains to climb on, and lakes for boats, etc. Furthermore, to this more or less explicit and coherent artificialism there corresponds a latent animism which endows everything with the will to play its role and with just the force and awareness needed to act with regularity.

Thus the causal egocentrism, which on the sensorimotor plane disappears gradually under the influence of spatialization and objectification, reappears from the time of the beginnings of thought in almost as radical a form. Doubtless the child no longer attributes personal causality to others or to things, but while endowing objects with specific activities he centers all these activities on man and above all on himself. It seems clear that in this sense we may speak of temporal displacement from one plane to another and that the phenomenon is thus comparable to the phenomena which characterize the evolution of space and object.

But it is in a still deeper sense that the primitive schemata of causality are again transposed in the child's first reflective representations. If it is true that from the second year of life the child attributes causality to others and to objects instead of reserving a monopoly on them for his own activity, we have still to discover how he represents to himself the mechanism of these causal relations. We have just recalled that corresponding to the egocentric artificialism which makes the universe gravitate around man and child is an animism capable of explaining the activity of creatures and things in this sort of world. This example is precisely of a kind to help us understand the second kind of temporal displacement of which we now speak: if the child renounces considering his actions as the cause of every event, he nevertheless is unable to represent to himself the action of bodies except by means of schemata drawn from his own activity. An object animated by a "natural" movement like the wind which pushes clouds, or the moon which advances, thus seems endowed with purposefulness and finality, for the child is unable to conceive of an action without a conscious goal. Through lack of awareness, every process involving a relation of energies, such as the rising of the water level in a glass in which a pebble has been dropped, seems due to forces copied from the model of personal activity; the pebble "weighs" on the bottom of the water, it "forces" the water to rise, and if one held the pebble on a string midway of the column of the water the level would not change. In short, even though there is objectivity on the practical plane, causality may remain egocentric from the representative point of view to the extent that the first causal conceptions are drawn from the completely subjective consciousness of the activity of the self. With regard to spatialization of the causal connection the same temporal displacement between representation and action is observable. Thus the child can acknowledge in practice the necessity for a spatial contact between cause and effect, but that does not make causality geometric or mechanical. For example, the parts of a bicycle all seem necessary to the child long before he thinks of establishing irreversible causal series among them.

However, subsequent to these primitive stages of representation during which one sees reappear on the plane of thought forms of causality relative to those of the first sensorimotor stages and which seem surpassed by the causal structures of the final stages of sensorimotor intelligence, one witnesses a truly reflective objectification and spatialization, whose progress is parallel to that which we have described on the plane of action. Thus it is that subsequent to the animism and dynamism we have just mentioned, we see a gradual "mechanism" taking form, correlative to the principles of conservation described in §3 and to the elaboration of a relative space. Causality, like the other categories, therefore evolves on the plane of thought from an initial egocentrism to a combined objectivity and relativity, thus reproducing, in surpassing, its earlier sensorimotor evolution.

With regard to time, concerning which we have tried to describe on the purely practical plane of the first two years of life the transformation from subjective series into objective series, there is no need to emphasize the parallelism of this evolution with that which, on the plane of thought, is characterized by the transition from internal duration, conceived as the sole temporal model, to physical time constituted by quantitative relations between spatial guidemarks and external events. During the first phases of representative thought the child does not succeed in estimating either concrete duration or even rates of speed except by referring them to mere psychological time. Subsequently, on the contrary, he constructs in thought, and no longer only in action, objective series connecting internal duration to physical time and to the history of the external universe itself. For instance, if one draws in front of a child two concentric figures one of which describes a big circle and the other a much smaller one, and if one makes two automobiles of the same dimensions cover these two trajectories at the same time, the youngest subjects cannot avoid believing that the automobile following the small circle went "faster" than the other. "Faster" in this case simply means "more easily," "with less effort," etc., but the child does not take into account the relation between time and the space covered. For adults, on the contrary, speed is measured by this relation, and the expression "faster" loses its subjective meaning. So also, the expressions "more time" or "less time" have no objective meaning for little children and acquire it for adults, etc.

§ 5. CONCLUSION

The formation of the universe, which seemed accomplished with that of sensorimotor intelligence, is continued throughout the development of thought, which is natural, but is continued while seeming at first to repeat itself, before truly progressing to encompass the data of action in a representative system of the totality. This is the information we have just gained from a comparison of our present observations with the results of examining the representations of the child of three to twelve years of age.

To understand the scope of such a fact we must amplify what we said in §1 of these conclusions about the relations between intellectual assimilation and accommodation, by applying these reflections to the processes of thought itself.

We have tried to show how, on the sensorimotor plane, assimilation and accommodation, at first undifferentiated but pulling behavior in opposite directions, gradually became differentiated and complementary. From what we have seen with regard to space, object, causality, and time it is clear that on the plane of representative thought, which is at the same time that of social relationships or coordination among individual minds, new assimilations and accommodations become necessary and these in turn begin with a phase of chaotic undifferentiation and later proceed to a complementary differentiation and harmonization.

During the earliest stages of thought, accommodation remains on the surface of physical as well as social experience. Of course, on the plane of action the child is no longer entirely dominated by the appearance of things, because through sensorimotor intelligence he has managed to construct a coherent practical universe by combining accommodation to objects with assimilation of objects to intercoordinated structures. But when it is a question of transcending action to form an impersonal representation of reality, that is, a communicable image destined to attain truth rather than mere utility, accommodation to things finds itself at grips with new difficulties. It is no longer a matter only of acting but of describing, not only of foreseeing but of explaining, and even if the sensorimotor schemata are already adapted to their own function, which is to insure the equilibrium between individual activity and the perceived environment, thought is obliged to construct a new representation of things to satisfy the common consciousness and the demands of a conception of totality. In this sense the first contact of thought, properly so called, with the material universe constitutes what may be called "immediate experience" in contradistinction to experimentation which is scientific or corrected by the assimilation of things to reason.

Immediate experience, that is, the accommodation of thought to the surface of things, is simply empirical experience which considers, as objective datum, reality as it appears to direct perception. In the numerous cases in which reality coincides with appearance this superficial contact with the object suffices to lead to truth. But the further one departs from the field of immediate action to construct an adequate representation of reality, the more necessary it is, to understand the phenomena, to include them in a network of relations becoming increasingly remote from appearance and to insert appearance in a new reality elaborated by reason. In other words, it becomes more and more necessary to correct appearance and this requires the formation of relationships among, or the reciprocal assimilation of, various points of view. In the example we cited in §3 of the groups of displacements relating to mountains, it is obvious that a whole structuring of experience, that is, a rational assimilation and co-ordination of many possible points of view, is indispensable to make the child understand that, despite appearance, mountains do not displace themselves when one moves in relation to them and that the various perspectives on them do not exclude the permanence of their form. The same applies to attributing stationary banks to a river or a lake when the boat advances and, in a general way, to organizing distant space no longer depending on direct action. Concerning objects let us consider the difference between immediate experience relating to the stars, that is, simple accommodation of perception to their apparent size and movements, from the real experience which the mind acquires when it combines that accommodation with an assimilation of the same data to the activity of reason. From the first of these points of view, the stars are little balls or spots located at the same height as clouds; their movements depend on our own walking and their permanence is impossible to determine (even with respect to the sun, there are children who believe in its identity with the moon when they do not, on the contrary, affirm the existence of several suns and moons). From the second point of view, on the contrary, real dimensions and distances no longer have any relation to appearance, the actual trajectories correspond with the apparent movements only through relationships of increasing complexity, and the identity of celestial bodies becomes the function of this system of totality. What is true on a large scale of the stars is always true, on every scale, of objects on which direct action does not bear. With regard to causality, the first example seen, like that of the floating of boats so suggestive to the child, gives rise to the same considerations. By following the course of immediate experience the child begins by believing that small boats float because they are light; but when he sees a tiny piece of lead or a little pebble gliding along at the bottom of the water, he adds that these bodies are doubtless too light and small to be held back by the water; moreover big boats float because they are heavy and can thus carry themselves. In short, if one remains on the surface of things, explanation is possible only at the price of continuous contradictions, because, if it is to embrace the sinuosity of reality, thought

must constantly add apparent connections to one another instead of coordinating them in a coherent system of totality. On
the contrary, the contact of the mind with real experience leads
to a simple explanation, but on condition of completing this elementary accommodation of thought to the immediate data of
perception by a correlative assimilation of these data to a system
of relationships (between weight and volume, etc.) which reason succeeds in elaborating only by replacing the appearance
of things with a real construction. Let us also be satisfied, in
the realm of time and duration, with a single example, that of the
dissociation of the concept of speed into relations between the
concepts of time and the space traversed. From the point of
view of immediate experience, the child succeeds very soon in
estimating speeds of which he has direct awareness, the spaces
traversed in an identical time or the "before" and "after" in arrival at a goal in cases of trajectories of the same length. But
there is a considerable gap between this and a dissociation of the
notion of speed to extract a measurement of time, for this would
involve replacing the direct intuitions peculiar to the elementary accommodation of thought to things by a system of relations involving a constructive assimilation.

In short, thought in all realms starts from a surface contact
with the external realities, that is, a simple accommodation to
immediate experience. Why then, does this accommodation remain, in the true sense of the word, superficial, and why does it
not at once lead to correcting the sensory impression by rational
truth? Because, and this is what we are leading up to, primitive
accommodation of thought, as previously that of sensorimotor
intelligence, is undifferentiated from a distorting assimilation of
reality to the self and is at the same time oriented in the opposite direction.

During this phase of superficial accommodation to physical and
social experience, we observe a continuous assimilation of the universe not only to the impersonal structure of the mind—which
is not completed except on the sensorimotor plane—but also and
primarily to the personal point of view, to individual experience,
and even to the desires and affectivity of the subject. Considered
in its social aspect, this distorting assimilation consists, as we
have seen (§2), in a sort of egocentrism of thought so that

thought, still unsubmissive to the norms of intellectual reciprocity and logic, seeks satisfaction rather than truth and transforms reality into a function of personal affectivity. From the point of view of the adaptation of thought to the physical universe this assimilation leads to a series of consequences of interest to us here. In the domain of space, for example, it is evident that, if the child remains dominated by the immediate experience of the mountain which is displaced and by the other superficial accommodations we have discussed, it is because these remain undifferentiated from a continual assimilation of reality to the personal point of view; thus the child believes that his own displacements govern those of the mountains, the sky, etc. The same is true of objects. To the extent the child has difficulty, for example, in constituting the identity of the moon and the stars in general because he does not transcend the immediate experience of their apparent movements, it is because he still believes he is followed by them and thus assimilates the image of their displacements to his own point of view, exactly like the baby whose universe is ill objectified because it is too closely centered on his own activity. With regard to causality, if the child has difficulty in integrating his explanations into a coherent system of relations, this is again because accommodation to the qualitative diversity of reality remains undifferentiated from an assimilation of phenomena to personal activity. Why, for instance, are boats conceived as heavy or light in themselves, without consideration of the relation of weight and volume, if not because weight is evaluated as the function of the subject's muscular experience instead of being transformed into an objective relationship? So also, the primacy of internal duration over external time attests to the existence of a distorting assimilation which necessarily accompanies primitive accommodaton of the mind to the surface of events.

The superficial accommodation of the beginnings of thought and the distorting assimilation of reality to the self are therefore at first undifferentiated and they operate in opposite directions. They are undifferentiated because the immediate experience which characterizes the former always, in the last analysis, consists in considering the personal point of view as the expression of the absolute and thus in subjecting the appearance of things to an egocentric assimilation, just as this assimilation is necessarily on a par with a direct perception that excludes the construction of a rational system of relations. But at the beginning, however undifferentiated may be these accommodative operations and those in which assimilation may be discerned, they work in opposite directions. Precisely because immediate experience is accompanied by an assimilation of perceptions to the schemata of personal activity or modeled after it, accommodation to the inner workings of things is constantly impeded by it. Inversely, assimilation of things to the self is constantly held in check by the resistances necessitating this accommodation, since there is involved at least the appearance of reality, which is not unlimitedly pliant to the subject's will. So also, on the social plane, the constraint imposed by the opinion of others thwarts egocentrism and vice versa, although the two attitudes of imitation of others and assimilation to the self are constantly coexistent and reveal the same difficulties of adaptation to reciprocity and true cooperation.

On the contrary, gradually, as the child's thought evolves, assimilation and accommodation are differentiated and become increasingly complementary. In the realm of representation of the world this means, on the one hand, that accommodation, instead of remaining on the surface of experience, penetrates it more and more deeply, that is, under the chaos of appearances it seeks regularities and becomes capable of real experimentations to establish them. On the other hand, assimilation, instead of reducing phenomena to the concepts inspired by personal activity, incorporates them in the system of relationships rising from the more profound activity of intelligence itself. True experience and deductive construction thus become simultaneously separate and correlative, whereas in the social realm the increasingly close adjustment of personal thought to that of others and the reciprocal formation of relationships of perspectives insures the possibility of a cooperation that constitutes precisely the environment that is favorable to this elaboration of reason.

Thus it may be seen that thought in its various aspects reproduces on its own plane the processes of evolution we have observed in the case of sensorimotor intelligence and the structure of the initial practical universe. The development of reason, outlined on the sensorimotor level, follows the same laws, once social life and reflective thought have been formed. Confronted by the obstacles which the advent of those new realities raises, at the beginning of this second period of intellectual evolution assimilation and accommodation again find themselves in a situation through which they had already passed on the lower plane. But in proceeding from the purely individual state characteristic of sensorimotor intelligence to the cooperation which defines the plane on which thought will move henceforth, the child, after having overcome his egocentrism and the other obstacles which impede this cooperation, reecives from it the instruments necessary to extend the rational construction prepared during the first two years of life and to expand it into a system of logical relationships and adequate representations.

THE BASIC CLASSICS IN PSYCHIATRY

This series presents major thinkers in writings of paramount importance to present day psychiatric theory and technique.

Selected Papers of Sandor Ferenczi, M.D., Volume I
SEX IN PSYCHOANALYSIS
Introduction by Clara Thompson, M.D.

Ferenczi's great pioneering work, dealing in part with psychosexual impotence, homosexuality, masturbation and obscene words. "A book for every serious student of human behavior. It will be found to be richly informative and will probably provoke many new and original lines of thought in the reader." *Mental Hygiene.* $3.50

Selected Papers of Sandor Ferenczi, M.D., Volume II
Further Contributions to
THE THEORY AND TECHNIQUE OF PSYCHOANALYSIS

90 papers and briefer pieces, predominantly clinical and concerned with technique, by this brilliant associate of Freud. "The scope of these papers is extremely wide; there are few aspects of psychoanalysis on which he has not something illuminating or stimulating to say." *Edward Glover, M.D.* $6.00

EGO PSYCHOLOGY AND THE PSYCHOSES
By Paul Federn, M.D.
Edited and with an introduction by Edoardo Weiss, M.D.

"The important work of one of the modest great in the field of medical psychology. As an aid to understanding the conscious and 'intellectual' part of the human mentality, and of schizophrenia . . . from the dynamic point of view, I know of no work to surpass this of Federn's." *Newton Bigelow, M.D.* $6.00

SELECTED PAPERS ON PSYCHOANALYSIS
By Karl Abraham, M.D.
Introduction by Ernest Jones, M.D.

30 clinical papers, including Abraham's important contributions on the oral period of development, character formation, manic-depressive psychosis, female castration complex. "His theoretical contributions to psychoanalysis were crystallizations from a saturated solution of clinical experience. . . . Here is the work of a master craftsman." *Edward Glover, M.D.* $6.00

BASIC BOOKS, INC., *Publishers, 59 Fourth Avenue, New York 3*

DATE DUE			
APR 25 '78	APR 26 '78		
FE 23 '82	FEB 24 '82		
MY 1 '84	MAY 3 '84		
GAYLORD			PRINTED IN U.S.A.